A note from
Karen

Robert this is
a Present for your
Birthday sorry
It's a little but I
hope you enjoy it
and find it of
Some use.

God Bless

APRIL
2000

Prayers for the People

Prayers for the People

LEADER'S EDITION

Edited by

MICHAEL PERRY

with PATRICK GOODLAND *and* ANGELA GRIFFITHS

MARSHALL PICKERING

An imprint of HarperCollins *Publishers*

JUBILATE   CPAS

Also edited by the Jubilate group:

Hymns for Today's Church
Church Family Worship
Carols for Today
Carol Praise*
Let's Praise!*
Come Rejoice!*
The Wedding Book*
The Dramatised Bible*
Psalms for Today
Songs from the Psalms
Hymns for the People

* *Available from HarperCollins*

First published in Great Britain in 1992 by Marshall Pickering
Marshall Pickering is an imprint of
HarperCollins*Religious*
Part of HarperCollins*Publishers*
77–85 Fulham Palace Road, London W6 8JB

Compilation Copyright © 1992 Michael Perry

The Compilers assert the moral right to be identified as the compilers of this work

Designed by Claire Brodmann

Printed and bound in Great Britain by HarperCollins Manufacturing, Glasgow

A catalogue record for this book is available from the British Library

ISBN 0 551 01990–5 (People's)
ISBN 0 551 01 991–3 (Leaders')

Contents

Contents

Preface to the Leader's Edition

Prayers for the People is offered for worship in today's churches. It is designed to meet a whole variety of situations. The People's Edition has the appearance of a contemporary Christian song book and is produced relatively inexpensively so that eventually each member of the congregation can have one. The Leader's Edition offers a fund of resources for every occasion, and its indexes and thematic sections will enable the leader or minister quickly to find the relevant item.

INVOLVING THE PEOPLE

The Free Churches have always enjoyed a liberating theology: all Christians are 'kings and priests' - a royal priesthood; there is no fundamental distinction between minister and congregation, apart from the calling of ordination and the pastoral authority it confers. And even this authority expresses the 'servanthood' of Jesus, so that the minister is there to help the people in their praying, and not the other way round.

That Free Churches have shunned prayer books is a consequence of history, stemming from the days when they fled forced subservience to an ecclesiology their conscience could not accept. *The Book of Common Prayer* remained an inspiration, but it did not fully reflect their theology and suggested that which many feared, 'vain repetition'. Hymn books had no such taboo, and the irony is that Free Churches became attached to denominational hymn books in a way that Anglicans never did.

This prayer-book shyness found easy acceptance in a day when few were able to read fluently, and the format of education imbued congregations with the notion that it was godly to be seen and not heard - except in the hymns! As to vain repetition, a new danger lurked in the ministerial cliché.

Education patterns have changed. Now, young people at least, want to take part, and to articulate their prayers in words which may not be the minister's. And it would seem to be theologically correct for them to do so. But how? Not everyone is a budding poet, and totally informal prayer - though desirable and attractive at times - can often sit uneasily in a public service. How, too, to involve a whole congregation in simultaneous response beyond the pervasive 'Amen', 'Alleluia', or even 'Praise the Lord'?

That it is right for the congregation to respond is evident from the Psalms (see especially Psalms 24 and 118), where the people plainly took part in Hebrew celebratory worship; and from the New Testament, when so many statements of faith and doctrine have become rounded into responsive or credal forms (see, for instance, the Beatitudes, or the opening verses of 1 Corinthians 13).

Among its many resources, *Prayers for the People* seeks to provide 'rounded' prayers and 'responsive' prayers for leader/minister and people - so that they might play a full (but necessarily unrehearsed) part in the prayerful public worship of God. *Prayers for the People* does not prescribe fixed forms but offers a variety of examples according to season and subject, many of them firmly based on Bible usage.

CHAPTERS

The chapters of *Prayers for the People* enclose within them prayer for a wide spectrum of subjects indicated by the chapter title. For instance, it will be possible for the leader/minister to follow through chapter 18, *The Caring Church, Healing*, choosing prayers, readings etc on either of those main subjects and more.

The grouping of items together like this enables a congregation to stay within a chapter for any one service. On the other hand, it is perfectly possible for the leader or minister simply to use *Prayers for the People* as a 'chorus'-book in the best sense; choosing various items to suit the purpose of the occasion. One warning: jumping around too much - especially backwards and forwards - in a book like this does tend to weary a congregation, and so detract from their spirit of prayerfulness. Selective use of *Prayers for the People* should be more like the use of a hymn or song book.

SEQUENCES

Within each chapter, items are arranged in the likely order of use: Greeting, Approach, Confession, Absolution, Theme Prayer, Psalm, Reading, Creed, Intercession for Others, Intercession for Ourselves, Thanksgiving, Acclamation, Blessing. There will often be several examples of each type of prayer, offering differences of style and variation of theme.

All the items in which the congregation plays a part are printed in the People's Edition; these are also indicated by an arrowhead 'dingbat' in the Leader's Edition. The arrowhead will alert the Leader/Minister that the people have the prayer in front of them and can be expected to join in. The absence of an arrowhead shows that the people do not have the prayer in their books.

Prayers not included in the People's Edition are those which because of style or function (for instance, a benediction) are more appropriate to the leader. The Leader's Edition also contains in each chapter a selection of dramatised readings. These, too, enable participation, but not usually so widely as to require them to be printed in the People's Edition.

THE LEADER LEADING

There will be times when the leader wants to use a prayer without congregational involvement; a glance will show how this can be done by the omission of the petition (such as 'Lord in your mercy:') and the response (such as 'hear our prayer'). It will be noticed that prayers designed for leader alone (those not indicated by the arrowhead) have straight edges, both right and left, in the text - they are fully 'justified'.

Prayers and parts of prayers intended for the congregation are set in 'speech-equivalent' lines, breaking and returning to the margin where the sense allows and a natural pause is possible. Often, especially in the responsive psalm versions, rhythm has been introduced to congregational lines in order to assist the flow of worship. If the leader appreciates this, it will help him keep the congregation moving together in harmony.

The Psalm versions are those used in *The Dramatised Bible, Psalms for Today* and *Songs from the Psalms* under the title *The Jubilate Liturgical Psalms*. Some of the responses are divided into parts ("A", "B" etc.). It is advisable not to attempt this distinction with a more formal congregation except, say, on a festive occasion. If parts are used with children present, it is wise to have a leader for each division.

Sometimes, prayers set for leader/minister alone are in the first person singular. These are always marked 'a personal prayer' so that the minister may be alerted to tell the congregation before embarking upon it. Worshippers appreciate being told if they are about to be asked to make an individual statement of faith. "Here is a personal prayer that we may make our own", or some such similar warning from the leader, gives them the opportunity to decide if they want to be associated with the prayer's sentiments, and then, if they assent, to pray with true commitment.

HOME AND GROUP USE

The minister may wish to commend *Prayers for the People* for private use apart from the context of congregational worship. It is often possible for the individual to substitute mentally "I" for "We" etc., and so identify with the prayer; this can be recommended, along with the suggested omission of petition and response (see above). Many of the prayers based on Bible text (those marked here with an obelisk '†') are available in a sister compendium *Bible Praying*; some may be found there in two versions, 'second person singular' as well as 'first person plural'. In Bible Praying, prayers are arranged first in order of type - so that all the Confessions are together, all the Blessings are together, etc. - and then in Bible order.

Within a home group, or in other informal situations, otherwise reluctant participants can be encouraged to lead in prayer, given the support which *Prayers for the People* offers. If someone in the group has the Leader's Edition there is the obvious advantage of more material available - but limited use can be made with the People's Edition alone.

SHORT SERVICES

Another way of using *Prayers for the People* in public worship is to stay with the 'Short service' or the short 'Communion Service' at the back, augmenting from within the main volume (but not too erratically!). Not all churches have complete freedom to employ their own chosen words. The Church of England, for example, has a legal framework for its liturgy. But part of that discipline is a freedom now given under the canons, and with due authority, to use appropriately devised forms for circumstances where none is provided by law. Over the years, many Church of England clergy have successfully met in this way the needs of Family Services, Guest Services, Celebration Services, Conference Services, Holiday Services, Healing Services, etc.

With the coming of the *Alternative Service Book 1980* a new freedom was granted. *ASB 1980* rubrics (regulatory paragraphs in the text) often provide for the minister to pray in "the form below . . or other suitable words". Elsewhere, the rubrics provide for wholesale omissions of the service text. By and large, clergy have not made use of these freedoms, often because they have not read the rubrics! The Liturgical Commission in an effort to encourage flexibility have published various documents - especially *Patterns for Worship*; a path which was pioneered by our musical volume *Church Family Worship*, and its predecessors.

Church of England clergy, may therefore use *Prayers for the People* with a clear conscience in places where the rubrics allow; and, given a willing Bishop and supportive Parochial Church Council, on occasions when the canons permit.

ACKNOWLEDGEMENTS

A full set of practical acknowledgements appears at the back of each edition, but I would especially like to thank Rev Patrick Goodland MBE, of the Baptist denomination, and Rev John Moore, General Director of the Church Pastoral Aid Society who asked me to get this book published. To my colleagues in editing - both Patrick Goodland and Angela Griffiths - may I express my fullest appreciation for their talented and inspirational assistance. Together, we dedicate this volume to the service of the churches and to the glory of our Lord and Saviour.

MICHAEL PERRY
Epiphany 1992

New Year, Thanksgiving for the Old Year

▶ **1.1** GREETING
From Romans 15†

The God of peace be with you all.
Amen.

1.2 SENTENCE
Psalm 31. 14,15

We trust in you, O Lord; we say, 'You are our God'. Our times are in your hands.

1.3 SENTENCE
Psalm 90.4

Lord, a thousand years in your sight are just like yesterday.

1.4 SENTENCE
Philippians 3. 13,14

Forgetting what is behind and reaching for what is ahead, we press on towards the goal to win the prize for which God has called us heavenwards in Christ Jesus.

1.5 SENTENCE
Hebrews 13.8

Jesus Christ is the same yesterday and today and for ever.

▶ **1.6** RESPONSE
From Revelation 1†

The Lord God says 'I am Alpha and Omega, who is, and who was, and who is to come, the Almighty'. **Amen!**

▶ **1.7** RESPONSE
From Psalm 89†

O Lord, we will sing always of your constant love:
we will proclaim your faithfulness for ever!

We know that your love will last for all time:
that your faithfulness is founded in heaven.

Praise be to the Lord for ever:
Amen and Amen!

▶ **1.8** RESPONSE
From 2 Corinthians 5†

Anyone in Christ is a new creation:
the old has gone, the new has come! Amen.

▶ **1.9** RESPONSE
From Psalm 90†

Lord, you have been our rock in every generation:
from everlasting to everlasting you are our God.

1.10 APPROACH
Editors

Loving God, our provider and sustainer, we come to you as people
who are being made whole through your Son, Jesus Christ; we come
sincerely, loving, longingly. Our hearts are overwhelmed with praise
as we recall your creation of each one of us; and as we believe that
we are to enjoy you and adore you in heaven. You have given us a
mind to understand your character and your works, you have given
us a heart to love you and a will to serve you. Because you have
made such rich provision for us, increase our knowledge, our love
and our obedience, that we may grow in the likeness of our Lord
Jesus Christ, for his sake. **Amen.**

1.11 APPROACH
From Psalm 105†

O Lord, we thank you for your greatness; we witness to the
wonderful things you have done and we are glad that we belong to

you: today we come to you for strength, for you are our God; your justice is for all the world, your covenant with us is for ever, and your promises for a thousand generations: praise be to you, O Lord our God. **Amen.**

▶ **1.12** PRAISE
From Psalm 75†

We give you thanks, O God;
we give you thanks.

We proclaim how great you are,
and tell of the wonderful things you have done. Amen.

▶ **1.13** CONFESSION
Diocese of Sheffield, adapted

We look to God for forgiveness, knowing that in this last year we have often grieved him through our failures and sins:

Where we have not cared enough for you:
forgive us, O God.

Where we have not cared enough for your world:
forgive us, O God.

Where we have been content with ourselves as we are:
forgive us, O God.

**Give us the will and the power
to live in the Spirit of Jesus;
now and always. Amen.**

▶ **1.14** CONFESSION
Editors

Help us, O Lord, and forgive us when we offer you less than the best of our loyalty and service:

When we resent your loving correction, when we grudge giving to the work of your kingdom, when we fail to value the fellowship of your people; in your tender mercy:
forgive us, Lord, and help us.

When through pride we will not admit our mistakes, when we make it easier for others to do wrong, when we bring upon them anxiety →

and needless worry; in your tender mercy:
forgive us, Lord, and help us.

For every unkind word we have spoken, for every action which has hurt another person, for every wrong desire we have harboured in our minds; in your tender mercy:
forgive us, Lord, and help us.

Lord have mercy upon us and forgive us,
that we may live close to you now
and be with you for ever in your eternity;
through Jesus Christ our Lord. Amen.

1.15 ABSOLUTION
From Psalm 140†

The Lord *your* God hears *your* cry for mercy; the Sovereign Lord is *your* strong deliverer; he will shield *your* head, and *you* shall not die; for the sake of Jesus Christ our Lord. **Amen.**

▶ **1.16**   COLLECT
Lent 2, ASB 1980

Lord God almighty,
grant your people grace
to withstand the temptations
of the world, the flesh, and the devil,
and with pure hearts and minds
to follow you, the only God;
through Jesus Christ, our Lord. **Amen.**

▶ **1.17**   PSALM
From Psalm 90†

Lord, you have been our home through all generations; before the mountains were born, before you gave birth to the earth and its people, from everlasting to everlasting:
you are our God!

A thousand years in your sight are like a day gone by:
like a dream in the night.

The length of our days is seventy years – or eighty if we are strong enough:

they quickly pass, and we fly away.

Teach us to count our days:
to gain a heart of wisdom.

Satisfy us every morning with your unfailing love that we may sing for joy:
and be glad the whole day long.

Make up for our bad days with as many days of happiness:
with as many happy years as our years of sorrow.

Show us, your servants, your wonderful deeds:
show your glory to our children.

O Lord our God, let your favour rest upon us; bless our work and make it endure:
yes, Lord, establish the work of our hands. Amen.

▶ **1.18** PSALM
Psalm 136.1–26†

The congregation must divide at A, B *and* C *saying the whole stanza,* OR *both ministers and congregation should divide*

A Give thanks to God, for he is good:
A **his love shall last for ever!**

B Give thanks to him, the God of gods:
B **is love shall last for ever!**

C Give thanks to him, the Lord of lords:
C **his love shall last for ever!**

A For God alone works miracles:
A **his love shall last for ever!**

B The skies were made at his command:
B **his love shall last for ever!**

C He spread the seas upon the earth:
C **his love shall last for ever!**

A He made the stars to shine at night:
A **his love shall last for ever!**

B He made the sun to shine by day:
B **his love shall last for ever!**

c He brought us out from slavery:
c **his love shall last for ever!**

a He leads us onward by his grace:
a **his love shall last for ever!**

b He saves us from our enemies:
b **his love shall last for ever!**

c Give thanks to God, for he is good:
c **his love shall last for ever!**

ALL **Amen!**

▶ **1.19** PSALM
Psalm 147.1–20†

The congregation may divide at a, b *and* c

O praise the Lord, sing out to God:
such praise is right and good.

The Lord restores Jerusalem:
a **he brings the exiles home.**

He heals all those with broken hearts:
b **he bandages their wounds.**

He counts the number of the stars:
c **he calls them each by name.**

How great and mighty is the Lord:
a **immeasurably wise!**

He raises up the humble ones:
b **and brings the mighty down.**

Sing hymns of triumph to his name:
c **make music to our God!**

He spreads the clouds across the sky:
a **he showers the earth with rain.**

He sends the animals their food:
b **he feeds the hungry birds.**

His true delight is not the strong:
c **but those who trust his love.**

Extol the Lord, Jerusalem:
a **let Zion worship God!**

For God shall keep your people safe:
B **and bring your harvest home.**

He gives commandment to the earth:
C **his will is quickly done.**

He spreads like wool the falling snow:
A **how cold the frosty air!**

He sends the wind, the warming rain:
B **and melts the ice away.**

His laws he gives to Israel:
C **and Judah hears his word.**

He does not favour other lands:
ALL **so, praise the Lord. Amen!**

1.20 READING: WARNING AGAINST BOASTING
James 4.13–17

Cast: James, Voice 1, Voice 2

James
Now listen to me, you that say:

Voice 1 (*confident*)
Today or tomorrow we will travel to a certain city, where we will stay a year and go into business and make a lot of money.

James
You don't even know what your life tomorrow will be! You are like a puff of smoke, which appears for a moment and then disappears. What you should say is this:

Voice 2 (*humble*)
If the Lord is willing, we will live and do this or that.

James
But now you are proud, and you boast; all such boasting is wrong. So then, the person who does not do the good he knows he should do is guilty of sin.

Cast
[This is] the word of the Lord.
All
Thanks be to God.

7

FURTHER BIBLE READINGS

Readings appropriate to this theme will be found listed in our companion volume, 'The Dramatised Bible' (published by HarperCollins) on index page 420.

▶ **1.21**   CREED
From 2 Corinthians 1†

All God's promises are 'yes' in Christ; through him we give glory to God and say, 'Amen':

It is Christ
to whom we belong.

It is the Father
who assures us of our salvation
 and anoints us for his service.

It is the Spirit
by whom we are sealed in love for evermore.

We believe in one God:
Father, Son, and Holy Spirit. Amen.

▶ **1.22**   FOR THE PRESENCE OF GOD
From Psalms 143†

O God,
as we remember days gone by,
and think about all you have done for us,
our souls thirst for you
and we lift our hands to you in prayer.
Answer us now, O Lord;
don't hide yourself from us,
remind us each morning of your constant love:
for we put our trust in you,
through Jesus Christ our Lord. **Amen.**

1.23   FOR OUR LEADERS
Editors

God, our Leader and our Lord, you have taught us in the Scriptures to pray for our nation and those who have the privilege and responsibility of leadership: bless our Queen, and grant to her grace

and wisdom that she may ever be an example to her people of how they ought to walk in life's way; strengthen the royal family that they too may always give the best example; bless all members of Parliament and those who administer the cities, the towns and the villages of this land. Help them to set the good of the people above the success of their party; and the welfare of the nation above any personal ambition. We ask this in the name of the Lord Jesus Christ. **Amen.**

1.24   FOR PEACE IN OUR WORLD
Frank Colquhoun, adapted

O God of love, in whose will is our peace: so set your peace in human hearts that the nations of the world may learn to live as members of one family, and children of one God and Father, to the glory of your name; through Jesus Christ our Lord. **Amen.**

▶ 1.25   FOR THE SICK AND THE SAD
Editors

O Lord, as we think of other people hear our prayer.

For all who are ill (*especially* . . .), we ask your healing. Lord in your mercy:

hear our prayer.

For those who are lonely, frightened, and unhappy, we ask your help. Lord, in your mercy:

hear our prayer.

For those who are suffering from war, and for refugees, we ask your care. Lord, in your mercy:

hear our prayer.

For children who are handicapped, we ask your protection. Lord, in your mercy:

hear our prayer.

For those who are in trouble through foolish behaviour, we ask your correction and restoration. Lord, in your mercy:

hear our prayer.

For those who are hungry or homeless or in inadequate housing, we ask your compassion. Lord, in your mercy:

hear our prayer.

→

For your church in every part of the world, we ask for your compassion. Lord, in your mercy:
hear our prayer.

For all who labour for the peace of the world and the freedom of all peoples, we ask your guidance and strength. Lord, in your mercy:
hear our prayer.

Lord, you promise to hear
those who are gathered to pray in your name:
receive our prayer for all in need,
and grant your salvation to them and to us;
through our Saviour, Jesus Christ. Amen.

1.26 FOR FORGIVENESS
St Bartholomew's, Oxford

O God, our loving Father, we are very sorry for all the things we have done which make you sad: we have sometimes been selfish or bad-tempered or disobedient. And we are sorry for the things we have failed to do: for the work we did not finish, the thank-you we forgot to say, the friends we did not help, the quarrel we never made up. For these and all our failings, forgive us, through Jesus Christ our Lord. **Amen.**

1.27 FOR STRENGTH AGAINST TEMPTATION (MORNING)
From 'A New Zealand Prayer Book'
* *'year' may be substituted for 'day'*

Father, we thank you for bringing us to the beginning of another *day.* Help us through your Holy Spirit, so that we may not fall into sin, but may do everything that pleases you, through Jesus Christ our Lord. **Amen.**

1.28 FOR OUR WORK
Paul Simmonds

O God, we thank you for the gifts you have given to each of us, and for the satisfaction of a task well done – whether for ourselves, for our family, for our church, for our employer, or for a friend: help us to do all that we do, as Jesus did, to bring honour and glory to your name. **Amen.**

1.29 ABOUT THE OLD YEAR
George Appleton, adapted

Lord, looking back on our journey so far, we see how your love and goodness have been with us – through many failings and dangers, in many joys and adventures. We have received much love from friends, enjoyed so many good and lovely things, been guided and inspired by the wisdom and encouragement of many teachers and writers. Often we have felt your presence near, and sometimes we have had to walk by faith. Forgive our slowness, our failures in faith, the smallness of our love, our poor use of your grace. Accept our heart's thanks for a growing knowledge of you, for an increasing assurance of your purposes of love and for a deepening understanding of the things that are eternal. As we turn again to the journey ahead, it is bright with the remembrance of past mercies: dear Father and Saviour, we bring you eternal praise, through Jesus our Lord. **Amen.**

1.30 FOR EVERY DAY
Editors

This is the day which the Lord has made; let us rejoice and be glad in it:

Heavenly Father, help us to be aware of your presence each new morning; teach us your ways and let us respond to you with love and complete trust. Thank you for the precious gift of life: let us use each day to fulfil your divine purpose. Our times are in your hand: hold us fast for Jesus' sake. **Amen.**

▶ **1.31** FOR GOD'S HELP IN THE NEW YEAR
Christopher Idle, adapted

O God our Father, at the beginning of this new year, look upon our Christian family. We come to you in prayer with our hopes and resolutions. And we come also with our doubts and fears, knowing the power of the world, the flesh and the devil. Yet we pray that you will help us not to fall. At the beginning of the new year,
Lord, hear our prayer.

Look upon us as we do our work, face our exams, run our households, look for jobs, earn our wages, maintain our business, enjoy our leisure. At the beginning of the new year,
Lord, hear our prayer.

Look upon our church as it loves and cares and serves, as it learns and worships and witnesses. At the beginning of the new year,
Lord, hear our prayer.

Look upon your world, with all its waste and war and sorrow, yet all its joys as well. At the beginning of the new year,
Lord, hear our prayer.

Father, grant us your presence and your peace;
keep us safe in the knowledge of Jesus Christ our Lord. Amen.

1.32   FOR TRUST IN JESUS
Editors

Lord, you told us not to be anxious about tomorrow; but we confess there are times when we worry needlessly, and slip into the shadow of doubt: please help us to trust you completely and bring our burdens to you whatever the circumstances; teach us how to take your yoke upon us and and learn from you, our Master; for we can find true rest only in you, Jesus, Lord and Saviour. **Amen.**

▶ **1.33**   THANKSGIVING
Editors

For the year that is past:
Lord, we thank you.

For your mercies every day:
Lord, we thank you.

For new discoveries of your grace, and fresh opportunities to do your work:
Lord, we thank you.

For your strength to survive hurt and sorrow, and that you pick us up when we fall:
Lord, we thank you.

For our life in Christ which gives us hope for the future:
Lord, we thank you.

Lord, we thank you that you walk beside us –
your mighty hand to uphold us,
your heart of love to guide us,
your outstretched arms to meet us at our journey's end;
through Jesus our redeemer. Amen.

▶ **1.34** THANKSGIVING (CONCLUSION)
From Ephesians 5†

We give thanks for everything to God the Father:
in the name of our Lord Jesus Christ. Amen.

1.35 FOR ALL OUR FUTURES
Editors

God of new beginnings, we offer joyful thanks to you for the year ahead: help us to use it and not waste any part of it; may we live each day with Jesus as our friend and guide; teach us to value all that is good in the days to come, and help us to cope with any difficult times – we know you are with us in sunshine and shadow. Show us how to care and share, to give and forgive, and let the beauty of Christ touch us so that each day we may reflect his perfect love. This new year is the start of our future – thank you for giving it to us: we commit ourselves to you, for the sake of your dear Son, Jesus Christ. **Amen.**

1.36 DEDICATION
Minnie Haskins, adapted

'I said to the man who stood at the Gate of the Year, "Give me a light that I may tread safely into the unknown." And he replied, "Go out into the darkness and put your hand into the hand of God. That shall be to you better than light and safer than a known way."' May that Almighty hand guide and uphold us all; through Jesus Christ our Lord. **Amen.**

▶ **1.37** ASCRIPTION
From Jude†

Now to him who is able to keep us from falling
and to present us before his glorious presence
without fault and with great joy –
to the only God our Saviour
be glory, majesty, power and authority,
through Jesus Christ our Lord,
before all ages, now, and for evermore! **Amen.**

▶ **1.38** DOXOLOGY
Liturgical Commission

In a world of change and hope,
of fear and adventure:
faithful God,
glorify your name. **Amen.**

1.39 BLESSING
From Numbers 6†

The Lord bless and watch over *you*, the Lord make his face shine
upon *you* and be gracious to *you*, the Lord look kindly on *you* and
give *you* peace; and the blessing of God almighty, the Father, the Son,
and the Holy Spirit, be among *you* and remain with *you* always.
Amen.

1.40 BLESSING
From Philippians 4†

Rejoice in the Lord always, let everyone know your gentleness, do
not be anxious, make your needs known to God; and the peace of
God guard *your* hearts in Christ Jesus. **Amen.**

Epiphany, The Wise Men, The Escape to Egypt

▶ **2.1** GREETING
From 2 John†

Grace, mercy and peace from God the Father and from Jesus Christ, the Father's Son, be with you in truth and love. **Amen.**

2.2 SENTENCE
Isaiah 60.1

Arise, shine, Jerusalem, for your light has come, and the glory of the Lord has risen upon you.

2.3 SENTENCE
Matthew 2.11

On coming into the house, the wise men saw the child with his mother, Mary, and they bowed down and worshipped him.

2.4 SENTENCE
Luke 2. 29, 32

Sovereign Lord, as you have promised, you now dismiss your servant in peace, for my eyes have seen your salvation, which you have prepared in the sight of all people a light for revelation to the Gentiles and for the glory of your people, Israel.

2.5 SENTENCE
Malachi 1.11

From the rising of the sun to its setting, my name is great among the nations, says the Lord.

2.6 SENTENCE
Matthew 3.17

There came a voice from heaven: this is my Son, the Beloved, in whom I am well pleased.

15

▶ **2.7** RESPONSE
From Isaiah 60†

Arise, shine, for your light has come:
the glory of the Lord has risen upon you.

▶ **2.8** RESPONSE
From Matthew 2†

We have seen his star in the East:
and have come with gifts to worship the Lord. Amen.

▶ **2.9** RESPONSE
From John 1†

We have seen his glory:
glory as of the only Son from the Father. Amen.

2.10 APPROACH
From Psalm 118†

Lord, this is the day you made; we rejoice and are glad in it. Save us,
prosper us, bless us, as we come into your house. Lord God, you
have made your light to shine upon us: we celebrate, and join to
worship you. You are our God: we give you thanks and exalt you.
Thank you, Lord, that you are good and that your love endures for
ever. **Amen.**

▶ **2.11** APPROACH
From John 1, Colossians 1, Hebrews 1†

In the beginning was the Word, and the Word was with God, and the
Word was God. Through him all things were made. In him was life
and that life was the light of us all. The light shines in the darkness:
We have seen his star in the East
and have come to worship him.

Christ is the image of the invisible God, the first-born over all
creation. He is before all things, and in him all things hold together:
We have seen his star in the East
and have come to worship him.

The Word became flesh and lived for a while among us. We have seen his glory, the glory of the one and only Son, who came from the Father, full of grace and truth:
**We have seen his star in the East
and have come to worship him.**

In the past God spoke to our forefathers through the prophets, but in these last days he has spoken to us by his Son, who is the radiance of his glory and the exact representation of his being:
**We have seen his star in the East
and have come to worship him.**

God, who said, 'Let light shine out of darkness,' made his light shine in our hearts to give us the light of the knowledge of the glory of God in the face of Christ:
**We have seen his star in the East
and have come to worship him. Amen.**

▶ **2.12** PRAISE
From Psalm 94†

Come, let us worship the Lord:
let us worship the Lord.

Let us bow down in the presence of our maker:
he is the Lord our God.

▶ **2.13** PRAISE
From Psalm 96†

Sing a new song to the Lord;
sing to the Lord, all the earth!

Sing to the Lord, praise his name;
proclaim his triumph day by day!

Worship the Lord in the splendour of his holiness;
tremble before him all the earth!

For great is the Lord, and worthy to be praised.
Amen.

▶ **2.14** CONFESSION
Editors

Lord Jesus Christ, wise men from the East worshipped and adored you; they brought you gifts – gold, incense, and myrrh.

We too have seen your glory, but we have often turned away. Lord, in your mercy,
forgive us and help us.

We too have gifts, but we have not fully used them or offered them to you. Lord, in your mercy,
forgive us and help us.

We too have acclaimed you as King, but we have not served you with all our strength. Lord, in your mercy,
forgive us and help us.

We too have acknowledged you as God, but we have not desired holiness. Lord, in your mercy,
forgive us and help us.

We too have welcomed you as Saviour, but we have failed to tell others of your grace. Lord, in your mercy,
forgive us and help us.

Make our trust more certain,
make our love more real,
make our worship more acceptable to you;
for your glory's sake. Amen.

▶ **2.15** CONFESSION
Editors

Lord Jesus Christ, you continually reveal your truth to us. Our privilege is the measure of our responsibility to share your good news with the world.

When all too easily we receive from you and neglect to tell others of your coming to give eternal life: Lord, in your mercy,
forgive us and strengthen us.

When we receive your gracious gifts, and clutch them to ourselves, and forget to share them with others: Lord, in your mercy,
forgive us and strengthen us.

When we know your guidance but trust in our own desires and selfish opinions: Lord, in your mercy,
forgive us and strengthen us.

When by our own choice, we walk in spiritual darkness, and do not recognise your nearness: Lord, in your mercy,
forgive us and strengthen us.

Lord, you alone can dispel our darkness:
help us to worship you,
to come into the fullness of your light,
then go out to work for you in a darkened world,
for the sake of Jesus Christ our Lord. Amen.

2.16 ABSOLUTION
From Psalm 118†

The Lord is good; his love endures for ever. The Lord is with *you:* do not be afraid. He has heard the cry of *your* heart, and has set *you* free from *your* sins. In the name of the Lord they are cut off from *you; you will* not die, but live and proclaim what the Lord has done; through Jesus Christ. **Amen.**

▶ 2.17 COLLECT
Christmas 2 (year 2), ASB 1980

Eternal God,
who by the shining of a star
led the wise men
to the worship of your Son:
guide by his light
the nations of the earth,
that the whole world
may behold your glory;
through Jesus Christ our Lord. **Amen.**

▶ 2.18 COLLECT
Holy Innocents, Church of Ireland APB 1984

Heavenly Father,
whose children suffered at the hands of Herod
though they had done no wrong:
help us to defend all your children
from cruelty and oppression;
in the name of Jesus Christ who suffered for us,
but is alive and reigns with you and the Holy Spirit,
one God, now and for ever. **Amen.**

▶ **2.19** PSALM
Psalm 95. 1–7†

The congregation may divide at A and B, the ministers at M and N

M Come, let's joyfully praise our God, acclaiming the Rock of our salvation.

N Come before him with thanksgiving, and greet him with melody.

A **Our God is a great God –**
B **a king above all other gods.**
A **The depths of the earth are in his hands –**
B **the mountain peaks belong to him.**
A **The sea is his – he made it!**
B **His own hands prepared the land.**

M Come, bow down to worship him;
N kneel before the Lord who made us.
A&B **We are his people, the sheep of his flock.**

M&N You shall know his power today –
N if you listen to his voice. **Amen**

2.20 READING: VISITORS FROM THE EAST
Matthew 2. 1–11[12]

Cast: Narrator, Magi, Chief Priest, Teacher (can be the same as Chief Priest), Prophet, Herod

Narrator
After Jesus was born in Bethlehem in Judaea, during the time of King Herod, Magi from the east came to Jerusalem and asked:

Magi
Where is the one who has been born king of the Jews? We saw his star in the east and have come to worship him.

Narrator
When King Herod heard this he was disturbed, and all Jerusalem with him. When he had called together all the people's chief priests and teachers of the law, he asked them where the Christ was to be born. They replied:

Chief Priest
In Bethlehem in Judaea.

Teacher

For this is what the prophet has written:

Prophet

But you, Bethlehem, in the land of Judah, are by no means least among the rulers of Judah; for out of you will come a ruler who will be the shepherd of my people Israel.

Narrator

Then Herod called the Magi secretly and found out from them the exact time the star had appeared. He sent them to Bethlehem [and said]:

Herod

Go and make a careful search for the child. As soon as you find him, report to me, so that I too may go and worship him.

Narrator

After they had heard the king, they went on their way, and the star they had seen in the east went ahead of them until it stopped over the place where the child was. When they saw the star, they were overjoyed. On coming to the house, they saw the child with his mother Mary, and they bowed down and worshipped him. Then they opened their treasures and presented him with gifts of gold and of incense and of myrrh. [And having been warned in a dream not to go back to Herod, they returned to their country by another route.]

Cast
[This is] the word of the Lord.   OR   This is the Gospel of Christ/
This is the Gospel of the Lord.

All
Thanks be to God.   **Praise to Christ our Lord/**
Praise to you, Lord Jesus Christ.

2.21   READING: THE ESCAPE INTO EGYPT
Matthew 2. 13–18

Cast: Narrator, Angel, Prophet, Jeremiah

Narrator

When the Magi had gone, an angel of the Lord appeared to Joseph in a dream:

Angel

Get up. Take the child and his mother and escape to Egypt. Stay there until I tell you, for Herod is going to search for the child to kill him.

Narrator

So he got up, took the child and his mother during the night and left for Egypt, where he stayed until the death of Herod. And so was fulfilled what the Lord had said through the prophet:

Prophet

Out of Egypt I called my son.

Narrator

When Herod realised that he had been outwitted by the Magi, he was furious, and he gave orders to kill all the boys in Bethlehem and its vicinity who were two years old and under, in accordance with the time he had learned from the Magi. Then what was said through the prophet Jeremiah was fulfilled:

Jeremiah

A voice is heard in Ramah,
weeping and great mourning,
Rachel weeping for her children
and refusing to be comforted,
because they are no more.

Cast

[This is] the word of the Lord.   OR   This is the Gospel of Christ/
                                                        This is the Gospel of the Lord.

All

Thanks be to God.   **Praise to Christ our Lord/**
                                                              Praise to you, Lord Jesus Christ.

2.22   READING: THE RETURN FROM EGYPT
Matthew 2. 19–23

Cast: Narrator, Angel, Prophet

Narrator

After Herod died, an angel of the Lord appeared in a dream to Joseph in Egypt:

Angel

Get up, take the child and his mother, and go back to the land of Israel, because those who tried to kill the child are dead.

Narrator

So Joseph got up, took the child and his mother, and went back to Israel.

But when Joseph heard that Archelaus had succeeded his father Herod as king of Judaea, he was afraid to go there. He was given more instructions in a dream, so he went to the province of Galilee and made his home in a town named Nazareth. And so what the prophets had said came true:

Prophet

He will be called a Nazarene.

Cast

[This is] the word of the Lord.   OR   This is the Gospel of Christ/
This is the Gospel of the Lord.

All

Thanks be to God.   **Praise to Christ our Lord/
Praise to you, Lord Jesus Christ.**

2.23   READING: THE PREACHING OF JOHN THE BAPTIST
Matthew 3. 1–12

Cast: Narrator, John, Isaiah.

Narrator

John the Baptist came to the desert of Judaea and started preaching.

John

Turn away from your sins, because the Kingdom of heaven is near!

Narrator

John was the man the prophet Isaiah was talking about when he said:

Isaiah

Someone is shouting in the desert, 'Prepare a road for the Lord; make a straight path for him to travel!'

Narrator

John's clothes were made of camel's hair; he wore a leather belt round his waist, and his food was locusts and wild honey. People came to him from Jerusalem, from the whole province of Judaea, and from all the country near the River Jordan. They confessed their sins, and he baptized them in the Jordan. (PAUSE)

When John saw many Pharisees and Sadducees coming to him to be baptized, he said to them:

John

You snakes – who told you that you could escape from the punishment God is about to send? Do those things that will show that you have turned from your sins. And don't think you can escape punishment by saying that Abraham is your ancestor. I tell you that God can take these stones and make descendants for Abraham! The axe is ready to cut down the trees at the roots; every tree that does not bear good fruit will be cut down and thrown in the fire. I baptize you with water to show that you have repented, but the one who will come after me will baptize you with the Holy Spirit and fire. He is much greater than I am; and I am not good enough even to carry his sandals. He has his winnowing shovel with him to thresh out all the grain. He will gather his wheat into his barn, but he will burn the chaff in a fire that never goes out.

Cast

    [This is] the word of the Lord.   OR   This is the Gospel of Christ/
                                            This is the Gospel of the Lord.

All

    Thanks be to God.   **Praise to Christ our Lord/**
                                            Praise to you, Lord Jesus Christ.

FURTHER BIBLE READINGS
Readings appropriate to this theme will be found listed in our companion volume, 'The Dramatised Bible' (published by HarperCollins) on index pages 420–421.

▶ **2.24**   CREED
From Titus 2 and 3†

We believe the grace of God has dawned upon us with healing for all the world, and so we rejoice to declare our faith in him:

**We trust in God the Father,
who has revealed his love and kindness to us,**

and in his mercy saved us,
not for any good deed of our own,
but because he is merciful.

We trust in Jesus Christ,
who gave himself up for us
to free us from our sin,
and set us apart for himself –
a people eager to do good.

We trust in the Holy Spirit,
whom God poured out on us generously
through Christ our saviour,
so that justified by grace
we might become heirs
with the hope of eternal life. Amen.

▶ **2.25**   FOR PEOPLE IN NEED
Source unknown, adapted Editors

O God, the Father of our Lord Jesus Christ, you came to bring good news to the poor, sight to the blind, freedom to the oppressed, and salvation to your people. Come to us now by your Holy Spirit and break down the barriers which divide, that we may truly love one another:

Persecuted minorities, all oppressed by sectarian or cold religious attitudes, all oppressed by racist politics and government, all oppressed by force or by intimidation: our God and Father,
these we bring before you.

Those who seek to remove oppression by patience, persuasion, courage and love: our God and Father,
for these we ask your grace.

All who feel compelled to turn to violence to oppose violence – that they may not be corrupted or oppressive themselves: our God and Father,
for these we pray.

All who are not whole – the hungry, the diseased, the homeless, those in poverty, depression, degradation, all who cannot find community: our God and Father,
for these we shout aloud.

Those who give their lives to bring to others wholeness and salvation: our God and Father,
for these we ask your strength.

Lord Jesus,
make us one in heart and mind,
give us a spirit of service
and true faith in Jesus Christ our Lord. Amen.

2.26 ABOUT OUR RESPONSE
Christopher Idle

Remember, O merciful God, all those in need: people with no good food or proper clothes, no home of their own or no work to do, no family or friends, or no knowledge of your love. Move us to respond to their plight, and strengthen us to help them; through Jesus Christ, our Lord. **Amen.**

2.27 FOR REFUGEES
Editors

Loving Father, we pray for millions of silent people today: the homeless, the refugees – forced to live in tents or shacks, often in camps, herded together. We pray for people whose harvest has failed for years, who must listen to the sobs of children with daily hunger pains. Strengthen every missionary, every church organisation, every national fund seeking to help the forgotten millions; and show us how we can best love these our neighbours in need. Hear our prayer and enliven our response; for Jesus' sake. **Amen.**

▶ **2.28** LITANY
Editors

Christ, born in a stable,
give courage to all who are homeless.

Christ, who fled into Egypt,
give comfort to all refugees.

Christ, who fasted in the desert,
give relief to all who are hungry.

Christ, who hung in torment on the cross,
give strength to all who suffer.

Christ, who died to save us,
give us the assurance of your forgiveness.

**Save us today,
and use us in your loving purposes;
for your glory's sake. Amen.**

▶ **2.29**   THAT WE MAY HAVE LIGHT
Editors

Lord Jesus, we acknowledge you as the Light of the World:
Lord, lead us from darkness to light.

Lord Jesus, we acknowledge you as a light to the nations:
Lord, help us to reflect the light of your love.

Lord Jesus, we acknowledge you as the true light from heaven:
Lord, may we always live in the light of your holiness.

Lord Jesus, we acknowledge you as the light that overcomes the
darkness:
Lord, guide us and shine your light on our daily path.

Lord Jesus, we acknowledge you as the eternal light of our life:
**Lord, we are your children of light,
aglow and ever praising you, our
Sun of Righteousness for ever. Amen.**

2.30   DEDICATION
Editors

Father, God of love, long ago, wise men followed a star to find your
Son, the Christ child. They worshipped him and presented gifts to
him. Now, Father, we are drawn by your radiant light to the Bright
Morning Star, our Saviour Jesus Christ. We worship him with
exceeding joy, and with humble heart we present ourselves. **Amen.**

▶ **2.31**   THANKSGIVING
Editors

Eternal God, our loving heavenly Father, you are perfection, yours is
the fullness of majesty, power and glory. Yours are the heavens and
the earth. Here we bow before you:
and praise you for your greatness.

Through the ages you have concerned yourself with men and women, your creatures on this earth. Within the immensity of this universe our little world has been your delight. Here we bow before you:
and praise you for your greatness.

You have revealed to us glimpses of your eternal glory in your Son our Saviour, Jesus Christ. He is Lord of time and of eternity; he is the living Word who became flesh and lived among us. We have seen his glory, full of grace and truth. Here we bow before you:
and praise you for your greatness.

You, Lord God, have commanded the light to shine out of darkness. You have lit up our minds and our emotions, and we are receiving knowledge of you and your gracious dealing through Jesus Christ. Eternal God:
we praise you, adore you, and bless your holy name;
through Jesus Christ our Lord. Amen.

2.32 BLESSING
From 'Still Waters, Deep Waters'

The Lord be within *you* to strengthen *you*: around *you* to ward off *your* spiritual foes on every side, under *you* to hold *you* up along the way, behind *you* to guard *you* from the assaults of the past, before *you* to lead *you* on; and the blessing of God – Father, Son and Holy Spirit – be upon *you* and remain with *you* always. **Amen.**

The People of God, Covenant and Unity

▶ **3.1** GREETING
From Galatians 6†

Peace and mercy to the people of God. **Amen.**

3.2 SENTENCE
Exodus 19.6

God said to his people 'Although the whole earth is mine, you will be for me a kingdom of priests and a holy nation'.

3.3 SENTENCE
Isaiah 41.10

God says to his people, 'Do not fear, for I am with you; do not be dismayed, for I am your God. I will strengthen you and help you; I will uphold you with my righteous right hand'.

3.4 SENTENCE
Deuteronomy 15.5

If you fully obey the voice of the Lord your God . . . then he will richly bless you.

3.5 SENTENCE
Ephesians 2.19

We are no longer foreigners and aliens, but fellow-citizens with God's people.

3.6 SENTENCE
1 Peter 2.9

You are a chosen people, a royal priesthood, a holy nation, a people belonging to God, that you may declare the praises of him who called you out of darkness into his wonderful light.

3.7   SENTENCE
John 10.16

Jesus said 'I am the good shepherd: I have other other sheep that I must bring also. They too will listen to my voice, and there shall be one flock and one shepherd'.

3.8   SENTENCE
John 17.11

Jesus said 'Holy Father, protect by the power of your name those you gave me out of the world so that they may be one as we are one'.

3.9   SENTENCE
Ephesians 2.18

Through Christ Jesus we have access to the Father by one Spirit.

3.10   SENTENCE
Daniel 9.9

Compassion and forgiveness belong to the Lord our God, though we have rebelled against him.

▶ **3.11**   RESPONSE
From Psalm 95†

Come, let us bow down in worship, let us kneel before the Lord our maker:
for he is our God;
we are the sheep of his pasture,
the people of his care. Amen.

▶ **3.12**   RESPONSE
From Psalm 100†

Know that the Lord is God:
It is he who made us, and we are his,
we are his people, the sheep of his pasture.

3.13 APPROACH
From Psalm 100†

Almighty Lord, all the earth shouts with joy; and we your people come before you with joyful songs. We know that you are God; you made us, and we are yours – we are your people and the sheep of your pasture. (Today) we enter your gates with thanksgiving and come into your presence with praise – we give you thanks and praise your name. For you, Lord, are good; you are faithful to every generation, and your love endures for ever and ever. **Amen.**

3.14 APPROACH
Editors

Our gracious and eternal heavenly Father, it is our joy to come together as your children around you, to know that you give power to the faint, and increase strength to those who feel weak.

You have made all things; your creation astounds us. Though you are God and all things come from you, yet you have promised to look to the one who is humble and contrite in Spirit, who trembles at your word.

We come as your believing children – called by your grace to be members of your family.

We come to give you our praise for your gracious goodness and constant provision for our needs.

Help us to be quiet, relaxed and receptive today, accepting the inpouring of your love, so that in the depths of our nature and being, your healing grace may take from us all anxious cares, all unwholesome thoughts and ingratitude.

We affirm your presence. We know you are absolutely dependable: our forbears trusted and were not disappointed. We trust and find life and purpose in our Lord Jesus Christ, whom you have sent to be our saviour. To you be glory for ever and ever. **Amen.**

3.15 APPROACH (UNITY)
Editors

God of love and unity, we come to you now to pray for your Church, the Body of Christ on earth. Forgive us for the sin of disunity: forgive us for the times when we have allowed personal preferences to become more important than Christ's message of love and salvation; forgive us for the times when we have been intolerant and over-critical of one another – forgive us for our judgemental attitudes. Forgive us for wounding Christ's body again and again; and causing you grief.

Lord, we ask you to cleanse us and lead us into the full light of your Holy Spirit, so that we may cast aside distrust and truly embrace all our sisters and brothers. Fill our hearts with your love so that we shall be ready to accept any difference and learn from each other with meekness and humility. Let every decision and action be the fruit of our shared love for you; let this love be paramount in every cherished hope or plan. Grant us the grace and courage to worship in unity beneath your canopy of love and peace. Father, make us one, for our dear Lord's sake. **Amen.**

▶ **3.16** PRAISE
From Psalm 117†

Praise the Lord, all you nations;
extol him, all you peoples!

For his love protecting us is strong;
his faithfulness endures for ever! Amen.

▶ **3.17** PRAISE
From Psalm 72†

Praise the Lord, the God of Israel:
he alone does marvellous things.

Praise his glorious name for ever;
let his glory fill the earth! Amen. Amen.

▶ **3.18** PRAISE
From Revelation 19†

Praise our God, all you his servants, you who fear him both small and great:
Alleluia!

Alleluia!
Salvation and glory and power

belong to our God,
for true and just are his judgements.
Alleluia! Amen!

▶ **3.19** CONFESSION
Editors

Father God, we thank you for calling us and making us your children:

In bringing us out of spiritual darkness and giving us light, you desire that we should be clearly seen as your people. When we fail to live up to your expectations – Father, be merciful:
forgive us and help us.

When we show uncaring attitudes; when our selfish desires are revealed in our life-style – Father, be merciful:
forgive us and help us.

When we become mesmerised by trivial things of this world, and forget important things which belong to your kingdom – Father, be merciful:
forgive us and help us.

When we hold on to petty differences in the practice of our faith, and fail to show the unity of your family – Father, be merciful:
forgive us and help us.

Father, purify us continually;
make us die to self
and rise to newness of life
in Jesus Christ our Lord. Amen.

▶ **3.20** CONFESSION
From Daniel 9†

O Lord our God, you brought your people out of slavery with a mighty hand, and made for yourself a name which endures to this day:

We have sinned, we have done wrong. O Lord, hear:
O Lord, forgive!

In keeping with all your righteous acts, turn away your anger from your people. O Lord, hear:
O Lord, forgive!

Our sins have made us despised by those around us. O Lord, hear:
O Lord, forgive!

We do not come before you because we are righteous, but because of your great mercy. O Lord, hear:
O Lord, forgive!

O Lord our God, do not delay
but send your holy Spirit
to revive your church,
because your people bear the name of Christ. Amen.

▶ **3.21** CONFESSION
From Isaiah 59†

O God,
our offences are many in your sight,
and our sins testify against us;
our wrongdoing is ever with us,
and we acknowledge our iniquities;
we have rebelled against you
and acted treacherously towards you
turning our backs on you:
O God, forgive us,
through Jesus Christ our Lord. Amen.

3.22 ABSOLUTION
From Isaiah 12†

Praise the Lord: although he was angry with *you*, in the name of Jesus his anger is turned away and he will comfort *you*. God is *your* salvation – (let us) trust and do not be afraid. **Amen.**

▶ **3.23** COLLECT
Sixth Sunday before Christmas, ASB 1980

Lord God our redeemer,
you heard the cry of your people
and sent your servant Moses
    to lead them out of slavery:

free us from the tyranny of sin and death
and, by the leading of your Spirit,
bring us to our promised land;
through Jesus Christ our Lord. **Amen.**

▶ **3.24** COLLECT
Seventh Sunday before Easter, ASB 1980

Merciful Lord,
grant to your faithful people pardon and peace:
that we may be cleansed from all our sins
and serve you with a quiet mind;
through Jesus Christ our Lord. **Amen.**

▶ **3.25** COLLECT
Pentecost 2, Church of Ireland APB 1984

Almighty and eternal God,
you have called us to be your people:
bring us to closer unity and fellowship
with you and one another,
so that every member of your Church
may serve you in holiness and truth;
through our Lord and Saviour Jesus Christ. **Amen.**

▶ **3.26** PSALM
Psalm 105.1–45†

The congregation – and ministers/leaders – may divide at A, B *and* C

Give thanks to the Lord, praise his name:
A **tell the nations what he has done.**

Sing to him, sing praise to him:
B **tell of all his wonderful deeds.**

Glory in his holy name:
C **let all who worship him rejoice.**

Go to the Lord for help:
A **and worship him for ever.**

Remember the wonders he does:
B **the miracles he performs.**

35

He is the Lord our God:
c **he judges the whole wide earth.**

He keeps his word and covenant:
A **for a thousand generations.**

The covenant he made with Abraham:
B **the oath he swore to Israel.**

He brought them out of Egypt:
c **and none of them was lost.**

He gave a cloud for covering:
A **a pillar of fire by night.**

He gave them bread from heaven:
B **and water from the rock.**

He brought his people out rejoicing:
c **his chosen ones with shouts of joy.**

ALL **Praise the Lord! Amen**

3.27 READING: JOSHUA SPEAKS TO THE PEOPLE
From Joshua 24. 14–25

Cast: [Narrator], Joshua, Person 1, Person 2, Person 3 (Persons 1–3 can be the same)

[Narrator
Joshua said:]

Joshua
Now then, honour the Lord and serve him sincerely and faithfully. Get rid of the gods which your ancestors used to worship in Mesopotamia and in Egypt, and serve only the Lord. If you are not willing to serve him, decide today whom you will serve, the gods your ancestors worshipped in Mesopotamia or the gods of the Amorites, in whose land you are now living. As for my family and me, we will serve the Lord.

[Narrator
The people replied:]

Person 1
We would never leave the Lord to serve other gods!

Person 2
The Lord our God brought our fathers and us out of slavery in Egypt –

Person 3

And we saw the miracles that he performed.

Person 2

He kept us safe wherever we went among all the nations through which we passed.

Person 3

As we advanced into this land, the Lord drove out all the Amorites who lived here.

Person 1

So *we also* will serve the Lord; he is our God.

Joshua

But you may not be *able* to serve the Lord. He is a holy God and will not forgive your sins. He will tolerate no rivals, and if you leave him to serve foreign gods, he will turn against you and punish you. He will destroy you, even though he was good to you before.

Person 1

No –

Persons 2 and 3

We *will* serve the Lord!

Joshua (*firmly*)

You are your own witnesses to the fact that you have chosen to serve the Lord.

Persons 1 and 2

Yes –

Person 3

We are witnesses.

Joshua (*demanding*)

Then get rid of those foreign gods that you have, and pledge your loyalty to the Lord, the God of Israel.

Person 1

We will serve the Lord our God.

Person 2

We will obey his commands.

Narrator

So Joshua made a covenant for the people that day.

Cast
    [This is] the word of the Lord.

All
    Thanks be to God.

FURTHER BIBLE READINGS
Readings appropriate to this theme will be found listed in our companion volume, 'TheDramatised Bible' (published by HarperCollins) on index page 421.

▶ **3.28**   CREED
From 1 Corinthians 8 and 12†

There is one God and Father:
from him all things come.

There is one Lord Jesus Christ:
through him we come to God.

There is one Holy Spirit:
in him we are baptised into one body.

We believe and trust in one God:
Father, Son and Holy Spirit. Amen.

▶ **3.29**   CREED
From Ephesians 4†

As God's people, let us declare our faith:

There is one body and one Spirit,
just as we were called to one hope;
one Lord, one faith, one baptism:
one God and Father of all,
who is over all, and through all,
and in all. Amen.

3.30   FOR UNITY
From 'New Every Morning'

Father, we pray for your Church throughout the world, that it may share to the full in the work of your Son, revealing you to men and women and reconciling all to you and to one another; that we and all

Christian people may learn to love one another as you have loved us, and your Church may more and more reflect the unity which is your will and your gift in Jesus Christ our Lord. **Amen.**

3.31 FOR UNITY
For the Unity of the Church, ASB 1980

Heavenly Father, you have called us in the Body of your Son Jesus Christ to continue his work of reconciliation and reveal you to mankind. Forgive us the sins which tear us apart; give us the courage to overcome our fears and to seek that unity which is your gift and your will; through Jesus Christ our Lord. **Amen.**

3.32 FOR UNITY IN CHRIST
Editors

Lord Jesus Christ, you are the Vine, we are the branches: help us to grow towards your light; feed, nurture and direct us, for the sake of your Church which is rooted in divine love and grace. Cut away our misguided attitudes and make us truly sorry for the blight and shame of Christian disunity. Gentle Lord, direct us again to your Cross, where we may bury our pride; drench us with the dew of heaven, that we may bring forth new fruit and worship you as one. **Amen.**

▶ **3.33** UNITY IN THE SPIRIT
From Romans 1†

God our Father,
always when we pray
we thank you for our fellowship
with others whom you love
and have called to be your own people:
help us to share our spiritual blessings with them,
and so to be made strong together –
our faith helping them
and their faith helping ours;
through Jesus Christ our Lord. **Amen.**

3.34 FOR UNITY AND PEACE
Editors

Father of all, we acknowledge you as the source of life and love; help us to remember that we are sisters and brothers and this is your world, help us to understand how you have spoken to us through your dear Son, and help us to respond to your message of love: for it is only when we learn to walk in peace with each other and live at peace with you, that we find sanctity and discover the true joy of living; thank you, Lord. **Amen.**

▶ **3.35** FOR GOD'S GRACE
Editors

O God, we are your people: in your Son you have redeemed us; by your Spirit you have sealed us as your own.

Make our hearts respond to your love. Lord, receive our praise,
and hear our prayer.

Make our lives bear witness to your mercy. Lord, receive our praise,
and hear our prayer.

Make our wills ready to obey. Lord, receive our praise,
and hear our prayer.

Show us your glory,
that we may delight in your presence,
and walk with you faithfully all our days. Amen.

3.36 FOR FREEDOM FROM OUR PREJUDICES
Ian Bunting

O Lord Jesus Christ, prince of peace, break down the barriers which separate us from each other and from God. Teach Christians to love each other across the walls of colour, class and creed; forgive us, too, the excuses we make for our own prejudice. And lead us captive in your cause of peace and goodwill on earth; for your name's sake. **Amen.**

3.37 FOR FORGIVENESS AND LOVE
Editors

Come, Lord Jesus, forgive us for our divisions and unite us in your love; break down the barriers we have built, and draw us together in the bond of peace. All our hope is in you, Lord Jesus: help us to see where we fail you, and forgive us for our short-sighted and wilfull attitudes; help us to live, work and worship in harmony with one another, and so bring honour to your name; fill our hearts with divine love and grant us new opportunities to share that love with our sisters and brothers across the world; for your glory and the sake of your Kingdom. **Amen.**

▶ ### 3.38 FOR FORGIVENESS
From Exodus 34†

Lord, the only God,
compassionate and gracious,
slow to anger, full of love:
be with us now.
Judge of the guilty:
though we have been stubborn,
though we have rebelled against you,
yet forgive our wickedness and sin
and receive us as your own;
through Jesus Christ our Lord. **Amen.**

3.39 FOR THE JOURNEY OF LIFE
Editors

Our gracious God and heavenly Father, you are the source of all life and vitality. You provided Israel of old with food, and sustained your people with your presence as they travelled through the wilderness; you saved them from desolation and dejection, and gave them a purpose for toiling onward to their destiny. Thank you that you feed us in Christ today, and are present with us through the Holy Spirit. We ask you to bless those who are tired and despondent; assure them that you will make provision for rest and refreshment, and grant us all a vision of your eternal purpose; through Jesus Christ our Lord. **Amen.**

▶ **3.40** THANKSGIVING
From 1 Corinthians 12†

We thank God for our unity in diversity.

There are different kinds of gifts:
but the same Spirit.

There are different kinds of service:
but the same Lord.

There are different kinds of working:
but the same God.

**Praise to God almighty,
Father, Son and Holy Spirit,
who works in us in all these ways. Amen.**

3.41 FOR GOD'S PRESENCE
From Isaiah 35†

O God, lead us in the way of holiness, cleanse us for our journey and teach us to be wise; guard your redeemed, crown your ransomed ones with everlasting joy; let sorrow and sighing flee away, and gladness overtake us; in Jesus Christ our Lord. **Amen.**

3.42 THANKSGIVING
Editors

O God, we thank you that your divine adequacy is able to meet every human need; we praise you that as the whole caravan of humanity and time journeys purposefully on – seeking, dreaming, stretching, strengthening – you are with us, the almighty, loving God. In Jesus Christ you control the creativeness of life, confirming in us this day your lordship over time and eternity; for your glory. **Amen.**

▶ **3.43** DEDICATION (UNITY)
Unkown

**God our Father,
in the name of Christ
and in the power of the Spirit,
we commit ourselves**

to you and to one another,
to live, work and pray
as one body in Christ;
to do apart
nothing which we can do together,
and to do together
what we cannot do apart.

Give us vision,
give us courage,
and give us joy,
that the world may believe
that Jesus is Lord
to your eternal glory. Amen.

▶ **3.44**   THE TEN COMMANDMENTS
From Exodus 20/Deuteronomy 5†

Let us hear the decrees and the laws of the Lord, learn them, and be
sure to follow them:

'You shall have no other gods but me':
Lord, help us to love you
with all our heart, all our soul,
all our mind and all our strength.

'You shall not make for yourself any idol':
Lord, help us to worship you
in spirit and in truth.

'You shall not dishonour the name of the Lord your God':
Lord, help us to honour you with reverence and awe.

'Remember the Lord's day and keep it holy':
Lord, help us to celebrate Christ
risen from the dead,
and to set our minds on things above,
not on things on the earth.

'Honour your father and your mother':
Lord, help us to live as your servants,
giving respect to all,
and love to our brothers and sisters in Christ.

'You shall not murder'
Lord, help us to be reconciled with each other,
and to overcome evil with good.

'You shall not commit adultery':
**Lord, help us to realise
that our body is a temple of the Holy Spirit.**

'You shall not steal':
**Lord, help us to be honest in all we do,
and to care for those in need.**

'You shall not be a false witness':
Lord, help us always to speak the truth.

'You shall not covet anything which belongs to your neighbour':
**Lord, help us to remember Jesus said,
'It is more blessed to give than to receive',
and help us to love our neighbours as ourselves;
for his sake. Amen.**

▶ **3.45** DEDICATION
From Deuteronomy 26†

Choose for yourselves this day whom you will serve:
We will serve the Lord!

You are witnesses against yourselves that you have chosen to serve the Lord:
Yes, we are witnesses.

Serve no other gods; yield your hearts to the Lord your God:
We will serve the Lord our God and obey him. Amen.

▶ **3.46** ACT OF COMMITMENT (THE TEN COMMANDMENTS)
From Exodus 20/Deuteronomy 5†

Let us resolve to follow the decrees and the laws of the Lord:

Lord, we will have no other God but you.

**Lord, we will not make idols for ourselves,
nor will we worship them.**

Lord, we will not dishonour your name.

Lord, we will remember your day and keep it holy.

Lord, we will honour our father and our mother.

Lord, we will do no murder.

Lord, we will not commit adultery.

Lord, we will not steal.

Lord, we will not be a false witness.

Lord, we will not covet anything that belongs to another.

May the awe of your presence
and the vision of your glory
keep us from sinning,
for the sake of Jesus our redeemer. Amen.

3.47 EXHORTATION (Following recital of commandments)
From Deuteronomy 26†

You have declared this day that the Lord is your God and that you will walk in his ways, that you will keep his decrees, commands and laws, and that you will obey him. And the Lord declares that you are his people, his treasured possession – holy to the Lord your God, as he promised in Jesus our Redeemer.

Thanks be to God. **Amen.**

▶ **3.48** ASCRIPTION
From Revelation 5†

You are worthy, O Lord our God:
to receive glory and honour and power.

For you created all things:
and by your will they existed
and were created.

Your are worthy, O Christ, for you were slain:
and by your blood
you ransomed us for God.

From every tribe and tongue and people and nation:
you made us a kingdom of priests
to serve our God.

To him who sits upon the throne, and to the Lamb
be blessing and honour
and glory and might
for ever and ever. Amen.

▶ **3.49**   ASCRIPTION (BEFORE SONG)
From Exodus 5†

Who is like you, O Lord, our God – majestic in holiness, awesome in glory, working wonders?

In your unfailing love you will lead your redeemed;
in your strength you will guide us, Lord.

Let us sing to the Lord for he is highly exalted:
the Lord will reign for ever and ever. Amen.

▶ **3.50**   NIGHT PRAYER
Jim Cotter

O God of love and mercy,
grant us, with all your people,
rest and peace. **Amen.**

▶ **3.51**   BLESSING
1 Kings 8†

Praise to the Lord, who has given rest to his people:
not one word of all his promises has failed.

May the Lord your God be with *you:*
**may he never leave us
or forsake us.**

May he turn *your* hearts to him, to walk in his ways and to keep his commandments:
**may the words we have prayed
before the Lord our God
be near him day and night.**

Let all the people of the earth know the Lord is God:
there is no other! Amen.

3.52   BLESSING
From Romans 15†

The God of patience and encouragement give you a spirit of unity among yourselves as you follow Christ Jesus, that with one mind and one mouth you may glorify the God and Father of our Lord Jesus Christ; and the blessing of God almighty, the Father, the Son and the Holy Spirit be with you always. **Amen.**

3.53 BLESSING
From 1 Corinthians 16†

Be on your guard, stand firm in the faith, be people of courage, be strong, do everything in love; and the grace of the Lord Jesus be with you. **Amen.**

3.54 BLESSING
2 Corinthians 11†

Be of one mind, live in peace: and the God of love and peace be with you always. **Amen.**

3.55 BLESSING
From Numbers 6†

The Lord bless *you* and keep *you*, the Lord make his face to shine upon *you* and be gracious to *you*, the Lord lift up his countenance upon *you* and give *you* peace; and the blessing of God the Father, Son and Holy Spirit be among *you* and remain with *you* always. **Amen.**

3.56 BLESSING
From Deuteronomy 10†

Fear the Lord your God, walk in his ways, love him with all your heart, serve him with all your soul, obey his commandments; and the blessing of God almighty, the Father, the Son and the Holy Spirit be with you always. **Amen.**

▶ **3.57** BLESSING
From Psalm 128†

The Lord bless *you* all the days of *your* life; may *your* community prosper; may *your* families flourish:
peace be upon the Lord's people.

The blessing of God the Father, God the Son and God the Holy Spirit be with *you* always. **Amen.**

3.58   BLESSING (UNITY)
From Romans 15†

God who gives *you* endurance and encouragement, give *you* a spirit of unity among *yourselves* as *you* follow Christ Jesus, so that with one heart and mouth *you* may glorify the God and Father of our Lord Jesus Christ. **Amen.**

3.59   BLESSING (UNITY)
From Romans 15†

The God of strength and encouragement grant you to live in such harmony with each other, that together you may with one voice glorify the God and Father of our Lord Jesus Christ; and the blessing of God the Father, God the Son, and God the Holy Spirit be with you always. **Amen.**

▶ **3.60**   BLESSING
From 2 Corintians 13†

Strive for perfection, listen to wisdom, agree with one another, live in peace; and the God of love and peace be with you always. **Amen.**

Following Jesus, Jesus' Teaching

▶ **4.1** GREETING
From Ephesians 6†

Grace to all who love our Lord Jesus Christ with an undying love.
Amen.

4.2 SENTENCE
John 14.6

Jesus answered, 'I am the way and the truth and the life. No one comes to the Father except through me'.

4.3 SENTENCE
John 8.12

Jesus said, 'I am the light of the world. Whoever follows me will never walk in darkness, but will have the light of life'.

4.4 SENTENCE
John 10, 14

Jesus said, 'I am the good shepherd, and know my sheep, and am known by mine'.

4.5 SENTENCE
Luke 24.27

Beginning with Moses and all the Prophets, Jesus explained to them what was said in all the Scriptures concerning himself.

4.6 SENTENCE
Mark 1.17

Jesus said to the fisherman, 'Follow me, and I will make you fishers of men'.

4.7 SENTENCE
Matthew 11.29, [30]

[Jesus said,] 'Take my yoke upon you and learn from me, for I am gentle and humble in heart, and you will find rest for your souls. [For my yoke is easy and my burden is light]'.

▶ **4.8** RESPONSE
From John 6†

Lord, to whom shall we go?
you have the words of eternal life.

▶ **4.9** RESPONSE
From 2 Timothy 1†

God did not give us a spirit of timidity:
but of power, of love
and of self-discipline. Amen.

▶ **4.10** RESPONSE
From Hebrews 12†

Let us fix our eyes on Jesus:
the author and goal of our faith. Amen.

▶ **4.11** APPROACH
From 'New Every Morning'

Heavenly Father, from our hearts we thank you for the light of this new day. May we so spend its hours in the perfect freedom of your service, that when evening comes we may again give you thanks. Direct and control us in every part of our life:

Our tongues, that we speak no false or angry words –
Lord, keep us from wrong-speaking.

Our actions, that we may do nothing to shame ourselves or hurt others –
Lord, keep us from wrong-doing.

Our minds, that we may think no evil or bitter thoughts –
Lord, keep us from wrong-thinking.

Our hearts, that they may be set only on pleasing you –
Lord, keep us in your love,
through Jesus Christ our Lord. Amen.

▶ **4.12** PRAISE
From Psalm 113†

Praise the Lord, you servants of the Lord;
praise the name of the Lord.

Blessed be the name of the Lord;
both now and evermore. Amen.

▶ **4.13** CONFESSION
Editors.

Almighty God, our Father, we come to you with humble hearts, to confess our sins:

For turning away from you, and ignoring your will for our lives: Father, forgive us,
save us and help us.

For behaving just as we wish, without thinking of you: Father, forgive us,
save us and help us.

For failing you – not only by what we do, but also by our thoughts and words: Father, forgive us,
save us and help us.

For letting ourselves be drawn away from you by temptations in the world about us: Father, forgive us,
save us and help us.

For acting as if we were ashamed to belong to your dear Son Jesus: Father, forgive us,
save us and help us.

Father, we have failed you often, and humbly ask your forgiveness:
help us so to live
that others may see your glory;
through Jesus Christ our Lord. Amen.

▶ **4.14**   CONFESSION
From Psalm 101†

Lord God, our hearts are guilty,
we have been dishonest,
we have looked on evil,
we have clung to our selfish ways.
We have talked about others behind their backs
with haughty eyes and a proud heart.
Lord, forgive us and help us;
renew us in righteousness every morning:
make our lives faithful and our talk blameless
that we may live in your presence for ever
through Jesus Christ our Lord. Amen.

▶ **4.15**   A PERSONAL CONFESSION
Editors

Jesus, my strength, my love, my life,
I have sinned against you
and I now humbly confess it.
I am sorry, Jesus.
Please forgive me and restore me to spiritual health:
for in you I find my rest, my peace, my joy –
in you I am complete. Amen.

4.16   ABSOLUTION
From Psalm 116†

The Lord knows *your* voice; the Lord hears *your* cry for mercy; the Lord turns his ear toward *you*. The Lord is gracious and righteous, he is full of compassion; in *your* need he has saved you. [Let us] be at peace, *your* God forgives *you*; through Jesus Christ. **Amen.**

▶ **4.17**   COLLECT
9 before Easter, ASB 1980

Eternal God,
whose Son Jesus Christ is for all people
the way, the truth and the life:
grant us to walk in his way,
to rejoice in his truth,

and to share his risen life;
who is alive and reigns with you and the Holy Spirit,
one God, now and for ever. **Amen.**

▶ **4.18**   COLLECT
Pentecost 18, ASB 1980

Almighty God,
you have made us for yourself,
and our hearts are restless
till they find their rest in you:
teach us to offer ourselves to your service,
that here we may have your peace,
and in the world to come
    may see you face to face;
through Jesus Christ our Lord. **Amen.**

▶ **4.19**   PSALM
Psalm 40.4–16†

The congregation – and ministers – may divide at A *and* B

Happy are those who trust in God:
who do not worship idols.

Sacrifice and offering you do not desire:
A **but you want my ears to be open.**

So I said, 'Lord I come:
B **obedient to your word.'**

I delight to do your will, O God:
A **and keep your teaching in my heart.**

I'll tell the world your saving news:
B **you know my lips will not be sealed.**

I have not hid your righteousness:
A **but speak of all your salvation, Lord.**

I do not hide your faithful love:
B **but share your mercy with them all.**

May all who come to you be glad; may all who know your
saving power for ever say:
ALL **How great is the Lord! Amen.**

4.20   READING: JESUS MAKES UP HIS TEAM
From John 1 and Matthew 4 and 9

Cast: Narrator, Jesus, Philip, Nathanael, Pharisee.

Narrator
Jesus decided to go to Galilee. He found Philip [and said]:

Jesus
Come with me!

Narrator
Philip found Nathanael [and told him]:

Philip
We have found the one whom Moses wrote about in the book of the Law, and whom the prophets also wrote about. He is Jesus son of Joseph, from Nazareth.

[Narrator
Nathanael asked:]

Nathanael
Can anything good come from Nazareth?

Philip
Come and see.

Narrator
When Jesus saw Nathanael coming to him, he said about him:

Jesus
Here is a real Israelite; there is nothing false in him!

Nathanael
How do you know me?

Jesus
I saw you when you were under the fig-tree before Philip called you.

Nathanael
Teacher, you are the Son of God! You are the King of Israel.

Narrator
As Jesus walked along the shore of Lake Galilee, he saw two brothers who were fishermen, Simon – called Peter – and his brother Andrew, catching fish in the lake with a net. [Jesus said to them:]

Jesus

Come with me, and I will teach you to catch men.

Narrator

At once they left their nets and went with him. (PAUSE)

He went on and saw two other brothers, James and John, the sons of Zebedee. They were in their boat with their father Zebedee, getting their nets ready. Jesus called them, and at once they left the boat and their father, and went with him.

As Jesus walked along, he saw a tax collector, named Matthew, sitting in his office. [He said to him:]

Jesus

Follow me.

Narrator

Matthew got up and followed him. (PAUSE)

While Jesus was having a meal in Matthew's house, many tax collectors and other outcasts came and joined Jesus and his disciples at the table. Some Pharisees saw this and asked his disciples:

Pharisee

Why does your teacher eat with such people?

Narrator

Jesus heard them [and answered]:

Jesus

People who are well do not need a doctor, but only those who are sick. I have not come to call respectable people, but outcasts.

Cast

[This is] the word of the Lord.   OR   This is the Gospel of Christ/
                                        This is the Gospel of the Lord.

All

Thanks be to God.   **Praise to Christ our Lord/
                                          Praise to you, Lord Jesus Christ.**

▶ **4.21** READING: THE BEATITUDES
Matthew 5.3–12

LEADER Happy are those who know they are spiritually poor:
ALL **The Kingdom of heaven belongs to them!**

LEADER Happy are those who mourn:
ALL **God will comfort them!**

LEADER Happy are those who are humble:
ALL **They will receive what God has promised!**

LEADER Happy are those whose greatest desire is to do what God requires:
ALL **God will satisfy them fully!**

LEADER Happy are those who are merciful to others:
ALL **God will be merciful to them!**

LEADER Happy are the pure in heart:
ALL **They will see God!**

LEADER Happy are those who work for peace:
ALL **God will call them his children!**

LEADER Happy are those who are persecuted because they do what God requires:
ALL **The Kingdom of heaven belongs to them!**

LEADER Happy are you when people insult you and persecute you and tell all kinds of evil lies against you because you are Christ's disciples. Be happy and glad, for a great reward is kept for you in heaven.

LEADER [This is] the word of the Lord.
ALL **Thanks be to God.**

OR This is the Gospel of Christ/This is the Gospel of the Lord.
Praise to Christ our Lord/Praise to you, Lord Jesus Christ.

FURTHER BIBLE READINGS
Readings appropriate to this theme will be found listed in our companion volume, 'The Dramatised Bible' (published by HarperCollins) on index pages 421–422.

▶ **4.22** CREED
From 1 Corinthians 8 and 12†

There is one God and Father:
from him all things come.

There is one Lord Jesus Christ:
through him we come to God.

There is one Holy Spirit:
in him we are baptized into one body.

We believe and trust in one God:
Father, Son, and Holy Spirit. Amen.

▶ **4.23** FOR STRENGTH TO FOLLOW JESUS
Unknown

Jesus said: 'If one of you wants to be great, he must be the servant of
the rest' – Master, we hear your call:
help us to follow.

Jesus said: 'Unless you change and become humble like little
children, you can never enter the Kingdom of heaven' – Master, we
hear your call:
help us to follow.

Jesus said: 'Happy are those who are humble; they will receive what
God has promised' – Master, we hear your call:
help us to follow.

Jesus said: 'Be merciful just as your Father is merciful; love your
enemies and do good to them' – Master, we hear your call:
help us to follow.

Jesus said: 'Love one another, just as I love you; the greatest love a
person can have for his friends is to give his life for them' – Master,
we hear your call:
help us to follow.

Jesus said: 'Go to all peoples everywhere and make them my
disciples, and I will be with you always, to the end of the world' –
Master, we hear your call:
help us to follow.

Lord, you have redeemed us and called us to your service:
give us grace to hear your word and to obey your command;
for your mercy's sake. Amen.

▶ **4.24** ABOUT OUR DISCIPLESHIP
From 'New Every Morning'

Lord Jesus, you have called us to the life of discipleship: make us
better disciples. You have taught us something of your truth: teach
us still more. O Lord, hear us:
Lord, hear us and help us.

Give us at all times openness of mind and humility of heart, that we
may learn your will and follow you more closely. O Lord, hear us:
Lord, hear us and help us.

As you have called us to be your disciples, so make us ready to learn
all that you wish to teach us. O Lord, hear us:
Lord, hear us and help us.

Open our eyes to your truth,
open our ears to your call;
and in the tasks of life
strengthen us to seek your will and serve your kingdom. Amen.

▶ **4.25** FOR STRENGTH TO OBEY JESUS
From Matthew 22 and John 13†

We pray for God's strength to keep Jesus' commandment:

'Love the Lord your God with all your heart, with all your mind,
with all your soul, and with all your strength':
Lord, help us to obey.

'Love your neighbour as yourself':
Lord, help us to obey.

'Love one another as I have loved you':
Lord, help us to obey.

In your mercy strengthen us
and move our hearts to do your will. Amen.

4.26 FOR OUR CHARACTER
Editors

Lord, we live as your creatures in this your world so magnificent yet
so often abused. We live among people who reject spiritual things;
their jokes depress us, their values are so flimsy, their superficiality
saddens us, they seem so insensitive to the real and beautiful, they

are oblivious to your love, and careless of their responsibility to others. Lord, you lived among people who were uncouth in speech, hypocrites; who were double-tongued and two-faced; you lived for thirty-three years among the grasping – those who were only out for things which rust and decay. Yet you went on loving, forgiving, helping – hating the sin yet loving the sinner, facing people with themselves and taking the consequence. Help us to follow you. **Amen.**

4.27 FOR STRENGTH TO LIVE FOR JESUS
Editors

Lord Jesus, so often our minds are bombarded with sad and evil things, our tongues speak unkind and negative words, our hearts are cold and sometimes callous in the face of human need. Help us, we pray, to speak carefully and to act wisely. Cleanse us from selfish living, and in your strength enable us to serve you with integrity. So may we love you well who first loved us, Jesus Christ our Lord. **Amen.**

▶ 4.28 FOR OUR DAILY LIVES
Editors

Lord God our Father, grant us to know your control throughout this day. Give us grace that we may live each hour conscious of your presence.

Guard our tongues from careless and unhelpful words, from all false and uncontrolled speaking; Lord, have mercy on us:
guard us today.

Fill our minds with your truth, that we may think no bitter, unkind or evil thoughts; Lord, have mercy on us:
fill us today.

Save us from actions which hurt and bring discredit upon ourselves, our families and you; Lord, have mercy on us:
save us today.

Let your word of truth live in us richly, and let the mind of Jesus captivate our minds:
enable us to please you
and bring honour to your name;
through Jesus Christ our Saviour. Amen.

4.29 FOR OUR DAILY WALK WITH GOD
Editors

O God, give us a living faith, warm hearts and minds open to truth. Save us from wasting our energy in foolish speaking, in negative thinking, in unkind criticism. Help us to give as well as to receive, to serve as well as to be served, to test anew what we believe. Give us your strength in the Holy Spirit to live graciously, compassionately, considerately; for your glory's sake. **Amen.**

4.30 IN TROUBLE
Editors

Lord Jesus Christ, you were poor and in distress, a captive and forsaken. You know all our troubles, you stay with us when others fail us, you remember and seek us; it is your will that we should know you and turn to you. Lord, we hear your call and follow. **Amen.**

4.31 FOR SELF-CONTROL
(Variant of 4.28) Editors

Lord God, our strong heavenly Father, grant us to know your control in the hours of this day; guard our tongues from hurtful and unhelpful words, and from all false and careless speaking. Discipline our minds with your truth, that we may think no evil, bitter or unkind thoughts. Save us from actions which hurt and bring discredit upon ourselves or our families or society. Let your true word in all its richness live in us, and let the mind of Jesus captivate and control our minds. By your Spirit enable us to please you, and bring honour to your glorious name; through Christ our Lord. **Amen.**

▶ **4.32** TO BE DISCIPLES
Editors

Lord Jesus, when Peter, James and John heard your voice, they left their nets to follow you. We want to be followers too:
teach us your ways,
show us the right path
and, if we are slow to obey,
draw closer and call us again, Lord. Amen.

▶ **4.33** FOR OUR DAILY WALK WITH CHRIST
Editors

Lord Jesus,
help us to be aware of your presence each day
so that we do not squander
    a single moment of our lives;
keep us eager to hear your voice
so that we are ready to obey you when you call.
Jesus, please make us a blessing in the world,
and let us follow in the steps of our beloved Master,
to whom be all glory for ever. **Amen.**

▶ **4.34** FOR FAITH IN GOD'S LEADING
From 'A New Zealand Prayer Book'

Holy and eternal God,
give us such trust in your sure purpose,
that we measure our lives
not by what we have done or failed to do,
but by our faithfulness to you;
in Jesus our Redeemer. **Amen.**

4.35 THE WAY, THE TRUTH AND THE LIFE:
        A PERSONAL PRAYER
Editors

Lord Jesus, you are the Way: lead me through life's journey, for
without you I am lost. Lord Jesus, you are the Truth: illuminate my
path, help me to travel in your light. Lord Jesus, you are the Life: live
in me, and be my power for living, for in your love I am blessed and
made new. **Amen.**

▶ **4.36** COMING TO CHRIST: A PERSONAL PRAYER
Editors

Lord, in your love and mercy you are still calling sinners to repentance, calling stray sheep to the fold, calling prodigal sons to come home, calling all who labour and are heavy laden, calling new disciples to follow you:

Lord of Glory,
in your love and mercy say the word –
and I will come. Amen.

▶ **4.37** FOR OUR DAILY WALK WITH CHRIST
Attribute to Richard of Chichester

Lord Jesus Christ,
redeemer, friend and brother:
may we know you more clearly,
love you more dearly,
and follow you more nearly,
day by day. **Amen.**

4.38 THANKSGIVING FOR VISION
Alan Gaunt

Living God, thank you for every event, painful or pleasant, that has opened our eyes, lifted our hearts, brought us to life, pointed us beyond itself to some deep truth of nature or humanity, or given us a glimpse of your passing presence which calls us to follow to brave new adventures for you and all our fellow men and women; through Jesus Christ our Lord. **Amen.**

▶ **4.39** THANKSGIVING FOR JESUS' PRESENCE
Editors

Lord Jesus,
thank you for being our friend:
when we are weak, you strengthen us,
when we are lonely you speak to us,
when we are sad you comfort us,
when we are glad you rejoice with us;
you are our guide and keeper,
our shepherd and shield;
your presence is our constant joy. **Amen.**

▶ **4.40** THANKSGIVING
Editors

For the wonder of creation, we give you thanks, O Lord:
and praise your holy name.

For Christ, your Living Word, through whom we are taught the
perfect way of life, we give you thanks, O Lord:
and praise your holy name.

For the gifts and talents with which each of us is endowed, we give
you thanks, O Lord:
and praise your holy name.

For the blessing of home and family life, for companionship and true
friendship, we give you thanks, O Lord:
and praise your holy name.

**Glory to the Father and to the Son and to the Holy Spirit
as it was in the beginning
is now, and shall be for ever. Amen.**

▶ **4.41** FOR OBEDIENCE
From 'The Promise of His Glory'

Lord Jesus Christ,
Son of the Living God:
teach us to walk in your way more trustfully,
accept your truth more faithfully,
and share your life more lovingly;
so that we may come
by the power of the Holy Spirit
as one family
to the kingdom of the Father
where you live for ever and ever. **Amen.**

▶ **4.42** DEDICATION
Editors

Father,
we dedicate ourselves to serve you faithfully
and to follow Christ,
to face the future with him,
seeking his special purpose for our lives.

Send us out to work and to witness
    freely, gratefully and hopefully,
in the power of the Spirit,
and for the honour and glory of your Son,
Jesus our Lord. **Amen.**

▶ **4.43** DEDICATION
From Deuteronomy 10†

O Lord our God,
we want to fear you,
to walk in your ways,
to love and serve you with all our heart
    and all our soul,
and to obey your commandments;
for you are God of gods and Lord of lords,
the great one, mighty and awesome:
you are our God, and we praise you for ever. **Amen.**

4.44 BLESSING
From Hebrews 12†

[Let us Fix *your* eyes on Jesus, the author and finisher of *your* faith, who for the joy set before him endured the cross, scorning its shame, and sat down at the right hand of the throne on high; and the blessing of God almighty, Father, Son and Holy Spirit be with *you* always. **Amen.**

4.45 BLESSING
Unknown

The love of the Lord Jesus draw *you* to himself, the power of the Lord Jesus strengthen *you* in his service, the joy of the Lord Jesus fill *your* hearts. And the blessing of God almighty, the Father, the Son and the Holy Spirit be upon *you* and remain with *you* always. **Amen.**

4.46 BLESSING
2 Corinthians 11†

Be of one mind, live in peace; and the God of love and peace be with you always. **Amen.**

4.47 BLESSING
From 1 Timothy 6†

Strive for righteousness, godliness, faith, love, endurance and gentleness; run the race of faith, take hold of eternal life to which God called you when you confessed his name before the world; and the blessing of God almighty, Father Son and Holy Spirit will be with you always. **Amen.**

The Life of Prayer, Forgiveness

▶ **5.1** GREETING
From 2 Timothy 4†

The Lord be with your spirit:
grace be with you. Amen.

5.2 SENTENCE
Isaiah 65.24

The Lord says, 'Before you call I will answer; while you are still speaking I will hear'.

5.3 SENTENCE
1 Chronicles 16.11

Look to the Lord and his strength: seek his face always.

5.4 SENTENCE
Mark 1.35

Very early in the morning, while it was still dark, Jesus got up, left the house and went off to a solitary place, where he prayed.

5.5 SENTENCE
Philippians 4.6

In everything, by prayer and petition, with thanksgiving, make your requests known to God.

5.6 SENTENCE
Matthew 26.41

Watch and pray that you do not fall into temptation: the spirit is willing, but the body is weak.

▶ **5.7** RESPONSE
From Hebrews 10†

We have a great High Priest over the house of God:
let us draw near to God
with a sincere heart
in full assurance of faith. Amen.

▶ **5.8** RESPONSE
From Ephesians 6†

Pray in the Spirit on all occasions with all kinds of prayers and requests:
be alert and always keep on praying.

▶ **5.9** RESPONSE
From Psalm 51†

The sacrifice of God is a broken spirit:
a broken and contrite heart, O God you will not despise.

▶ **5.10** RESPONSE
From Daniel 9†

The Lord our God is merciful and forgiving:
even though we have rebelled against him.

▶ **5.11** RESPONSE
From Lamentations 3†

The Lord's compassions never fail; they are new every morning:
Great is your faithfulness, O Lord.

The Lord is good to those whose hope is in him; to the one who seeks him:
It is good to wait quietly for the salvation of the Lord.

▶ **5.12** RESPONSE
From 1 Corinthians 15†

The sting of death is sin, and the power of sin is the law:
But thanks be to God:
he gives us the victory
through our Lord Jesus Christ. Amen.

5.13 APPROACH
From Psalm 139†

O Lord, you have searched us and you know us; you know when we sit down and when we get up; you see us go out, you see us lie down. You know just what we are like. Before the word is off our lips, you know what we were going to say. You are all around us and your hand is upon us. Wherever we go, you are there with us – your hand guiding us, holding us fast. However dark it gets, it is not dark to you – your eyes follow us, you can see us. For you created us, formed us before ever we were born – how wonderfully you made us: we praise you, Lord! And you knew then each day that would come to be – how much you know, Lord! Each day when we awake, you are still with us.

O God, search our hearts, be with us in our anxieties, take away our sin, and lead us in your eternal way; through Jesus Christ our Lord. **Amen.**

5.14 APPROACH
Editors

Our Lord God, we come to you knowing that our words are inadequate, but that your Spirit can express our deepest desires; and we praise you that there is profound love and sympathy in your heart. You are always more ready to listen than we are to pray – so, Lord God, pour your life into us this day, that we may have a greater desire for your glory: we want our lives to overflow with your joy. We praise you that we can offer our worship and prayers in the name of Jesus Christ our Lord. **Amen.**

▶ **5.15** PRAISE
From Psalm 80†

Turn to us, almighty God;
look down from heaven and see!

Renew us, O Lord God almighty;
show us your mercy that we may be saved!

▶ **5.16** CONFESSION
Editors

Gracious God, we confess our shortcomings and our sins. How slow
we are to do good! In your mercy:
Lord, forgive us.

How easily we are deceived by passing values of the world! In your
mercy:
Lord, forgive us.

How weak is our hold on things which are eternal! In your mercy:
Lord, forgive us.

How glibly we blame and criticise others, and how slow we are to
blame ourselves! In your mercy:
Lord, forgive us.

Give us your pardon;
give us liberty;
help us not to be slaves to insecurity, doubt, and guilt;
help us to claim your promises as we confess our sins;
through Jesus our Lord. Amen.

▶ **5.17** CONFESSION
From Psalm 51†

The sacrifices of God are a broken spirit; a broken and contrite heart,
O God, you will not despise. O God, in your unfailing love:
have mercy on us.

We know our transgressions and our sin is ever before us; against
you only have we sinned and done what is evil in your sight. O God,
in your unfailing love:
have mercy on us.

According to your great compassion blot out our transgressions,

wash away all our iniquity and cleanse us from our sin. O God, in your unfailing love:
have mercy on us.

Cleanse us, and we shall be clean;
wash us, and we shall be whiter than snow;
through Jesus Christ our Lord. Amen.

5.18 ASSURANCE OF FORGIVENESS
From John 8 and Romans 8†

Jesus said 'I do not condemn you: go and sin no more'. There is no more condemnation for those who are in Christ Jesus. **Amen.**

5.19 ABSOLUTION
From Psalm 31†

The Lord have mercy upon *you* in *your* distress; the Lord deliver *you* from *your* sins and shelter *you* in all temptation; the Lord make his face shine upon *you* and save *you* in his unfailing love. **Amen.**

5.20 ABSOLUTION
From Psalm 103†

God who is merciful and loving will not punish *you* as *you* deserve or repay *you* for *your* sins and wrong-doing. As high as the sky is above the earth, so great is his love for *you*; as far as the east is from the west, so far will he remove *your* sins from *you*; through Jesus Christ our Lord. **Amen.**

▶ **5.21 COLLECT**
Pentecost 22, Church of Ireland APB 1984

Almighty God,
you gave your Son Jesus Christ
to break the power of evil:
free us from all darkness and temptation,
and bring us to eternal light and joy;
through the power of him
who lives and reigns
with you and the Holy Spirit,
one God, now and ever. **Amen.**

▶ **5.22** COLLECT
From Concluding Prayers, ASB 1980

Almighty God,
the fountain of all wisdom,
you know our needs before we ask,
and our ignorance in asking:
have compassion on our weakness,
and give us those things
which for our unworthiness we dare not,
and for our blindness we cannot ask,
for the sake of your Son, Jesus Christ our Lord. **Amen.**

▶ **5.23** PSALM
Psalm 80.1–19†

Ministers/leaders may divide at A, B *and* C

A Hear us, O Shepherd of Israel, leader of your flock.

B Hear us from your throne above the cherubim.

C Shine forth, awaken your strength, and come to save us.
Bring us back, O God, and save us,
make your face to shine upon us.

A O Lord God almighty, how long will you be angry with your people's prayers?

B You have given us sorrow to eat and tears to drink.

C You have made us a source of contention to our neighbours, and our enemies insult us.
Bring us back, O God, and save us,
make your face to shine upon us.

A Return to us, O God Almighty, look down from heaven and see.

B Look on this vine that you planted with your own hand, this child you raised for yourself.

C Let your hand rest upon the people you have chosen, then we will not turn away from you; revive us, and we shall praise your name.
Bring us back, O God, and save us,
make your face to shine upon us. Amen.

5.24   READING: THE PHARISEE AND THE TAX COLLECTOR
Luke 18.9–14

Cast: Narrator, Jesus, Pharisee, Tax Collector

Narrator
   Jesus told this parable to people who were sure of their own goodness and despised everybody else:

Jesus
   Once there were two men who went up to the Temple to pray: one was a Pharisee, the other a tax collector.

Narrator
   The Pharisee stood apart by himself and prayed:

Pharisee (*haughtily*)
   I thank you, God, that I am not greedy, dishonest, or an adulterer, like everybody else. I thank you that I am not like that tax collector over there. I fast two days a week, and I give you a tenth of all my income.

Jesus
   But the tax collector stood at a distance and would not even raise his face to heaven, but beat on his breast and said:

Tax collector (*humbly*)
   God, have pity on me, a sinner!

Jesus
   I tell you, the tax collector, and not the Pharisee, was in the right with God when he went home. For everyone who makes himself great will be humbled, and everyone who humbles himself will be made great.

Cast
   [This is] the word of the Lord.   OR   This is the Gospel of Christ/
                                              This is the Gospel of the Lord.

All
   Thanks be to God.   **Praise to Christ our Lord/**
                                              Praise to you, Lord Jesus Christ.

FURTHER BIBLE READINGS
Readings appropriate to this theme will be found listed in our companion volume, 'The Dramatised Bible' (published by HarperCollins) on index pages 422–423.

▶ **5.25**   CREED
From Hebrews 4†

Let us hold firmly to the faith we profess:

**We have a high priest
able to understand our weaknesses
who has gone into heaven:
Jesus, the Son of God.
He was tempted in every way,
just as we are –
yet without sin.**

**Therefore we approach
the throne of grace
with confidence,
to receive mercy
and find grace to help us
in our time of need. Amen.**

5.26   BEFORE PRAYER
From Hebrews 4†

Let us have confidence and approach God's throne where we will
receive mercy and grace to help us when we need it. [Let us pray.]

▶ **5.27**   AFTER PRAYER
From the Lima Liturgy

Into your hands, O Lord,
we commend all for whom we pray,
trusting in your mercy;
through your Son, Jesus Christ, our Lord. **Amen.**

5.28   FOR A HUNGER TO PRAY
Editors

Lord God, we acknowledge you as our Creator and loving Father,
and we thank you for the precious gift of prayer; it is wonderful to
know that you are ready to listen whenever we speak to you: help it
to be ready to listen whenever you speak to us. Thank you, Lord, for
prayer, which is our lifeline in every situation; for we know that you
are always present with us as we pray, even when our prayers are

not made of words. In prayer help us to receive your love, your forgiveness, your cleansing, your healing, your comfort, your peace, your power, your guidance, your grace – and your Spirit of holiness. Then shall we praise you with joy in our hearts, rejoicing in Christ's name. **Amen.**

▶ **5.29** FOR FRANKNESS BEFORE GOD
From 'A New Zealand Prayer Book'

All-seeing God,
teach us to be open with you about our needs,
to seek your support in our trials,
to admit before you our sins,
and to thank you for all your goodness;
for Jesus' sake. **Amen.**

▶ **5.30** FOR FORGIVENESS
From 'A New Zealand Prayer Book'

God of infinite love,
grant that we who know your mercy
may rejoice in your forgiveness
and gladly forgive others;
for the sake of Jesus Christ our Saviour. **Amen.**

5.31 FOR PENITENCE
Dick Williams, adapted

O God you made us and you love us; thank you for being so willing to forgive us: make us quick to own up to you whenever we do wrong, so that we may quickly be forgiven; then our day will not be spoilt by worry, and we shall live in your peace, through Jesus Christ our Lord. **Amen.**

5.32 FOR THE WILL TO FORGIVE
Eileen Wheeler

Heavenly Father, when we want your forgiveness for ourselves we can find so many reasons for our sinfulness; excuses, circumstances that seem to lessen our guilt.

Help us to be at least as willing to understand others – those whom we find offensive, distressing, infuriating – so that we may come to forgive them as much as we want to be forgiven by you.

Help us to put their past offences behind us, and let us learn to forgive each other as you have forgiven us for Christ's sake. **Amen.**

5.33 ABOUT TEMPTATION
From Psalm 141†

O Lord, hear us when we call to you – come quickly to save us; may our prayers rise up before you like incense, and the lifting of our hands like the evening sacrifice. Lord, set a guard over what we say; keep watch over the door of our lips. Don't let our heart be drawn to what is evil, to do wicked things; make us take notice of good people that we may let them correct us. Above all, keep our eyes fixed on you, for you alone are able to protect us from the snares of death and to make us live in safety; for your name's sake. **Amen.**

5.34 FOR STRENGTH IN TEMPTATION (LENT)
Unknown

Lord, we confess to you what we are: we like the path of life to be easy; we like every step to be free from fear; we like the world to be at our feet. Lord, by all the grace of your forty desert days, arm us against those temptations, alert us to their corruption, forgive us our sins, and teach us to tread the way that Jesus takes, for his sake. **Amen.**

5.35 FOR GOD'S HELP
Editors

Father, we need your help to fight our sins; we need your help to stop us saying or doing hurtful things: please bless us with the constant presence of your Holy Spirit, so that we can live clean and honest lives; show us how to make amends for any hurt we have caused, grant us the courage to say sorry, give us the grace to forgive others that we may be forgiven, and be able to forgive ourselves. Your love comforts us, Father; you are our strength and our song, our peace, our freedom and our joy; through Jesus, your Son, our Lord. **Amen.**

▶ **5.36   THAT WE MAY LIVE IN GOD**
From Philippians 4†

O God of peace,
cause us to rejoice in you always,
make us gentle to everyone;
keep us from being anxious about anything –
help us to ask you for what we need,
    with thanksgiving;
and let your peace
guard our hearts and minds
in Jesus Christ our Lord. **Amen.**

5.37   FOR A SENSE OF HUMOUR
Michael Hollings and Etta Gullick

Give us a sense of humour, Lord and also things to laugh about; give
us the grace to take a joke against ourselves, and to see the funny
side of the things we do; save us from annoyance, bad temper,
resentfulness against our friends. Help us to laugh even in the face of
trouble, fill our minds with the love of Jesus; for his name's sake.
Amen.

5.38   THAT WE MAY PRAY EFFECTIVELY
Editors

Holy Lord God, give us the grace of humility as we pray to you. You
don't listen to the proud, haughty or conceited; you will not hear the
vain words of hypocrites: help us to come to you in lowliness of
heart and with the simplicity of a little child.

Stir up in us those graces of character which please you; give us
strength to lay hold on your promises with faith; save us from
expecting to win victories without being willing for the fight.

Grant us that transparent, honest, faith that can overcome the spirit
of the world. Lord, teach us to pray: to agonise in prayer, to sacrifice
for prayer, to hunger for prayer. Draw our hearts and minds ever
toward yourself, that we may find your way and see you ever more
clearly; through Jesus Christ our Saviour. **Amen.**

▶ **5.39**   LITANY
From 'Contemporary Parish Prayers'

By the prayers of Jesus,
Lord, teach us how to pray.

By the grace of Jesus,
Lord, teach us how to give.

By the labours of Jesus,
Lord, teach us how to work.

By the love of Jesus,
Lord, teach us how to love.

By the cross of Jesus,
Lord, teach us how to live. Amen.

▶ **5.40**   A MORNING PRAYER
From Isaiah 33†

O Lord,
be gracious to us –
we long for you.
Be our strength every morning,
our salvation in time of distress.
Thank you, Lord. **Amen.**

5.41   IN THE MORNING: A PERSONAL PRAYER
Editors

O God, early in the morning I cry to you: help me to pray and to
concentrate my thoughts on you; I cannot do this alone. In me there
is darkness, but with you there is light; I am lonely, but you do not
leave me; I am feeble in heart, but with you there is help; I am
restless, but with you there is peace; in me there is bitterness, but
with you there is patience; I do not understand your ways, but you
know the way for me. O God, early in the morning I cry to you.
Amen.

▶ **5.42** AN EVENING PRAYER
Frank Colquhoun

O God of all life,
thank you for looking after us today
and for all your goodness to us:
bless us tonight with your forgiveness,
send your peace into our hearts,
and take us and all we love into your care;
for Jesus Christ our Saviour's sake. **Amen.**

5.43 A NIGHT PRAYER
Editors

O Lord our God, thank you for bringing this day to a close; thank you for giving us rest in body and soul. Your hand has been over us and has guarded and preserved us: forgive our lack of faith, and any wrong that we have done today, and help us to forgive all who have wronged us. Let us sleep in peace under your protection, and keep us from all the temptations of darkness. Into your hand we commend our loved ones and all who dwell around us; to you we entrust ourselves, body and soul. O God, your holy name be praised. **Amen.**

5.44 NIGHT PRAYER
Jim Cotter

Lord, it is night. The night is for stillness. Let us be still in the presence of God. It is night after a long day. What has been done has been done; what has not been done has not been done: let it be. The night is dark: let our fears of the darkness of the world, and of our own lives, rest in you. The night is quiet: let the quietness of your peace enfold us, all dear to us, and all who have no peace. The night heralds the dawn: let us look expectantly to a new day, new joys, new possibilities. In your name we pray. **Amen.**

▶ **5.45** THANKSGIVING
From Psalm 118†

God our Father, we thank you,
for you are good,
and your love endures for ever;

we thank you that you have heard our cry to you
    and set us free;
we thank you that you are with us,
and we need not be afraid;
we thank you that you have answered us
and become our salvation;
through Jesus our Lord. **Amen.**

▶ **5.46** ASCRIPTION
From Jude†

Now to him who is able to keep us from falling,
and to present us faultless
before the presence of his glory,
with exceeding joy;
to the only wise God, our Saviour,
be glory and majesty, dominion and power,
both now and for ever. **Amen.**

OR

5.47 BLESSING
From Jude†

Now to him who is able to keep *you* from falling, and to present *you*
faultless before the presence of his glory, with exceeding joy, to the
only wise God, our Saviour, be glory and majesty, dominion and
power; and the blessing of God – Father, Son and Holy Spirit, be
upon *you* now and for ever. **Amen.**

5.48 BLESSING
From Psalm 102†

The Lord hear *your* prayer; the Lord turn his face towards *you*; the
Lord show *you* his compassion; the Lord build *you* up, and reveal to
you his glory; the Lord look down from heaven and bring *you* peace.
Amen.

5.49   BLESSING
From Philippians 4†

Rejoice in the Lord always, let everyone know your gentleness, do not be anxious, make your needs known to God; and the peace of God guard your hearts in Christ Jesus. **Amen.**

5.50   BLESSING
From Colossians 3†

Forgive each other as the Lord has forgiven you; over all virtues put on love; let the peace of Christ rule your hearts, and be thankful; let the word of Christ dwell in you richly; do all in the name of the Lord Jesus; and the blessing of God almighty – the Father, the Son and the Holy Spirit – be with you always. **Amen.**

5.51   BLESSING
From 'Still Waters, Deep Waters'

Go, and know that the Lord goes with you: let him lead you each day into the quiet place of your heart, where he will speak with you; know that he loves you and watches over you – that he listens to you in gentle understanding, that he is with you always, wherever you are and however you may feel: and the blessing of God – Father, Son and Holy Spirit – be yours for ever. **Amen.**

▶ **5.52**   CONCLUDING PRAISE
From Exodus 33†

Lord God almighty, you have revealed your goodness to us and proclaimed your name among us:
show us your glory.

You will have mercy on us, and compassion; in Christ you will forgive our sins:
**hide us in the cleft of the Rock,
cover us with your hand.**

Lord, you know us by name; in Christ we have found favour in your sight:
**now let your presence go with us,
and give us rest. Amen.**

The Family, Parents and Children, Mothering Sunday

▶ **6.1** GREETING
From 3 John†

Peace to you . . . greet your friends by name. **Amen.**
(We greet each other)

6.2 SENTENCE
Psalm 128.1

Blessed are those who fear the Lord; who walk in his ways.

6.3 SENTENCE
Exodus 20.12

Honour your father and your mother, so that you may live long in the land your God is giving you.

6.4 SENTENCE
2 Corinthians 13.11

Be of one mind, live in peace, and the God of peace will be with you.

6.5 SENTENCE
Deuteronomy 30.19

I have set before you life and death, blessings and curses: now choose life that you (and your children) may live.

6.6 SENTENCE
Isaiah 66.13

'As a mother comforts her child, so will I comfort you, and you shall be comforted,' says the Lord.

6.7 SENTENCE
1 John 2.12,13

Children, your sins have been forgiven on account of Jesus' name; parents, you have known him who is from the beginning; young people, you are strong because the word of God lives in you and you have overcome the evil one.

▶ **6.8** RESPONSE
From Ephesians 3†

I bow my knees before the Father:
from whom every family in heaven and on earth is named.

▶ **6.9** RESPONSE
From Psalm 16†

We have set the Lord always before us:
because he is at our right hand, we will not be shaken.

6.10 APPROACH
After C. S. Woodward

O God, we have come to this house of prayer: help us to remember that you are here with us, to pray to you and sing your praise with all our hearts, and to listen to your word with open ears; through Jesus Christ our Lord. **Amen.**

▶ **6.11** APPROACH
From Deuteronomy 12†

Lord, our God,
this is the place where we may worship you;
you have set your name here.
Here in your presence our families shall rejoice,
because you have blessed us;
here we present to you
the offering of our lives;
here we promise to obey your laws;
here we pray for our children,
that we and they
may do what is right in your sight;
through Jesus our Redeemer. **Amen.**

6.12 APPROACH
Editors

O God, who sees us from heaven, we come to you this day praising you for every experience we have of your loving care. We thank you for Jesus Christ our Saviour, who came to demonstrate and fulfil your love towards us, your created children. We are amazed and wonder as we see your self-giving in his life's teaching, his dying, and his resurrection. We thank you for all who, in the same spirit of caring, concern themselves with us in human relationship: for our parents, and the love which brought us into the world – and especially this day for our mothers. We thank you for all mothers who give themselves to the welfare of their children and their homes; for their comforting love, care and thoughtfulness, for wise training, and good examples given to us in early years. For all your gracious family gifts, we praise and thank you, now and always, through Jesus our Lord. **Amen.**

▶ **6.13** PRAISE
From Psalm 95†

Come, let us sing for joy to the Lord;
let us shout to the Rock of our salvation.

Come before him with thanksgiving;
sing him joyful songs of praise! Amen.

▶ **6.14** CONFESSION
From Ephesians 5 and 6, Editors†

*The bracketed section may be omitted.

O God, the Father of us all, we come to you in sorrow, for we have often failed you:
ALL **Lord, forgive us, and help us to obey.**

MINISTER You have taught us: 'Honour your father and mother, that it may go well with you and that you may enjoy long life on the earth.' We have often failed you:
ALL **Lord, forgive us, and help us to obey.**

[A CHILD] You have taught us as children: 'Obey your parents in the Lord, for this is right.' We have often failed you:
CHILDREN **Lord, forgive us, and help us to obey.**

[A FATHER] You have taught us as fathers: 'Do not exasperate your children; instead, bring them up in the training and instruction of the Lord.' We have often failed you:

FATHERS **Lord, forgive us, and help us to obey.**

[A MOTHER] You have taught us as mothers to live with sincere faith and bring our children to Christ. We have often failed you:

MOTHERS **Lord, forgive us, and help us to obey.**

*[A HUSBAND You have taught us as husbands: 'Love your wives as you love yourselves.' We have often failed you:

HUSBANDS **Lord, forgive us, and help us to obey.**

A WIFE You have taught us as wives: 'Respect your husbands.' We have often failed you:

WIVES **Lord, forgive us, and help us to obey.]**

[MINISTER] You have taught us as the Christian family: 'Submit to one another out of reverence for Christ.' We have often failed you:

ALL **Lord, forgive us, and help us to obey.**
Father, help us all to hear your word, and to obey it; for Jesus' sake. Amen.

▶ **6.15** CONFESSION
Editors

Our Father, forgive us this day for times when we fail to honour our parents. Your desire is that we may live in family love and unity: forgive our arrogance and indifference to your commandments. Father of mercy, we put our trust in you:
forgive us and help us.

Forgive us for our anger and the harsh words we sometimes speak to those who are near to us in our family homes. Help us to know your strength as we discipline our tongues. Father of mercy, we put our trust in you:
forgive us and help us.

Forgive us for our unthankful spirit at home; for taking the warmth, comfort and provision as a right, and forgetting that all good gifts come from you. Father of mercy, we put our trust in you:
forgive us and help us for Jesus' sake. Amen.

6.16 ABSOLUTION
From Psalm 145†

God is gracious and compassionate, slow to anger and rich in love;
he loves *you* and will keep his promise to forgive *you*; he will lift *you*
up when *you* fall, and hear *your* cry and save *you*; through Jesus
Christ our Lord. **Amen.**

▶ **6.17** COLLECT
Pentecost 14, Church of Ireland APB 1984

God our Father,
your Son Jesus Christ
lived in a family at Nazareth:
grant that in our families on earth
we may so learn to love and to live together
that we may rejoice as one family
in your heavenly home;
through Jesus Christ our Lord. **Amen.**

▶ **6.18** COLLECT
From The Marriage Service, ASB 1980, adapted

Lord and Saviour Jesus Christ,
who shared at Nazareth the life of an earthly home:
reign in our homes as Lord and King;
give us grace to serve others as you have served us,
and grant that by deed and word
we may be witnesses of your saving love
to those among whom we live;
for the sake of your holy name. **Amen.**

▶ **6.19** PSALM
Psalm 128.1–6†

The congregation may divide at A *and* B

    The pilgrims' song:
A **Blessed are those who fear the Lord,**
B **who walk in his ways.**

    You will eat the fruit of your work; blessings and prosperity
    will be yours:

A **Blessed are those who fear the Lord,**
B **who walk in his ways.**

Your wife will be like a fruitful vine within your house; your children will be like young olive trees around your table:
A **Blessed are those who fear the Lord,**
B **who walk in his ways.**

May the Lord bless you all the days of your life; may you have prosperity; may you live to see your children's children:
ALL **Peace be with you. Amen.**

6.20 READING: THE BIRTH OF SAMUEL
From 1 Samuel 1.1–20

Cast: Narrator, Elkanah, Hannah, Eli

Narrator
There was a certain man from the hill-country of Ephraim, whose name was Elkanah. Year after year this man went up from his town to worship and sacrifice to the Lord Almighty at Shiloh. Whenever the day came for Elkanah to sacrifice, he would give his wife Hannah a double portion of the meat because he loved her, and the Lord had closed her womb. But whenever Hannah went up to the house of the Lord she wept and would not eat. Elkanah her husband would say to her:

Elkanah
Hannah, why are you weeping? Why don't you eat? Why are you downhearted? Don't I mean more to you than ten sons?

Narrator
Once when they had finished eating and drinking in Shiloh, Hannah stood up. Now Eli the priest was sitting on a chair by the doorpost of the Lord's temple. In bitterness of soul Hannah wept much and prayed to the Lord. And she made a vow:

Hannah
O Lord Almighty, if you will only look upon your servant's misery and remember me, and not forget your servant but give her a son, then I will give him to the Lord for all the days of his life.

Narrator
As she kept on praying to the Lord, Eli observed her mouth. Hannah was praying in her heart, and her lips were moving but

her voice was not heard. Eli thought she was drunk [and said to her:]

Eli (*severely*)
How long will you keep on getting drunk? Get rid of your wine.

Hannah (*sadly*)
Not so, my lord. I am a woman who is deeply troubled. I have not been drinking wine or beer; I was pouring out my soul to the Lord. Do not take your servant for a wicked woman; I have been praying here out of my great anguish and grief.

Narrator
Eli answered:

Eli (*with compassion*)
Go in peace, and may the God of Israel grant you what you have asked of him.

Hannah (*pleased*)
May your servant find favour in your eyes.

Narrator
Then she went her way and ate something, and her face was no longer downcast. Early the next morning they arose and worshipped before the Lord and then went back to their home. Hannah conceived and gave birth to a son. She named him:

Hannah (*slowly*)
Samuel – because I asked the Lord for him.

Cast
[This is] the word of the Lord.

All
Thanks be to God.

6.21   READING: SAMUEL'S DEDICATION
1 Samuel 1.21–28

Cast: Narrator, Hannah, Elkanah

Narrator
The time came again for Elkanah and his family to go to Shiloh and offer to the Lord the yearly sacrifice and the special sacrifice he had promised. But this time Hannah did not go. [She told her husband:]

Hannah (*to Elkanah*)

As soon as the child is weaned, I will take him to the house of the Lord, where he will stay all his life.

[Narrator

Elkanah answered:]

Elkanah

All right, do whatever you think best; stay at home until you have weaned him. And may the Lord make your promise come true.

Narrator

So Hannah stayed at home and nursed her child. (PAUSE)

After she had weaned him, she took him to Shiloh, taking along a three-year-old bull, ten kilogrammes of flour, and a leather bag full of wine. She took Samuel, young as he was, to the house of the Lord at Shiloh. After they had killed the bull, they took the child to Eli. [Hannah said to him:]

Hannah

Excuse me, sir. Do you remember me? I am the woman you saw standing here, praying to the Lord. I asked him for this child, and he gave me what I asked for. So I am dedicating him to the Lord. As long as he lives, he will belong to the Lord.

Narrator

Then they worshipped the Lord there.

Cast

[This is] the word of the Lord.

All

Thanks be to God.

6.22   READING: JESUS BLESSES LITTLE CHILDREN
Mark 10.[1], 13–16

Cast: Narrator, Jesus

Narrator

Jesus crossed the river Jordan. Crowds came flocking to him again, and he taught them, as he always did.

Some people brought children to Jesus for him to place his hands on them, but the disciples scolded the people. When Jesus noticed this, he was angry and said to his disciples:

Jesus

Let the children come to me, and do not stop them, because the Kingdom of God belongs to such as these. I assure you that whoever does not receive the Kingdom of God like a child will never enter it.

Narrator

Then he took the children in his arms, placed his hands on each of them, and blessed them.

Cast

[This is] the word of the Lord.   OR   This is the Gospel of Christ/
                                 This is the Gospel of the Lord.

All
Thanks be to God.   **Praise to Christ our Lord/**
                                      Praise to you, Lord Jesus Christ.

6.23 READING: THE CHRISTIAN FAMILY
From Ephesians 5.1–6.12

Cast: Minister/Leader, Wife, Husband, Child, Father

Minister/Leader

Be imitators of God, therefore, as dearly loved children and live a life of love, just as Christ loved us and gave himself up for us as a fragrant offering and sacrifice to God. Speak to one another with psalms, hymns and spiritual songs. Sing and make music in your heart to the Lord, always giving thanks to God the Father for everything, in the name of our Lord Jesus Christ. Submit to one another out of reverence for Christ.

Wife

Wives, submit to your husbands as to the Lord. For the husband is the head of the wife as Christ is the head of the church, his body, of which he is the Saviour. Now as the church submits to Christ, so also wives should submit to their husbands in everything.

Husband

Husbands, love your wives, just as Christ loved the church and gave himself up for her to make her holy, cleansing her by the washing with water through the word, and to present her to himself as a radiant church, without stain or wrinkle or any other blemish, but holy and blameless. In this same way, husbands ought to love their wives as their own bodies. He who loves his wife loves himself. After all, no-one ever hated his own body, but he feeds and cares for it, just as Christ does the church.

Minister/Leader

For this reason a man will leave his father and mother and be united to his wife, and the two will become one flesh. This is a profound mystery – but I am talking about Christ and the church. However, each one of you also must love his wife as he loves himself, and the wife must respect her husband.

Child

Children, obey your parents in the Lord, for this is right. 'Honour your father and mother' – which is the first commandment with a promise – 'that it may go well with you and that you may enjoy long life on the earth.'

Father

Fathers, do not exasperate your children; instead, bring them up in the training and instruction of the Lord.

Minister/Leader

Finally, be strong in the Lord and in his mighty power. Put on the full armour of God so that you can take your stand against the Devil's schemes. For our struggle is not against flesh and blood, but against the rulers, against the authorities, against the powers of this dark world and against the spiritual forces of evil in the heavenly realms.

Cast

[This is] the word of the Lord.

All

Thanks be to God.

FURTHER BIBLE READINGS

Readings appropriate to this theme will be found listed in our companion volume, 'The Dramatised Bible' (published by HarperCollins) on index pages 423–424.

▶ **6.24** PRESENTATION OF A BIBLE/NEW TESTAMENT
Editors

To the father:

It is your responsibility as the father of the family to teach them the word of God:
I will do this, the Lord helping me.

To the mother:

It is your duty as the mother to ensure that your child(*ren*) shall know the Holy Scriptures:
I will do this, the Lord helping me.

▶ **6.25** CREED
From Ephesians 3†

Let us declare our faith in God:

We believe in God the Father,
from whom every family
in heaven and on earth is named.

We believe in God the Son,
who lives in our hearts through faith,
and fills us with his love.

We believe in God the Holy Spirit,
who strengthens us with power from on high.

We believe in one God;
Father, Son, and Holy Spirit. Amen.

6.26 FOR OUR MOTHERS (WITH CHILDREN PRESENT)
David Cavil

Lord Jesus, you know the blessings of a mother's care: your mother, Mary, cared for you when you were a baby, when you travelled about with your disciples, and when you hung on the cross. Thank you for our mothers, who are always busy caring for us; who laugh with us in our happy times, comfort us when we are sad, and are always there when we need them. Remind us how much we owe to our mothers. Help us to say 'Thank you' to them by doing all we can to help them; through Jesus Christ our Lord. **Amen.**

6.27 FOR OUR MOTHERS
Christopher Idle

O God of grace and love, we thank you for all that you have given us
through the loving care and hard work of our mothers. We pray for
your richest blessing upon all mothers: for those with difficult
homes, whose children are more of a problem than a blessing; for
those with no husband or with husbands who find it hard to be
constant and loving; for those with loved ones far away and those
who are lonely; for those who find it hard to make ends meet, or
who go short themselves for the sake of their families; for those who
are nearly at the end of their tether; for those mothers who are trying
to make Christ real to their families; for those who do not know him
as their Saviour, nor how to cast their care on him. For each one
according to her need, hear our prayer, and draw all mothers closer
to you today; through your Son Jesus Christ our Lord. **Amen.**

▶ **6.28** FOR OUR MOTHERS
From 'A New Zealand Prayer Book'

Blessed are you, God of strength and patience;
yours is the love our mothers showed us,
yours the care we need;
as we learn to care for one another
and to share your love,
may it be with our mother we share it
    first of all. **Amen.**

▶ **6.29** ABOUT A MOTHER'S LOVE
From 'A New Zealand Prayer Book'

Ever–loving God,
your care for us is greater
even than a mother's love for her child;
teach us to value a mother's love
and see in it an expression of your grace,
that we may ever feel more deeply your love for us
in Christ Jesus our Saviour. **Amen.**

► **6.30**   FOR OUR FAMILIES (WITH CHILDREN PRESENT)
Angela Needham

Lord God, our heavenly Father:
for our families and homes – thank you,
for your love and care – thank you,
for everything you give us – thank you:
make us thoughtful at home,
make us helpful to our parents,
and above all,
teach us to love you more day by day;
for Jesus' sake. **Amen.**

6.31   FOR THOSE WITH WHOM WE LIVE
Editors

O God, you are the Father of all families: make our family like the
family where Jesus grew up, and our home like his home. Let us all
care for each other and share our things with each other, so that there
is enough for everyone. Show us what to do when we feel jealous, or
want our own way; and make us strong to be unselfish: through
Jesus Christ our Lord. **Amen.**

6.32   FOR FAMILIES IN CHURCH TODAY
James M Todd, adapted

God our Father, whose Son Jesus Christ shared in the home at
Nazareth: hear our prayer for every human family, and especially for
each home represented here, that they may be blessed by his
presence and united in his love. We ask this in his name. **Amen.**

6.33   FOR MUTUAL LOVE AND HELP AT HOME
Editors

Lord Jesus, you were refused the comfort of a home at your birth –
nobody really wanted to know your parents in Bethlehem when you
arrived in this world. Birds have nests, animals their places to go,
but you, the Son of Man, had nowhere to lay your head, no place
which you could call your own. You loved sitting with friends in
quietness; eating, resting, teaching, talking. Your close friends
reflected your love and were hospitable and caring. Whenever you

went to Bethany, you brought delight to the family of Lazarus, Mary and Martha; and they cared for you.

In your unchanging love, be with us in our homes and fill them with the sense of your being there. Let love, warmth, thoughtfulness and helpful words be a part of our daily living. Honour us with your presence, Lord Jesus. For your glory's sake. **Amen.**

6.34 FOR OUR FAMILIES, NEIGHBOURS AND COMMUNITY
From 'A New Zealand Prayer Book'

We pray for one another, for our families and friends, through whom we learn to love and to be loved. Thank you, Father, for all who care for us. Give us grace to serve Christ by serving our neighbours and our community, loving others as he loves us; for your name's sake. **Amen.**

▶ **6.35** ABOUT LIVING IN A FAMILY
From 'A New Zealand Prayer Book'

Gentle God,
grant that at home
where we are most truly ourselves,
where we are known at our best and worst,
we may learn to forgive and be forgiven. **Amen.**

▶ **6.36** FOR BLESSING IN A FAMILY
From 'A New Zealand Prayer Book'

God, the Father of us all,
you have created families and love of every kind.
Give us courage to listen to each other and to learn,
and grant us the gentle blessing
which a home can give. **Amen.**

6.37 FOR A NEWLY-MARRIED COUPLE
From 'Contemporary Prayers for Public Worship', adapted

Eternal God, creator of us all, we praise you for all the ways in which your love enters our lives, and for all the joys that can come to men and women through marriage. Today we especially pray for . . . and . . . as they begin their married life. With them we thank you for the love and care of their parents, which has guided them to maturity and prepared them for this commitment. Give them strength to keep the vows they have made, to be loyal and faithful to each other, and to support each other throughout their life, that they may bear each other's burdens and share each other's joys. Help them to be honest and patient with each other, (*to be wise and loving parents*) and to welcome both friends and strangers into their home. In all their future together may they enjoy each other and grow through the love they share, until, at the end of this life, you receive us all into your eternal kingdom, through Jesus Christ our Redeemer. **Amen.**

6.38   FOR NEW PARENTS
Editors

God our heavenly Father, we thank you for your creative power and love, through which these parents have been granted the gift of a child; and for the skill and care of all who have guarded the health of mother and baby. Grant that *N* and *N* may always remember your love for them, and serve you faithfully in all their responsibilities as parents. So may they give to *this child* a sure knowledge of that love, through Jesus Christ our Lord. **Amen.**

▶ 6.39   DEDICATION
From 1 Samuel 1†

Almighty God,
we present our child, *N*, before you.
We asked you for *him*,
and you granted what we asked of you:
so now we give *him* to you.
For *his* whole life
   he shall be given over to you.
O God, we worship and adore you;
through Jesus, our Lord. **Amen.**

6.40   ABOUT LOOKING AFTER CHILDREN
Editors

Almighty God, who has given to us the love and care of a mother, and has caused us to offer thanks this day: we pray for all who have the responsibility of looking after children; that, aware of their influence upon young lives, they may seek guidance and strength for their task, through Jesus Christ our Lord. **Amen.**

6.41 DEDICATION OF A CHILD
From 'Prayer, Poem and Songs'

Lord God, our Father, you have given your Son, Jesus Christ, to us as the good shepherd who knows us all by name. We thank you for your grace and your faithfulness – for the new life that you have created for this child who has been among us and whom you have entrusted to us. You have given *him* ears to hear with and eyes to see with. Bless too this child's mouth so that *he* may learn how to laugh and to speak. Bless also *his* hands and feet and may *he* learn from *his* own experience that everything you have made is good. We ask you to shelter this child and keep *him* safe in this rough world. Keep everything that is bad and cruel away from *him*, protect *him* from evil influences and never let *him* be perverted. May *he* be secure with *his* parents and may we who are mature and responsible never cause this child to stumble, but lead *him*, to the truth. If, however, sin should ever have power over *him*, be merciful to *him*, Lord God – you make good all human guilt and shortcomings and are yourself, even before this child is able to sin, the forgiveness of all sins, through Jesus Christ, our Lord. **Amen.**

6.42 AFTER DEDICATION/BAPTISM
Editors

Lord God, we thank you for this your *child* now dedicated/*baptised* into your name: hold *N* in your safe–keeping, and guide *him* into a future of blessing and goodness. Fill *N* with your Holy Spirit so that *he* can grow up to reflect your infinite truth, your divine beauty and your perfect love in Jesus Christ our Lord. **Amen.**

6.43 FOR GRACE TO GUIDE A CHILD
From 'The Book of Alternative Services of the Anglican Church of Canada'

God our Creator, thank you for the waiting and the joy, thank you for new life and for parenthood, thank you for the gift of *N*, entrusted to our care. May we be patient and understanding, ready to guide and forgive, that in our love *N* may know your love. May *he* learn to love your world and the whole family of your children; through Christ our life. **Amen.**

▶ **6.44** FOR CHILDREN
Editors

Dear Lord Jesus, hear us as we pray; bless our children, who are yours too:

We pray for all children who have not heard of you:
bless them, Lord Jesus.

We pray for all children who cannot see:
bless them, Lord Jesus.

We pray for all children who cannot hear:
bless them, Lord Jesus.

We pray for all children who cannot walk:
bless them, Lord Jesus.

We pray for all children who need to take medicine every day of their lives:
bless them, Lord Jesus.

We pray for all children everywhere who have special needs:
bless them, Lord Jesus.

Dear Lord Jesus,
hear us as we pray;
bless our children,
who are yours first of all. Amen.

▶ **6.45** PARENTS' PRAYER
From 'A New Zealand Prayer Book'

All-embracing God
the hope of every generation,
complete our joy by your presence;
give us quiet strength and patient wisdom
as we nurture N
in all that is good, and true, and just,
through Jesus Christ our friend and brother. **Amen.**

6.46 FOR DEPRIVED YOUNG PEOPLE
Editors

Thank you, Father, that we don't have to worry that our family has no money, thank you that we don't have to leave our families because they cannot afford to keep us. We pray for all young people everywhere who have to leave home to find a job: keep them from danger; may they come to know that you love them and you want the best for them. In Jesus' name. **Amen.**

6.47 FOR THOSE IN NEED
Editors

O God, we remember the ill and the unhappy: we ask you to be with those who have no family, and those who have few friends; we ask you to heal those who are ill and to comfort those in pain: help them to trust you, and give them strength to get better, through the power of Jesus Christ our Lord. **Amen.**

6.48 FOR HOMES IN DIFFICULTY
Leslie Weatherhead, adapted

We pray, loving Father, for those who are trying to bring up young children and are over-anxious about them: give them a peaceful trust in you. We pray for those in whose homes young people are growing up self-assertive, and hostile to all restraint or advice: give them a right understanding of liberty and a new belief in youth. We pray for those who are married but have ceased truly to love, who maintain an external confidence but conceal a bored distaste: make them willing to see the best in the one who has become unattractive; make them ready to end the pride that will not talk things out or confess failure; help them to realise that their partner is disappointed too, and had hoped that love would become a beautiful companionship. Lord, make your strength perfect in our weakness; through Jesus, our Lord. **Amen.**

6.49 FOR MARRIAGES UNDER STRESS
Susan Williams

O Lord God, we thank you for the gift of marriage – that gift which leads to the heights of shared joy or to the depths of shared bitterness. We pray for those who are suffering hurt in marriage; for those who inflict it, and for those whose greatest unhappiness stems from the closeness of their partner. O Lord who in love created the complexities of the human mind, and in power conquered the evil that invades it: bring unity to those who are divided, and wholeness to those who long for it, that we may all finally be united with you and with one another; through Jesus our redeemer. **Amen.**

6.50 FOR THE DIVORCED
Susan Williams

O Lord, we pray for all those who, full of confidence and love, once chose a partner for life, and are now alone after final separation. May they all receive the gift of time, so that hurt and bitterness may be redeemed by healing and love, personal weakness by your strength, inner despair by the joy of knowing you and serving others; through Jesus Christ our Lord. **Amen.**

6.51 FOR THE REMARRIED
Editors

God of mercy and new hope, we pray for all those who are remarried after the trauma of divorce, and for their partners. You read their hearts and minds; you know the inhibitions and the comparisons; you understand the readjustments they must continually make; you know the shadows of past failure and the weight of obligation to bygone unhappiness. In Christ you lift our burdens and sustain us: for such refreshment and strength we bring to you those whom you love; in Jesus' name. **Amen.**

6.52 ABOUT BELONGING (MARRIAGE)
Editors

Lord, we know that all our possessions are truly yours and, because our lives are in your hands, we have each other in trust from you. Grant us to regard each other as yours first of all, and so to honour and care for our partner as someone who belongs to God; someone whom we have been given to look after; in Jesus Christ our Lord. **Amen.**

6.53 ABOUT BELONGING (CHILDREN)
Editors

God, our Father, we are taught that children are a blessing and a gift from you: give us that perfect balance of care and trust which you show towards us; strengthening us both to protect them and to release them. When we can no longer guide them as we would, take them into your arms; through Jesus Christ our Lord. **Amen.**

▶ **6.54** FOR SAD FAMILIES
Zinnia Bryan

We pray for those who will be unhappy today:

For mothers who cannot provide for their children – Lord, in your mercy,
hear our prayer.

For fathers who cannot earn enough money for their families – Lord, in your mercy,
hear our prayer.

For children who are ill or frightened – Lord, in your mercy,
hear our prayer.

For all who are alone, and without people to love them – Lord, in your mercy,
hear our prayer.

Bless those who give their lives
in service to the poor and hungry,
and strengthen us to help
   in meeting their needs;
through Jesus Christ our Lord. Amen.

6.55 FOR THE FAMILIES OF PRISONERS
Elizabeth Goudge

Our God, we pray to you for the broken homes of prisoners, wives left without their husbands, children fatherless, whole families in fear as they face the loneliness and hardships that lie before them. Help us, O Lord, to help them; show us how to bring to them all the love and aid in our power, in whatever way is possible for us. Bless all that is done for them, comfort their fears, and give them peace through our Lord Jesus Christ. **Amen.**

6.56 FOR OBEDIENCE
From 'A New Zealand Prayer Book'

God of the humble and expectant, you bless those who believe when you promise; help us, like Mary and Elizabeth, simply to delight in the good things you prepare for us, and to say, 'Yes'. **Amen.**

▶ **6.57 THANKSGIVING FOR A CHILD**
From 'A New Zealand Prayer Book'

We thank you God for this new person,
child of your creation:
may the knowledge of you dawn on *him*,
may the love of you grow in *him*,
and may the grace of your Spirit
draw *him* to you. **Amen.**

6.58 THANKSGIVING FOR A CHILD
From 'The Book of Alternative Services of the Anglican Church of Canada'

God the creator of us all, we give you thanks for the life of N. Grant us accepting and understanding hearts, and the gifts of courage and patience to face the challenge of caring for *him*. Let your love for us be seen in our lives, that we may create an atmosphere in which *he* will live a life of dignity and worth. We ask this in the name of Jesus, the compassionate. **Amen.**

▶ **6.59 THANKSGIVING FOR OUR FAMILIES**
Editors

We thank God for giving us other people to be part of our lives:

For parents, and the love which brought us to birth: we praise you, O Lord,
and bring you thanks today.

For mothers who have cherished and nurtured us: we praise you, O Lord,
and bring you thanks today.

For fathers who have loved and supported us: we praise you, O Lord,
and bring you thanks today.

For brothers and sisters with whom we have shared our home: we praise you, O Lord,
and bring you thanks today.

For children, entrusted to our care as parents: we praise you, O Lord,
and bring you thanks today.

For other relatives and friends who have been with us in our hopes and our joys: we praise you, O Lord,
and bring you thanks today.

For all who first spoke to us of Jesus, and have drawn us into the family of our Father in heaven: we praise you, O Lord,
and bring you thanks today.

Help us to live
as those who belong to one another and to you,
now and always. Amen.

▶ **6.60** THANKSGIVING FOR OUR FAMILIES
Marjorie Hampson

Thank you, Lord, for our homes and families,
thank you for our health and happiness,
thank you for the good times,
thank you for helping us to cope
   with the times that are not so good.
Thank you for life itself –
and for your wonderful love
in Jesus Christ our Lord. **Amen.**

6.61 THANKSGIVING FOR FAMILY LIFE AND FELLOWSHIP
Patricia Mitchell

Father, we thank you that you have seen fit to establish us in families, so that we may live together, play together, work together, rejoice together, and grieve together. But above all we thank you that we are able to be members of your family the church; that through your Son Jesus Christ we are able to become your children.

We thank you that no matter how widely spread throughout the world our Christian family may be, our hearts can be united in prayer so that we are able to share one another's burdens, rejoice in one another's blessings and strengthen one another in the power of your Holy Spirit. And we thank you that in your wisdom you have set aside a day when we can gather together for praise and worship and, drawn aside from everyday living, be renewed together as a family by your Holy Spirit, through Jesus Christ our Lord. **Amen.**

▶ **6.62** THANKSGIVING FOR FAMILY AND FRIENDS
Editors

We thank you, God, for our family and our friends –
for those who understand us
    better than we understand ourselves,
for those who know us at our worst and still love us,
for those who have forgiven us
    when we had no right to expect forgiveness.
Help us to be true to our friends,
as we would expect them to be to us;
through Jesus Christ our Lord. **Amen.**

▶ **6.63** THANKSGIVING FOR OUR HOMES
Editors

Heavenly Father, we acknowledge you to be the giver of every good and perfect gift:

For the homes you have provided for us as places of rest and refreshment, as centres of fellowship and friendship:
our God, we thank you.

For the labour and skill of those who built them, for the comfort of the amenities provided:
our God, we thank you.

For all the love and affection, the joy and hope they can bring to those who come within their walls:
our God, we thank you.

Be present in our homes –
that no false thing may come there;
bless them with your love –
that your will alone may be done there:
accept our prayer and thanksgiving
through Jesus Christ our Lord. Amen.

▶ **6.64** THANKSGIVING FOR BLESSINGS OF EVERY AGE
Editors

Dear God, you are our Father; and, whatever our age, we are your children. We thank you for the joy and eagerness of being young, of having boundless energy; we thank you for the fascination of developing skills, and for faculties of sight, hearing and taste that are sharp and keen. For our early years:
thank you, Father.

We thank you for the years of maturity with their experience and steadiness, fortitude and hope that come with proving your goodness. For our middle years:
thank you, Father.

We thank you for the richness of growing old; for the wisdom, the sense of proportion and the humility that age can bring. For our final years:
thank you, Father.

**Father, we thank you
that, when our earthly years are spent,
there awaits us life in your presence
with our Lord Jesus Christ. Amen.**

6.65 DEDICATION
Lancelot Andrewes

We commend to you, O Lord, our souls and our bodies, our minds and our thoughts, our prayers and our hopes, our health and our work, our life and our death; our wives and husbands, our parents and brothers and sisters, our benefactors and friends, our neighbours, our fellow countrymen and women, and all Christian people, this day and always. **Amen.**

6.66 BLESSING
From Psalm 128†

The Lord bless *you* all the days of your life: may *you* have prosperity; may *you* live to see your children's children: and the love of God, the Father, Son and Holy Spirit enrich *you* always. **Amen.**

6.67 BLESSING
From Psalm 115†

The Lord who remembers us all – humble and great alike – bless you that fear him; the Lord prosper your way, the Lord bless your children; the Lord, the maker of heaven and earth bless you both now and evermore. **Amen.**

6.68 BLESSING
Based on 1 Corinthians 13

The grace of our Lord Jesus Christ make *you* gracious, the love of God make *you* loving and the fellowship of the Holy Spirit make *you* one with all God's people; now and always. **Amen.**

Palm Sunday (and Passion Readings)

▶ **7.1** GREETING
From Revelation 22†

The grace of the Lord Jesus be with God's people. **Amen.**

7.2 SENTENCE
Zechariah 9.9

Shout, daughter of Jerusalem! See, your king comes to you, righteous
and having salvation, gentle and riding on a donkey.

7.3 SENTENCE
Malachi 3.1

The Lord will suddenly come to his temple.

7.4 SENTENCE
Psalm 69.9 and John 2.17

The zeal of your house has consumed me.

7.5 SENTENCE
Philippians 2.5

Christ Jesus being found in appearance as a man, humbled himself
and became obedient to death – even death on a cross.

▶ **7.6** RESPONSE
From Psalm 24†

Fling wide the gates and open the ancient doors:
that the King of glory may come in.

▶ **7.7** RESPONSE
From Zechariah 9 and Mark 11†

Shout for joy, you people of Jerusalem! Look, your king is coming to you – triumphant and victorious, but humble and riding on a donkey:
Hosanna!
Blessed is he
who comes in the name of the Lord! Amen.

▶ **7.8** RESPONSE
From Matthew 21†

Say to the daughter of Zion, 'See, your king comes to you, gentle and riding on a donkey':
Hosanna to the Son of David,
blessed is he
who comes in the name of the Lord.
Hosanna in the highest!

▶ **7.9** RESPONSE
From Matthew 21†

Hosanna to the Son of David:
Blessed is he
who comes in the name of the Lord.
Hosanna in the highest!

7.10 APPROACH
Editors

Lord Jesus, you entered the city of Jerusalem in public and to joyful acclaim. We praise you for the mystery of your coming to us today in spirit. We open our hearts and minds gladly to you, and welcome you. We praise you that, though eternally divine, you did not flinch from coming to this world; humbling yourself, living our life and dying our death. You are the way for us to follow, the full, perfect and sufficient sacrifice for our sin. We praise you for the triumph of your coming into our lives, we adore you for the comfort of your presence, for the clarity of your word, for the constancy of your love, and for the confidence you give of your ultimate victory over all suffering, sorrow, injustice and oppression. To you be the glory for ever and ever. **Amen.**

▶ **7.11**   PRAISE
From Isaiah 12†

Shout aloud, and sing for joy, people of Zion:
Great is the Holy one of Israel. Amen.

▶ **7.12**   PRAISE
From Psalm 100†

Shout for joy to the Lord, all the earth;
serve the Lord with gladness!

Come before him with joyful songs;
give thanks to him and praise his name! Amen.

▶ **7.13**   CONFESSION
Editors

On Palm Sunday, the crowds worshipped Jesus; on Good Friday
they shouted for him to die. Let us who also worship him, confess
that we sometimes reject him, and ask his forgiveness:

Lord Jesus Christ, you come to us in peace, but we shut the door of
our mind against you. In your mercy:
forgive us and help us.

You come to us in humility, but we prefer our own proud ways. In
your mercy:
forgive us and help us.

You come to us in judgement, but we cling to our familiar sins. In
your mercy:
forgive us and help us.

You come to us in majesty, but we will not have you to reign over us.
In your mercy:
forgive us and help us.

Lord, forgive our empty praise,
fill our loveless hearts;
come to us
and make our lives your home for ever. Amen.

▶ **7.14** CONFESSION
From Isaiah 64†

Sovereign Lord,
we have continually sinned against you;
we have become unclean,
all our righteous acts are like filthy rags;
we shrivel up like leaves,
and our sins sweep us away.
Yet, O Lord, you are our Father:
do not remember our sins for ever.
We are your people:
look upon us, we pray,
and forgive us;
through Jesus our redeemer. Amen.

7.15 ABSOLUTION
From Isaiah 40†

Hear God's tender words of comfort for his people: your struggles are ended, your sin is paid for. God will show you his glory, [and you will] receive the grace of forgiveness at his hand; through Jesus Christ our Lord. **Amen.**

▶ **7.16** COLLECT
Palm Sunday, ASB 1980

Almighty and everlasting God,
who in your tender love towards the human race
sent your Son our Saviour Jesus Christ
to take upon him our flesh
and to suffer death upon the cross:
grant that we may follow the example
of his patience and humility,
and also be made partakers of his resurrection;
through Jesus Christ our Lord. **Amen.**

▶ **7.17**   PSALM
Psalm 24.1–10†

E– *enquirer,*   D– *director, or these lines may also be said by the minister.*

> The earth is the Lord's, and everything in it:
> **the world, and all who live here.**

> He founded it upon the seas:
> **and established it upon the waters.**

> E Who has the right to go up the Lord's hill;
> who may enter his holy temple?
> **Those who have clean hands**
> **and a pure heart,**
> **who do not worship idols**
> **or swear by what is false.**

> They receive blessing continually from the Lord:
> **and righteousness**
> **from the God of their salvation.**

> Such are the people who seek for God:
> **who enter the presence of the God of Jacob.**

> D Fling wide the gates, open the ancient doors:
> **that the king of glory may come in.**

> E Who is the king of glory?
> **The Lord, strong and mighty, the Lord mighty in battle.**

> D Fling wide the gates, open the ancient doors:
> **that the king of glory may come in.**

> E Who is he, this king of glory?
> **The Lord almighty, he is the king of glory. Amen.**

7.18   READING: THE APPROACH TO JERUSALEM
Luke 19.28–40

Cast: Narrator, Jesus, Owner, Disciple, Person 1 [can be the same as Disciple], Person 2 [can be the same as Owner], Pharisee.

Narrator
   As Jesus came near Bethphage and Bethany at the Mount of Olives, he sent two disciples ahead with these instructions:

Jesus
   Go to the village there ahead of you; as you go in, you will find a

colt tied up that has never been ridden. Untie it and bring it here. If someone asks you why you are untying it, tell him that the Master needs it.

Narrator

They went on their way and found everything just as Jesus had told them. As they were untying the colt, its owners said to them:

Owner

Why are you untying it?

Narrator

They answered:

Disciple

The Master needs it.

Narrator

And they took the colt to Jesus. Then they threw their cloaks over the animal and helped Jesus get on. As he rode on, people spread their cloaks on the road. (PAUSE)

When he came near Jerusalem, at the place where the road went down the Mount of Olives, the large crowd of his disciples began to thank God and praise him in loud voices for all the great things that they had seen:

Person 1 *(calling)*

God bless the king who comes in the name of the Lord!

Person 2

Peace in heaven and glory to God!

Narrator

Then some of the Pharisees in the crowd spoke to Jesus.

Pharisee

Teacher, command your disciples to be quiet!

Jesus

I tell you that if they keep quiet, the stones themselves will start shouting.

Cast
    [This is] the word of the Lord.   OR   This is the Gospel of Christ/
                                       This is the Gospel of the Lord.

All
    Thanks be to God.   **Praise to Christ our Lord/**
                                       Praise to you, Lord Jesus Christ.

7.19   READING: JESUS GOES TO THE TEMPLE
Luke 19.41–48

Cast: Narrator, Jesus

Narrator
Jesus came closer to the city, and when he saw it, he wept over it [saying]:

Jesus
If you only knew today what is needed for peace! But now you cannot see it! The time will come when your enemies will surround you with barricades, blockade you, and close in on you from every side. They will completely destroy you and the people within your walls; not a single stone will they leave in its place, because you did not recognize the time when God came to save you!

Narrator
Then Jesus went into the Temple and began to drive out the merchants [saying to them]:

Jesus *(firmly)*
It is written in the Scriptures that God said, 'My Temple will be called a house of prayer.' But you have turned it into a hideout for thieves!

Narrator
Every day Jesus taught in the Temple. The chief priests, the teachers of the Law, and the leaders of the people wanted to kill him, but they could not find a way to do it, because all the people kept listening to him, not wanting to miss a single word.

Cast
[This is] the word of the Lord.   OR   This is the Gospel of Christ/
                                                       This is the Gospel of the Lord.

All
Thanks be to God.   **Praise to Christ our Lord/**
                                                       Praise to you, Lord Jesus Christ.

FURTHER BIBLE READINGS
Readings appropriate to this theme will be found listed in our companion volume, 'The Dramatised Bible' (published by HarperCollins) on index page 424.

▶ **7.20**   CREED
From Philippians 2†

Let us affirm our faith in Jesus Christ the Son of God:

**Though he was divine,
he did not cling to equality with God,
but made himself nothing.
Taking the form of a slave,
he became as we are;
as a man he humbled himself,
and was obedient to death –
even the death of the cross.**

**Therefore God has raised him on high,
and given him the name above every name:
that at the name of Jesus
every knee should bow,
and every voice proclaim
that Jesus Christ is Lord,
to the glory of God the Father. Amen.**

▶ **7.21**   ADORATION
Based on 1 Corinthians 2†

O Lord, our God:
we worship and adore you.

You have revealed yourself to the simple and the innocent and have confounded the arrogant. O Lord, our God:
we worship and adore you.

You have chosen what the world considers foolish in order to shame the wise. O Lord, our God:
we worship and adore you.

You have used what the world considers weak in order to bring down the powerful. O Lord, our God:
we worship and adore you.

Jesus, Master, entering upon our world, gentle and majestic, clothed in humility, riding on a donkey, we acclaim you with our hosannas. O Lord, our God:
we worship and adore you.
Blessed is he who comes in the name of the Lord. Amen.

▶ **7.22**   INVITATION
Gordon Bates

Come into our *city*, Lord; bring hope and a cause for joy. Hosanna to the King
who comes in the name of the Lord!

Come into our *fellowship*, Lord; cleanse it of all that is not in accordance with your will. Hosanna to the King
who comes in the name of the Lord!

Come into our hearts, Lord; teach us your love and your truth. Hosanna to the King
who comes in the name of the Lord!

Lord Jesus,
as you entered into Jerusalem and its Temple,
so come to us
that we may be a holy people,
worthy of your presence,
bringing glory to your name. Amen.

7.23   FOR STEWARDS OF OUR CHURCH BUILDINGS
Editors

Lord God, you do not live in temples made with human hands, but you visit us with your righteous anger and cleansing power: bless all those who care for the buildings in which your name is honoured; let their hearts be open to the moving of your Spirit and shut against the desecration of selfishness, that your house may be a place of prayer for all the people, through Jesus Christ our Lord. **Amen.**

7.24   FOR OURSELVES
Editors

O God, our lives are temples of the Holy Spirit, but cluttered with the commerce of our selfishness: by the purity of Jesus cleanse us – throw over the tables of our deceit, throw out those influences that compete with you for our attention; by the presence of Jesus restore to our lives the serenity of prayer, and lift our hearts to worship and praise; for your glory evermore. **Amen.**

▶ **7.25** THANKSGIVING
After Lancelot Andrewes

Blessing and honour,
thanksgiving and praise,
more than we can utter,
more than we can conceive,
be to your glorious name, O God,
Father, Son and Holy Spirit,
by all angels, all people, all creation,
for ever and ever. **Amen.**

7.26 BLESSING
From Hebrews 12†

Fix your eyes on Jesus, the author and finisher of our faith, who for
the joy set before him endured the cross, scorning its shame, and sat
down at the right hand of the throne on high; and the blessing of our
God, Father, Son and Holy Spirit be with you always. **Amen.**

PASSION READINGS
From Mark's Gospel

CAST OF READERS
for dramatised Passion Readings

Narrator (*strong experienced voice*), **Voice 1**	**High Priest, Lawyer 1**
Jesus	**Disciple, Peter**
Pilate (*authoritative voice*)	**Judas, Lawyer 2, Commentator**
Priest, soldier, young man, Person 1, Bystander	**Girl, Person 2**
	Voice 2 (*to contrast with voice 1*)
	Crowd

The cast are best disposed about the building. For instance:
Jesus in the pulpit, **Narrator** at the lectern (if different), **Pilate**
(accompanied by **Jesus**) in a gallery or other place remote from
the **Crowd**. The **Crowd**, if well-rehearsed and co-ordinated, can
be placed about the congregation. Otherwise they are best in a
position opposite where **Pilate** and **Jesus** will be. It is most
effective if they rise from their seats to play their part.

Further dramatised readings are available in a companion volume, *The
Dramatised Bible* (published by HarperCollins).

7.27 READING: JESUS SPEAKS ABOUT HIS DEATH
Mark 10.32–34

Narrator

Jesus and his disciples were now on the road going up to Jerusalem. Jesus was going ahead of the disciples, who were filled with alarm; the people who followed behind were afraid. Once again Jesus took the twelve disciples aside and spoke of the things that were going to happen to him:

Jesus

Listen, we are going up to Jerusalem where the Son of Man will be handed over to the chief priests and the teachers of the Law. They will condemn him to death and then hand him over to the Gentiles, who will mock him, spit on him, whip him, and kill him; but three days later he will rise to life.

Narrator

[This is] the word of the Lord.　　OR　　This is the Gospel of Christ/
　　　　　　　　　　　　　　　　　　　　　　This is the Gospel of the Lord.

All

　Thanks be to God.　　　　　　　**Praise to Christ our Lord/**
　　　　　　　　　　　　　　　　　　Praise to you, Lord Jesus Christ.

HYMN: for example 'All glory, laud/praise and honour'

7.28　READING: JESUS ENTERS JERUSALEM AND THE TEMPLE
From Mark 11

Narrator

As they approached Jerusalem, near the towns of Bethphage and Bethany, they came to the Mount of Olives. Jesus sent two of his disciples on ahead with these instructions:

Jesus

Go to the village there ahead of you. As soon as you get there, you will find a colt tied up that has never been ridden. Untie it and bring it here. And if someone asks you why you are doing that, tell him that the Master needs it and will send it back at once.

Narrator

So they went and found a colt out in the street, tied to the door of a house. As they were untying it, some of the bystanders asked them:

Person 1

What are you doing – untying that colt?

Narrator

They answered just as Jesus had told them, and the men let them go. They brought the colt to Jesus, threw their cloaks over the animal, and Jesus go on. Many people spread their cloaks on the road, while others cut branches in the fields and spread them on the road. The people who were in front and those who followed behind began to shout:

Persons 1 and 2

Praise God!

Person 1

God bless him who comes in the name of the Lord!

Person 2

God bless the coming kingdom of King David, our father!

Persons 1 and 2

Praise God!

Narrator

When they arrived in Jerusalem, Jesus went to the Temple and began to drive out all those who were buying and selling. He overturned the tables of the money-changers and the stools of those who sold pigeons, and he would not let anyone carry anything through the temple courtyards. He then taught the people:

Jesus

It is written in the Scriptures that God said, 'My Temple will be called a house of prayer for the people of all nations.' But you have turned it into a hideout for thieves!

Narrator

The chief priests and the teachers of the Law heard of this, so they began looking for some way to kill Jesus. They were afraid of him, because the whole crowd was amazed at his teaching.

When evening came, Jesus and his disciples left the city. (PAUSE)

Narrator
[This is] the word of the Lord.   OR   This is the Gospel of Christ/
                                                                   This is the Gospel of the Lord.

All
Thanks be to God.   **Praise to Christ our Lord/**
                                                           Praise to you, Lord Jesus Christ.

HYMN: for example 'Ride on, ride on in majesty'

7.29   READING: THE PLOT AND THE PASSOVER
From Mark 14.1–21

Narrator

It was now two days before the Festival of Passover and Unleavened Bread. The chief priests and the teachers of the Law were looking for a way to arrest Jesus secretly and put him to death:

Priest

We must not do it during the festival.

Lawyer 1

The people might riot.

Narrator

Then Judas Iscariot, one of the twelve disciples, went off to the chief priests in order to betray Jesus to them. They were pleased to hear what he had to say, and promised to give him money. So Judas started looking for a good chance to hand Jesus over to them.

On the first day of the Festival of Unleavened Bread, the day the lambs for the Passover meal were killed, Jesus' disciples asked him:

Disciple

Where do you want us to go and get the Passover meal ready for you?

Narrator

Then Jesus sent two of them with these instructions:

Jesus

Go into the city, and a man carrying a jar of water will meet you. Follow him to the house he enters, and say to the owner of the house: 'The Teacher says, Where is the room where my disciples and I will eat the Passover meal?' Then he will show you a large upstairs room, prepared and furnished, where you will get everything ready for us.

Narrator

The disciples left, went to the city, and found everything just as Jesus had told them; and they prepared the Passover meal. (PAUSE)

When it was evening, Jesus came with the twelve disciples. While they were at the table eating, Jesus said:

Jesus

I tell you that one of you will betray me – one who is eating with me.

Narrator

The disciples were upset and began to ask him, one after the other:

Disciple

Surely you don't mean me, do you?

Jesus

It will be one of you twelve, one who dips his bread in the dish with me. The Son of Man will die as the Scriptures say he will; but how terrible for that man who betrays the Son of Man! It would have been better for that man if he had never been born!

Narrator

[This is] the word of the Lord.

All

Thanks be to God.

HYMN: for example 'No weight of gold or silver' – Passion Chorale

7.30 READING: THE LORD'S SUPPER
Mark 14.22–26

Narrator

While they were eating, Jesus took a piece of bread, gave a prayer of thanks, broke it, and gave it to his disciples. [He said:]

Jesus

Take it, this is my body.

Narrator

Then he took a cup, gave thanks to God, and handed it to them; and they all drank from it.

Jesus

This is my blood which is poured out for many, my blood which seals God's covenant. I tell you, I will never again drink this wine until the day I drink the new wine in the Kingdom of God.

Narrator

Then they sang a hymn and went out to the Mount of Olives.

Narrator

[This is] the word of the Lord.

All

Thanks be to God.

PSALM VERSION: for example Psalm 22

7.31 READING: JESUS IS DESERTED AND ARRESTED
Mark 14.27–52

Narrator
Jesus said to them:

Jesus
All of you will run away and leave me, for the scripture says, 'God will kill the shepherd, and the sheep will all be scattered'. But after I am raised to life, I will go to Galilee ahead of you.

Narrator
Peter answered:

Peter
I will never leave you, even though all the rest do!

Jesus (*to Peter*)
I tell you that before the cock crows twice tonight, you will say three times that you do not know me.

Peter (*insistently*)
I will never say that, even if I have to die with you!

Narrator
And all the other disciples said the same thing.

They came to a place called Gethsemane, and Jesus said to his disciples:

Jesus
Sit here while I pray.

Narrator
He took Peter, James, and John with him. Distress and anguish came over him:

Jesus
The sorrow in my heart is so great that it almost crushes me. Stay here and keep watch.

Narrator
He went a little farther on, threw himself on the ground, and prayed that, if possible, he might not have to go through that time of suffering:

Jesus
Father, my Father! All things are possible for you. Take this cup of suffering away from me. (PAUSE) Yet not what I want, but what you want.

Narrator

Then he returned and found the three disciples asleep. He said to Peter:

Jesus

Simon, are you asleep? Weren't you able to stay awake even for one hour?

Jesus (*looking round*)

Keep watch, and pray that you will not fall into temptation. The spirit is willing, but the flesh is weak.

Narrator

He went away once more and prayed, saying the same words. (PAUSE) Then he came back to the disciples and found them asleep; they could not keep their eyes open. And they did not know what to say to him. (PAUSE) He came back the third time ...

Jesus

Are you still sleeping and resting? Enough! The hour has come! Look, the Son of Man is now being handed over to the power of sinful men. Get up, let us go. Look, here is the man who is betraying me!

Narrator

Jesus was still speaking when Judas, one of the twelve disciples, arrived. With him was a crowd armed with swords and clubs, and sent by the chief priests, the teachers of the Law, and the elders. The traitor had given the crowd a signal:

Judas

The man I kiss is the one you want. Arrest him and take him away under guard.

Narrator

As soon as Judas arrived, he went up to Jesus . . .

Judas

Teacher!

Narrator

. . . and kissed him. So they arrested Jesus and held him tight. But one of those standing there drew his sword and struck at the High Priest's slave, cutting off his ear. Then Jesus spoke up:

Jesus

Did you have to come with swords and clubs to capture me, as though I were an outlaw? Day after day I was with you teaching in the Temple, and you did not arrest me. But the Scriptures must come true.

Narrator

Then all the disciples left him and ran away. (PAUSE)

A certain young man, dressed only in a linen cloth, was following Jesus. They tried to arrest him, but he ran away naked, leaving the cloth behind.

Narrator

[This is] the word of the Lord.

All

Thanks be to God.

HYMN: for example 'It is a thing most wonderful'

7.32 READING: JESUS BEFORE THE HIGH PRIEST
Mark 14.53–72

Narrator

Jesus was taken to the High Priest's house, where all the chief priests, the elders, and the teachers of the Law were gathering. Peter followed from a distance and went into the courtyard of the High Priest's house. There he sat down with the guards, keeping himself warm by the fire. The chief priests and the whole Council tried to find some evidence against Jesus in order to put him to death, but they could not find any. Many witnesses told lies against Jesus, but their stories did not agree.

Then some men stood up and told this lie against Jesus:

Man

We heard him say, 'I will tear down this Temple which men have made, and after three days I will build one that is not made by men.'

Narrator

Not even they, however, could make their stories agree.

The High Priest stood up in front of them all and questioned Jesus:

High Priest

Have you no answer to the accusation they bring against you?

Narrator

But Jesus kept quiet and would not say a word. Again the High Priest questioned him:

High Priest

Are you the Messiah, the Son of the Blessed God?

Jesus

I am, and you will all see the Son of Man seated on the right of the Almighty and coming with the clouds of heaven!

Narrator

The High Priest tore his robes:

High Priest

We don't need any more witnesses! You heard his blasphemy. What is your decision?

Narrator

They all voted against him: he was guilty and should be put to death.

Some of them began to spit on Jesus, and they blindfolded him and hit him:

Man

Guess who hit you!

Narrator

And the guards took him and slapped him.

Peter was still down in the courtyard when one of the High Priest's servant-girls came by. When she saw Peter warming himself, she looked straight at him:

Girl

You, too, were with Jesus of Nazareth.

Peter *(denying)*

I don't know . . . I don't understand what you are talking about.

Narrator

And he went out into the passage. Just then a cock crowed. (PAUSE)

The servant-girl saw him there and began to repeat to the bystanders:

Girl

He is one of them!

Narrator

But Peter denied it again. (PAUSE)

A little while later the bystanders accused Peter again:

Bystander

You can't deny that you are one of them, because you, too, are from Galilee.

Peter

I swear that I am telling the truth! May God punish me if I am not! I do not know the man you are talking about!

Narrator

Just then a cock crowed a second time, and Peter remembered how Jesus had said to him, 'Before the cock crows twice, you will say three times that you do not know me.' And he broke down and cried.

Narrator

[This is] the word of the Lord.

All

Thanks be to God.

HYMN: *for example 'He stood before the court'*

7.33 READING: JESUS BEFORE PILATE
Mark 15.1–15

Narrator

Early in the morning the chief priests met hurriedly with the elders, the teachers of the Law, and the whole Council, and made their plans. They put Jesus in chains, led him away, and handed him over to Pilate. Pilate questioned him:

Pilate

Are you the king of the Jews?

Jesus

So you say.

Narrator

The chief priests were accusing Jesus of many things, so Pilate questioned him again:

Pilate

Aren't you going to answer? Listen to all their accusations!

Narrator

Again Jesus refused to say a word, and Pilate was amazed. (PAUSE)

At every Passover Festival Pilate was in the habit of setting free any one prisoner the people asked for. At that time a man named Barabbas was in prison with the rebels who had committed murder in the riot. When the crowd gathered and began to ask Pilate for the usual favour, he asked them:

Pilate (*calling*)

Do you want me to set free for you the king of the Jews?

Narrator

He knew very well that the chief priests had handed Jesus over to him because they were jealous.

But the chief priests stirred up the crowd to ask, instead, for Pilate to set Barabbas free for them. Pilate spoke again to the crowd:

Pilate

What, then, do you want me to do with the one you call the king of the Jews?

Crowd (*shouting*)

Crucify him!

Pilate

But what crime has he committed?

Crowd (*louder*)

Crucify him!

Narrator

Pilate wanted to please the crowd, so he set Barabbas free for them. Then he had Jesus whipped and handed him over to be crucified.

Narrator

[This is] the word of the Lord.

All

Thanks be to God.

HYMN: for example 'There is a green hill'

7.34 READING: JESUS IS CRUCIFIED
Mark 15.16–32

Narrator

The soldiers took Jesus inside to the courtyard of the governor's palace and called together the rest of the company. They put a purple robe on Jesus, made a crown out of thorny branches, and put it on his head. Then they began to salute him:

Soldier(s)

Long live the King of the Jews!

Narrator

They beat him over the head with a stick, spat on him, fell on their knees, and bowed down to him. When they had finished mocking him, they took off the purple robe and put his own clothes back on him. Then they led him out to crucify him. (PAUSE)

On the way they met a man named Simon, who was coming into the city from the country, and the soldiers forced him to carry Jesus' cross.

Commentator

(Simon was from Cyrene and was the father of Alexander and Rufus.)

Narrator

They took Jesus to a place called Golgotha, which means 'The Place of the Skull'. There they tried to give him wine mixed with a drug called myrrh, but Jesus would not drink it. Then they crucified him and divided his clothes among themselves, throwing dice to see who would get which piece of clothing. It was nine o'clock in the morning when they crucified him. The notice of the accusation against him said:

Voice of Pilate (*slowly*)

The King of the Jews.

Narrator

They also crucified two bandits with Jesus, one on his right and the other on his left.

People passing by shook their heads and hurled insults at Jesus:

Persons 1 and 2

Aha!

Person 1

You were going to tear down the Temple and build it up again in three days!

Person 2

Now come down from the cross and save yourself!

Narrator

In the same way the chief priests and the teachers of the Law jeered at Jesus, saying to each other:

Lawyer 1

He saved others, but he cannot save himself!

Lawyer 2

Let us see the Messiah, the king of Israel, come down from the cross now, and we will believe in him!

Narrator

And the two who were crucified with Jesus insulted him also.

Narrator

[This is] the word of the Lord.

All

Thanks be to God.

CHORAL: for example 'A purple robe'; 'Were you there'

7.35   READING: THE DEATH OF JESUS
Mark 15.33–39

Narrator

At noon the whole country was covered with darkness, which lasted for three hours. At three o'clock Jesus cried out with a loud shout:

Jesus

Eloi, Eloi, lema sabachthani?

Narrator

Which means: My God, my God, why did you abandon me? Some of the people there heard him:

Person 1

Listen, he is calling for Elijah!

Narrator

One of them ran up with a sponge, soaked it in cheap wine, and put it on the end of a stick. Then he held it up to Jesus' lips:

Person 2

Wait! Let us see if Elijah is coming to bring him down from the cross! (PAUSE)

Narrator

With a loud cry Jesus died. (PAUSE)

The curtain hanging in the Temple was torn in two, from top to bottom. The army officer who was standing there in front of the cross saw how Jesus had died:

Soldier

This man was really the Son of God!

Narrator

[This is] the word of the Lord.

All

Thanks be to God.

PRAYER: reflecting on the Passion story

SONG in respsonse to prayers : for example 'Jesus, name above all names'

7.36   READING: CHRIST AND US
1 Peter 2.21–24

Voice 1

Christ himself suffered for you and left you an example, so that you would follow in his steps.

Voice 2

He committed no sin, and no one has ever heard a lie come from his lips.

Voice 1

When he was insulted, he did not answer back with an insult:

Voice 2

When he suffered, he did not threaten, but placed his hopes in God, l the righteous Judge.

Voice 1 and 2

Christ himself carried our sins in his body to the cross, so that we might die to sin and live for righteousness.

Voice 2

It is by his wounds that you have been healed.

Narrator

[This is] the word of the Lord.

All

Thanks be to God.

HYMN: for example 'When I survey the wondrous cross'

Passiontide, Good Friday, Easter Eve

▶ 8.1 GREETING
From Galatians 1†

Grace and peace be with you from God our Father and the Lord Jesus Christ, who gave himself for our sins according to the will of our God and Father; to whom be glory for ever and ever. **Amen.**

8.2 SENTENCE
John 12.33

Jesus said 'When I am lifted up from the earth I will draw all people to myself'. He said this to show the kind of death he was going to die.

8.3 SENTENCE
Matthew 26.42

Jesus said, 'Father, if this cup may not pass from me, but I must drink it, your will be done'.

8.4 SENTENCE
Philippians 2.8

Christ Jesus, being found in human form, humbled himself: and became obedient even to death, death on a cross.

8.5 SENTENCE
John 12.23

The hour has come for the Son of Man to be glorified.

8.6 SENTENCE
1 Peter 2.24

Christ himself bore our sins in his body on the tree, so that we might die to sins and live for righteousness; by his wounds you have been healed.

8.7 SENTENCE
1 Peter 3.18

Christ died for our sins once for all, the righteous for the unrighteous, to bring you to God.

8.8 SENTENCE
Colossians 2. 13,14

God forgave us all our sins, cancelling the laws that stood against us by nailing them to the cross.

8.9 SENTENCE
Colossians 2.15

God disarmed the evil powers and authorities and made a public spectacle of them, triumphing over them by the cross.

8.10 SENTENCE
Colossians 1. 19, 20

God was pleased through our Lord Jesus Christ to reconcile to himself all things, whether things on earth or things in heaven, by making peace through his blood, shed on the cross.

8.11 SENTENCE
1 John 3.16

This is how we know what love is: Jesus Christ laid down his life for us.

▶ **8.12** RESPONSE
From 2 Corinthians 5†

Jesus died for all:
**that we who live should no longer live for ourselves
but for him who for our sake died
and was raised to life. Amen.**

▶ **8.13** RESPONSE
From Ephesians 2†

You who once were far away have been brought near through the blood of Christ:
he himself is our peace!

▶ **8.14** RESPONSE
From Romans 5†

God demonstrates his own love for us in this:
while we were still sinners, Christ died for us.

8.15 APPROACH
Alan Gaunt

Living God, we come with joy and awe to the Cross, where we are met by your love, persistent and profound. We praise you for the mixture of joy and sorrow we feel on this day – joy for your love which gave your Son to the world; sorrow for our sin which nailed him to the cross. We praise you for the sorrow because it makes us conscious of our need; we praise you for the joy because it keeps our hope alive. Let the joy and sorrow combine in our act of worship, so that we may go back into the world to diminish the sorrow and increase the joy, not only for ourselves but for everyone; in the name of Jesus Christ our Lord. **Amen.**

8.16 APPROACH
Editors

Jesus, Son of God, we come to you in worship and thanksgiving: suffering servant, pioneer of our salvation, sacrifice for our sins, example of perfect forgiveness, God sharing our humanity, obedient even to the death of the cross, made to be a curse for us to take away our curse, victor over the powers of darkness, achieving our peace, reconciling us to the Father, bread of our life and blood of our deliverance, Lamb of God, redeemer, by your death sealing God's new covenant of love by which the sins of many are forgiven, drawing all people to yourself by the glory of your cross, raised high for the healing of the nations, that all who see you might believe and be saved: glory be to you, Jesus, Son of God. **Amen.**

▶ **8.17** CONFESSION
From Psalm 143†

O Lord, we have let you down,
darkness overtakes us,
our spirits fail
and our hearts are dismayed;
your face is hidden from us
and we wait for your word of love:
hear our prayer,
listen to our cry for mercy;
in your faithfulness and righteousness
come to our relief;
do not bring us to judgement –
for no-one living is righteous before you;
show us the way we should go,
teach us to do your will
and let your Spirit lead us;
through Jesus Christ our Lord. Amen.

▶ **8.18** CONFESSION
Editors

Lord Jesus, we feel the burden of Good Friday, for we know that on this day you suffered, bled and died for us. For our sin:
Lord, forgive us.

In our weakness:
Lord, strengthen us.

We are totally unable to earn or merit your forgiveness and your renewing love. We can only recall with wonder your sacrifice, and seek you with penitence and faith. For our sin:
Lord, forgive us.

In our weakness:
Lord, strengthen us.

We so often fail you and betray you – by our silence, by our neglect, and in our fear of being hurt. For our sin:
Lord, forgive us.

In our weakness:
Lord, strengthen us.

We confess our disobedience and our spirit of neglect. Help us not to shirk our duty to bear your cross, or seek to avoid our responsibilities as your redeemed in the world. For our sin:
Lord, forgive us.

In our weakness:
Lord, strengthen us.

Cleanse us from our sin by your precious blood,
and graciously restore us to your service
for your glory and your praise. Amen.

8.19   ABSOLUTION
From 'A New Zealand Prayer Book'

Through the cross of Christ, God have mercy on you, pardon you and set you free. Know that you are forgiven and be at peace: God strengthen you in all goodness and keep you in life eternal. **Amen.**

8.20   ABSOLUTION
From Psalm 51†

God in his goodness have mercy on you, wash you clean from your guilt and purify you from your sin; the Lord the righteous judge remove your sins from you and make you whiter than snow; through Jesus our redeemer. **Amen.**

▶ ### 8.21   PRAISE
From Psalm 103†

Praise the Lord and do not forget his blessings:
he heals our diseases and rescues our life from hell.

He crowns us with love and compassion:
he satisfies us with good things.

Praise the Lord! Amen.

▶ **8.22** CONFESSION
Editors

Lord Jesus Christ, we confess we have failed you as did your disciples, and we ask for your mercy and your help:

When we are tempted to betray you for the sake of selfish gain: Christ, have mercy;
Lord, forgive us and help us.

When we do not keep watch in prayer, and will not share the pain of your suffering: Christ, have mercy;
Lord, forgive us and help us.

When we allow the world to silence you, and run away from those who abuse you: Christ, have mercy;
Lord, forgive us and help us.

When we will not confess your name, and fear the consequences of being known to belong to you: Christ, have mercy;
Lord, forgive us and help us.

When we spurn your dying love, and will not offer you the sacrifice of our lives: Christ, have mercy;
Lord, forgive us and help us.

Cleanse us from our sins by your precious blood,
and graciously restore us to your service;
for your praise and glory. Amen.

▶ **8.23** COLLECT
Good Friday, ASB 1980

Almighty Father,
look with mercy on this your family
for which our Lord Jesus Christ
was content to be betrayed
    and given up into the hands of the wicked,
and to suffer death upon the cross;
who is alive and glorified
    with you and the Holy Spirit,
one God, now and for ever. **Amen.**

▶ **8.24** PSALM
From Psalm 22†

I am poured out like water, and all my bones are out of joint; my heart has turned to wax – it has melted away within me. My strength is dried up and my tongue sticks to the roof of my mouth; you lay me in the dust of death. Dogs have surrounded me; a band of evil men has encircled me, they have pierced my hands and my feet. I can count all my bones; people stare and gloat over me. They divide my garments among them and cast lots for my clothing. But you, O Lord, be not far off; O my strength, come quickly to help me.

All the ends of the earth will remember
and turn to the Lord,
and all the families of the nations
will bow down before him,
for dominion belongs to the Lord
and he rules over the nations.

My God, my God, why have you forsaken me? Why are you so far from saving me, so far from the words of my groaning? O my God, I cry out by day, but you do not answer, by night, and am not silent. Yet you are enthroned as the Holy One; you are the praise of Israel.

In you our fathers put their trust;
they trusted and you delivered them.
They cried to you and were saved;
in you they trusted
and were not disappointed.

But I am a worm and not a man, scorned by men and despised by the people. All who see me mock me; they hurl insults, shaking their heads:
He trusts in the Lord –
let the Lord rescue him;
let him deliver him
since he delights in him!

Posterity will serve him; future generations will be told about the Lord:
they will proclaim his righteousness to a people yet unborn
for he has done it. Amen.

▶ **8.25** CANTICLE
From Isaiah 53†

The people reply:

Who has believed our message:
to whom has the arm of the Lord been revealed.

He grew up before him like a tender shoot:
and like a root out of dry ground.

He was despised and rejected:
a man of sorrows and familiar with grief.

Surely he took up our infirmities:
and carried our sorrows.

He was pierced for our transgressions;
he was crushed for our iniquities.

The punishment that brought us peace was upon him:
and by his wounds we are healed.

He was led like a lamb to the slaughter, and as a sheep before her shearers is silent:
so he did not open his mouth.

He was assigned a grave with the wicked:
and with the rich in his death.

We all, like sheep have gone astray;
each of us has turned to our own way:
and the Lord has laid on him the iniquity of us all. Amen.

8.26 READING: JESUS IS CRUCIFIED
John 19. 17–30

Cast: Narrator, Pilate, Priest, Soldier 1, Soldier 2, Psalmist [can be the same as Priest], Jesus

Narrator
Jesus went out, carrying his cross, and came to 'The Place of the Skull', as it is called. In Hebrew it is called 'Golgotha'. There they crucified him; and they also crucified two other men, one on each side, with Jesus between them. Pilate wrote a notice and had it put on the cross.

Pilate
Jesus of Nazareth, the King of the Jews.

Narrator

Many people read it, because the place where Jesus was crucified was not far from the city. The notice was written in Hebrew, Latin, and Greek. The chief priests said to Pilate:

Priest

Do not write 'The King of the Jews', but rather, 'This man said, I am the King of the Jews.'

Pilate

What I have written stays written.

Narrator

After the soldiers had crucified Jesus, they took his clothes and divided them into four parts, one part for each soldier. They also took the robe, which was made of one piece of woven cloth without any seams in it. [The soldiers said to one another:]

Soldier 1 (*to Soldier 2*)

Let's not tear it.

Soldier 2 (*to Soldier 1*)

Let's throw dice to see who will get it.

Narrator

This happened in order to make the scripture come true:

Psalmist

They divided my clothes among themselves and gambled for my robe.

Narrator

And this is what the soldiers did. (PAUSE)

Standing close to Jesus' cross were his mother, his mother's sister, Mary the wife of Clopas, and Mary Magdalene. Jesus saw his mother and the disciple he loved standing there; so he said to his mother:

Jesus

He is your son.

Narrator

Then he said to the disciple:

Jesus

She is your mother.

Narrator

From that time the disciple took her to live in his home. (PAUSE)

Jesus knew that by now everything had been completed; and in order to make the scripture come true, he said:

Jesus
I am thirsty.

Narrator
A bowl was there, full of cheap wine; so a sponge was soaked in the wine, put on a stalk of hyssop, and lifted up to his lips. Jesus drank the wine and said:

Jesus
It is finished! (PAUSE)

Narrator
Then he bowed his head and died.

Cast
[This is] the word of the Lord. OR This is the Gospel of Christ/
This is the Gospel of the Lord.

All
Thanks be to God.

**Praise to Christ our Lord/
Praise to you, Lord Jesus Christ.**

FURTHER BIBLE READINGS
Readings appropriate to this theme will be found listed in our companion volume, 'The Dramatised Bible' (published by HarperCollins) on index pages 424–425.

▶ **8.27** CREED
From Galatians 2†

**We have been crucified with Christ
and we no longer live,
but Christ lives in us.
The life we live in the body
we live by faith in the Son of God,
who loved us and gave himself for us. Amen.**

▶ **8.28** CREED
From 1 Peter 3†

Let us confess our faith in Christ:

**Christ died for sins
once for all,
the just for the unjust,
to bring us to God:
he was put to death in the body,
but made alive by the Spirit;
he has gone up on high,
and is at God's right hand,
ruling over angels
    and the powers of heaven. Amen.**

▶ **8.29** FOR JESUS' HELP: A PERSONAL PRAYER
From 'A New Zealand Prayer Book'

Your cross, Jesus, remains like a tree on a hill:
you show me where I am,
you take away my fear,
and set me on my course again;
help me to watch for you night and day. **Amen.**

▶ **8.30** FOR THOSE IN NEED
Alan Warren, adapted

Lord Christ,
shine upon all who are in the darkness
    of suffering or grief,
that in your light
they may receive hope and courage,
in your mercy obtain relief and comfort,
and in your presence
find their rest and peace;
for your love's sake. **Amen.**

8.31 FOR THOSE WITH NERVOUS TROUBLES
Leslie Weatherhead, adapted

Our Saviour, we remember that you suffered anguish of spirit in the
Garden of Gethsemane, and we pray for all who are frightened and

unhappy because they are nervously ill; we lift up our hearts for those who are a prey to anxious fears – who cannot get their minds off themselves, and for whom every demand made upon them fills them with foreboding. Give them the comfort of knowing that this feeling is illness, not cowardice; that millions have felt as they feel, that there is a way through their dark valley and a light at the end of it; lead them to others who will listen and show them the pathway of renewed health. You are the Saviour who understands and can give them courage; help them to rest their minds in you, Jesus Christ our Lord. **Amen.**

8.32   FOR PRISONERS
From 'New Every Morning'

Lord God, we pray for all who have been imprisoned by their fellow men and women; for those who are in prison for crimes they have committed, that they may resolve to follow a new way of life, and find in you the help they need when they are released; for those who are in prison for conscience sake, that they may stand firm for what they believe to be right, and be sustained with courage and hope. We ask this in Christ's name. **Amen.**

8.33   FOR YOUNG PRISONERS AND FIRST OFFENDERS
Elizabeth Goudge

O Lord Jesus Christ, yourself a prisoner for our sakes and sinless in your bonds, we bring to your great love and unending compassion all prisoners who are young and all who are first offenders, those who have come where they are through misfortune or sudden temptation and are afraid and bewildered. Lord, uphold them in their shame and confusion, protect them from evil and bring to their help those who will steady and comfort them. We beseech you, O Lord, may the days pass hopefully for them and may they come to their freedom again unembittered and unharmed. **Amen.**

8.34   FOR POLITICAL PRISONERS
Elizabeth Goudge

O Lord Jesus Christ, you were unjustly taken prisoner and unjustly tried and condemned. We pray to you today for those men and women, all over the world, who are in prison for their faith. From one country to another, though their beliefs may differ and be at variance, you see the integrity of their souls, their courage and loyalty: these we beg you to preserve for them in strength and purity. Comfort them, O Lord of compassion, in loneliness and despair; and comfort and help those who love them and must fend without them. To all who have the care of them, O Lord, grant wisdom and kindness, and that respect for a differing faith that you asked of us with your command that we should love our enemies. And to all of us, O Lord, grant the light of your Holy Spirit that shall lead us into all truth. **Amen.**

▶ **8.35** ABOUT SELF-SACRIFICE
Alan Gaunt

Living God,
whose Son died on the cross
for everyone who lives:
show us by his dying
how the place of defeat
can be the place of victory;
and help us to take up our own cross
whatever form it takes,
so that women and men
may recognise your love in us
and come to you, with Christ,
in Resurrection glory. **Amen.**

8.36 ABOUT OBEDIENCE
Alan Gaunt

Living God, as your Son, Jesus Christ, went through the darkness of death for our sakes, and came out triumphant; help us, leaving sin and guilt behind, to follow him for other people's sake, and bring us at last with them to share his perfect joy, praising you for ever. **Amen.**

8.37 FOR HUMILITY
Maundy Thursday collect, ASB 1980

Almighty Father, whose Son Jesus Christ has taught us that what we do for the least of our brothers and sisters we do also for him: give us the will to be the servant of others as he was the servant of all, who gave up his life and died for us, yet is alive and reigns with you and the Holy Spirit, one God, now and for ever. **Amen.**

▶ **8.38** PRAYER OF REFLECTION
Based on Matthew 26 and 27, Editors

'Greetings, master!'. Lord, deliver us from Judas' duplicity – follower until the going was rough and the money ran out. Grant us an obedience which seeks the eternal kingdom. 'Greetings, master!' In your service:
Lord, make us faithful.

'Do we need any more witnesses?' Lord, deliver us from the High Priest's deviousness, following prejudice in the name of piety. Grant us a religion open to the Spirit and full of love. 'Do we need any more witnesses?' In our religion:
Lord, make us honest.

'I do not know the man!' Lord, deliver us from Peter's denial – following at a distance until the human cost became too great. Grant us a courage which will not hesitate to acknowledge our master. 'I do not know the man!' In our discipleship:
Lord, make us true.

'What shall I do with him?' Lord, deliver us from Pilate's dereliction of duty, following neither truth nor the promptings of conscience. Grant us a social awareness that does not wash its hands of justice. 'What shall I do with him?'. In our care for others:
Lord, make us merciful.

For Jesus' sake. Amen.

8.39 ABOUT SUFFERING FOR CHRIST
From 1 Peter 1†

O God, Father of our Lord Jesus Christ, shield us through our faith and by your power. If we are called upon to suffer grief in any kind of trial, help us to rejoice greatly and to know that it comes so that our faith – more precious than perishable gold which is refined by fire – may prove enduring to the praise and glory and honour of Jesus Christ our Lord. **Amen.**

▶ **8.40** FOR OURSELVES
Salvator mundi

O Saviour of the world,
by your cross and precious blood,
you have redeemed us:
Save us and help us,
we humbly beseech you, O Lord. Amen.

▶ **8.41** INTERCESSION ON EASTER EVE
Editors

Lord Jesus, we pray this night for all who look for your light, for all who have no hope in this world, for those who have rejected you, and for those who have denied you. Lord in your mercy:
hear our prayer.

We pray this night for all who are tired or hungry, for all who are anxious or ill, for those who are afraid of dying, and for those who do not believe in the resurrection from the dead. Lord in your mercy:
hear our prayer.

We pray this night for all who trust/*are baptized* in you, for the fellowship of those we love, for all in other lands who celebrate his rising, and for those who are persecuted for their faith. Lord in your mercy:
hear our prayer.

Lord Jesus, on this night
we lift to you our hands and our hearts,
looking for the dawn of a new day
and the everlasting hope of heaven
in the faith of your resurrection. Amen.

8.42 THANKSGIVING
Michael Botting

Heavenly Father, we thank you for giving your Son to die on the cross that we might be forgiven. Help us to understandthe extent of our sin, and the greatness of his love, so that we may trust him as our saviour and serve him as our Lord. **Amen.**

▶ **8.43** THANKSGIVING
Editors

The word in brackets may also be spoken by another voice, or omitted.

O God our Father, you loved the world so much that you sent your only Son to die that we might live through him.

('Forgive them . . .for they do not know what they are doing'.) For Jesus' willingness to forgive in the face of bitter hatred, Father, we thank you,
and praise your holy name.

('Today you shall be with me in paradise.') For Jesus' promise of heaven to the forgiven sinner, Father, we thank you,
and praise your holy name.

('Mother . . . behold your son.') For the example of Jesus' compassion to the last, Father, we thank you,
and praise your holy name.

('I thirst . . . ') For Jesus' sharing in our physical suffering and longing, Father, we thank you,
and praise your holy name.

('Why have you forsaken me?') For Jesus' entering into our mental suffering and loneliness, Father, we thank you,
and praise your holy name.

('It is finished?') For the completion of Jesus' saving work, and for the covenant of love between God and his world, Father, we thank you,
and praise your holy name.

('Into your hands I commit my spirit.') For Jesus' triumph over death and the certainty of eternal life, Father, we thank you,
and praise your holy name.

Father, God, as you loved us,
so by your grace
help us to love one another,
through Jesus Christ our Lord. Amen.

8.44 THANKSGIVING
Editors

Lord Jesus Christ, when you died on the cross at Calvary you brought life to us through your wounded hands, your wounded feet, your wounded side, your thorn-crowned head, your broken heart. By your blood freely given we are made whole, set free to serve, and lifted on wings of love to praise you for ever. Thank you, Jesus. **Amen.**

8.45 GOOD FRIDAY THANKSGIVING
Richard Hughes

Lord, it seems so strange to call a day like this Good Friday: so many lies, so much hate, so much pain. And yet through it all you went on loving; loving the liars, loving the haters, loving the people who gave you pain – with love so strong that nothing could overcome it. Thank you, Lord Jesus Christ. **Amen.**

▶ **8.46** THANKSGIVING
Richard of Chichester, adapted

Thanks to you, Lord Jesus Christ,
for all the cruel pains and insults you have borne for us;
for all the many blessings you have won for us.
Holy Jesus, most merciful Redeemer, friend and brother,
may we know you more clearly, love you more dearly,
and follow you more nearly, day by day. **Amen.**

▶ **8.47** DEDICATION
Editors

Lord, draw us to your Cross which brings forgiveness:
that we may be cleansed.

Lord, draw us to your Cross which brings light:
that we may have vision.

Lord, draw us to your Cross which brings love:
that we may have compassion.

Lord, draw us to your Cross which brings Life:
that we may live for you.

Lord, draw us to yourself
and to each other;
one Body in heaven and on earth. Amen.

▶ **8.48** ASCRIPTION
From Revelation 1†

To him who loves us,
and has freed us from our sins by his blood,
and has made us to be a kingdom and priests
to serve his God and Father –
to him be glory and power
for ever and ever. **Amen.**

8.49 BLESSING
From 'Still Waters, Deep Waters'

The dying Saviour's love, the risen Saviour's power, the ascended
Saviour's blessing, and the returning Saviour's glory be the joy and
comfort of *your* hearts now and for ever. **Amen.**

8.50 BLESSING
From 'Still Waters, Deep Waters'

May you experience the peace of God in your trouble, hope when
you are tempted to despair, joy through your pain, faith and
courage when the heavens seem silent, and the sure knowledge that
the Lord has been through it all too, he understands, he cares, and
he loves you very much. And (may) the blessing of God our
saviour, the Father, the Son and the Holy Spirit, be with *you* always.
Amen.

Easter, Resurrection

▶ **9.1** GREETING
From Revelation 1†

Grace and peace to you from Jesus Christ, who is the faithful witness, the first-born from the dead. **Amen.**

▶ **9.2** GREETING
From Revelation 1† (alternative)

Grace and peace to you from God who is, and who was, and who is to come, and from Jesus Christ, the faithful witness, the first-born from the dead. **Amen.**

9.3 SENTENCE
Mark 16.2

Very early in the morning, on the first day of the week, they came to the tomb, just as the sun was rising.

9.4 SENTENCE
Luke 24.1

On the first day of the week, the disciples went to the tomb and they found the stone rolled away.

9.5 SENTENCE
John 20.19

In the evening of that same day, the first day of the week, Jesus came and stood among the disciples, and said to them: 'Peace be with you'.

9.6 SENTENCE
2 Corinthians 5.15

Jesus died for all: so that we who live should live no longer for ourselves, but for him who died and was raised to life for us.

9.7 SENTENCE
2 Corinthians 4.14

We know that God who raised the Lord Jesus from the dead will also raise us with Jesus.

9.8 SENTENCE
Colossians 1.15

Jesus Christ is the beginning and the first-born from among the dead. (Alleluia!)

▶ **9.9** RESPONSE
From Romans 6†

Christ raised from the dead will never die again:
death no longer has power over him: Alleluia!

▶ **9.10** RESPONSE
From Luke 24†

Why do you look for the living among the dead?
He is not here, he is risen!

▶ **9.11** RESPONSE
From Acts 2†

God has raised this Jesus to life:
we are all witnesses.

▶ **9.12** RESPONSE
From 2 Corinthians 1†

All God's promises are 'Yes!' in Christ, and through him we reply 'Amen', to the glory of God: **Amen.**

▶ **9.13** RESPONSE
From 2 Corinthians 13†

In weakness Christ was put to death on the Cross:
by God's power he lives!

▶ **9.14**   RESPONSE
From Romans 7†

Who will rescue us from this body of death?
Thanks be to God – through Jesus Christ our Lord!

▶ **9.15**   RESPONSE
From Galatians 5†

Freedom is ours;
Christ has set us free.
Alleluia! Amen.

▶ **9.16**   RESPONSE
From 1 Peter 1†

Praise be to the God and Father of our Lord Jesus Christ!
In his great mercy he has given us new birth into a living hope
through the resurrection of Jesus Christ from the dead. Amen.

▶ **9.17**   RESPONSE
Frank Colquhoun, adapted

We are risen with Christ –
the Lord is risen!

Eternal life is ours –
the Lord is risen!

Death has met its master –
the Lord is risen!

The way to heaven is open –
the Lord is risen!

He is risen indeed –
Alleluia! Amen.

▶ **9.18**   APPROACH
Editors

Our God and Father, as this new morning breaks, and there dawns
the full light of another Resurrection day, we have come to worship
you. In your presence we begin to understand the energy of your

Spirit and the power of your love. Our hearts are warmed again, and you renew our confidence. Heavenly Father, on Easter Day:
we praise and adore you.

Lord Jesus, Easter morning tells us that you are alive; that nothing can separate us from your love. We join the countless number in heaven and on earth who proclaim your victory. Risen Lord Jesus, nothing can hold you now from fulfilling your work on earth through your Church. Lord Jesus, Saviour, on Easter Day:
we praise and adore you.

Holy Spirit of God, we come to renew our hearts and minds so that in daily contact with those who know our friendship, or share our place of employment, or live with us in the intimacy of our homes, we may realise our partnership with you: meeting the needs of the world with the power of Jesus' Resurrection. Holy Spirit of God, on Easter Day:
we praise and adore you.

O Lord our God,
Father, Son and Holy Spirit,
yours is the kingdom, the power and the glory,
for ever and ever. Amen.

▶ **9.19**   PRAISE
From Psalm 86†

O Lord our God,
we will praise you with all our heart.

O Lord our God,
we will proclaim your greatness for ever.

Great is your constant love for us;
you have saved us from the grave itself! Amen.

▶ **9.20**   CONFESSION
Alternative Confession, ASB 1980

Almighty God, our heavenly Father,
we have sinned against you,
through our own fault,
in thought and word and deed,
and in what we have left undone.

For your Son our Lord Jesus Christ's sake,
forgive us all that is past;
and grant that we may serve you in newness of life
to the glory of your name. Amen.

▶ **9.21** CONFESSION
Editors

O Jesus Christ, risen master and triumphant Lord, we bow before you in sorrow for our sins, and confess to you our weakness and unbelief:

We have lived by our own strength, and not by the power of your resurrection. In your mercy, forgive us:
Lord, hear us and help us.

We have lived by the light of our own eyes, as faithless and not believing. In your mercy, forgive us:
Lord, hear us and help us.

We have lived for this world alone, and doubted our home in heaven. In your mercy, forgive us:
Lord, hear us and help us.

Lift our minds above earthly things,
set them on things in heaven;
show us your glory and your power,
that we may serve you gladly all our days. Amen.

9.22 ABSOLUTION
From Isaiah 53†

Receive God's forgiveness through our Lord Jesus Christ: he has taken up your infirmities and carried your sorrows; he was pierced for your transgressions and crushed for your iniquities; upon him was the punishment that brings you peace, and by his wounds you are healed. **Amen.**

▶ **9.23** COLLECT
9 before Easter, ASB 1980

Eternal God,
whose Son Jesus Christ is for all people
the way, the truth and the life:

grant us to walk in his way,
to rejoice in his truth,
and to share his risen life;
who is alive and reigns with you and the Holy Spirit,
one God, now and for ever. **Amen.**

▶ **9.24** COLLECT
Easter, ASB 1980

Lord of all life and power,
who through the mighty resurrection of your Son
overcame the old order of sin and death
to make all things new in him:
grant that we, being dead to sin
and alive to you in Jesus Christ,
may reign with him in glory;
to whom with you and the Holy Spirit
be praise and honour, glory and might,
now and in all eternity. **Amen.**

▶ **9.25** PSALM
Psalm 126.1–6†

When the Lord brought us back from slavery:
we were like those who dream.

Our mouths were filled with laughter:
our tongues with songs of joy.

Then those around us said, 'The Lord has done great things for
them':
**The Lord has done great things for us,
and we are filled with joy.**

Those who sow in tears
shall reap with songs of joy. Amen.

9.26 READING: THE EMPTY TOMB
John 20.1–10 [11–18]

Cast: Voice 1, Voice 2 [can be the same as Voice 1], Mary, Angel(s), Jesus

Voice 1
Early on Sunday morning, while it was still dark, Mary Magdalene

went to the tomb and saw that the stone had been taken away from the entrance. She went running to Simon Peter . . .

Voice 2

And the other disciple, whom Jesus loved.

Mary

They have taken the Lord from the tomb, and we don't know where they have put him!

Voice 1

Peter and the other disciple went to the tomb. The two of them were running.

Voice 2

But the other disciple ran faster than Peter and reached the tomb first. He bent over and saw the linen wrappings, but he did not go in.

Voice 1

Behind him came Simon Peter, and he went straight into the tomb. He saw the linen wrappings lying there and the cloth which had been round Jesus' head. It was not lying with the linen wrappings but was rolled up by itself.

Voice 2

Then the other disciple, who had reached the tomb first, also went in; he saw and believed.

Voice 1

They still did not understand the scripture which said that he must rise from death. Then the disciples went back home. (PAUSE)

Voice 2

Mary stood crying outside the tomb. While she was still crying, she bent over and looked in the tomb and saw two angels there dressed in white, sitting where the body of Jesus had been, one at the head and the other at the feet. [They asked her:]

Angel(s)

Woman, why are you crying?

Mary

They have taken my Lord away, and I do not know where they have put him!

Voice 2

Then she turned round and saw Jesus standing there; but she did not know that it was Jesus.

Jesus

Woman, why are you crying? Who is it that you are looking for?

Voice 1

She thought he was the gardener.

Mary

If you took him away, sir, tell me where you have put him, and I will go and get him.

Jesus

Mary!

Mary

Rabboni! Teacher!

Jesus

Do not hold on to me, because I have not yet gone back up to the Father. But go to my brothers and tell them that I am returning to him who is my Father and their Father, my God and their God.

Voice 2

So Mary Magdalene went and told the disciples that she had seen the Lord and related to them what he had told her.

Cast
    [This is] the word of the Lord.   OR   This is the Gospel of Christ/
                                         This is the Gospel of the Lord.

All
    Thanks be to God.   **Praise to Christ our Lord/**
                                            Praise to you, Lord Jesus Christ.

9.27   READING: JESUS APPEARS TO HIS DISCIPLES
John 20. 19–23

Cast: Narrator, Jesus.

Narrator

It was late that Sunday evening, and the disciples were gathered together behind locked doors, because they were afraid of the Jewish authorities. Then Jesus came and stood among them. [He said:]

Jesus

Peace be with you.

Narrator

After saying this, he showed them his hands and his side. The disciples were filled with joy at seeing the Lord. [Jesus said to them again:]

Jesus

Peace be with you. As the Father sent me, so I send you.

Narrator

Then he breathed on them [and said]:

Jesus

Receive the Holy Spirit. If you forgive people's sins, they are forgiven; if you do not forgive them, they are not forgiven.

Cast

[This is] the word of the Lord.   OR   This is the Gospel of Christ/
                                                          This is the Gospel of the Lord.

All

Thanks be to God.   **Praise to Christ our Lord/**
                                                          Praise to you, Lord Jesus Christ.

9.28   READING: JESUS AND THOMAS
John 20.24–29

Cast: Narrator, Disciple(s), Thomas, Jesus

Narrator

One of the twelve disciples, Thomas (called the Twin), was not with them when Jesus came. So the other disciples told him:

Disciple(s)

We have seen the Lord!

[Narrator

Thomas said to them:]

Thomas

Unless I see the scars of the nails in his hands and put my finger on those scars and my hand in his side, I will not believe.

Narrator

A week later the disciples were together again indoors, and Thomas was with them. The doors were locked, but Jesus came and stood among them [and said]:

Jesus

Peace be with you.

[Narrator
Then he said to Thomas:]

Jesus *(to Thomas)*
Put your finger here, and look at my hands; then stretch out your hand and put it in my side. Stop your doubting, and believe!

Thomas
My Lord and my God!

Jesus
Do you believe because you see me? How happy are those who believe without seeing me!

Cast
[This is] the word of the Lord.   OR   This is the Gospel of Christ/
This is the Gospel of the Lord.

All
Thanks be to God.   **Praise to Christ our Lord/**
Praise to you, Lord Jesus Christ.

9.29   READING: JESUS APPEARS TO SEVEN DISCIPLES
John 21. 1–14

Cast: Narrator, Peter, Disciple, Jesus, John [can be the same as Disciple]

Narrator
Jesus appeared once more to his disciples at Lake Tiberias. This is how it happened. Simon Peter, Thomas – called the Twin, Nathanael – the one from Cana in Galilee, the sons of Zebedee, and two other disciples of Jesus were all together. Simon Peter said to the others:

Peter
I am going fishing.

Disciple
We will come with you.

Narrator
So they went out in a boat, but all that night they did not catch a thing. As the sun was rising, Jesus stood at the water's edge, but the disciples did not know that it was Jesus. [Then he asked them:]

Jesus *(calling)*
Young men, haven't you caught anything?

Disciple
Not a thing.

Jesus *(calling)*
Throw your net out on the right side of the boat, and you will catch some.

Narrator
So they threw the net out and could not pull it back in, because they had caught so many fish. (PAUSE) The disciple whom Jesus loved said to Peter:

John
It is the Lord!

Narrator
When Peter heard that it was the Lord, he wrapped his outer garment round him – for he had taken his clothes off – and jumped into the water. The other disciples came to shore in the boat, pulling the net full of fish. They were not very far from land, about a hundred metres away. When they stepped ashore, they saw a charcoal fire there with fish on it and some bread. [Then Jesus said to them:]

Jesus
Bring some of the fish you have just caught.

Narrator
Simon Peter went aboard and dragged the net ashore full of big fish, a hundred and fifty-three in all; even though there were so many, still the net did not tear. [Jesus said to them:]

Jesus
Come and eat.

Narrator
None of the disciples dared ask him, 'Who are you?' because they knew it was the Lord. So Jesus went over, took the bread, and gave it to them; he did the same with the fish.

This, then, was the third time Jesus appeared to the disciples after he was raised from death.

Cast
[This is] the word of the Lord.　　OR　　This is the Gospel of Christ/
　　　　　　　　　　　　　　　　　　　　　This is the Gospel of the Lord.

All
　　Thanks be to God.　　　　　　　　　**Praise to Christ our Lord/Praise to you,
　　　　　　　　　　　　　　　　　　　　　Lord Jesus Christ.**

FURTHER BIBLE READINGS
Readings appropriate to this theme will be found listed in our companion volume, 'The Dramatised Bible' (published by HarperCollins) on index page 425.

▶ **9.30** CREED
From 1 Corinthians 15†

Let us declare our faith in the resurrection of our Lord Jesus Christ:

**Christ died for our sins
in accordance with the scriptures;
he was buried;
he was raised to life on the third day
in accordance with the scriptures;
afterwards he appeared to his followers,
and to all the apostles:
this we have received, and this we believe. Amen.**

▶ **9.31** CREED
From 1 Peter 1, Romans 4 and 8†

Let us proclaim our faith:

**We believe in God the Father,
by whose great mercy
we have been born again
to a living hope,
through the resurrection of Jesus Christ
from the dead.**

**We believe in God the Son,
who died for our sin,
and rose again for our justification.**

**We believe in God the Holy Spirit,
who bears witness with our spirit
that we are the children of God.**

**We believe in one God:
Father, Son, and Holy Spirit. Amen.**

▶ **9.32** FOR JESUS' PRESENCE AND POWER
Michael Botting, adapted

Lord Jesus, our risen Saviour,
we rejoice in your mighty victory over sin and death:
you are the Prince of Life;
you are alive for evermore.
Help us to know your presence in our worship,
and to receive your power in our lives;
until we rise to live with you for ever. **Amen.**

▶ **9.33** FOR THE CHURCH
Editors

O God, our Father,
we give you thanks for our Church:
shed the light of your Holy Spirit here,
that all who enter in may find you.
Bless us with your presence;
let love reach out and be met with love,
rest your hand on all who minister for you;
for the sake of Jesus,
our Saviour and risen Lord. **Amen.**

▶ **9.34** FOR FAITH
David Silk

Grant to us, Lord God,
to trust you not for ourselves alone,
but for those also whom we love
and who are hidden from us by the shadow of death;
that, as we believe your power
    to have raised our Lord Jesus Christ from the dead,
so we may trust your love
    to give eternal life to all who believe in him;
through Jesus Christ our Lord,
who is alive and reigns with you and the Holy Spirit,
one God, now and for ever. **Amen.**

▶ **9.35** FOR OUR FAITH
Editors

Gracious Father, God of Love,
we rejoice in the glorious resurrection of your Son, Jesus Christ;
we praise you and thank you for our Saviour,
who triumphed over death
to reign as Lord of life.
Strengthen us, Father;
grant us a firm faith,
that we may know the presence of Jesus
our Wonderful Counsellor and true friend:
all glory and honour to his name! **Amen.**

9.36 FOR OBEDIENCE
Alan Gaunt

Living God, as your Son, Jesus Christ, went through the darkness of
death for our sakes, and came out triumphant; help us, leaving sin
and guilt behind, to follow him for other people's sake, and bring us
at last with them to share his perfect joy, praising you for ever.
Amen.

▶ **9.37** THANKSGIVING
Editors

We give thanks to our Lord Jesus Christ for the hope of Easter:

For your penetrating love which has pierced the darkness and
redeemed the utter despair of humanity, we give you thanks, Lord
Jesus.
We praise you, risen Christ.

That you have taken our sorrows, our failures and our weaknesses,
and have transformed them by the power and radiance of your
resurrection, we give you thanks, Lord Jesus.
We praise you, risen Christ.

For your church, to whom you have given the message of
reconciliation to proclaim to the world, we give you thanks, Lord
Jesus.
We praise you, risen Christ.
Alleluia! Amen.

▶ **9.38** THANKSGIVING
Richard Hughes

Our Lord Jesus Christ, risen from death, we praise you for changed lives and new hopes at Easter:

You came to Mary in the garden, and turned her tears into joy. For your love and your mercy:
we give you thanks, O Lord.

You came to the disciples in the upper room, and turned their fear into courage. For your love and your mercy:
we give you thanks, O Lord.

You came to the disciples by the lakeside, and turned their failure into faith. For your love and your mercy:
we give you thanks, O Lord.

You came to the disciples on the Emmaus road, and turned their despair into hope. For your love and your mercy:
we give you thanks, O Lord.

You come to us in our unworthiness and shame, and turn our weakness into triumph. For your love and your mercy:
we give you thanks, O Lord.

Lord Jesus,
wherever there are tears,
or fear, or failure,
or despair, or weakness:
come, reveal to us your love, your mercy,
   and your risen power;
for the glory of your name.
Alleluia! Amen.

▶ **9.39** THANKSGIVING
From 1 Peter 1†

Praise be to you, O God our Father:
for in your great mercy
you have given us new birth into a living hope
through the resurrection from the dead
of Jesus Christ our Lord. **Amen.**

9.40 EASTER THANKSGIVING
Richard Hughes

Lord, we watch the news and sometimes it seems that evil and death always have the last word. There is so much fighting, so much pain, so many deaths. There seems so little we can do, except stand and watch from afar like the disciples. But nothing could stop the power of Jesus' love – even on the cross he forgave his enemies; his love broke the power of evil and death, his love had the last word. On Easter Day the tomb is empty and he is risen. That's the best news of all. Thank you for it. **Amen.**

▶ **9.41** RESURRECTION THANKSGIVING
From 'New Every Morning', adapted

Because you have broken for us the chains of sin and brought us into fellowship with our heavenly Father:
thanks be to you, our Lord Jesus Christ.

Because you overcame death and opened for us the gates of eternal life:
thanks be to you, our Lord Jesus Christ.

Because when two or three gather in your name you are present with them:
thanks be to you, our Lord Jesus Christ.

Because you ever live to intercede for us:
thanks be to you, our Lord Jesus Christ.

For these and all other benefits
  of your glorious resurrection,
thanks be to you, Lord Jesus Christ. Amen.

9.42 EASTER COMMISSION
From John 21†

Jesus asks each one of us, 'Do you truly love me?'
Yes, Lord, you know that I love you.

'Feed my lambs'. (PAUSE) Jesus asks us each by name, 'Do you truly love me?'
Yes, Lord, you know that I love you.

163

'Take care of my sheep'. (PAUSE) Jesus asks us the third time, 'Do you love me?'
Lord, you know all things, you know that I love you.

Jesus tells us, 'Feed my sheep! Follow me!'
Amen.

9.43   BLESSING
From Hebrews 13†

The God of peace, who by the blood of the eternal covenant brought again from the dead our Lord Jesus Christ, that great shepherd of the sheep, make you perfect in every good work, working in you that which is pleasing and good, through Jesus Christ, to whom be glory for ever and ever. **Amen.**

9.44   BLESSING
From John†

The Lord bless you and keep you: behold your Lord, receive his peace, in the name of the Father, the Son and the Holy Spirit. **Amen.**

9.45   BLESSING
From 2 John 21†

God the Father and Jesus Christ, the Father's Son, give *you* grace, mercy and peace; may they be *yours* in truth and love. **Amen.**

God's Creation

▶ **10.1** GREETING
From 1 Peter 1†

Grace and peace be yours in full measure. **Amen.**

10.2 SENTENCE
Genesis 1.1

In the beginning God created the heavens and the earth.

10.3 SENTENCE
Genesis 1.31

God looked at everything he had made, and it was very good.

10.4 SENTENCE
Matthew 6. 28–30

See how the lilies of the field grow – not even Solomon in all his glory was dressed like one of these – that is how God clothes the grass of the field!

10.5 SENTENCE
Romans 1.20

Since the creation of the world, God's invisible qualities – his eternal power and divine nature – have been clearly seen, being understood from what has been made.

10.6 SENTENCE
Colossians 1.15

Christ is the first-born over all creation. By him all things in heaven and on earth were created.

▶ **10.7** RESPONSE
From Genesis 1†

God saw all that he had made:
it was very good.

▶ **10.8** RESPONSE
From Psalm 19†

The heavens declare the glory of God:
the skies proclaim the work of his hands.

▶ **10.9** RESPONSE
From Isaiah 45†

The Lord who created the heavens, who fashioned and made the earth:
he is God!

▶ **10.10** RESPONSE
From Psalm 8†

O Lord, our Lord:
how majestic is your name in all the earth!

10.11 INVITATION
From Nehemiah 9†

Stand up and praise the Lord your God,
who is from everlasting.

Blessed be his glorious name, let it be exalted above all blessing and praise: Stand up and praise the Lord your God,
who is from everlasting.

He alone is the Lord, he made the highest heavens and all their starry host, the earth and all that is on it, the seas and all that is in them: Stand up and praise the Lord your God,
who is from everlasting.

He gives life to everything, and the multitudes of heaven worship him: Stand up and praise the Lord your God,
who is from everlasting.

We praise you O God
for you have created all things
and made us anew
in Jesus Christ our Lord. Amen.

▶ **10.12** INVITATION
From Song of Songs 2†

See, the winter is past:
the snows are over and gone.

Flowers appear on the earth:
the season of singing has come.

The trees are beginning to bud:
the blossom has spread its fragrance.

The cry of the birds is heard in our land. Arise, come and worship.
Amen.

10.13 APPROACH
From Psalm 148†

O God, we come to worship you, Lord of all creation. The skies
praise you in the heights above; all the angels praise you, your
heavenly army; the sun, the moon and the shining stars all praise
you – they praise your name, for you commanded and they were
created. You set them in place for ever; you made a decree that will
not pass away. From the earth, the great sea-creatures praise you –
unfathomable ocean depths. Lightning, hail, snow and clouds – all
obey you; mountains, hills and trees; wild animals, cattle, little
creatures, birds on the wing – all praise you. Men, women and
children, we too praise you – here as your people, holy and close to
your heart – we praise you. O Lord God, we come to worship you.
Amen.

▶ **10.14** APPROACH
Editors

Gracious God, the variety of beauty and colour in the world often
leaves us speechless; the rolling hills, the mighty seas, the desert
plains and the succulent green pastures, all proclaim your power
and creative provision. O Lord our God:
we praise and adore you.

We praise you for the warming sun, the growth-making rain, the freshness of a new morning and the calm of a still evening: all proclaim your purpose and your pleasure. O Lord our God:
we praise and adore you.

We praise you for your Son, our Saviour, Jesus Christ: through him we have received pardon for our sin and the joy of salvation; for he lived and died and rose again to redeem us. O Lord our God:
we praise and adore you.

For all the work of your hands,
and for every gift from your heart of love,
we exalt your holy name for ever and ever. Amen.

▶ **10.15** PRAISE
From Psalm 8†

O Lord our God, how glorious is your name in all the earth:
high above the heavens your majesty is praised. Amen.

▶ **10.16** CONFESSION
From 'Worship Now'

Almighty God, we confess that we have often misused and ill-treated your creation: hear us, and in your mercy save us and help us.

For every act of carelessness that has treated the world merely as a playground: Father, forgive us –
save us and help us.

For every act of wastefulness that forgets the crying of the needy: Father, forgive us –
save us and help us.

For every act of selfishness that defies your just rule over our lives: Father, forgive us –
save us and help us.

Cleanse us from our sins
through the love of Christ,
and set us free for his service
through the power of the Spirit;
for the glory of your name. Amen.

▶ **10.17** CONFESSION
From Psalm 106†

O Lord our God,
we have not obeyed your commands,
we have not always done what is right;
we have sinned through our human nature,
we have done wrong and acted wickedly;
we have forgotten your many kindnesses
and we have rebelled against you:
O Lord, forgive us and save us
bring us back and restore us;
that we may give thanks to your holy name
and glory in your praise. Amen.

10.18 ABSOLUTION
From Psalm 103†

The Lord, whose love for those who seek him is as great as the heavens are high above the earth, remove your sins from you as far as the east is from the west and remember them no more; through Jesus Christ, our Lord. **Amen.**

▶ **10.19** COLLECT
Rogation Days, ASB 1980

Almighty God,
you have provided
the resources of the world
to maintain the life of your children,
and have so ordered our life
that we are dependent upon each other.
Bless us all in our daily work
and, as you have given us
    the knowledge to produce plenty
so give us the will
to bring it within reach of all;
through Jesus Christ our Lord. **Amen.**

10.20 COLLECT

Rogation Days, ASB 1980

Almighty God, whose will it is that the earth should bear its fruit in their seasons; direct the labours of those who work on the land that they may employ the resources of nature to your glory, for our own well-being, and for the relief of those in need; through Jesus Christ our Lord. **Amen.**

▶ **10.21** PSALM
Psalm 67.1–7†

The congregation may divide at A *and* B

> May God be gracious to us and bless us:
> A **and make his face to shine upon us.**
>
> Let your ways be known upon earth:
> B **your saving grace to every nation.**
>
> Let the peoples praise you, O God:
> ALL **let the peoples praise you.**
>
> Let the nations be glad:
> A **and sing aloud for joy.**
>
> Because you judge the peoples justly:
> B **and guide the nations of the earth.**
>
> Let the peoples praise you, O God:
> ALL **let all the peoples praise you.**
>
> Then the land will yield its harvest:
> A **and God, our God, will bless us.**
>
> God will bless us:
> B **and people will fear him**
> ALL **to the ends of the earth. Amen.**

▶ **10.22** PSALM
Psalm 148. 1–14†

The congregation may divide at A *and* B

Praise the Lord!

Praise the Lord from the heavens:
praise him in the heights above.

Praise him, all his angels:
A **praise him, all his heavenly host.**

Praise him, sun and moon:
B **praise him, all you shining stars.**

Let them praise the name of the Lord:
ALL **Praise the Lord!**

Praise the Lord from the earth:
A **praise him, great sea creatures.**

Praise him, storms and clouds:
B **praise him, mountains and hills.**

Praise him, fields and woods:
A **praise him, animals and birds.**

Praise him, rulers and nations:
B **praise him, old and young.**

Let them praise the name of the Lord:
ALL **Praise the Lord! Amen.**

10.23   READING: GOD'S CREATION
From Genesis 1.1–2.4

Cast: Narrator, God

Narrator
In the beginning, when God created the universe, the earth was formless and desolate. The raging ocean that covered everything was engulfed in total darkness, and the power of God was moving over the water. Then God commanded:

God
Let there be light.

Narrator
And light appeared. God was pleased with what he saw. Then he separated the light from the darkness, and he named the light:

God
Day.

Narrator
And the darkness:

God

Night.

Narrator

Evening passed and morning came – that was the first day. Then God commanded:

God

Let there be a dome to divide the water and to keep it in two separate places.

Narrator

And it was done. So God made a dome, and it separated the water under it from the water above it. He named the dome:

God

Sky.

Narrator

Evening passed and morning came – that was the second day. Then God commanded:

God

Let the water below the sky come together in one place, so that the land will appear –

Narrator

And it was done. He named the land:

God

Earth.

Narrator

And the water which had come together he named:

God

Sea.

Narrator

And God was pleased with what he saw. Then he commanded:

God

Let the earth produce all kinds of plants, those that bear grain and those that bear fruit.

Narrator

And it was done. So the earth produced all kinds of plants, and God was pleased with what he saw. Evening passed and morning came – that was the third day. Then God commanded:

God

Let lights appear in the sky to separate day from night and to show the time when days, years, and religious festivals begin; they will shine in the sky to give light to the earth.

Narrator

And it was done. So God made the two larger lights, the sun to rule over the day and the moon to rule over the night; he also made the stars. He placed the lights in the sky to shine on the earth, to rule over the day and the night, and to separate light from darkness. And God was pleased with what he saw. Evening passed and morning came – that was the fourth day. Then God commanded:

God

Let the water be filled with many kinds of living beings, and let the air be filled with birds.

Narrator

So God created the great sea-monsters, all kinds of creatures that live in the water, and all kinds of birds. And God was pleased with what he saw. He blessed them all and told the creatures that live in the water to reproduce, and to fill the sea, and he told the birds to increase in number. Evening passed and morning came – that was the fifth day. Then God commanded:

God

Let the earth produce all kinds of animal life: domestic and wild, large and small.

Narrator

And it was done. So God made them all, and he was pleased with what he saw. Then God said:

God

And now we will make human beings; they will be like us and resemble us. They will have power over the fish, the birds, and all animals, domestic and wild, large and small.

Narrator

So God created human beings, making them to be like himself. He created them male and female, blessed them, and said:

God

Have many children, so that your descendants will live all over the earth and bring it under their control. I am putting you in charge of the fish, the birds, and all the wild animals. I have provided all kinds of grain and all kinds of fruit for you to eat; but for all the wild animals and for all the birds I have provided grass and leafy plants for food.

Narrator
And it was done. God looked at everything he had made, and he was very pleased. Evening passed and morning came – that was the sixth day. And so the whole universe was completed. By the seventh day God finished what he had been doing and stopped working. He blessed the seventh day and set it apart as a special day, because by that day he had completed his creation and stopped working. And that is how the universe was created.

Cast
[This is] the word of the Lord.

All
Thanks be to God.

FURTHER BIBLE READINGS
Readings appropriate to this theme will be found listed in our companion volume, 'The Dramatised Bible' (published by HarperCollins) on index page 425.

▶ **10.24** CREED
From Isaiah 44†

We believe in one God who made all things;
he alone stretched out the heavens
and spread out the earth:
he formed us in the womb.
He is our king and our redeemer –
the Lord almighty.

We belong to the Lord –
we are his people
and are called by his name;
he pours out his Spirit upon us
as water on a thirsty land.

We believe in one God, the almighty,
Father, Son and Holy Spirit. Amen.

OR

▶ **10.25** CREED
From Isaiah 44†

We believe in one God who made all things:

Did he stretch out the heavens, spread out the earth, and form us in the womb?
He did!

Is he the Lord almighty, our King and our Redeemer?
He is!

Are we his own people, called by his name?
We are!

Does he pour his Spirit on us as on a dry and thirsty land?
He does!

We believe in one God, the almighty, Father Son and Holy Spirit.
Amen.

▶ **10.26** CREED
From Colossians 1†

Christ is the image of the invisible God,
the first-born over all creation.
By him all things were created:
things in heaven and on earth,
visible and invisible;
all things were created by him and for him.
He is before all things
and in him all things hold together.
He is the head of the body, the Church;
he is the beginning and the first-born from among the dead.
Amen.

10.27 FOR FARMING COMMUNITIES
Editors

Father, you provide all our needs. We thank you for all who work in the agricultural industry, harvesting the earth's resources. We pray for all who are engaged in farming throughout the world. We thank you for their energies and skills, and we ask that they may use them wisely. Help them to feel a deep responsibility to hold the balance between profitability and the care and conservation of the soil. We pray for farming communities where the countryside is being encroached upon for development because of the need for housing land. Strengthen those who farm in difficult conditions, who shepherd their flocks on remote hills and lonely moors. Let all perceive your hand in creation and realise their stewardship. Help your church in rural areas to be a welcoming, uniting community: this we ask in the name of the great Shepherd, Jesus Christ our Lord. **Amen.**

▶ **10.28**   FOR FORGIVENESS
Alan Gaunt

For our misuse of the world, our wanton destruction of life and our thoughtless pollution of the atmosphere:
Lord, forgive us.

For our greed of gain, our poverty of spirit and our lust for power:
Lord, forgive us.

For our loss of nerve, our lapses into despair, and our failure to unite the human family:
Lord, forgive us,
for the sake of Jesus Christ our Saviour. Amen.

▶ **10.29**   ABOUT OURSELVES AND GOD'S CREATION
Michael Botting

Lord of the universe,
we praise you for your creation;
for the wonder of space,
the beauty of the world
and the value of earth's resources:
keep us from spoiling these your gifts
    by our selfishness
and help us to use them for the good of all people
and the glory of your name. **Amen.**

10.30   FOR OUR STEWARDSHIP
Frank Colquhoun, adapted

Almighty God, Creator and Lord of all things, we thank you for the vast resources of the earth and the sea, and for the hidden forces of nature now brought within our grasp by scientific discovery: help us to use your gifts wisely and faithfully for the benefit of humanity, that all may rejoice in your goodness; through Jesus Christ our Lord. **Amen.**

10.31   FOR OUR RESPONSIBILITY
Editors

O God, our Father, thank you for the world in which we live. Thank you for all the beautiful things in it, for all the interesting things in it, for all the useful things in it. Help us never to do anything which would make the world uglier or sadder; help us always to add something to the world's beauty and to the world's joy: through Jesus Christ our Lord. **Amen.**

10.32   ABOUT ANIMALS
Editors

Loving Creator, who designed and made everything, we thank you for all the earth's animals and birds. Your wonderful creation is a cause for celebration! When we see the exquisite patterns and shapes and colours of wildlife, we are given a glimpse of your grand sovereignty, your authority over all the universe. Show us how to look after all creatures: the domestic – both pets and working animals; and the wild – the rare species and the ordinary. Give us pity, Lord; help us to prevent their needless suffering, and to make their existence happy. So may we fulfil our stewardship of your creation to the glory of our Creator and Redeemer. **Amen.**

▶ ### 10.33   FOR OURSELVES
From 'Prayers and Hymns for Junior Schools'

O Lord,
open our eyes to see what is beautiful,
our minds to know what is true,
and our hearts to love what is good;
for Jesus' sake. **Amen.**

10.34   ABOUT OUR SENSES
Editors

God, our Creator, we thank you for the gateway of our senses which open to us rich and formative experiences.

For sight, through which we appreciate the beauty of nature and the elegance of art, and with which we behold those who are dear to us. For hearing, by which we can appreciate language, conversation, and the experiences of music and sound. For touch, which brings us into contact with the texture of materials, and gives us the joys of human closeness and friendship. For taste, with which we enjoy newly-baked bread or the fruits of the earth – deeply satisfying and a blessing to our lives. For smell, which saves us from disasters of fire and smoke, yet beckons us to appreciate the sensation of polished furniture or alluring perfume. O God, how thoughtfully you have designed us!

Above all we praise you for the sense of your presence and our spiritual well-being in Christ: keep us ever thankful for your love and ever true to your purpose; for the glory of your name. **Amen.**

10.35   FOR GOOD LIVES
Editors. See responsive version at 10.40

Creator God, you have provided a wonderful world for us to enjoy. We are so glad to be alive and able to appreciate some of the wonders of nature; the careful ordering of times and seasons and the variety of human and animal life. We thank you that in Jesus you have shown us that you are the Lord of life and death: please go on helping us to change our ways; and by the power of your Holy Spirit strengthen our wills, that we may love to do what is right. Discipline our lives for your glory and the good of those with whom we share this world. We ask this in the name of Jesus Christ our Lord. **Amen.**

10.36   THANKSGIVING FOR THE WORLD
Editors

Our God and Father, we thank you for everything that ministers to us in your wonderful world: for the inspiration of morning mists, for the dew on field and flower, for the whispering wind and purifying rain, for sunshine, warmth and colour; for the calm seas reflecting the beauty of the skies, and the flying spume of lashing waves that speak of your power and might. For all that we see in the world around us, we thank you in Jesus' name. **Amen.**

10.37 THANKSGIVING FOR THE UNIVERSE
Editors

Lord God, maker of all worlds, we praise and adore you: thank you for our beautiful planet moving in space; thank you for light, and warmth, and food, and life in all its forms; thank you for magnificent rainbows and night skies patterned with stars; thank you for a glimpse of your majestic universe; thank you for humankind, and for creating each one of us in your image; thank you for Jesus, whose name is over all. **Amen.**

▶ **10.38** THANKSGIVING FOR OUR SENSES
Editors

O Lord of love and creation, we thank you for the privilege and blessing of living in a world filled with beauty, excitement and variety:

For the gift of loving and being loved, for friendship and understanding, we lift up our hearts:
and give you our thanks, O Lord.

For the beauty of forest and marshes, for the green of meadows and trees, we lift up our hearts:
and give you our thanks, O Lord.

For the sound of waterfalls and rippling streams, for the happy cries of children and the interest they bring, we lift up our hearts:
and give you our thanks, O Lord.

For the delight of music and words, for the stimulus of others' thoughts and conversation, for their books to read – by the fireside, or in bed with the rain falling on the roof or the snow blowing past outside the window – we lift up our hearts:
and give you our thanks, O Lord.

For all your providence and generosity,
we thank you, O Lord our God. Amen.

▶ **10.39** GENERAL THANKSGIVING
From 'Contemporary Prayers for Public Worship', adapted

Let us thank God for all his goodness to us:

For creating the world and for preserving it until now: we give you thanks, O Lord,
and praise your holy name.

For the regular return of day and night, and of the seasons: we give you thanks, O Lord,
and praise your holy name.

For the wonder of nature and the beauty of the earth: we give you thanks, O Lord,
and praise your holy name.

For our memory, which enables us to build on the experience of the past: we give you thanks, O Lord,
and praise your holy name.

For our imagination, which admits us to a wider world than we could otherwise know: we give you thanks, O Lord,
and praise your holy name.

For the grace by which you have revealed yourself to us: we give you thanks, O Lord,
and praise your holy name.

For your patience with our waywardness and your forgiveness for our sinfulness: we give you thanks, O Lord,
and praise your holy name.

Above all
we thank you for the promise of all things made new,
and for our re-creation in your dear Son,
Jesus Christ our Lord. Amen.

10.40 THANKSGIVING FOR GOD'S CARE
Editors

Lord God Almighty, when we look at the night sky, and think of the countless numbers of stars and the immensity of space, we have some idea of your great power and eternal Majesty. And yet you are interested in the details of this earth: you know our names, and the number of hairs on our head; you even know when a sparrow falls to the ground. Lord, thank you for caring about all of your creation;

thank you for loving the world so much that you gave us the precious gift of your Son, Jesus Christ, to be our saviour. **Amen.**

▶ **10.41**   PRAISE FOR CREATION
Editors. See prose version at 10.35

Our God and Father, we praise you for everything that ministers to us in your wonderful world.

For the inspiration of morning mists:
our God, we praise you.

For the dew on field and flower:
our God, we praise you.

For the whispering wind and purifying rain:
our God, we praise you.

For sunshine, warmth and colour:
our God, we praise you.

For the calm seas reflecting the beauty of skies:
our God, we praise you.

For the flying spume and the lashing waves that speak of your power and might:
our God, we praise you.

For all that we see in the world around us,
we praise you,
in Jesus' name, Amen.

▶ **10.42**   PRAISE FOR ALL GOD'S GIFTS
Edward Smalley

For creation with its order and beauty; for the rhythm of the seasons – summer, winter, spring, and autumn – and for all that sustains our life on earth: our God we thank you,
and bring you praise today.

For all that makes the earth our home, for other people whose labours and skills contribute to our needs, for institutions of society which provide for our health and security: our God we thank you,
and bring you praise today.

For families and the love of partners, for our parents and our children, for the concern and interest of those who anticipate our

needs and provide for our well-being, for the loyalty of friends and all who encourage and sustain us by their words and examples: our God we thank you,
and bring you praise today.

For work and leisure, hobbies and sport; for literature, music and art, radio and television, and for every medium by which we draw upon the treasury of others' thoughts: our God we thank you,
and bring you praise today.

For the Christian church with its opportunities of friendship, service and worship, for the communion of saints; for your word of life in Jesus our Lord, for the Holy Spirit ever present to guide and to enable; for the hope of heaven and for life eternal: our God we thank you,
and bring you praise today.

[Especially for . . . , our God we thank you,
and bring you praise today.]

Praise the Lord:
praise his holy name. Amen.

▶ **10.43** ASCRIPTION
Jim Cotter

To God the Creator,
who loved us first
and gave this world to be our home;
to God the Redeemer,
who loves us
and by dying and rising
pioneered the way of freedom;
to God the Sanctifier,
who spreads the divine love in our hearts,
be praise and glory for time and for eternity. **Amen.**

▶ **10.44** ASCRIPTION
From Nehemiah 9†

Blessed be your glorious name, O Lord our God;
may it be exalted above all human worship and praise.
You alone are the Lord,
you made the skies and the universe beyond;

182

you made the earth and all that is on it,
the sea and all that is in it;
you give life to everything.
You are the Lord our God;
with the hosts of heaven we worship you. **Amen.**

▶ **10.45** DOXOLOGY
Thomas Ken, adapted

Praise God
   from whom all blessings flow,
in heaven above and earth below;
one God, three persons, we adore –
to him be praise for evermore! **Amen.**

▶ **10.46** DOXOLOGY
From Psalm 63†

Lord God, our God,
we have seen you in the sanctuary,
we have looked on your power and your glory.
Because your love is better than life
our lips will glorify you,
we will praise you as long as we live,
and in your name we will lift up our hearts;
through Jesus Christ our Lord. **Amen.**

10.47 BLESSING (ROGATION)
From Deuteronomy 28†

May the Lord our God open his storehouse of heaven and send his
blessing on our land: bless us in the city, bless us in the country; bless
our homes with children; bless our farms with crops, our orchards
with fruit; bless our industry with produce, our commerce with
trade; bless us in our coming in and going out; bless us in obedience
to his will, grant us his prosperity, and lead us to follow him alone
for ever. **Amen.**

10.48 BLESSING
From Psalm 19†

God, whose glory the heavens declare, whose handiwork the skies proclaim, who speaks through his creation, revive *your* spirit(s) by his word, make *you* wise by his laws and give *you* joy through his commands, now and for ever. **Amen.**

10.49 BLESSING
From Psalm 121†

The Lord who made heaven and earth, watch over you, the Lord be close by your side, the Lord guard your life and keep you from harm, the Lord protect you as you come and go, and bless you now and evermore. **Amen.**

10.50 BLESSING
From Romans 1†

God, whose invisible qualities – his eternal power and divine nature, are clearly seen in his creation since the beginning, grant *you* to know his righteousness in Christ Jesus and his eternal peace, and to enjoy the works of his hands: and the blessing of the Father, the Son and the Holy Spirit, one God, be with *you* always. **Amen.**

Jesus is the Lord, Ascension

▶ **11.1** GREETING
From 2 Timothy 1†

Grace, mercy and peace from God the Father and Christ Jesus our Lord. **Amen.**

11.2 SENTENCE
Ephesians 1.19

By his mighty power God has raised Christ from the dead and has seated him at his right hand in heaven.

11.3 SENTENCE
Hebrews 4.14

We have a great high priest who has passed through the heavens, Jesus the Son of God.

11.4 SENTENCE
Hebrews 8.1

We have a high priest who sat down at the right hand of the throne of the majesty in heaven.

11.5 SENTENCE
Acts 7.56

'Look, I see heaven open and the Son of Man standing at the right hand of God.'

11.6 SENTENCE
Psalm 45. 6,7 and Hebrews 1. 8,9

'Your throne, O God, will last for ever and ever; a sceptre of justice will be the sceptre of your kingdom. [You love righteousness and hate wickedness; therefore God, your God, has set you above your companions by anointing you with the oil of joy.]'

▶ **11.7** RESPONSE
From Acts 2 and Philippians 2†

Be assured of this – God has made this Jesus both Lord and Christ:
God has exalted him,
and given him a name above every name. Amen.

▶ **11.8** RESPONSE
From Revelation 11†

We give you thanks, Lord God Almighty, the One who is and who
was, because you have taken your great power and have begun to
reign. **Amen.**

▶ **11.9** RESPONSE
From Revelation 11†

The kingdom of this world has become the kingdom of our Lord and
of his Christ:
and he will reign for ever and ever. Amen.

▶ **11.10** RESPONSE
From Revelation 12†

Now have come the salvation and the power and the kingdom of
our God, and the authority of his Christ. **Amen.**

▶ **11.11** APPROACH
From 'Companion to the Lectionary', adapted

God our Father, King of heaven:
all honour and glory and power are yours by right.

Jesus Christ, crucified, risen, ascended Lord:
all honour and glory and power are yours by right.

Spirit of God, lighting upon us, filling our lives with love, spurring
us to greater deeds:
all honour and glory and power are yours by right.

Our glorious and holy God, we praise you for all that makes the
unseen heaven a reality to us while we live on earth: for word and
sacrament, for faithful Christians past and present, for fellowship in

the Church, and for times of deep awareness that Jesus is with us always.
One God, Father, Son and Holy Spirit:
all honour and glory and power are yours by right. Amen.

▶ **11.12** PRAISE
From Psalm 68†

Sing to God, O kingdoms of the earth;
sing praises to the Lord!

Sing to God, O kingdoms of the earth;
proclaim his mighty power!

Praise the Lord! **Amen.**

▶ **11.13** CONFESSION
Editors

Lord Jesus Christ,
crucified, risen and ascended for us:
we have not loved you as our Redeemer,
nor obeyed you as our Lord;
we have not brought our prayers to you,
nor heeded your tears shed over the world.
Forgive us, we pray;
breathe into us a new spirit of service,
and make us joyfully obedient to your will:
for your glory's sake. Amen.

▶ **11.14** CONFESSION/PRAYER FOR FORGIVENESS
Editors

For our failure to appreciate and enjoy the good things you provide for our lives, in your mercy:
Lord, forgive us.

For our insensitivity to the needs of others, and for our over-sensitivity when we are hurt by them, in your mercy:
Lord, forgive us.

For becoming consumed in the business of life, and for losing faith in your sovereignty and power, in your mercy:
Lord, forgive us.

For moods of disobedience and for outright rejection of your will, in
your mercy:
Lord, forgive us.

For consenting to wrong practices by our cool silence, and for
listening to scandal, in your mercy:
Lord, forgive us.

**Reform our will,
reinforce our courage:
create in us a new heart, O God,
and put your righteousness in us;
through Jesus Christ our Lord. Amen.**

▶ **11.15** CONFESSION
From Lamentations 5†

**Remember, O Lord, your people in their sorrow;
look, and see our disgrace:
joy is gone from our hearts;
our dancing has turned to mourning,
we are no longer proud –
the crown has fallen from our head –
for we have sinned.
You, O Lord, reign for ever,
your throne endures to every generation:
do not forget us now,
do not forsake us for long:
forgive us, restore us and renew us
through our redeemer Jesus Christ. Amen.**

11.16 ABSOLUTION
From Psalm 140†

The Lord hears your cry for mercy; the Sovereign Lord is your strong
deliverer; he will shield your head, and you shall not die; in the
name of Jesus. **Amen.**

▶ **11.17** COLLECT
John Austin, adapted

O God, you have exalted the crucified Saviour your Son
by a triumphant resurrection and ascension into heaven.
May his triumphs and glories so shine in our hearts and minds,
that we may be able to understand more readily his sufferings,
and more courageously face our own;
through Jesus Christ our Lord
who, with you and the Spirit lives and reigns,
one God for ever and ever. **Amen.**

▶ **11.18** PSALM
Psalm 47.1–9†

The congregation may divide at A *and* B

Clap your hands, all you nations:
shout to God with cries of joy.

How awesome is the Lord most high:
A **the King who rules the whole wide earth!**

God has ascended to his throne:
B **with shouts of joy and sound of trumpets.**

Sing praises to our God, sing praises:
A **sing praises to our King, sing praises.**

For God is king of all the earth:
B **sing to him a psalm of praise.**

God is seated on his throne:
A **he rules the nations of the world.**

The leaders of the nations come:
B **as subjects of our holy God.**

The lords of earth belong to God:
ALL **he reigns supreme. Amen.**

▶ **11.19** PSALM
Psalm 99.1–9†

The congregation may divide at A *and* B

The Lord reigns:
A **let the nations tremble!**

He sits enthroned on high:
B **let the earth shake!**

Great is the Lord our God:
ALL **exalted over all the world.**

Let the nations praise his awesome name, and say:
A **God is holy!**

Praise the Lord our God, and worship at his feet:
B **God is holy!**

Exalt the Lord our God, and worship on his holy mountain:
ALL **The Lord our God is holy! Amen**

11.20   READING: JESUS IS TAKEN UP TO HEAVEN
From Acts 1.4–11

Cast: Narrator, Jesus, Apostle, Angel

Narrator
When his apostles came together, Jesus gave them this order:

Jesus
Do not leave Jerusalem, but wait for the gift I told you about, the gift my Father promised. John baptized with water, but in a few days you will be baptized with the Holy Spirit.

Narrator
When the apostles met together with Jesus, they asked him:

Apostle
Lord, will you at this time give the Kingdom back to Israel?

Jesus
The times and occasions are set by my Father's own authority, and it is not for you to know when they will be. But when the Holy Spirit comes upon you, you will be filled with power, and you will be witnesses for me in Jerusalem, in all Judaea and Samaria, and to the ends of the earth.

Narrator

After saying this, he was taken up to heaven as they watched him and a cloud hid him from their sight. They still had their eye fixed on the sky as he went away, when two men dressed in white suddenly stood beside them and said:

Angel

Galileans, why are you standing there looking up at the sky? This Jesus, who was taken from you into heaven, will come back in the same way that you saw him go to heaven.

Cast

[This is] the word of the Lord.

All

Thanks be to God.

11.21 READING: CHRIST'S HUMILITY AND GREATNESS
Philippians 2.1–11

Cast: Paul, Reader 1, Reader 2, Reader 3, Reader 4

Paul

Your life in Christ makes you strong, and his love comforts you. You have fellowship with the Spirit, and you have kindness and compassion for one another. I urge you, then, to make me completely happy by having the same thoughts, sharing the same love, and being one in soul and mind. Don't do anything from selfish ambition or from a cheap desire to boast, but be humble towards one another, always considering others better than yourselves. And look out for one another's interests, not just for your own. The attitude you should have is the one that Christ Jesus had:

Reader 1

He always had the nature of God.

Reader 2

But he did not think that by force he should try to become equal with God. Instead of this, of his own free will he gave up all he had, and took the nature of a servant.

Reader 1

He became like man and appeared in human likeness.

191

Reader 2
He was humble and walked the path of obedience all the way to death – his death on the cross.

Reader 3
For this reason God raised him to the highest place above.

Reader 4
And gave him the name that is greater than any other name.

Reader 3
And so, in honour of the name of Jesus all beings in heaven, on earth, and in the world below will fall on their knees.

Reader 4
And all will openly proclaim:

Readers 1–4
Jesus Christ is Lord –

Reader 4
To the glory of God the Father.

Cast
[This is] the word of the Lord.

All
Thanks be to God.

FURTHER BIBLE READINGS
Readings appropriate to this theme will be found listed in our companion volume, 'The Dramatised Bible' (published by HarperCollins) on index pages 425–426.

▶ **11.22** CREED
From 'Te Deum', Editors

Let us confess our faith in Christ:

**We believe in Christ
the King of glory,
the eternal Son of the Father:
he became man to set us free,
and did not despise the Virgin's womb;
he overcame death,
and opened the kingdom of heaven to all believers;
he is seated at God's right hand in glory,
and will come to be our judge. Amen.**

▶ **11.23** CREED
From Ephesians 2†

Let us declare our faith in the resurrection and reign of Christ:

By his mighty power,
God raised from the dead our Lord Jesus Christ
and seated him at his right hand in heaven,
far above all rule and authority,
power and dominion,
and every title that can be given,
not only in the present age but also in the age to come.

God placed all things under his feet
and appointed him to be head over everything for the Church,
which is his body,
the fullness of him who fills everything
everywhere and always. Amen.

▶ **11.24** CREED
From Colossians 1†

Let us declare our faith in the supremacy of Christ:

Christ is the image of the invisible God,
the first-born over all creation.
For by him all things were created:
things in heaven and on earth,
visible and invisible;
thrones, powers, rulers and authorities –
all things were created by him and for him.
He is before all things,
and in him all things hold together.

He is the head of the body, the Church;
he is the beginning and the first-born
    from among the dead,
so that in everything he might have the supremacy.

God was pleased to have all his fullness dwell in him,
and through him to reconcile to himself all things;
things on earth and things in heaven,
by making peace through his blood shed on the cross.
Alleluia. Amen.

▶ **11.25** FOR CONFIDENCE IN CHRIST
From Hebrews 4†

O Jesus, Son of God,
our high priest who has gone into the heavens,
you are able to understand our weaknesses;
for you have been tempted in every way,
just as we are – yet without sin:
give us confidence
that we may approach the throne of grace
to receive mercy
and find grace to help us in our time of need:
to the glory of God the Father. **Amen.**

▶ **11.26** FOR STRENGTH
Michael Botting

Lord Jesus Christ,
we thank you that you ascended as king of heaven and earth,
and that you are in control of all things:
help us to trust you in joy and in sorrow,
and to obey you always;
for the honour of your name. **Amen.**

11.27 A PERSONAL PRAYER AT ASCENSIONTIDE
Editors

Lord Jesus Christ, when I think of you newly born, lying in the manger at Bethlehem, I want to shield and protect you from the world.

Lord Jesus Christ, when I think of you working in the carpenter's shop at Nazareth, I want to work at the bench with you and help you.

Lord Jesus Christ, when I think of you walking on the shore at Galilee, I want to walk with you and listen and learn.

Lord Jesus Christ, when I think of you transfigured in light on Mount Hermon, I want to fall at your feet and worship you.

Lord Jesus Christ, when I think of you praying in the olive grove at Gethsemane, I want to stay close and keep watch and pray with you.

Lord Jesus Christ, when I think of you nailed to the cruel Cross at Calvary, I want to reach out and comfort you with love.

Lord Jesus Christ, when I think of you outside the empty tomb in the Easter garden, I want to proclaim the news of your wonderful resurrection.

Lord Jesus Christ, when I think of you now, reigning in majesty with God the Father, I want to dance and sing songs of pure joy. Alleluia Jesus! King of Glory! **Amen.**

11.28 THANKSGIVING
From Philippians 2†

We praise you, O God, because you have exalted your Son Jesus Christ to your right hand in glory, and given him the name above every name, that at the name of Jesus every knee should bow. So, our Father, accept our worship – our love and thanksgiving; and grant that we, with those of every tongue, may confess that Jesus Christ is Lord, to your glory and honour. **Amen.**

▶ ## 11.29 THANKSGIVING
From Revelation 1†

Jesus Christ,
faithful witness, firstborn from the dead,
ruler of the powers of this world:
we thank you that you love us,
and by your sacrificial death
have freed us from our sins
and made us a kingdom of priests
to serve our God and Father:
to you, Lord Jesus
be glory and power for ever and ever! **Amen.**

▶ **11.30** THANKSGIVING
Editors

O Lord our God, we thank you for the privilege of living in a world filled with variety and beauty, and for the challenge of its mysteries.

For the gift of loving and being loved, for friendship and mutual understanding: O Lord, we give you thanks,
and lift up our hearts in praise.

For the richness of our world; for forests and fields, for mountains and oceans: O God, we give you thanks,
and lift up our hearts in praise.

For the delights of music and poetry, for other people's thoughts and conversations, and for all good books and reading: O God, we give you thanks,
and lift up our hearts in praise.

For the refreshing power of the falling rain, for the strength and vitality of the shining sun, and for every life-giving source: O God, we give you thanks,
and lift up our hearts in praise.

Above all,
we thank you for the grace of your Spirit
flowing into our lives and recreating them
in the image of Jesus our redeemer. Amen.

▶ **11.31** ACCLAMATION
Unknown, adapted

We praise our ascended and exalted Lord:

Name above every name: Jesus, Lord,
we worship and adore you.

King of righteousness, king of peace, enthroned at the right hand of Majesty on high: Jesus, Lord,
we worship and adore you.

You are our great high priest; you are the pioneer of our salvation: Jesus, Lord,
we worship and adore you. Amen.

▶ **11.32**   ASCRIPTION
From Revelation 4 and 5†

Let us give glory to God:

Our Lord and God, you are worthy to receive glory, honour, and power; for you created all things, and by your will they were given existence and life:
Glory to God in the highest!

O Lamb of God, you are worthy to receive wisdom, strength, and praise, for by your death you bought for God people from every tribe, language, nation and race:
Glory to God in the highest!

You have made them a kingdom of priests to serve our God, and they shall rule on earth:
Glory to God in the highest!

**To him who sits upon the throne
and to the Lamb,
be praise and honour,
glory and power, for ever and ever! Amen.**

▶ **11.33**   ADORATION
Editors

Lord Jesus Christ,
thank you for your unfailing mercy and infinite love:
through our sweet communion with you
we have seen the Father.
Lord, King of heaven and earth,
we worship and adore you,
today, tomorrow and for ever. **Amen.**

11.34   BLESSING
From Philippians 4†

Rejoice in the Lord always, show gentleness to all; do not be anxious about anything but bring your prayers to God with thanksgiving; and God's peace [shall] guard your hearts and your minds in Christ Jesus our Lord, now and for ever. **Amen.**

11.35 BLESSING
From Colossians 3†

Set your heart on things above where Christ is seated at the right hand of God; and the blessing of God almighty, the Father, the Son and the Holy Spirit be with you always. **Amen.**

11.36 BLESSING
From 1 Thessalonians 3†

God himself, our Father, and our Lord Jesus Christ direct your way together; the Lord make your love increase and overflow for each other and for everyone else, the Lord strengthen your hearts so that you will be blameless and holy in the presence of our God and Father at the coming of our Lord Jesus Christ. **Amen.**

11.37 BLESSING
From Hebrews 12†

[*Let us*] fix *your* eyes on Jesus, the author and finisher of our faith, who for the joy set before him endured the cross, scorning its shame, and sat down at the right hand of the throne on high; and the blessing of God almighty, Father, Son and Holy Spirit be upon *you* always. **Amen.**

The Holy Spirit

▶ **12.1** GREETING
From 2 Timothy 4†

The Lord be with your spirit:
grace and peace be with you. Amen.

12.2 SENTENCE
Joel 2.29, 32 and Acts 2. 18, 21

'In those days' says the Lord, 'I will pour out my Spirit on my servants, both men and women. And everyone who calls on the name of the Lord will be saved'.

OR

12.3 SENTENCE
Joel 2.28 and Acts 2.17

'I will pour out my Spirit on all people,' says the Lord. 'Your sons and your daughters will prophesy, your old men will dream dreams and your young men will see visions.'

12.4 SENTENCE
John 14.26

Jesus said, 'The Holy Spirit . . . shall teach you all things and will remind you of everything I have said.'

12.5 SENTENCE
Acts 2.1–4

When the day of Pentecost came, they were all together in one place. Suddenly a sound like the blowing of a violent wind came from heaven and filled the whole house where they were sitting. All of them were filled with the Holy Spirit.

12.6   SENTENCE
Romans 8.16

The Spirit himself testifies with our spirit that we are God's children.

12.7   SENTENCE
1 John 4.13

We know that we live in him and he in us, because he has given us of his Spirit.

▶ **12.8**   RESPONSE
From Acts 2 and Romans 5†

'In the last days,' God says, 'I will pour out my Spirit on all people':
God's love has been poured out into our hearts by the Holy Spirit whom he has given us. Amen.

▶ **12.9**   RESPONSE
From Galatians 5†

The fruit of the Spirit is love, joy, peace, patience, kindness, goodness, faithfulness, gentleness and self-control:
since we live by the Spirit,
let us walk in the Spirit. Amen.

▶ **12.10**   APPROACH
Editors

With joy and gladness we celebrate your power and presence, Holy Spirit of God. By your energy the world was formed and made, darkness gave place to light, men and women were fashioned and became living beings, able to know God, to hear God speaking, and to respond to God calling. From you, Holy Spirit, the word of God has come to us through prophets and preachers; by your inspiration poets and musicians have composed works of praise; by your operation, faith and hope in Jesus Christ has been born in us, your Church has sprung to life, your gifts and graces have been distributed, new life and wholeness has come to Christ's body:

To you, Holy Spirit –
giving eternal life,
glorifying Jesus,

exalting God our heavenly Father –
be glory now and for evermore. Amen.

▶ **12.11**   PRAISE
From Psalm 103†

Praise the Lord, O my soul,
all my being, praise his name!

Praise the Lord, O my soul,
and forget not all his blessings!

Praise the Lord, O my soul.
Praise the Lord. Amen.

▶ **12.12**   CONFESSION
Editors

**Almighty God,
we confess that we have sinned against you:
for we have denied**
your saving presence in our lives,
**and we have grieved your Holy Spirit.
Come to us in the fire of your love,
and set our minds
on the things of the Spirit,
that we may share his gifts and bear his fruit
in love and joy and peace;
through Jesus Christ our Lord. Amen.**

12.13   CONFESSION
Editors

O God, we come before you and confess our failure and
unworthiness. Our minds are darkened, and by ourselves we cannot
find or know the truth. Our wills are weak, and by ourselves we
cannot resist temptation, or bring to completion good things we
resolve to do. Our hearts are fickle, and by ourselves we cannot give
you the loyalty which is your due. Our steps are faltering, and by
ourselves we cannot walk in your straight way. So this day we ask
you: enlighten us, strengthen us, and guide us by your Spirit, that
we may know you, love you, and follow you, all the days of our life,
through Jesus our Lord. **Amen.**

12.14 ABSOLUTION
From Psalm 51†

Hear the words of God's forgiveness:

The Lord hide his face from your sins and blot out all your iniquity; the Lord create in you a pure heart, and renew within you a steadfast spirit; the Lord comfort you by his Holy Spirit and restore to you the joy of your salvation; through Jesus our Redeemer. **Amen.**

12.15 COLLECT
Pentecost 4, ASB 1980

Almighty God, you have broken the tyranny of sin and have sent the Spirit of your Son into our hearts whereby we call you Father. Give us grace to dedicate our freedom to your service, that many may be brought to the glorious liberty of the children of God; through Jesus Christ our Lord. **Amen.**

▶ **12.16** PSALM
Psalm 51.6–12 and Psalm 143.6–10†

O Lord, I spread my hands out to you:
I thirst for you like dry ground.

Teach me to do your will, for you are my God:
let your good Spirit lead me in safety.

You require sincerity and truth in me:
fill my mind with your wisdom.

Create in me a pure heart, O God:
renew a faithful spirit in me.

Do not cast me from your presence:
or take your Holy Spirit from me.

Give me again the joy of your salvation:
and make me willing to obey. Amen.

▶ **12.17** PSALM
Psalm 104.1–4, 29–30†

O Lord our God, you are very great:
you are clothed with splendour and majesty.

You make winds your messengers:
and flashes of fire your servants.

How many are your works:
the earth is full of your creatures!

When you hide your face, they are afraid:
when you take away their breath, they die.

When you send your Spirit they are created:
and you renew the face of the earth. Amen.

12.18 READING: THE HOLY SPIRIT
From Acts 2, 1–21

Cast: Narrator, Person 1, Person 2, Peter, Joel [can be the same as Peter]

Narrator
> When the day of Pentecost came, all the believers were gathered together in one place. Suddenly there was a noise from the sky which sounded like a strong wind blowing, and it filled the whole house where they were sitting. Then they saw what looked like tongues of fire which spread out and touched each person there. They were all filled with the Holy Spirit and began to talk in other languages, as the Spirit enabled them to speak. There were Jews living in Jerusalem, religious men who had come from every country in the world. When they heard this noise, a large crowd gathered. They were all excited, because each one of them heard the believers speaking in his own language. [In amazement and wonder they exclaimed:]

Person 1 (*amazed*)
> These people who are talking like this are Galileans! How is it, then, that all of us hear them speaking in our own native languages about the great things that God has done?

Narrator
> Amazed and confused, they kept asking each other:

Persons 1 and 2
> What does this mean?

Narrator
> Others made fun of the believers:

Person 2
> These people are drunk!

Narrator

Then Peter stood up with the other eleven apostles and in a loud voice began to speak to the crowd:

Peter

Fellow-Jews and all of you who live in Jerusalem, listen to me and let me tell you what this means. These people are not drunk, as you suppose; it is only nine o'clock in the morning. Instead, this is what the prophet Joel spoke about:

Joel

God says: This is what I will do in the last days,
I will pour out my Spirit on everyone.
Your sons and daughters will proclaim my message;
your young men will see visions,
and your old men will have dreams.
Yes, even on my servants, both men and women,
I will pour out my Spirit in those days,
and they will proclaim my message.
I will perform miracles in the sky above
and wonders on the earth below.
There will be blood, fire, and thick smoke;
the sun will be darkened,
and the moon will turn red as blood,
before the great and glorious Day of the Lord comes.
And then, whoever calls out to the Lord for help will be saved.

Cast

[This is] the word of the Lord.

All

Thanks be to God.

FURTHER BIBLE READINGS

Readings appropriate to this theme will be found listed in our companion volume, 'The Dramatised Bible' (published by HarperCollins) on index page 426.

▶ **12.19** CREED
From Revelation 1†

Let us declare our faith in God:

We believe in God the Father;
the almighty, who was, and is, and is to come.

We believe in Jesus Christ;
the faithful witness,
the firstborn from the dead,
the King of kings,
who loves us,
and has freed us from our sins by his blood.

We believe in the Spirit;
giver of many gifts,
proceeding from the throne on high.

We believe in one God:
   Father, Son, and Holy Spirit. Amen.

▶ **12.20** FOR THE HOLY SPIRIT
Editors

O Holy Spirit of God,
come to us and cleanse us, we pray:
fill us with your love and truth and wisdom,
and make us your temples of holiness and peace;
grant us your precious gift of faith,
so that bonded with Christ we may know the joy of serving him.
Spirit divine, draw us into your pure light;
bless us and possess us,
for the sake of our Saviour, Jesus Christ. **Amen.**

12.21 FOR THE POWER OF THE HOLY SPIRIT
Michael Botting

We praise you, O God, because you gave the Holy Spirit to the first
Christians, making Jesus real to them, teaching them the truth and
giving them the power to witness boldly: fill us with the same Spirit
that we may know their experience and follow their example, in the
service of your Son Jesus, our Lord and saviour. **Amen.**

12.22   FOR THE HOLY SPIRIT'S BLESSING
Editors

Holy Spirit, we meet you in countless ways and find you in many forms: breath, wind, fire, water, dove. Often you comfort us, often you inspire us, sometimes you surprise us, always you bless us. Holy Spirit, enfold us, so that we are an echo of God's love, a reflection of Christ's light, and a pathway for your peace. **Amen.**

▶ **12.23   FOR THE SPIRIT'S POWER**
Editors

O Lord God, fill us, we pray, with the power of your Holy Spirit:

Grant us your peace, that we may stand firm and remain quiet in trouble. Lord,
grant us your peace.

Grant us your courage, that we may speak of you and of your love when the time is ripe. Lord,
grant us your courage.

Grant us your calmness to think clearly and wisely in the face of crisis or pressure. Lord,
grant us your calmness.

Grant us your confidence to know that in all things you are finally in charge and that nothing can separate us from your love. Lord,
grant us your confidence.

Grant us your obedience to accept what has to be in our lives and to put aside resentment, bitterness and envy which destroys. Lord,
grant us your obedience.

O God, pour out upon us all these graces
  of your Holy Spirit
that we may hold firm to our faith,
and to our life's end
be good witnesses to our Lord Jesus Christ. Amen.

▶ **12.24** FOR GOD'S SPIRIT
Based on Galatians 5

We pray that God's Holy Spirit may direct our lives:

'The fruit of the Spirit is love, joy and peace' – Father, we know that our world needs love and harmony: come to bless us,
and fill us with your Spirit.

'The fruit of the Spirit is patience, kindness and goodness' – Father, we know that our world is starved of compassion and true fellowship: come to bless us,
and fill us with your Spirit.

'The fruit of the Spirit is faithfulness, gentleness and self-control' – Father, we know that our world is short of truth and justice: come to bless us,
and fill us with your Spirit.

Send us out in his power
to live and work
  to your praise and glory;
through him to whom we belong,
Jesus Christ our Lord. Amen.

12.25 FOR OUR WITNESS AND SERVICE
Editors

God, our Father, at Pentecost long ago you poured out your Holy Spirit on the Church: by your Holy Spirit bless your children all over the world; cleanse us by your power and fill us with your love, help us to share the Good News and be a blessing to others wherever we go, take our lives and use us for the glory of your kingdom; in Jesus' name. **Amen.**

▶ **12.26** THANKSGIVING FOR THE SPIRIT
Editors

'The Spirit of God was hovering over the waters.' For your Spirit's power in creation, bringing life and light to birth; for his creative power in us today, O God, we thank you:
from our hearts we thank you.

'The Spirit of God came upon them.' That your Spirit energised the prophets to speak your word, and guided the leaders of your people; that he speaks and leads today, O God, we thank you:
from our hearts we thank you.

'The Spirit descended on him like a dove.' That your Spirit identified your Son Jesus, and filled him for ministry; that he reveals him to us and leads us into all truth, O God, we thank you:
from our hearts we thank you.

'All of them were filled with the Holy Spirit.' That on the day of Pentecost the Spirit came to your waiting disciples, enriching them with your gifts and driving them out to work and witness for you; that he renews and empowers your Church today, equipping us for service by many gifts, O God, we thank you:
from our hearts we thank you.

'The Spirit of God is living in us.' That your Spirit is in each of us, giving life to our mortal bodies, putting to death our sinful nature, proving to us that we are God's children and heirs of his grace, helping us in our weakness, interceding for us in prayers beyond words, O God, we thank you:
from our hearts we thank you.

Spirit of God, Spirit of Jesus,
creator Spirit, life-giving Spirit,
encouraging Spirit, cleansing Spirit,
healing Spirit, gracious Spirit,
O holy Spirit, come! Amen.

▶ **12.27** THANKSGIVING
Editors

We rejoice, our God, in the multitude of gifts you have given. For music, in all its variety and harmony, which expresses our deep feelings and desires, thank you:
to you be the glory, O Lord.

For art in all its forms, portraying nature, expressing inward beauty, evoking our response, satisfying our emotions, thank you:
to you be the glory, O Lord.

For your life-creating and sustaining Spirit, in these last days poured out upon us your family to energise our service and to lead us into all truth, thank you:
to you be the glory, O Lord.

Receive our thanks for all your gifts,
and let them be used
for the glory of your name. Amen.

▶ **12.28**   THANKSGIVING
Editors

O God, we are your people, you are our creator; your loving
kindness is without end; your faithfulness abounds. Almighty God:
we praise you and adore you.

We can never praise you enough for the presence of the Lord Jesus in
this world: the majesty of your being is displayed in him; the way
into your presence we find through him. Almighty God:
we praise you and adore you.

You flow into our lives by the Holy Spirit whose coming brings us
joy and peace. Our weakness and shallowness is transformed by his
strength, our darkest moments enlightened by his presence.
Almighty God:
we praise you and adore you.

To you, our God, be praise now and for ever,
Father, Son and Holy Spirit. Amen.

▶ **12.29**   THANKSGIVING
Christopher Idle

We thank you, God our Father,
for sending your Holy Spirit
to guide and strengthen us,
to help us understand the Bible,
and love and serve the Lord Jesus;
for his sake. **Amen.**

12.30   THANKSGIVING
Editors

Father, God of heaven and earth: we praise you for our Lord Jesus
Christ who is now ascended and reigns with you in glory; we thank
you for the promise made by Jesus, that he would give us his Holy
Spirit, so that we are never alone in the world.

Father, we know the Holy Spirit is here: when we are anxious he strengthens us, when we feel lost he guides us, when we are sad he comforts us, when we are glad he rejoices with us.

Father, one day we will see you face to face: until that day we will serve you gladly in the power of your Spirit, seal of your unfathomable love and source of our unending joy; in Jesus Christ our Lord. **Amen.**

▶ **12.31**   FOR HOLINESS: A PERSONAL PRAYER
Editors

Breathe on me, Holy Spirit;
cleanse and sanctify me,
so that I may offer
   all my praise,
   all my service,
   all my devotion,
   all my love,
through Jesus the Son
to God the Father. **Amen.**

▶ **12.32**   DEDICATION: A PERSONAL PRAYER
Editors

Ever-gracious Holy Spirit:
come to me in your perfect power,
and take possession of my life;
help me to understand more about Jesus
   and his sacrifice on the Cross,
and help me to live out my gratitude.
Draw me ever nearer to my Lord and Saviour,
and never let me stray from his side.
Spirit of God, receive me as I receive you,
in Jesus' name. **Amen.**

12.33   BLESSING
From 1 Thessalonians 5†

Go in peace, be very courageous, hold on to what is good, do not return evil for evil, strengthen the faint-hearted, support the weak, help the afflicted, honour all people, love and serve the Lord, rejoicing in the power of the Holy Spirit; and the grace of the Lord Jesus be with you. **Amen.**

12.34 BLESSING
From Ephesians 5†

In the name of our Lord Jesus Christ, be filled with the Spirit, sing and make music in your hearts to the Lord, always give thanks to our God and Father for everything; and the blessing of God – Father, Son and Holy Spirit be with you always. **Amen.**

12.35 BLESSING
From 'Still Waters, Deep Waters', adapted

May the love of God be poured out into *your* heart(s) by his Holy Spirit; may the knowledge of God be deeply impressed upon *your* mind, may God's strength enable *you* to persevere: and the blessing of the holy Trinity be with *you* always. **Amen.**

The Holiness and Majesty of God, Trinity

▶ **13.1** GREETING
From 2 Thessalonians 1†

Grace and peace to you from God our Father and the Lord Jesus
Christ. **Amen.**

13.2 SENTENCE
Isaiah 6.3

'Holy, holy, holy is the Lord Almighty; the whole earth is full of his
glory'!

13.3 SENTENCE
1 Chronicles 17.20

There is no-one like you, O Lord, and there is no God but you!

13.4 SENTENCE
Ezekiel 1.28

Like the appearance of a rainbow in the clouds on a rainy day, so
was the radiance around the Lord.

13.5 SENTENCE
Ezekiel 1.29

When I saw the appearance of the likeness of the glory of the Lord I
fell face down and I heard the voice of one speaking.

13.6 SENTENCE
2 Chronicles 2.12

Praise be to the Lord, the God of Israel, who made heaven and earth!

13.7 SENTENCE
Ezekiel 1. 3,24

The word of the Lord came like the sound of wings, like the roar of rushing waters, like the tumult of an army – the voice of the Almighty!

▶ **13.8** RESPONSE
From Romans 11†

Oh, the depth of the riches of the wisdom and knowledge of God!
How unsearchable his judgements,
and his paths beyond tracing out!

▶ **13.9** RESPONSE
From Isaiah 6†

Holy, holy, holy is the Lord almighty:
the whole earth is full of his glory. Amen.

▶ **13.10** RESPONSE
From Psalm 104†

O Lord our God, you are very great:
you are clothed with splendour and majesty.

Praise the Lord, O my soul:
Praise the Lord. Amen.

13.11 APPROACH
From Psalm 113†

Lord, we your servants worship you as we come before you now – from sunrise to sunset your name be praised. You are exalted over all the nations; your glory fills the skies. Who is like you, enthroned on high? Yet you stoop down to look at our world; you raise up the poor and lift up the needy: praise be to your name. **Amen.**

13.12 APPROACH
From Ecclesiastes 52†

O God, we have come to your house; we tread with guarded steps, we draw near to listen. We do not plead our merit, for we know we have done wrong: help us to be silent before you, to think before we speak. You are in heaven and we are on earth, so we choose our words with care. Here we make our vows to you: let us fulfil them without delay. Lord, do not let our mouth lead us into sin; nor let us go back on our promises, but stand in awe of you, our judge, our redeemer, and our Lord for ever. **Amen.**

▶ **13.13** APPROACH
Editors

Great and mighty is our Lord God,
his wisdom cannot be measured.
He takes pleasure in those who honour him,
in those who trust in his constant love.

Lord God, our loving Father in heaven, creator of this magnificent world – all your works praise you in all places of your dominion. Lord, you are great and mighty:
your wisdom cannot be measured.

We rejoice this day in your goodness, we are amazed at every indication of your interest in us. You are the Lord of the universe, the King of kings, yet you care for all your creatures. You are the Lord of lords and yet you reach down in loving compassion and tender mercy even to the most contemptible of human sinners. Lord, you are great and mighty:
your wisdom cannot be measured.

You have inexhaustible desires to bless your people; yours is a mercy that knows no bounds, a love which penetrates all barriers, a forgiveness which reaches to all our guiltiness. Lord, you are great and mighty:
your wisdom cannot be measured.

We gladly and fervently offer you our worship and praise. We join the whole creation in heaven and on earth to acknowledge your sovereignty, and we rest wholly in your salvation revealed in Jesus Christ our Lord. **Amen.**

▶ **13.14** APPROACH
Editors

This is the day that the Lord has made:
let us rejoice and be glad in it.

O give thanks to the Lord for he is good:
his steadfast love endures for ever.

We praise you our God. We acknowledge you to be the Lord. You are eternal and perfect, our minds reach upward to know you. Give us a true spirit of worship that gazes in wonder at the richness of your personality and love. Help us to experience you today as our loving heavenly Father, as our glorious Redeemer and as our powerful Comforter; to acknowledge you as Creator, Saviour and Sanctifier, that we with the great company of your people on earth and in heaven may bring you praise and glory both now and for eternity.
Amen.

▶ **13.15** PRAISE
From Revelation 19†

Praise our God, all you his servants, you who fear him, both small and great:
Alleluia!
For our Lord God almighty reigns.

Let us rejoice and be glad and give him the glory: **Amen.**

▶ **13.16** PRAISE
From Psalm 104†

Praise the Lord, O my soul;
praise the Lord!

O Lord my God, how great you are;
robed in majesty and splendour.

Praise the Lord, O my soul;
praise the Lord! Amen.

▶ **13.17**   CONFESSION
From Isaiah 6†

O Lord our God,
enthroned on high,
filling the whole earth with your glory:
holy, holy, holy is your name.
Our eyes have seen the King,
the Lord almighty;
but our lips are unclean.
We cry to you in our sinfulness
to take our guilt away,
through Jesus Christ our Lord. Amen.

▶ **13.18**   CONFESSION
From Isaiah 57†

O God,
you are eternal, and your name is holy;
you live in a high and holy place –
yet also with the humble and penitent:
revive our spirits,
renew our hearts;
do not accuse us, nor be angry for ever.
We confess our greed and our wilful ways:
you have punished us
and you have hidden your face from us:
O God, forgive us, through Jesus Christ our Lord. Amen.

▶ **13.19**   CONFESSION
Editors

Others may help the minister in leading this prayer at A, B *and* C

We confess to you, our Father, our small-mindedness and
limited appreciation of your greatness and almighty power.

A We confess that we scarcely consider your mighty movements
at the beginning of time, creating the heavens and the earth.
Lord, we have sinned:
forgive us, and enlarge our understanding.

B We confess that the life and death and resurrection of our Lord
   Jesus Christ do not infuse our thinking as they should; we are
   so hemmed in by transitory interests and temporal pursuits
   that we lose sight of the essential and eternal issues. Lord, we
   have sinned:
   forgive us, and deepen our love.

C We confess that we do not value, and often do not welcome, the
   gift of your Holy Spirit to liberate our tongues to praise you and
   our lives to serve you. Lord, we have sinned:
   forgive us, and set us free.

   Father, forgive us for our failures and our sins,
   through the love of our Lord Jesus;
   and help us by the power of your Holy Spirit. Amen.

13.20 ABSOLUTION
From Lamentations 5†

The Lord who reigns for ever, whose throne endures from generation
to generation has not forgotten you, nor has he forsaken you: he
forgives the sins you have confessed to him. The Lord will restore
you to himself and renew your days; through our saviour Jesus
Christ. **Amen.**

▶ **13.21** COLLECT
Trinity Sunday, ASB 1980

Almighty and eternal God,
you have revealed yourself
as Father, Son, and Holy Spirit,
and live and reign in the perfect unity of love.
Hold us firm in this faith,
that we may know you in all your ways
and evermore rejoice in your eternal glory,
who are three Persons in one God,
now and for ever. **Amen.**

▶ **13.22** PSALM
Psalm 8.1–9†

The congregation may divide at A, B *and* C

O Lord, our Lord:
how great is your name in all the world!
A **Your glory fills the skies.**
B **Your praise is sung by children.**
C **You silence your enemies.**

I look at the sky your hands have made, the moon and stars you put in place:
ALL **Who are we that you care for us?**

You made us less than gods:
ALL **to crown us with glory and honour.**

You put us in charge of creation:
A **the beasts of the field.**
B **the birds of the air.**
C **the fish of the sea.**

O Lord, our Lord:
ALL **how great is your name in all the world! Amen.**

▶ **13.23** PSALM
Psalm 97.1–12†

The congregation may divide at A, B *and* C

The Lord is king:
the Lord is king!

Let the whole wide earth rejoice:
A **let the islands all be glad.**

Thunder-clouds encircle him:
B **truth and justice are his throne.**

Fire shall go before the Lord:
C **burning up his enemies.**

Lightning strikes the darkened world:
A **all the people see and fear.**

Mountains melt before our God:
B **he is Lord of all the earth.**

Skies proclaim his righteousness:
c **nations see his glory now.**

Idol-worshippers are shamed:
A **gods bow down before the Lord.**

Let Jerusalem rejoice:
B **in your faithful judgements, Lord!**

Sovereign of the universe:
c **mightier still than all the gods!**

Yet you help your saints, O Lord:
A **saving them from wicked men.**

Light will shine upon the good:
B **gladness fill the righteous heart.**

Now recall what God has done:
c **thank him,**
B **praise him,**
ALL **and rejoice! Amen.**

13.24 READING: GOD CALLS ISAIAH TO BE A PROPHET
Isaiah 6.1–8

Cast: Isaiah, Creature 1, Creature 2, Young Isaiah, The Lord

Isaiah

In the year that King Uzziah died, I saw the Lord. He was sitting on his throne, high and exalted, and his robe filled the whole Temple. Round him flaming creatures were standing, each of which had six wings. Each creature covered its face with two wings, and its body with two, and used the other two for flying. They were calling out to each other:

Creature 1

Holy, holy, holy!

Creature 2

The Lord Almighty is holy!

Creatures 1 & 2

His glory fills the world.

Isaiah

The sound of their voices made the foundation of the Temple shake, and the Temple itself was filled with smoke.

I said:

Young Isaiah

There is no hope for me! I am doomed because every word that passes my lips is sinful, and I live among a people whose every word is sinful. And yet, with my own eyes, I have seen the King, the Lord Almighty!

Isaiah

Then one of the creatures flew down to me, carrying a burning coal that he had taken from the altar with a pair of tongs. He touched my lips with the burning coal and said:

Creature 1

This has touched your lips, and now your guilt is gone, and your sins are forgiven.

Isaiah

Then I heard the Lord say:

The Lord

Whom shall I send? Who will be our messenger?

Isaiah

I answered:

Young Isaiah

I will go! Send me!

Cast

[This is] the word of the Lord.

All

Thanks be to God.

FURTHER BIBLE READINGS

Readings appropriate to this theme will be found listed in our companion volume, 'The Dramatised Bible' (published by HarperCollins) on index pages 426–427

▶ **13.25** CREED
From Psalm 145†

We believe in God
who is gracious and compassionate,
slow to anger and rich in love.

We believe in God,
whose kingdom is everlasting,
whose dominion endures for ever.

We believe in God,
who is faithful to all his promises,
and loving towards all he has made.

We believe in God,
who opens his hand
and satisfies the needs
of all things living. Amen.

▶ **13.26** CREED
From 'The Athanasian Creed', Editors

Let us declare the universal Christian Faith:

We worship one God in trinity,
and trinity in unity;
neither confusing the persons
nor dividing the nature of God.
For there is one person of the Father,
another of the Son,
and another of the Holy Spirit;
but the Godhead of the Father,
of the Son, and of the Holy Spirit is all one –
the glory equal,
the majesty co-eternal:
what the Father is, so is the Son
and so is the Holy Spirit. Amen.

▶ **13.27** FOR HOLINESS
From 'Contemporary Parish Prayers', adapted

Father, Son and Holy Spirit,
Lord of majesty,
Trinity of love and power:
accept and make holy
   all that we are,
   all that we have,
   and all that we offer you.
Keep us firm in our faith
and strong in your service;
create in us a new heart,
that we may respond to your great mercy:
one God, our saviour,
now and for ever. **Amen.**

13.28 THANKSGIVING
Editors

God our maker and redeemer, we give you thanks for the wonder of creation, for the gift of life, and that together we may become your children; we praise you for Christ, your living Word, through whom we are taught the perfect way and the privilege of service; and for your Spirit, who offers rich gifts to us for the common good. We praise you, our God; Father, Son and Spirit for ever. **Amen.**

▶ **13.29** THANKSGIVING
Editors

Three persons A, B *and* C *may lead this prayer*

   A Father Almighty, for your majesty and your mercy – loving us still in our waywardness, forgiving us in our unworthiness: we bring you our worship
   and offer you thanksgiving.

   B Jesus, our Redeemer, for your humility and your sacrifice – sharing our joys and sorrows, dying and rising for our salvation: we bring you our worship
   and offer you thanksgiving.

c Holy Spirit of God, for your guidance and your encouragement – inspiring and empowering the church, revealing to us all truth: we bring you our worship
and offer you thanksgiving.

**God of gods –
Father, Son and Holy Spirit,
eternal Lord, Three-in-One:
to you be glory, honour and praise,
for ever and ever. Amen.**

▶ **13.30** THANKSGIVING
Editors

Two persons, A and B, may lead this prayer

A We praise and adore you, our heavenly Father, that in your grace and providence you richly fill our lives.

B You created the world, commanding light to shine out of darkness, making us in your moral image; and you have shone into our minds and hearts, bringing wisdom and power.

A&B Father, we thank you:
ALL **we worship and adore you.**

A We praise and adore you, Lord Jesus Christ, who on the first day of the week rose from the dead in triumph.

B You brought immortality to light; you have shown us the dawn beyond the darkness. Your word and your power have brought to us the Kingdom of God.

A&B Jesus, we thank you:
ALL **we worship and adore you.**

A We praise and adore you, Holy Spirit, for you revealed your power on the day of Pentecost; and today you are at work in our lives, filling us with the love of the Father, giving us understanding and wisdom.

B You illumine the Scriptures, bringing understanding to our darkened minds; you share your gifts among us to build your church into a spiritual household; you confirm your presence within our lives, giving us love for one another.

A&B Holy Spirit, we thank you:
ALL **we worship and adore you.**

ALL **God almighty, Father, Son and Holy Spirit,
to you be praise for ever and ever. Amen.**

▶ **13.31** THANKSGIVING
Editors

Father, we thank you:
we worship and adore you.

Jesus, we thank you:
we worship and adore you

Holy Spirit, we thank you:
we worship and adore you.

**O God almighty,
Father, Son and Holy Spirit,
to you be praise for ever and ever. Amen**

▶ **13.32** ASCRIPTION
From Revelation 15†

Great and marvellous are your deeds,
    Lord God almighty;
just and true are your ways,
    King of the ages.
Who will not fear you, O Lord,
and bring glory to your name?
For you alone are holy;
all nations will come and worship before you,
for your righteous acts have been revealed. **Amen.**

13.33 ASCRIPTION
From 1 Timothy 6†

To God, the blessed and only Ruler, the King of kings and Lord of
lords, who alone is immortal and who lives in unapproachable light:
to him be honour and might for ever. **Amen.**

▶ **13.34** ASCRIPTION
From Revelation 15†

Glory be to you, O God,
Father, Son, and Holy Spirit,
you have power, wisdom and majesty:
receive from us
honour, glory, worship and blessing.
Great and marvellous are your works,
just and true are your ways:
blessing and honour and glory and power
be to him who reigns upon the throne,
and to the Lamb,
through the one eternal Spirit,
now and for ever. **Amen.**

13.35 ASCRIPTION
Lancelot Andrewes, adapted

Blessing and honour, thanksgiving and praise, more than we can
utter, more than we can conceive, be to your glorious name, O God,
Father, Son and Holy Spirit, by all angels, all people, all creation, for
ever and ever. **Amen.**

▶ **13.36** DOXOLOGY
From Romans 11†

O Lord our God, how profound are the riches of your wisdom and
knowledge; how unsearchable your judgements, and your paths
beyond tracing out!
Who has known your mind, O Lord;
who has been your counsellor?
Who has ever given to you,
that you should repay?

For from you and through you and to you are all things:
yours be the glory for ever! Amen.

▶ **13.37** DOXOLOGY
Alan Gaunt

You are the one and only God; there is none like you, Lord; you are great and your name is holy:
glorify your name.

By the worship of your Church in every generation, by our worship today:
glorify your name.

By the proclamation of the coming of Jesus, by his reception in our hearts:
glorify your name.

By the winning of the world and the reconciliation of all people:
glorify your name.

By the living of our lives in faith, by the labour of our love and by our hope in the Lord Jesus Christ:
glorify your name.

Our Lord God,
you have glorified it
and you will glorify it again:
glorify your name in us. Amen.

▶ **13.38** DOXOLOGY
From A New Zealand Prayer Book'

Great is the Lord and worthy of all praise:
Amen! Praise and glory and wisdom,
thanksgiving and honour, power and might,
be to our God for ever and ever! Amen.

13.39 BLESSING
From Psalm 8†

God who made the heavens, who set the moon and stars in place, who crowned *you* with glory and honour, making *you* to rule over the works of his hands, whose name is majestic in all the earth, the Father, the Son and the Holy Spirit grant *you* his blessing evermore.
Amen.

13.40 BLESSING
From 'Still Waters, Deep Waters'

God the Father enrich *you* with his grace, God the Son make *you* holy in his love, God the Holy Spirit strengthen *you* with his joy; the Lord bless *you* and keep *you* in eternal life. **Amen.**

Sea Theme, Holidays

▶ **14.1** GREETING
From Titus 1†

Grace and peace from God the Father and Christ Jesus our Saviour. **Amen.**

14.2 SENTENCE
Psalm 93.4

Mightier than the thunder of the great waters, mightier than the breakers of the sea—the Lord on high is mighty.

14.3 SENTENCE
Mark 6.31

Jesus said, 'Come with me by yourselves to a quiet place and rest awhile'.

14.4 SENTENCE
Matthew 11.28

[Jesus says,] 'Come to me, all you who are weary and burdened, and I will give you rest'.

14.5 SENTENCE
Mark 4.37

The waves broke over the boat: Jesus was in the stern, sleeping on a cushion.

14.6 SENTENCE
Psalm 107.9

It is the Lord who satisfies the thirsty and fills the hungry with good things.

▶ **14.7** RESPONSE
From Psalm 24†

The earth is the Lord's and everything in it:
the world and all who live here.

▶ **14.8** RESPONSE
From Psalm 104†

There is the sea, vast and spacious, teeming with creatures beyond
number—living things both large and small:
how many are your works, O Lord!
in wisdom you have made them all.

▶ **14.9** RESPONSE
From Mark 4†

Jesus rebuked the wind and said to the waves: 'Be quiet!' The
disciples said:
Who is this?
Even the wind and the waves obey him!

▶ **14.10** RESPONSE
From Psalm 107†

Those who went out to the sea in ships, merchants on the mighty
waters, were glad when the Lord guided them to their desired
haven:
Let them give thanks to the Lord
for his unfailing love. Amen.

14.11 APPROACH
From Job 38†

Lord, you laid the earth's foundations; you placed its cornerstone
while the morning stars sang together and all the angels shouted for
joy; you set limits for the sea and said 'This far and no further!' You
gave orders to the morning and showed the dawn its place; you
moulded the earth until it took shape. You alone know the springs of
the sea; you alone comprehend the vastness of the universe; you
alone know the laws of heaven. Lord, give wisdom to our hearts and
understanding to our minds. **Amen.**

► **14.12** APPROACH
Unknown, adapted Editors

Three persons A, B *and* C *may assist with leading this prayer*

We have come to worship God our Father; to acknowledge his power and authority, to give thanks for his care and keeping, and to offer ourselves in the service of Christ:

A He is Creator of the world:
he gives us life and breath.

B He is Preserver of all life:
he sustains us day by day.

C He is Redeemer of his people:
he shows us his love in Christ.

A, B and C He is Lord of lords:
he controls all things.

O God our Father,
we bring you our love and praise
and give you thanks for all your goodness,
through Jesus Christ our Lord. Amen.

14.13 APPROACH
Editors

Lord, we come this morning with gladness, joy and singing. You have made our lives rich with mercy, bright with hope and vibrant with love. Once we were in darkness, but now we are children of the light and of the day. Once we were blind and could not see the beauty of your ways, but now our hearts and minds can see you at work in your world. The gracefulness of the trees, the luxurious green grass, the rich variety of colour in the hedgerow, the majesty of the seas and skies seem to cry out, What a wonderful God we have! You have made yourself known to successive generations, and now you have revealed yourself to us—we are so grateful. You have come to us in your Spirit showing us Jesus your son, our Saviour. You are working out your purposes in our lives: Jesus Christ is at work in us. We are flesh of his flesh, bone of his bone. Sometimes in the Spirit we feel the warmth of his presence and the gentle touch of his hand, and it thrills us.

So in nature and in our nature you touch our lives with your beauty: O Lord we give you all our thanks and praise and offer you the service of our lives: to the honour and glory of your name. **Amen.**

▶ **14.14**   PRAISE
From Psalm 98†

Sing to the Lord a new song,
for he has done marvellous things!

Sing for joy to the Lord, all the earth;
praise him with songs and shouts of joy! Amen.

▶ **14.15**   CONFESSION
C S Woodward, adapted

O God, our gracious Father,
we confess that we have sinned against you
and done many things to grieve you:
we have often been selfish,
we have sometimes forgotten to pray to you,
and we have not loved you as we should.
For these and all other sins
forgive us, we pray,
through him who died for us,
Jesus Christ our Lord. Amen.

▶ **14.16**   CONFESSION
Editors

Creator God, we confess that we fail to value your creation. We take so much for granted without thanking you, the giver of every good thing; we exploit the world, we abuse its resources; we pollute the earth, the sky, the sea. O God, forgive us:
have mercy on us.

We confess that we fail to heed the Bible's teaching about the earth—that it is the good work of your hands, given into our care, waiting for redemption. And we forget that we shall be called to account for our stewardship. O God, forgive us:
have mercy on us.

231

We confess that we think too little of the new creation in our Lord Jesus Christ. We are slow to follow him, we do not firmly trust in his forgiveness, we do not fully share in his resurrection life. O God, forgive us:
have mercy on us.

Help us in your mercy to receive your forgiveness,
and strengthen us to serve you well;
for the sake of Jesus Christ our Lord. Amen.

▶ **14.17** CONFESSION
From Psalm 130†

Out of the depths, O Lord, we cry to you. O Lord, hear our voice:
listen to our cry for mercy.

If you kept a record of our sins, who could stand before you? O Lord, hear our voice:
listen to our cry for mercy.

But you offer forgiveness, and therefore we fear you. O Lord, hear our voice:
listen to our cry for mercy.

We wait for you, O Lord, and in your promise we put our hope. O Lord, hear our voice:
listen to our cry for mercy.

We long for you, O Lord, more than the sleepless long for the morning. O Lord, hear our voice:
listen to our cry for mercy.

O God, we put our trust in you,
because with you there is unfailing love
and full redemption from all our sins
through our Saviour Jesus Christ. Amen.

14.18 ABSOLUTION
From Isaiah 59 †

The arm of God is not too short to save, nor his ear too dull to hear: the Lord your redeemer will come to you when you repent of your sins.

In the name of Jesus your sins are forgiven; God's Spirit and his word will not leave you from this time on for ever. **Amen.**

▶ **14.19** COLLECT
From 'The Scottish Prayer Book', adapted

Almighty God,
you led your people through the sea,
and made a path for them in deep waters:
be near all those
who face the dangers of the seas;
protect them from disaster,
help them on their way,
and bring them safely to their desired haven
with hearts thankful for your mercy;
through Jesus Christ our Lord. **Amen.**

▶ **14.20** PSALM
Psalm 93. 1–5†

The congregation may divide at A *and* B

    The Lord reigns, robed in majesty:
A **he arms himself with power.**

    The earth is firmly set in place:
B **it never can be moved.**

    Your throne was founded long ago:
A **before all time began.**

    The oceans raise their voice, O Lord:
B **and lift their roaring waves.**

    The Lord is mightier than the sea:
A **he rules supreme on high.**

    His laws stand firm through endless days:
B **his praise for evermore.**

ALL **Amen.**

▶ **14.21** PSALM
Psalm 107. 1–31†

The congregation may divide at A *and* B

Give thanks to the Lord, for he is good:
his love endures for ever.

Repeat these words in praise to the Lord:
all those he has redeemed.

Some sailed the ocean in ships:
A **they earned their way on the seas.**

They saw what the Lord can do:
B **his wonderful deeds in the deep.**

For he spoke and stirred up a storm:
A **and lifted high the waves.**

Their ships were thrown in the air:
B **and plunged into the depths.**

Their courage melted away:
A **they reeled like drunken men.**

They came to the end of themselves:
B **and cried to the Lord in their trouble.**

He brought them out of distress:
A **and stilled the raging storm.**

They were glad because of the calm:
B **he brought them safely to harbour.**

Let them give thanks to the Lord:
ALL **for his unfailing love. Amen**

14.22 READING: JESUS CALMS THE STORM
Luke 8. 22–25

Cast: Narrator, Jesus, Disciple 1, Disciple 2

Narrator
One day Jesus got into a boat with his disciples and said to them:

Jesus
Let us go across to the other side of the lake.

Narrator
So they started out. As they were sailing, Jesus fell asleep. Suddenly a strong wind blew down on the lake, and the boat began to fill with water, so that they were all in great danger. The disciples went to Jesus and woke him up [saying]:

Disciple 1 *(calling)*
Master, Master!

Disciple 2
We are about to die!

Narrator
Jesus got up and gave an order to the wind and the stormy water; they died down, and there was a great calm. Then he said to the disciples:

Jesus
Where is your faith?

Narrator
But they were amazed and afraid, and said to one another:

Disciple 1 *(amazed)*
Who is this man?

Disciple 2
He gives orders to the winds and waves, and they obey him!

Cast
[This is] the word of the Lord.   OR   This is the Gospel of Christ/
This is the Gospel of the Lord.

All
Thanks be to God.

**Praise to Christ our Lord/
Praise to you, Lord Jesus Christ.**

FURTHER BIBLE READINGS
Readings appropriate to this theme will be found listed in our companion volume, 'The Dramatised Bible' (published by HarperCollins) on index page 427.

▶ **14.23** CREED
From 'Te Deum', Editor

Let us acclaim the Lord our God:

**We believe in God
the eternal Father;
heaven and earth are full of his glory.**

**We believe in Jesus Christ,
his true and only Son;
he became man to set us free.**

**We believe in the Holy Spirit;
he is our advocate and guide.**

**We believe in one God:
Father, Son, and Holy Spirit. Amen.**

14.24 FOR RE-CREATION
Editors

Our Lord God, we thank you for our holiday about to begin: we have looked forward to it so much. We pray that our tired minds and bodies will be refreshed: please help us to make the most of time away from regular routine; bring to mind the many blessings we have in our day-to-day life. While we are away help us to unwind and discover again the sounds and colours of your beautiful creation; grant us opportunities to be quiet and still, listening for your voice. When we return from our holiday, renewed by your love, show us how to value the gift of life and the future you hold for us in Jesus our life-giver. **Amen.**

14.25 FOR BLESSING ON HOLIDAY
Editors

Father God, our holidays are about to begin, so we ask for your blessing on this time of rest and recreation: show us how to love and value one another while we are away, and grant us the opportunity to meet new people and make new friends. Help us not to forget to pray: even though our routine will be different, we want to share each new venture and discovery with you. Father, please enrich us through this holiday; bind us closer together in your love, so that we are able to live and work in joyful harmony in the days to come. We ask this in Jesus' name. **Amen.**

14.26   FOR SEAFARERS
Missions to Seamen

O God, the sea is yours, and you made it; your hands prepared the dry land: grant that those who travel by sea and sail in deep waters may be aware of the works of their Creator, responsive to the moving of your Holy Spirit, and alert to the calling of him who once spoke across the waves, Jesus Christ our Lord. **Amen.**

14.27   FOR SEAFARERS
Apostleship of the Sea

O Lord our heavenly Father, we commend to your keeping all who sail the seas: enrich them with your presence, guard them in danger, protect them in temptation, sustain them in loneliness, and support them in sickness and anxiety. Bless those who minister to them, and guide us all to the haven of eternal life; through Jesus Christ our Lord. **Amen.**

14.28   FOR SEAFARERS
From 'New Every Morning'

We pray, O God, for all seafarers as they fulfil their duties and face the dangers of their calling: the officers and men of the Royal Navy and Merchant Navy; the keepers of lighthouses, the crews of lightships and weatherships, the pilots of our ports; all who carry out the services of docks and harbours; and those who crew lifeboats and guard our coasts. Grant them your strength and protection, and keep them in the hour of special need; for Jesus Christ's sake. **Amen.**

14.29   FOR TRAVELLERS
Unknown

We pray for those soaring into the skies, ploughing across the seas, and driving on the roads. Give strength and wisdom to all who use the machines of travel, and those who have responsibility for other people's lives. Save us all from selfishness and from taking undue risks; give us patience and the ability to move in this world in peace. We ask this for our health's sake, and for the glory of the Lord of life, our Saviour Jesus Christ. **Amen.**

▶ **14.30** FOR TRAVELLERS
From 'New Every Morning'

O God, our Father,
we commend to your keeping
those who travel by land or sea or air:
give them your protection on their way,
and bring them safely to their journey's end;
through Jesus Christ our Lord. **Amen.**

14.31 ABOUT AIR TRAVEL
Dick Williams

O God, who has given to humankind the spirit and the powers
which express themselves in flight, bless all who are engaged in
travel by air: bless aircraft designers, that in them knowledge and
invention may continually combine to produce aircraft which are
better and safer; bless all who operate commercial airlines, that they
may faithfully put public safety before private profit; bless all who
devise routes and schedules, that they may make constantly revised
allowances for error; bless those who co-ordinate departures and
arrivals at busy airports, that they may apply skill and sure
judgement within the safest limits; bless all aircrews, that they may
work with skill of mind, strength of body, and peace of heart; and
bless all travellers, that they may be brought safely to their journey's
end; through Jesus Christ our Lord. **Amen.**

14.32 FOR ALL ON HOLIDAY
Christopher Idle

O God, the giver of all things, we pray for those who go away on
holiday, that they may set out in peace and return in safety, refreshed
in body, mind and spirit; and that seeing the glory of your works
they may remember to give you their thanks and praise, for Jesus
Christ's sake. **Amen.**

14.33 FOR OUR HOLIDAYS
Unknown

Father God, thank you for holidays; for the excitement of preparing
and packing, for interesting places to explore, for new people to
meet, for time to be with our families and friends. Give rest to all

who are tired or overworked and are not able to have a holiday away from home. Help us to use our holidays to make new friends and to learn new things; through Jesus Christ our Lord. **Amen.**

▶ **14.34** THANKSGIVING
Editors

We thank God for the wonderful world he has given to us, and for all his love and care:

For the warmth of the sun, O God of love,
we give you thanks and praise.

For the rain which makes things grow, O God of love,
we give you thanks and praise.

For the woods and the fields, O God of love,
we give you thanks and praise.

For the sea and the sky, O God of love,
we give you thanks and praise.

For the flowers and the animals, O God of love,
we give you thanks and praise.

For families and holidays, O God of love,
we give you thanks and praise.

For all your gifts, O God of love,
we give you thanks and praise.

Everything around us rejoices:
therefore give us joyful hearts to praise you in your glory;
through Jesus Christ our Lord. Amen.

▶ **14.35** DOXOLOGY
From Romans 11†

O Lord our God
how profound are the riches
of your wisdom and knowledge;
how unsearchable your judgments,
and your paths beyond tracing out!
Who has known your mind, O Lord;
who has been your counsellor?

239

**Who has ever given to you,
that you should repay?**

For from you and through you and to you are all things:
yours be the glory for ever! Amen.

▶ **14.36** ASCRIPTION
From 1 Chronicles 29†

Lord God, may you be praised for ever and ever:

**You are great and powerful,
glorious, splendid and majestic;
everything in heaven and earth is yours
and you are king,
supreme ruler over all;
all riches and wealth come from you;
you rule everything
by your strength and power;
you alone are able to make anyone great and strong:
now, our God, we give you thanks
and praise your glorious name. Amen.**

14.37 A PERSONAL PRAYER OF TRUST
Editors

Jesus, sweet saviour and merciful friend, lift up your hand and calm the storm around me, then let your divine peace dwell in me. Stay close by my side always to bless me with strength and courage and wisdom: for you are my beloved companion, my true guide through life and into eternity. **Amen.**

14.38 BLESSING
Editors

God the Father keep *you* in his care, the Lord Jesus Christ be *your* constant friend, and the Holy Spirit guide *you* in all *you* do, now and always. **Amen.**

God's Love to Us, Our Response

▶ **15.1** GREETING
From Jude†

You are loved by God the Father and kept by Jesus Christ:
mercy, peace and love be ours for ever. Amen.

15.2 SENTENCE
1 John 4.9

God showed his love for us by sending his only Son into the world,
so that we might have life through him.

15.3 SENTENCE
John 3.16

God so loved the world that he gave his only Son, that whoever
believes in him shall not perish but have eternal life.

15.4 SENTENCE
Romans 5.8

God showed his love for us in that while we were still sinners Christ
died for us.

15.5 SENTENCE
Jeremiah 31.3

This is what the Lord says, 'I have loved you with an everlasting
love, I have drawn you with loving kindness'.

15.6 SENTENCE
Romans 8. 38,39

Neither death nor life, neither angels nor demons, neither the
present nor the future, nor any powers, neither height nor depth, nor
anything else in all creation, will be able to separate us from the love
of God that is in Christ Jesus our Lord.

▶ **15.7** RESPONSE
From Psalm 103†

The steadfast love of the Lord is from everlasting to everlasting upon those who fear him:
his righteousness to our children's children. Amen.

▶ **15.8** RESPONSE
From Psalm 145†

The Lord is gracious and merciful:
his compassion is over all that he has made.

▶ **15.9** RESPONSE
From 1 John 4†

Dear friends, since God so loved us, we ought also to love one another:
if we love one another,
God lives in us,
and his love is made perfect in us. Amen.

▶ **15.10** RESPONSE
From 1 John 4†

God loved us:
and sent his Son
to be the means by which
our sins are forgiven.

15.11 APPROACH (MORNING)
From Psalm 108†

O God, in you is our trust: we sing and praise you with all our heart. Our instruments of praise wake up the morning! We will praise you among those who do not know you; we will sing to you in front of the world. For your love is as great as the heavens are high, and your faithfulness as measureless as the skies. O God, show your glory in the heavens and your majesty upon earth; through Jesus Christ our Lord. **Amen.**

15.12 APPROACH
Editors

Father in heaven, our loving Father, you invite us to come to you in the name of Jesus Christ, our one and only Saviour. We cannot see you, but we feel your presence. We know how near you are because your love is in our hearts, and our minds are lifted up above the mundane and the material to know things heavenly and eternal. We cry out for love and affection: help us to look to you to satisfy our deepest needs. We are perplexed: enable us to unravel, in your presence, some of the mysteries of life. Whatever the magnitude of our need, help us to believe that you are greater; that your love is so strong it is able to hold us secure even when we feel most vulnerable. Make us sensitive to your call and open to your word, that we may know and feel your grace sustaining and strengthening us. We ask this in the name of our risen Lord Jesus. **Amen.**

15.13 APPROACH
Editors

Lord God our Father in heaven, we come to you today feeling our way into your presence: you are incomprehensible, yet we can know you; you are majestic and absolutely pure, so that we find ourselves with a sense of unworthiness as we approach you.

We are selfish sinners: we come asking your help to worship you, for we feel so inadequate. We have been busy with many things through the past week. Tired of work, we come seeking renewal of mind and refreshment of body; burdens rest heavily on many of us, worries and concerns make us tense and over-anxious. Give us your strength and your guidance; lift our eyes to see things which are eternal; prise open our cold hearts with the radiance of your great love. Help us to know we are not alone in this world, help us to understand that divine love and care which you offer to us, and give us faith to believe you are near at hand to help; grant us the joy of sharing our hopes and perplexities with you, so that we may find your way to do your will; through our saviour Jesus Christ. **Amen.**

▶ **15.14**   PRAISE
From Psalm 92†

It is good to praise you, Lord,
and make music to your name:

To proclaim your constant love in the morning,
and tell your faithfulness in the evening

For you, O Lord, are exalted for ever.
Amen.

▶ **15.15**   PRAISE
From Psalm 106†

Give thanks to the Lord, for he is good;
his love endures for ever.

Tell of all his mighty acts;
and make his praises heard.

Praise be to the Lord, the God of Israel:
from everlasting to everlasting.

Let all the people say, 'Amen':
Amen, praise the Lord!

▶ **15.16**   CONFESSION
Editors

Almighty God, we confess that too often we have taken the easy way of the world, rather than your way, and so have grieved your heart of love.

We have been slow to admit that we are not our own, but belong to you: in your mercy,
forgive us and help us.

We have been unwilling to see that we are bought with the price of Christ's blood: in your mercy,
forgive us and help us.

We have been unprepared to live out our lives as your servants: in your mercy,
forgive us and help us.

Raise us by the power of your love,
and fill us with the joy of your Spirit;
through Jesus Christ our Lord. Amen.

▶ **15.17** CONFESSION
Editors

Lord Jesus, as we confess our sins, help us to trust completely in your forgiveness:

For our lack of self-discipline that so often chooses what we wish rather than what we ought to do, in your mercy:
forgive us, dear Lord.

For our half-hearted obedience to your truth and to your way of life for your disciples, in your mercy:
forgive us, dear Lord.

For our failure to serve others, and for our neglect of those who are defeated by their poverty, their loneliness or their lack of opportunity, in your mercy:
forgive us, dear Lord.

For our sin and foolishness which has made it easier for others to neglect your truth and to doubt your everlasting love, in your mercy:
forgive us, dear Lord.

By your grace forgive us;
by your strength help us to amend our ways
and glorify you for ever. Amen.

▶ **15.18** CONFESSION
From Psalm 130†

O Lord, we cry to you
   from the depths of our being:
let your ears be open
   as we plead for mercy.
If you kept a record of our sins
none of us could stand before you;
but you alone can forgive us,
therefore we come to you in awe.
Lord, we wait for you
and in your promise we put our hope;
through our saviour Jesus Christ. Amen.

15.19 ABSOLUTION
From Psalm 130†

People of God, put your hope in the Lord, for with the Lord is unfailing love, and with him there is full redemption. Hear God's forgiveness:

The Lord himself will redeem you from all your sins through our Saviour, Jesus Christ. **Amen.**

▶ **15.20** COLLECT
Pentecost 16, ASB 1980

Almighty God,
you have taught us through your Son
that love is the fulfilling of the law.
Grant that we may love you with our whole heart
and our neighbours as ourselves;
through Jesus Christ our Lord. **Amen.**

▶ **15.21** COLLECT
From 'Morning Prayer', ASB 1980

Eternal God and Father,
you create us by your power
and redeem us by your love:
guide and strengthen us
    by your Spirit,
that we may give ourselves
    in love and service
to one another and to you;
through Jesus Christ our Lord. **Amen.**

▶ **15.22** PSALM
Psalm 36.5–9†

The congregation—and ministers—may divide at A *and* B

   Your love, O Lord, reaches the heavens:
A **your faithfulness extends to the skies.**

   Your righteousness is towering like the mountains:
B **your justice is like the great deep.**

How precious is your love, O God:
A **we find shelter beneath your wings!**

We feast on the food you provide:
B **we drink from the river of your goodness.**

For with you is the fountain of life:
ALL **in your light we see light. Amen.**

15.23   READING: THE LOST SON
Luke 15. 11–32

Cast: Jesus, Younger son, Father, Elder son, Servant

Jesus

There was once a man who had two sons. The younger one said to him:

Younger son

Father, give me my share of the property now.

Jesus

So the man divided his property between his two sons. After a few days the younger son sold his part of the property and left home with the money. He went to a country far away, where he wasted his money in reckless living. He spent everything he had. Then a severe famine spread over that country, and he was left without a thing. So he went to work for one of the citizens of that country, who sent him out to his farm to take care of the pigs. He wished he could fill himself with the bean pods the pigs ate, but no one gave him anything to eat. At last he came to his senses.

Younger Son

All my father's hired workers have more than they can eat, and here I am about to starve! (WITH RESOLVE) I will get up and go to my father and say, Father, I have sinned against God and against you. I am no longer fit to be called your son; treat me as one of your hired workers.

Jesus

So he got up and started back to his father. (PAUSE) He was still a long way from home when his father saw him; his heart was filled with pity, and he ran, threw his arms round his son, and kissed him. The son said:

Younger son

Father, I have sinned against God and against you. I am no longer fit to be called your son.

Jesus

But the father called his servants:

Father

Hurry! Bring the best robe and put it on him. Put a ring on his finger and shoes on his feet. Then go and get the prize calf and kill it, and let us celebrate with a feast! For this son of mine was dead, but now he is alive; he was lost, but now he has been found.

Jesus

And so the feasting began. (PAUSE) In the meantime the elder son was out in the field. On his way back, when he came close to the house, he heard the music and dancing. So he called one of the servants and asked him:

Elder son

What's going on?

[Jesus

The servant answered:]

Servant

Your brother has come back home, and your father has killed the prize calf, because he got him back safe and sound.

Jesus

The elder brother was so angry that he would not go into the house; so his father came out and begged him to come in. But he answered his father:

Elder son

Look, all these years I have worked for you like a slave, and I have never disobeyed your orders. What have you given me? Not even a goat for me to have a feast with my friends! But this son of yours wasted all your property on prostitutes, and when he comes back home, you kill the prize calf for him!

[Jesus

The father answered:]

Father

My son, you are always here with me, and everything I have is yours. But we had to celebrate and be happy, because your brother was dead, but now he is alive; he was lost, but now he has been found.

Cast
   [This is] the word of the Lord.   OR   This is the Gospel of Christ/
                                       This is the Gospel of the Lord.

All
   Thanks be to God.   **Praise to Christ our Lord/**
                                   Praise to you, Lord Jesus Christ.

FURTHER BIBLE READINGS
Readings appropriate to this theme will be found listed in our companion volume. 'The Dramatised Bible' (published by HarperCollins) on index pages 427–428.

▶ **15.24**   CREED
From John 1†

**We believe in God the Father,
who reveals his love to us in Christ.**

**We believe in God the Son,
who pours out his Holy Spirit on us.**

**We believe in the Holy Spirit,
who teaches us God's truth.**

**We believe in one God:
Father, Son, and Holy Spirit. Amen.**

▶ **15.25**   ADORATION
Editors

Lord God of earth and heaven, we praise you because you are the source of all life, all joy and all true love.

For your mighty power, creating the universe, stretching out the heavens, controlling the planets in their orbit, Lord God of earth and heaven,
we worship and adore you.

For your incessant searching and caring for us, though we are a selfish, rebellious and sinful people, Lord God of earth and heaven, **we worship and adore you.**

For your love revealed in Jesus Christ, which assaults the stubbornness of our unbelief; for the grace and truth which have come to us in him, and for our redemption, Lord God of earth and heaven,
we worship and adore you.

O Lord God eternal,
greater in majesty than we can imagine,
stronger than any power which we can comprehend,
closer to us than we can ever believe,
more aware of our needs than we can express in words;
Father, son and Holy Spirit,
we worship and adore you for ever and ever. Amen.

15.26   FOR THOSE WE LOVE
Frank Colquhoun

Heavenly Father, we bring to you in our prayers all whom we love, knowing that your love for them is so much greater than ours, and that your will for them is all that is for their good. So, guard them in your keeping, O Lord, and give them now and always your richest blessing; for Jesus Christ's sake. **Amen.**

15.27   FOR OUR FAMILIES
Marjorie Hampson

Thank you, Lord, for our homes and families; thank you for our health and happiness; thank you for the good times, and for helping us to cope with the times that are not so good. Thank you for life itself, and for your wonderful love in Jesus Christ our Lord. **Amen.**

15.28   FOR THE UNLOVED
Editors

Lord God our Father in heaven, you have sent your Son, our Saviour, Jesus Christ, to assure us of your everlasting love: give us faith in the love you have revealed. We thank you that nothing can separate from your love those for whom Christ has died—not the difficulties and dangers of life, not deprivation nor even death itself. Hear, as we pray for those who are unloved, uncared for, and unwanted; lonely people in large cities, isolated people in rural communities, and all who for any reason feel cut off from the joys of life and society. Help them to look to you, and to know that nothing can separate them from your love which is in Christ Jesus our Lord. **Amen.**

15.29 FOR LOVE
From Ephesians 3†

O God, you are the Father from whom the whole family in heaven and on earth is named: bless us with the riches of your glory, make us inwardly strong, and powerful in your Spirit, let Christ live in our hearts by faith; that, rooted in love and founded on it, we may surely grasp with all your people how broad and long, how high and deep is his love. So may we know that love which passes knowledge, and be filled with all your fulness; through Jesus our redeemer. **Amen.**

15.30 FOR GOD'S LOVE IN OUR LIVES
Editors

Our God and Father, you love us with an everlasting love. May that love which you have invested in our lives, reveal itself in increasing loyalty to you, in the service of others and in creating an atmosphere of helpfulness and joy. May we reflect your own love, and so influence people to consider Jesus Christ as the hope of the world, and confess him as their saviour and Lord. **Amen.**

15.31 FOR DAILY PROTECTION
Editors

Lord God, you are our protection, you are our complete saviour; we see the love you have for us in the mighty acts of Jesus Christ. There are times when we are harassed and overwhelmed, when we feel that our pilgrim path is full of thorns and briars, and we are walking in blindness with bare feet. Help us to know your comfort to be sure that if we have pain, you share it; to reflect that if the path is difficult, there is some reason because all things work together for good in those who love you, that with you we are safe and our wounds are only temporary. By your dealings with us deepen our faith, convince us of your kingship in our lives, and strengthen our service; that you may have the glory through our Lord Jesus Christ. **Amen.**

▶ **15.32** FOR CONTENTMENT IN CHRIST
Simon Baynes

O God, make us more thankful
for what we have received,
more content with what we have,
and more mindful of other people in need:
we ask it for his sake
who lived for us in poverty,
Jesus Christ our Lord. **Amen.**

▶ **15.33** THANKSGIVING
Editors

Heavenly Father, we thank you
for the beauty of the world around us;
for the love of parents and friends,
for work and play, for food and clothes,
for happiness, laughter and fun.
But most of all we thank you
for your redeeming grace:
for the birth of Jesus Christ your Son,
for the example of his life,
and the love which made him die for us.
Help us to serve him faithfully
all our days. **Amen.**

▶ **15.34** THANKSGIVING FOR ALL GOD'S GIFTS
Editors

O heavenly Father,
we thank you for the good things you so richly provide;
we thank you for your wisdom given when we ask you;
and we thank you for your love for us,
unasked and underserved.
Give us ever thankful hearts,
and always a sense of how much we owe you,
then help us to serve you as you deserve;
through Jesus Christ our Lord. **Amen.**

▶ **15.35** THANKFULNESS
Editors

'Bless the Lord, my soul, and do not forget all his blessings!' Each day we thank you, Lord:
and praise your name for ever.

For every ray of light you send into our darkened minds that we may recall our blessings, we thank you, Lord:
and praise your name for ever.

For every glimpse of beauty we have seen in this world, we thank you, Lord:
and praise your name for ever.

For every sign of your perfection and creative will, we thank you, Lord:
and praise your name for ever.

For every echo of your truth amid the world's deceit and hypocrisy, we thank you, Lord:
and praise your name for ever.

For every reflection of your love we have seen in family and friends, we thank you, Lord:
and praise your name for ever.

For every opportunity to serve you—even in small tasks and unrewarding duties—we thank you, Lord:
and praise your name for ever.

That you gave your Son to be our Saviour, and that with him you have freely given us all things, we thank you, Lord:
and praise your name for ever.

Lord, help us always to recall your blessings,
and to praise your name for ever. Amen.

▶ **15.36** THANKSGIVING
Editors

We praise you, heavenly Father, for the wonder of your love:

For the generous scale of creation, for the abundance of earth's resources, and for the number and variety of peoples you have made, we give you thanks today,
and praise you for your love.

That in your love you did not spare your only Son but freely gave him up to come as our Saviour into the world; that in love he lived among us and for us sinners died on the cross to effect our redemption; that he rose again on the third day to lead us to heaven, we give you thanks today,
and praise you for your love.

For your grace of forgiveness which covers our sin, for the variety of gifts of the Spirit given to your Church, and for sharing our pain, our sickness and our dying, we give you thanks today,
and praise you for your love.

**For these
and all your other gifts of providence and grace,
we thank you
in the name of the Lord Jesus Christ. Amen.**

▶ **15.37** THANKSGIVING FOR JESUS' FRIENDSHIP
Editors

Lord Jesus, thank you for being our friend:
when we are weak, you strengthen us,
when we are lonely you speak to us,
when we are sad you comfort us,
when we are glad you rejoice with us;
you are our guide, our keeper, our shepherd, our shield;
your presence is our constant joy,
our prayers are in your name. **Amen.**

OR, AS A PERSONAL PRAYER

Lord Jesus, thank you for being my friend:
when I am weak, you strengthen me,
when I am lonely you speak to me,
when I am sad you comfort me,
when I am glad you rejoice with me;
you are my guide, my keeper, my shepherd, my shield;
your presence is my constant joy,
my prayer is in your name. **Amen.**

▶ **15.38** THANKSGIVING FOR HUMAN LIFE
Editors

It is with a sense of deep gratitude, our Eternal God, that we bow head and heart in your presence; in creating us and bringing us to this moment are seen your measureless power and your limitless love:

For all your good gifts given freely to us, we praise you:
O Lord, we bless you, we thank and praise you!

For our minds, for the gift of thought that enables us to probe mysteries, and in some measure understand some of the wonderful things you have provided for us, we praise you:
O Lord, we bless you, we thank and praise you!

For the energy of youth, for its infectious quest after life; for visions and for dreams, we praise you:
O Lord, we bless you, we thank and praise you!

For the experience and maturity of judgement given to older people, whose lives have been moulded by your Holy Spirit, we praise you:
O Lord, we bless you, we thank and praise you!

For the gift of health—of body, mind and spirit, and for the harmony within us by which a thousand factors work together to produce freedom from pain and from distress of mind, we praise you:
O Lord, we bless you, we thank and praise you!

Accept our gratitude for all your blessings
and the response of our love and service
through Jesus our Lord. Amen.

▶ **15.39** DEDICATION
Editors

O God, we are your children and you love us:
so deep is your love
that nothing we have done, or thought to do,
shall take away the peace you give;
so strong is your love
that no passing trouble shall tear us from your arms;
so precious is your love
that all our life shall be lived in your service –
and yours shall be the glory,
through Jesus Christ our Lord. **Amen.**

15.40 BLESSING
Unknown

The love of the Lord Jesus draw *you* to himself, the power of the Lord Jesus strengthen *you* in his service, the joy of the Lord Jesus fill *your* hearts; and the blessing of God almighty, the Father, the Son and the Holy Spirit be upon *you* and remain with *you* always. **Amen.**

15.41 BLESSING
From a Scottish folk blessing

The Father's love enfold you, the grace of Christ uphold you, the Holy Spirit guide you; one God to walk beside you. **Amen.**

OR

▶ **15.42** BLESSING
From a Scottish folk blessing

The Father's love enfold us,
the grace of Christ uphold us,
the Holy Spirit guide us;
one God to walk beside us. **Amen.**

15.43 BLESSING
2 Thessalonians 3.5†

The Lord lead *your* hearts into the love of God, and the patience of Christ; and the blessing of God almighty, the Father, the Son and the Holy Spirit be among *you* and remain with *you* always. **Amen.**

15.44 BLESSING
From Isaiah 40†

The Lord our Shepherd tenderly care for *you*, gather *you* in his arms, carry *you* close to his heart and gently lead *you*; and the blessing of God the Father, God the Son and God the Holy Spirit be with *you* always. **Amen.**

Invitation to Faith

▶ **16.1** GREETING
From Titus 1†

Grace and peace from God our Father and Jesus Christ our Saviour.
Amen

16.2 SENTENCE
Revelation 3.20

The Lord says, 'I stand at the door and knock; if anyone hears my
voice and opens the door, I will come in'.

16.3 SENTENCE
Romans 10.9

If you confess with your mouth, 'Jesus is Lord' and believe in your
heart that God raised him from the dead, you will be saved.

16.4 SENTENCE
2 Corinthians 5. 6

[Listen!] This is the hour to receive God's favour; today is the day to
be saved!

16.5 SENTENCE
Matthew 7. 13,14

Jesus said, 'Enter by the narrow gate. For the gate is narrow and the
way is hard that leads to life, and those who find it are few'.

16.6 SENTENCE
Mark 10.15

Jesus said, 'I tell you the truth, anyone who will not receive the
kingdom of God like a little child will never enter it'.

16.7 SENTENCE
John 1.12

To all who received him, to those who believed in his name, he gave the right to become the children of God.

16.8 SENTENCE
Colossians 1. 25, 27

God has chosen to make known the mystery that has been kept hidden for ages, which is Christ in you, the hope of glory.

16.9 SENTENCE
1 John 1.3

That which we have seen and heard we proclaim to you, so that you may have fellowship with us; and our fellowship is with the Father and with his Son Jesus Christ.

16.10 SENTENCE
1 Corinthians 1.24

To those who are called, Christ is the power of God and the wisdom of God.

16.11 SENTENCE
Titus 3.4

God saved us, not because of righteous things we had done, but because of his mercy.

16.12 SENTENCE
2 Corinthians 6.2

Now is the time of God's favour; now is the day of salvation.

▶ **16.13** RESPONSE
From Romans 10†

Faith comes from hearing the message:
**and the message is heard
when Christ is proclaimed.**

258

▶ **16.14** RESPONSE
From Ephesians 2†

By grace you have been saved, through faith – and this not from yourselves, it is the gift of God – not by works, so that no-one can boast:
we are God's workmanship,
created in Christ Jesus to do good works,
which God prepared in advance
for us to do. Amen.

▶ **16.15** RESPONSE
From 2 Corinthians 5†

Anyone who is in Christ is a new creation:
the old has passed away –
see, the new has come!

▶ **16.16** RESPONSE
From Colossians 1†

God has rescued us from the power of darkness, and brought us safe into the kingdom of his dear Son:
in Christ our sins are forgiven,
we are set free. Amen.

▶ **16.17** RESPONSE
From Psalm 34†

Glorify the Lord with me:
let us praise his name together.

16.18 INVITATION
From Isaiah 55†

Come, all who are thirsty, come to the waters; and you who have no money, come buy and eat! Why spend money on that which is not bread, and your labour on what does not satisfy. Listen and eat what is good and your soul will delight in the richest of fare.

259

▶ **16.19** APPROACH
Editors

Our God, we come to you recognising that we fail; our human flesh is weak, our sins are many. But we are assured that sincere confession is met by your saving forgiveness:

Through your Son our sins are forgiven. For your mercies:
our God, we thank you.

Our guilt is dealt with, our burdens are lifted, our lives begin again. For your mercies:
our God, we thank you.

Through your Spirit we know your presence, our loneliness is shared; our blind eyes made to see, our love is rekindled. For your mercies:
our God, we thank you.

You and you alone can heal, restore, forgive. Your compassion and your understanding seep into us, your wisdom enlightens us, new courage grips us, and we find your Spirit at work in us bringing together everything which was fractured by our selfishness and sin.

**O Lord our God
to you be glory for ever and ever. Amen.**

16.20 APPROACH
From 'Companion to the Lectionary', Volume 3

Almighty Father, the source of all beauty, goodness and love: we come together to worship you; we are tiny people set in your vast and wonderful universe, too much absorbed by the transitory things of life; but today in this place we turn to you – to your eternity and greatness: widen our horizons, deepen our experience, and carry us out of ourselves: for in you alone is found joy, peace and salvation; through Jesus Christ our Lord. **Amen.**

▶ **16.21** PRAISE
From Isaiah 12†

The Lord is my strength and my song:
he has become my salvation.

Sing to the Lord, for he has done glorious things:
let it be known through all the world. Amen.

▶ **16.22** PRAISE
Editors

Praise be to God for his promise of pardon:
thanks be to him for his gift of new life!

O Lord release our hearts and minds:
our mouths will freely praise your name. Amen.

▶ **16.23** CONFESSION
Editors

Let us confess our sins to God and ask for his forgiveness:

For all the wrong things we have done: in your mercy,
forgive us, O God.

For forgetting what we ought to have remembered, for failing to do
as we promised, for turning away when we should have listened, for
being careless when we should have been diligent: in your mercy,
forgive us, O God.

For doing things we knew would annoy, for acting in ways we knew
would hurt, for behaving in ways we knew would disappoint: in
your mercy,
forgive us, O God.

**O God, when we look back
we can see how foolish and wrong we have been.
Forgive us,
and help us not to do the same things again;
through Jesus Christ our Lord. Amen.**

▶ **16.24** CONFESSION
From Ezra 9†

**O God,
we are too ashamed and disgraced
to lift up our faces to you,
because our sins are higher than our heads,
and our guilt has reached to the heavens.
O Lord you are righteous;
we are before you in our guilt,
not one of us can stand in your presence.
Forgive us in Jesus' name. Amen.**

▶ **16.25** CONFESSION
From Psalm 142†

Lord, we have sinned:
we lift up our voice to you
and cry for your mercy.
There is no-one else to whom we can go:
save us from our sins
and from temptations that are too strong for us.
Set us free,
that we may praise your name;
through Jesus Christ our Lord. Amen.

16.26 ABSOLUTION
From Ezra 9†

The Lord your God is gracious; he surrounds you with his love,
gives light to your eyes and freedom from your sins; God has not
deserted you – he shows you kindness and grants you new life in
Christ Jesus our Lord. **Amen.**

16.27 ABSOLUTION
From Hebrews 10†

Draw near with a sincere heart and a sure faith: you are purged from
your guilt and washed clean through the blood of Christ. Hold on to
your hope, and trust the promises of God. **Amen.**

16.28 ABSOLUTION
From 'A New Zealand Prayer Book'

Through the cross of Christ, God have mercy on you, pardon you
and set you free. Know that you are forgiven and be at peace. God
strengthen you in all goodness and keep you in life eternal. **Amen.**

▶ **16.29** COLLECT
Pentecost 6, ASB 1980

Almighty God,
without you we are not able to please you.
Mercifully grant that your Holy Spirit
may in all things direct and rule our hearts;
through Jesus Christ our Lord. **Amen.**

▶ **16.30** PSALM
Psalm 40.1–3†

I waited patiently for the Lord:
he turned and heard my cry.

He pulled me out of the slimy pit:
out of the mud and mire.

He set my feet upon a rock:
and made my step secure.

He put a new song in my mouth:
a hymn of praise to God.

Many will see it and fear;
and put their trust in the Lord. Amen.

16.31 READING: JESUS AND ZACCHAEUS
From, Luke 19.1–10

Cast: Narrator, Jesus, Grumbling person, Zacchaeus

Narrator
  Jesus went on into Jericho and was passing through. There was a
  chief tax collector there named Zacchaeus, who was rich. He was
  trying to see who Jesus was, but he was a little man and could not
  see Jesus because of the crowd. So he ran ahead of the crowd and
  climbed a sycomore tree to see Jesus, who was going to pass that
  way. When Jesus came to that place, he looked up.

Jesus
  Hurry down, Zacchaeus, because I must stay in your house today.

Narrator
  Zacchaeus hurried down and welcomed him with great joy.
  (PAUSE)

  All the people who saw it started grumbling:

Grumbling person
  This man has gone as a guest to the home of a sinner!

Narrator
  Zacchaeus stood up [and said to the Lord]:

Zacchaeus *(to Jesus)*
  Listen, sir! I will give half my belongings to the poor, and if I have
  cheated anyone, I will pay him back four times as much.

Jesus *(to Zacchaeus)*
> Salvation has come to this house today, for this man, also, is a descendant of Abraham. The Son of Man came to seek and to save the lost.

Cast
> [This is] the word of the Lord.   OR   This is the Gospel of Christ/
> This is the Gospel of the Lord.

All
> **Thanks be to God.**   **Praise to Christ our Lord/**
> **Praise to you, Lord Jesus Christ.**

FURTHER BIBLE READINGS
Readings appropriate to this theme will be found listed in our companion volume, 'The Dramatised Bible' (published by HarperCollins) on index pages 428–429.

▶ **16.32** CREED
From Galatians 2†

We have been crucified with Christ
and we no longer live,
but Christ lives in us.
The life we live in the body
we live by faith in the Son of God,
who loved us and gave himself for us. Amen.

▶ **16.33** CREED
From Titus 3†

Let us declare our faith in God's salvation:

God our Saviour saved us
not because of righteous things we had done,
but because of his mercy.
He saved us through the washing of rebirth
and renewal by the Holy Spirit,
whom he poured out on us generously
through Jesus Christ our Saviour
so that, having been justified by his grace,
we might become heirs
having the hope of eternal life.

This is a trustworthy saying. **Amen.**

▶ **16.34** CREED
From 1 Timothy 3†

Beyond all question the mystery of godliness is great:

The Son of God appeared in a body,
he was vindicated by the Spirit,
he was seen by apostles,
he was preached among the nations,
he was believed on in the world,
he was taken up to glory. Amen.

16.35 FOR THOSE SUFFERING FROM PHOBIA
Editors

We pray for all who are in bondage to phobias and fears, whose prisons are real. Holy Spirit of God, you can open the doors to freedom, in your own time: replace fears by faith in your upholding companionship, deal with apprehensiveness – and moments of sheer panic – by your calming presence. Give us all your patience, love and vital strength, that our tendency to be paralysed by circumstances may be met by our true confidence in Jesus Christ our Lord. **Amen.**

16.36 FOR SPIRITUAL STRENGTH
From 'Pray Every Day'

Lord of all power and might, you have called us to fight by your side against the tyranny of evil: arm us with the weapons of righteousness that we may be equipped to repulse all assaults of the enemy and to stand fast in the power of the Spirit; through Jesus Christ our Lord. **Amen.**

16.37 FOR THE DISAPPOINTED IN LIFE
Editors

We pray for those today who deeply feel the pain of disappointment: the forsaken and rejected partner – lonely and mystified, the parent whose child has been brought to court and who feels ashamed and a social failure, the couple who through the changing fortunes of economy find they can no longer meet their debts, the one who is suffering redundancy in the middle years and feels rejected and unvalued.

Lord Jesus, give them an understanding of life in which you share their hurt through your Sacrifice, and a faith which radiates hope through your Resurrection. Cause them, among the ashes of their disappointment, to look up to you and out into a new day. Equip your church to minister to such as these; through Jesus our redeemer. **Amen.**

▶ **16.38**   WE ASK FOR GOD'S FORGIVENESS
From 'Contemporary Parish Prayers', adapted

Most merciful God and Father,
give us true repentance for our sins.
Open our eyes
to recognise the truth about ourselves;
so that acknowledging our faults,
our weaknesses, and our failures,
we may receive your forgiveness,
and find in your love
the encouragement to make a new beginning;
for the sake of Jesus Christ our Lord. **Amen.**

▶ **16.39**   THAT WE MAY WALK IN GOD'S LIGHT
From 1 John 1†

O God, you are light,
and in you there is no darkness at all:
give us grace
no longer to walk in darkness,
but to walk in the light;
to live by the truth,
to have fellowship with you
and with one another,
purified from all sin
by the blood of your Son,
Jesus Christ our Lord. **Amen.**

16.40   IN TROUBLE AND PERPLEXITY
Editors

We thank you, our Loving Father, that you are concerned about the ruling of the stars in their orbits – and also for the tiny sparrow who falls to the ground. Your concern encourages us when we are surrounded by doubts and perplexities. We recognise our own weakness in that we so often seek to run our own lives without any reference to your purpose and plan. We grow weary of life's demands and yet we blunder on. We ask [this day] that you will give us a clear sense of your presence, an insight into your ways, and a sensitiveness to the unseen. We pray that you will help us to discern your light upon our own troubled pathway, and so find clearer direction. Give us courage, drive away our fears, make us brave, and restore to us the joy of salvation through faith in our Lord Jesus Christ. **Amen.**

▶ **16.41   FOR SAVING FAITH**
From John 3†

Holy Spirit of God,
invisible like the wind,
we do not see you moving among us,
but your effect we see:
come to our hearts
that we may be renewed and reborn.

Open our minds that we may
see your kingdom;
lift up our eyes
to where the cross of Christ stands
for our healing;
that we might believe,
and in believing not die
but have eternal life;
through your Son
who in your love for us
you sent into the world,
Jesus Christ our Lord. **Amen.**

▶ **16.42** FOR TRUST IN GOD
Søren Kierkegaard

Teach us, O God
not to torture ourselves,
not to make martyrs of ourselves
    through stifling reflection;
but rather teach us
to breathe deeply in faith,
through Jesus, our Lord. **Amen.**

▶ **16.43** FOR ASSURANCE
From Hebrews 11†

Living God,
give us faith to be sure of what we hope for,
and certain of what we do not see;
to believe that you are,
and that you reward those who truly seek you:
so may we please you,
and receive what you have promised;
in Jesus Christ our Lord. **Amen.**

16.44 REALITY IN GOD
Michael Hollings and Etta Gullick

'God', this word we call you by is almost dead and meaningless, transient and empty like all the words we misuse. We ask you to renew its force and meaning, to make it once again a name that brings your promise to us. Make it a living word which tells us that you will be for us as you have always been – trustworthy and hidden and very close to us, our God, now and for ever. **Amen.**

▶ **16.45** A PRAYER OF INDIVIDUAL FAITH
Maurice Wood

Lord Jesus, my saviour,
my heart is cold,
    warm it by your selfless love,
my heart is sinful,
    cleanse it by your precious blood,
my heart is weak,

268

strengthen it by your joyful Spirit,
my heart is empty,
   fill it with your divine presence;
Lord Jesus,
my heart is yours,
   possess it always and only for yourself. **Amen.**

▶ **16.46** COMMITMENT: A PERSONAL PRAYER
Editors

Lord Jesus Christ,
I am healed through the prayer of faith,
accepted by you and drawn to your open arms,
and so I come to you now in deep thankfulness.
I receive your gift of salvation and new life,
and I resolve to live for you in the power of your Spirit.
Thank you for the new peace in my heart
and for the joy of knowing
that one day I shall see you in all your heavenly splendour. **Amen.**

16.47 FOR GRACE
From Philippians 3†

God of grace, we have no righteousness of our own, but you give us
the righteousness which comes by faith in Christ: give us also the
mind which counts everything loss compared to his surpassing
greatness; may we gain him, and be found in him: may we know
him and the power of his resurrection; may we share the fellowship
of his sufferings, becoming like him in his death to attain the
resurrection from the dead in Jesus our Lord. **Amen.**

16.48 THANKSGIVING
Editors

Almighty God and gracious heavenly Father, we are overwhelmed
that you love the world so much that you did not spare your only
Son, but gave him for us all. We rejoice that he came, revealing your
ceaseless love and your mercy. We praise you that, though he is the
eternal Lord, he took our human flesh and lived among us as perfect
man. To see him and to understand him is our greatest joy and
fulfilment.

We thank you for his coming, his teaching, and his life. And praise you that he went through death, bearing all our sin; that we might be forgiven and brought back to eternal life, and that we might live in the warmth of your inexhaustible love. As we give you thanks, we give our lives to you afresh this day. Breathe new life and power into us, confirm our faith and establish us in your service, that Jesus' loving and giving may be seen in us, for your glory. **Amen.**

▶ **16.49** THANKSGIVING
Emmanuel Church, Northwood

Heavenly Father, we come before you with thanksgiving for all your mercy and your grace:

For the beauty of the world around us, we bring you our love,
and give you our thanks and praise.

For our parents and our families, we bring you our love,
and give you our thanks and praise.

For work and play, for food and clothes, we bring you our love,
and give you our thanks and praise.

For the joy of friends, and for the happiness we share, we bring you our love,
and give you our thanks and praise.

But most of all, for your Son Jesus Christ, for his wonderful birth, for the example of his life, for his death on the cross to save us, for raising him from the dead to be our living Lord, and for sending upon us your Holy Spirit, we bring you our love,
and give you our thanks and praise.

Help us to serve you gladly and faithfully
all our days,
until you call us
to worship you in heaven. Amen.

16.50 COMMITMENT
From Psalm 143†

O Lord God, make us to hear your voice in the morning, for in you shall be our trust; show us the way that we should walk in, for we lift up our souls to you; teach us to do the thing that pleases you, for you are our God. Let your loving Spirit lead us into the place of righteousness, for your name's sake. **Amen.**

▶ **16.51** PRAYER OF FAITH
Editors

Our Father in heaven,
we rejoice in the precious name of your Son,
the Lord Jesus Christ,
for we have heard the message of salvation
and we have understood it.
Now we receive Christ into our hearts by faith
with joy and thanksgiving.
Jesus, thank you for being our Saviour,
thank you for being our friend:
through your Holy Spirit we will live for you
and serve you gladly now and all our days. **Amen.**

▶ **16.52** DEDICATION
Editors

Lord Jesus Christ,
we give ourselves into your hands.
Grant us grace to see you,
to know your way,
to feel you near.
Find us now in the quiet,
and hold us fast in the haste of the day;
for your glory's sake. **Amen.**

▶ **16.53** DOXOLOGY
From Romans 11†

Oh, the depth of the riches of the wisdom and knowledge of God!
**How unsearchable his judgements,
and his paths beyond tracing out!**

Who has known the mind of the Lord?
Or who has been his counsellor?
Who has ever given to God, that God should repay?

For from him and through him and to him are all things.
To God be the glory for ever! Amen.

16.54   BLESSING
From Romans 15†

The God of hope fill you with all joy and peace in believing; and the blessing of God almighty, the Father, the Son and the Holy Spirit be with you always. **Amen.**

16.55   BLESSING
From Romans 15†

God our Father fill *you* with all joy and peace as *you* trust in Christ Jesus, that *you* may overflow with hope by the power of the Holy Spirit. **Amen.**

16.56   BLESSING
From Ephesians 1†

God, the glorious Father of our Lord Jesus Christ, give you the Spirit to make you wise and reveal Christ to you so that you may know him better; the eyes of your heart be opened to see his light, to know the hope to which he has called you, and the riches of glory he promises to his people, his power available to all who believe: and the blessing of God Almighty, the Father, the Son and the Holy Spirit be among you and remain with you always. **Amen.**

16.57   BLESSING
From 1 Timothy 6†

Strive for righteousness, godliness, faith, love, endurance and gentleness; run the race of faith, take hold of the eternal life to which God called you when you confessed his name before the world; and the blessing of God almighty, Father Son and Holy Spirit will be with you always. **Amen.**

The Witnessing Church, The Worldwide Church

▶ **17.1** GREETING
From Ephesians 6†

Peace to our brothers and sisters, and love with faith from God the
Father and the Lord Jesus Christ. **Amen.**

▶ **17.2** GREETING
From Ephesians 2†

Peace to those who are near, and peace to those who are far away:
through Christ
we all can approach the Father
by the one Holy Spirit, Amen.

17.3 SENTENCE
Matthew 29. 18, 19

Jesus said, 'All authority in heaven and on earth has been given to
me. Go, therefore, and make disciples of all nations'.

17.4 SENTENCE
Romans 10.17

Faith comes from hearing the message, and the message is heard
through the word of Christ.

17.5 SENTENCE
Acts 1.8

Jesus said, 'You shall receive power when the Holy Spirit has come
upon you, and you shall be my witnesses'.

17.6 SENTENCE
John 4.35

Lift up your eyes and see how the fields are already white for
harvest.

17.7 SENTENCE
Romans 10.14

How can they call on the one they have not believed in? And how can they believe in the one of whom they have not heard?

17.8 SENTENCE
Isaiah 45.22

The Lord says 'Turn to me and be saved, all you ends of the earth; for I am God, and there is no other'.

17.9 SENTENCE
Isaiah 66.18

The Lord declares 'I am about to come and gather all nations and tongues, and they will come and see my glory'.

17.10 SENTENCE
1 John 1.3

That which we have seen and heard we proclaim to you, so that you may have fellowship with us; and our fellowship is with the Father and with his Son Jesus Christ.

17.11 SENTENCE
2 Corinthians 6. 11–13

We have spoken frankly to you; we have opened *our* hearts wide: show us the same feelings we have for you. Open *your* hearts wide!

17.12 SENTENCE
Romans 1.8

I thank my God through Jesus Christ for all of you because the whole world is hearing about your faith.

17.13 SENTENCE
Acts 10. 34, 35

God does not show favouritism, but accepts people from every nation who fear him and do what is right.

▶ **17.14** RESPONSE
From John 20†

Jesus said, 'As the Father has sent me I am sending you – receive the Holy Spirit'. **Amen.**

▶ **17.15** RESPONSE
From Revelation 11†

The kingdom of the world has become the kingdom of our Lord and of his Christ:
and he will reign for ever and ever. Amen.

▶ **17.16** RESPONSE
From Revelation 1†

Jesus Christ has made us to be a kingdom and priests to serve his God and Father:
to him be glory and power for ever and ever. Amen.

▶ **17.17** RESPONSE
From Isaiah 48†

With songs of joy proclaim it; tell it to the ends of the earth:
the Lord has set his people free!

▶ **17.18** RESPONSE
From 1 Chronicles 16†

Let the heavens rejoice:
let the earth be glad.

Let them say among the people:
the Lord reigns! Amen.

17.19 APPROACH
Editors

*Here the minister inserts the purpose of the service (see over)

Lord God of heaven and earth, we praise you that you are the creator of all things; we acknowledge you to be the Lord of eternity and time – you control the nations of the world, and you are the maker of history. We thank you that nothing can frustrate your ultimate purposes of love and justice; you cause even human frailty to do your will. We rejoice in the authority and power of our Lord Jesus Christ and in his growing kingdom: and we come today to * . . . (*worship you*). To you (Lord God) be praise and glory for ever. **Amen.**

▶ **17.20** PRAISE
From Psalm 98†

Sing to the Lord, all the world,
for the Lord is a mighty God.

Sing a new song to the Lord,
for he has done marvellous things.

Proclaim his glory among the nations,
and shout for joy to the Lord our king!

▶ **17.21** PRAISE
From Deuteronomy 32†

We will proclaim the name of the Lord:
Oh praise the greatness of our God!

God is the Rock:
his works are perfect,
and all his ways are just.

▶ **17.22** CONFESSION
Editors

Lord God, our maker and redeemer, this is your world and we are your people: come among us and save us.

Where we have heard for ourselves the good news of Christ, but have not shared it with our generation nor taught it to our children, be merciful:
Lord, forgive us and help us.

Where we have failed to bring the love of Christ to the needy in our society, be merciful:
Lord, forgive us and help us.

Where we have not loved you with all our heart, nor our neighbours

as ourselves, be merciful:
Lord, forgive us and help us.

O God,
forgive us for our lack of love,
and in your mercy make us
what you would have us be,
through Jesus Christ our Lord. Amen.

▶ **17.23** CONFESSION
Alternative Confession, ASB 1980

Father eternal,
giver of light and grace,
we have sinned against you
in what we have thought,
in what we have said and done,
through ignorance, through weakness,
through our own deliberate fault.

We have wounded your love,
and marred your image in us.
We are sorry and ashamed,
and repent of all our sins.
For the sake of your Son Jesus Christ,
who died for us,
forgive us all that is past;
and lead us out from darkness
to walk as children of light. Amen.

17.24 ABSOLUTION
From Psalm 103†

The Lord, who is merciful and gracious, slow to be angry and full of love; who will not accuse us for ever, nor be angry with us always; who does not treat us as our sins deserve, or repay us according to our wrong-doing: have compassion on *you*, as a father has compassion on his children, and forgive *you your* sins; through Jesus Christ our Lord. **Amen.**

▶ **17.25** COLLECT
Pentecost, ASB 1980

Almighty God,
who on the day of Pentecost
sent your Holy Spirit to the disciples
with the wind from heaven and in tongues of flame,
filling them with joy and boldness to preach the gospel:
send us out in the power of the same Spirit
to witness to your truth and to draw all to the fire of your love;
through Jesus Christ our Lord. **Amen.**

▶ **17.26** COLLECT

Frank Colquhoun

Heavenly Father,
we thank you for making us in our baptism
members of your worldwide family the Church,
and for our brothers and sisters in every land
who love the Lord Jesus:
keep us loyal to one another,
faithful to our promises,
and active in your service,
for Jesus Christ's sake. **Amen.**

▶ **17.27** PSALM
Psalm 96. 1–13†

The congregation may divide at A *and* B

Sing to the Lord a new song:
A **sing to the Lord, all the earth.**

Sing to the Lord, praise his name:
B **proclaim his salvation each day.**

Declare his glory among the nations:
A **his marvellous deeds among the peoples.**

Great is the Lord, and worthy of praise:
B **honour him above all gods.**

Splendour and majesty surround him:
A **power and beauty fill his temple.**

Praise the Lord all people on earth:
B **praise his glory and might.**

Give him the glory due to his name:
A **bring an offering into his temple.**

Worship the Lord in his beauty and holiness:
B **tremble before him all the earth.**

Say to the nations:
ALL **The Lord is king!**

Let the heavens rejoice and the earth be glad:
A **let all creation sing for joy.**

For God shall come to judge the world:
B **and rule the people with his truth.**

ALL **Amen.**

17.28 READING: THE GREAT COMMISSION
Matthew 28. 16–20

Cast: Narrator, Jesus

Narrator
The eleven disciples went to the hill in Galilee where Jesus had told them to go. When they saw him, they worshipped him, even though some of them doubted. Jesus drew near [and said to them]:

Jesus
I have been given all authority in heaven and on earth. Go, then, to all peoples everywhere and make them my disciples: baptize them in the name of the Father, the Son and the Holy Spirit, and teach them to obey everything I have commanded you. And I will be with you always, to the end of the age.

Cast
[This is] the word of the Lord.   OR   This is the Gospel of Christ/
This is the Gospel of the Lord.

All
Thanks be to God.   **Praise to Christ our Lord/**
Praise to you, Lord Jesus Christ.

FURTHER BIBLE READINGS
Readings appropriate to this theme will be found listed in our companion volume, 'The Dramatised Bible' (published by HarperCollins) on index pages 429–430.

▶ **17.29** CREED
From Isaiah 43†

**We believe in the Lord God, the Holy One,
Father, Son and Holy Spirit;
we are his witnesses and his servants.**

**He alone is the Lord,
apart from him there is no saviour;
he has revealed and saved and proclaimed;
he is our creator, our redeemer
and our king;
it is he who blots out our transgressions
and remembers our sins no more. Amen.**

▶ **17.30** CREED

From 1 Corinthians 8 and 12†

There is one God and Father:
from him all things come.

There is one Lord Jesus Christ:
through him we come to God.

There is one Holy Spirit:
in him we are baptized into one body.

**We believe in one God:
Father, Son, and Holy Spirit. Amen.**

17.31 FOR THE CHURCH IN MISSION
Editors

We praise you, our God, for those who, following the resurrection of Jesus from the dead, proclaimed the gospel in face of distrust and opposition.

Be with all who witness to the faith of Christ, strengthen and enlarge your church where she is weak, guard the church where she is strong, give her humility where she is self-confident, grant that we may serve you with joy and fulfil your purposes with delight. Deepen the faith of your people as they proclaim the good news of the Kingdom of the Lord Jesus Christ. **Amen.**

► **17.32**   FOR HOSTAGES AND PRISONERS OF CONSCIENCE
Michael Walker, adapted

Lord of all freedom and peace, we pray for the victims of oppressors, for populations who are denied the freedom of political debate and intellectual enquiry, for men, women and children in the prisons and camps of oppressive regimes, and for all hostages.

Those who are in solitary confinement:
merciful Father,
we lift them to you in prayer.

(PAUSE)
Those who are being tortured:
merciful Father,
we lift them to you in prayer.

(PAUSE)
Those who have been imprisoned for many years:
merciful Father,
we lift them to you in prayer.

(PAUSE)
Families who suffer:
merciful Father,
we lift them to you in prayer.

(PAUSE)
Children of prisoners of conscience:
merciful Father,
we lift them to you in prayer.

(PAUSE)
Wives and husbands whose years of marriage are spent in waiting and praying for the day when prison doors will be opened:
merciful Father,
we lift them to you in prayer.

(PAUSE)
We pray for all who daily remind us of their plight and whose vigilance knows no rest:
in the name of Christ sustain them. Amen.

▶ **17.33 FOR MISSIONARIES**
Michael Botting

Heavenly Father,
we pray for those
who have gone to other countries
with the good news of Jesus:
when their work is difficult and tiring,
make them strong;
when they are lonely and homesick,
remind them that you are with them;
when they are uncertain what to do,
guide them.
Keep them at all times loving you;
for Jesus' sake. **Amen.**

17.34 FOR MINISTERS
Unknown, adapted Editors

Lord, keep the faith and vision of those who handle our religion professionally, alive and fresh. For any who have grown tired, disappointed or disillusioned, renew hope in your power and confidence in your grace. Keep their pastoral care loving and sensitive. Let their proclamation be in the power of the Spirit, and their teaching such as builds up your people in the faith and equips them for service.

We pray for our ministers of the future. Alert our congregations to discover in our members gifts for ministry, and to encourage those who are called. Let those who teach and those who learn in our colleges possess the wisdom, truth, love and learning in the Spirit. Grant, Lord Jesus, our requests for your glory. **Amen.**

17.35 FOR RELIEF WORKERS
Rita Snowden

Bless, O God, all who dedicate their powers today to the making of peace in the world; bless all who give their training and experience to the cause of feeding the hungry and housing the homeless. Bless all who lend their energies and skills to teach impoverished people to till their land, to sow, water and harvest it. Give us all a lively concern for the under-privileged, and show us practical ways of helping; for Christ's sake. **Amen**.

▶ **17.36** FOR CHRISTIAN WORKERS
Patricia Mitchell

We thank you Father for your gift of perfect love in Jesus Christ; we offer prayer for all who have accepted that gift and in whom your light shines:

For those who seek to improve the plight of the homeless and badly housed, Father, we thank you:
give them your strength.

For young people sharing their learning and energy freely through voluntary service at home and abroad, Father, we thank you:
give them your strength.

For all organisations helping to relieve suffering and distress in stricken lands, Father, we thank you:
give them your strength.

For missionaries living out your message in the midst of ignorance, fear and disease, Father, we thank you:
give them your strength.

For all those who freely offer time and energy to bring comfort, hope, and help to those in need, Father, we thank you:
give them your strength.

Your light shines on in the darkness,
and the darkness has not overcome it:
for this we thank you, Father,
through Jesus Christ our Lord. Amen.

17.37   FOR MISSION WORKERS
Editors

Our God and Father, we rejoice today that you have revealed yourself in Jesus Christ your Son. We thank you that your church has been sending, through all its history, messengers to tell the good news. We praise you for those who brought that gospel to our own land. We thank you for all who proclaim your truth in love today; by word of mouth and in kind deeds; in ministering food to the spiritually hungry, and healing to the sick in body and disturbed in mind. Give your servants wisdom, sensitivity and the assurance that you are renewing them daily by your Holy Spirit, that they may complete the work you have commanded them to do; in the name of your Son, our Lord Jesus Christ. **Amen.**

▶ **17.38**   FOR TEACHERS
Liturgical Commision

Bless those who teach,
that they may increase our understanding,
and be open to your word for them.

Jesus, Lord of your Church:
in your mercy hear us. Amen.

17.39   FOR EVANGELISTS
From 'A New Zealand Prayer Book'

Almighty God, we thank you for . . . , whom you called to preach the gospel to the people of . . .   Raise up in this and every land heralds and evangelists of your kingdom, that your Church may make known the immeasurable riches of our Saviour Christ, who lives and reigns with you and the Holy Spirit, one God now and for ever. **Amen**

▶ **17.40**   ABOUT THE GOOD NEWS
From 'A New Zealand Prayer Book'

Everlasting God,
your messengers have carried the good news of Christ
to the ends of the earth;
grant that we who commemorate the builders of your Church

may know the truth of the gospel in our hearts
and build well on the foundations they have laid;
through Jesus Christ our Lord. **Amen.**

17.41   FOR THE CHURCH
Editors

Lord of the church and of the church's mission: strengthen your church where she is weak, guard your church where she is strong, renew your church where she has lost her vision, give her humility where she is proud; grant that her members may serve you with joy and fulfil your purposes with delight; deepen the faith of your people as they proclaim the good news of the kingdom of our Lord Jesus Christ. **Amen.**

17.42   FOR RECONCILIATION
Timothy Dudley-Smith

God, who formed all humankind as a family to live in harmony and peace: we acknowledge before you our divisions, quarrels, hatreds, injustices and greed. Let your Church demonstrate before the world the power of the gospel to destroy divisions, so that in Christ Jesus there may be no barriers of wealth or class, age or intellect, race or colour, but all may be equally your children, members one of another and heirs together of your everlasting kingdom. To your name be glory for ever and ever. **Amen.**

▶ 17.43   FOR CHURCHES AND CONGREGATIONS
Unknown, adapted Editors

Lord Jesus, we pray that we may tell and live your good news wherever people are found:

That churches in the middle of cities where people come but do not live, where commerce and businesses flourish, may find how they can be effective centres of witness and worship, Lord, send your Holy Spirit:
bless your waiting people.

That churches in rural communities, where all are known to others, may find true fellowship in their smaller numbers and, by their lives, be true witnesses to you, Lord, send your Holy Spirit:
bless your waiting people.

That churches in towns and suburbs, where houses and work-places mingle, may provide caring communities for the lonely and needy to find acceptance, Lord, send your Holy Spirit:
bless your waiting people.

That all our churches may be centres of hope and love for those who have lost their way, or are overburdened with need, Lord, send your Holy Spirit:
bless your waiting people.

That we all may know his revitalising power, show holiness of life, and be ready to share his gifts, Lord, send your Holy Spirit:
bless your waiting people.

Hear our prayer
which we offer in the name of Jesus Christ our Lord. Amen.

17.44   FOR THE NATIONS OF THE WORLD
Editors

We praise you, Lord, that all kingdoms of this world are to become the kingdom of your Son. Purge out error in the nations, sweep out corruption; root out the powers of evil and establish us in grace and goodness. Lord, open the barred door of human hearts and lives; help us to let the King of Glory into our communities. So may justice and peace overwhelm injustice and hostility; so may the messengers of peace speedily take the Gospel to every land, that Jesus may be praised and glorified now and for ever. **Amen.**

17.45   FOR DIVIDED PEOPLES
Editors

You have told us in your word, our loving God, that we should commit our concern and heartaches to you, for you do great things – unsearchable wonders, marvellous and without number. We pray for every land and territory where there is segregation and bitter enmity; for families divided by politics and people forbidden by law to be friends because of their culture, or lovers because of the colour of their skin. Set your created people free; liberate your church from all prejudice, so that your redeemed children may be one in power and purpose, and may show Christ's reconciling love to all people everywhere. We ask this in the strong name of Jesus Christ our Lord. **Amen.**

17.46   IN A DIVIDED WORLD
Editors

Loving Father in heaven, we are so glad to be members of your worldwide family. Help us to express our unity and harmony. There are so many barriers erected between the different nations and people in this world: money divides rich from poor, the 'haves' from the 'have nots'; colour divides people who are called to live in one nation; pride, greed, snobbery, cause painful rifts. Heal us from prejudice and pride, help us to be peacemakers through the love and understanding which Jesus gives to us, and strengthen us to serve you in a divided world. We ask these things in the name of Jesus who is the Prince of peace: Lord, through Jesus hear our prayer. **Amen.**

17.47   FOR THE OPPRESSED
Christopher Idle

O God, we plead with you today for those nations where governments give little freedom: for their leaders, we ask that they may learn to govern in justice, mercy and truth; for their people, we ask that they may be able to hear your gospel and heed your words; for all your servants in these lands, we pray for great faithfulness, great courage and great love; through Jesus Christ our Lord. **Amen.**

17.48   FOR THE UNDER-PRIVILEGED
Unknown

Hasten the time, O Lord, when no one shall live in contentment knowing that others have need. Inspire in us and in people of all nations the desire for social justice; that the hungry may be fed, the homeless welcomed, the sick healed, and a just order established in the world; according to your gracious will made known in Jesus Christ, our Lord. **Amen.**

17.49   ABOUT JUSTICE AND TRUST
From 'A New Zealand Prayer Book'

God of nations, help us to reflect and share the goodness that surrounds us. Help us to win justice for poor and rich alike, and bring trust and friendship to all our different races. **Amen.**

17.50   FOR RACIAL HARMONY
St Michael-le-Belfrey, York

O Lord Jesus Christ, Prince of peace: break down the barriers which separate us from other people and from God; teach Christians to love each other across the walls of colour, class and culture; forgive us the excuses we make for our own prejudice; and make us all one in you, Jesus Christ our Lord. **Amen.**

17.51   FOR ETHNIC MINORITIES
Editors

Lord, we thank you that you have created great diversity in the human race. We praise you for its richness. Bless all ethnic minorities within our land. Grant that our prejudices and limited appreciation of others may be overcome. We pray for families trying to span two cultures, seeking to retain their traditional society in a western state. Enable young people growing up to overcome the tensions of multi-racial schooling. Give patience, grace and skill to those who administer job centres, and to those who keep law and order in areas where many of our ethnic brothers and sisters reside. Lord Jesus, you have broken down barriers of race and creed, colour and culture: help us to care as you care, and in your name to serve one another. To your name be glory for ever. **Amen.**

17.52   ABOUT OUR PREJUDICES
Editors

Lord of unity and love, teach us to recognise our own divisions and prejudices. Help us in our attempts to overcome them; enable us to move towards a greater understanding of our neighbours regardless of colour, nationality or belief. Through our own experiences, give us a deeper understanding of the problems of church partners overseas and so strengthen the reality of this partnership; that we may work together for the glory of your name. **Amen.**

17.53   THAT OTHERS MAY FORGIVE US
Editors

Give grace to all in the developing world, O Lord, who despise the western world for its arrogance. And forgive the many sins which we have inflicted upon Africa, Asia and South America; despicable slave trading, vicious forced labour, encouragement of the drink and tobacco trade, commercial exploitation, destruction of the environment. Lord, have mercy upon us all in Jesus name. **Amen.**

17.54   FOR STRENGTH TO PROCLAIM CHRIST
Editors

Our gracious God and Father, in Jesus Christ you have given eternal light and understanding to your people. Help us to acknowledge that there are millions in the world and in our land who have no understanding of you because they have never heard of your everlasting love and tender mercy. We have been given the light of the glorious gospel of truth: help us, Lord, to share your truth in humility – for all we know is through your grace. Fan the flame of spiritual desire within us that the world may see and know, and receive salvation; in the name of Jesus Christ our Lord. **Amen.**

▶ 17.55   FOR US AS GOD'S PEOPLE
Editors

O God, our Father, we ask that you will give a sense of the important in life:

From the trivial, the self-satisfaction and smugness with past achievement; from complacency with our present situation, Lord, save us:
Lord, in your mercy save us.

From tyranny of non-essentials which sap our energy, Lord, save us:
Lord, in your mercy save us.

From fear of new methods, especially in communicating your word, Lord, save us:
Lord, in your mercy save us.

From lack of imagination in using our resources with zeal and enthusiasm, Lord, save us:
Lord, in your mercy save us.

From all distrust of our partners in the work of your Kingdom, Lord, save us:
Lord, in your mercy save us.

Give us the gifts of patience and courage in all our living; determination to enjoy life and wisdom to select those pursuits which are your will for us. And let your gifts, so freely given, be used generously in our varied activities and occupations, so that others may become aware of your living Spirit and come to share in the life which is abounding and wonderfully fulfilling; even the fellowship of our Saviour, Jesus Christ. **Amen.**

▶ **17.56** FOR THE MISSION OF THE CHURCH
From 'A New Zealand Prayer Book'

Draw your Church together, O God,
into one great company of disciples;
together following our Lord Jesus Christ into every walk of life,
together serving him in his mission to the world,
and together witnessing to his love
on every continent and island. **Amen.**

17.57 FOR THE CHURCH IN CLOSED LANDS
Christopher Idle

O Lord Jesus Christ, you open so that none shall shut, and shut so that none shall open: we cry to you for your own people in countries which those in power have tried to close to your voice. We thank you that they are open to your Spirit and your love, to the message of the Bible which cannot be bound, and to the Church which cannot die. We pray that you will strengthen this part of your Church. Grant to its leaders and all its members a new reliance on you to whom all power is given, and a new commitment of themselves to share the gospel with others before it is too late; for the sake of your Kingdom and your glory. **Amen.**

17.58 FOR OUR WITNESS TO OTHERS
From Colossians 4†

O God, our Master in heaven, make us fair and just in our dealings with others; keep us determined in prayer, alert to their needs and constantly thankful; open doors for us to proclaim the message about the secret of Christ – help us to speak as we should, to make it clear; keep us wise in the way we act towards those who do not believe, help us always to make good use of every opportunity we have; let our speech always be attractive and interesting to them, and teach us how to give the right answer to everyone, through Jesus Christ our Lord. **Amen.**

▶ **17.59** FOR OUR WITNESS TO THE WORLD
Alan Gaunt

Fill us with your love
so that we may gladly
   speak for you,
   work for you,
   and live our whole life for you,
until all the nations of the earth
join with us in endless praise;
through Jesus Christ our Lord. **Amen.**

17.60 FOR OUR WITNESS
Editors

Lord, we have experienced the joy of sharing your life with others in this world: lift us into a new sense of life's meaning and dignity. We are only passing through this world into the vastness of your eternity, yet each day is a gift to be shared – each moment you want to release something of your greatness, power and love through our weakness. Make us channels of your peace and kindness, of your love and sympathy. Allow us to know your grace flowing through us, so that your attractiveness and your gifts may draw people to yourself for your glory's sake. So, enrich us as we wait upon you: we bless you and we worship you in Jesus' name. **Amen.**

17.61 FOR HUMILITY IN OUR WITNESS
Alan Gaunt

Living God, your power was made known in the one who hung helpless on the cross: so guide your church that through our humility the rulers of this world may learn the way that leads to peace, and by justice and integrity may open the way for every race and nation to live in unity; in the name of Jesus Christ our Lord. **Amen.**

17.62 FOR OUR DEDICATION TO CHRIST'S MISSION
Editors

Save us, O Lord, from being idle bystanders – looking on and attempting to interpret the dilemmas of a broken world, yet rarely willing to act. Give us compassion for the lost and confused, the weary and the oppressed. Save us from slick and simplistic answers to human problems, which offer words but no real help. Unsettle us, and move us on from viewing the plight of sin-scarred people, to actions which promote spiritual and inward healing and liberating forgiveness. Cleanse our lives, that they may be instruments worthy of conveying your truth of abundant and everlasting life through Jesus Christ the Lord. We ask in his name. **Amen.**

17.63 FOR PERSONAL DEDICATION TO MISSION
Editors

Lord God, you have told us to set our minds and hearts on the things which are everlasting – for we are citizens of heaven: help us to seek your will above every other earthly ambition; help us to value people above things; give us your eternal view, that we may be aware of what is most important; help us to live not seeking the favour of others but the glory of our Saviour Jesus Christ. **Amen.**

▶ **17.64** ABOUT OUR WITNESS
Michael Botting

O Lord God,
we are all called to be your witnesses:
help us to make Jesus our saviour known to others –
through our words and our lives,
through our prayers and our gifts;
for his sake. **Amen.**

17.65 FOR STRENGTH FROM GOD
Ian Bunting

Jesus said, 'When the Holy Spirit comes upon you, you will be filled with power, and you will be witnesses for me . . . to the ends of the earth':

We thank you, Lord Jesus, for your last words; we treasure them for the promise of your Holy Spirit to give us power: help us to obey your command to be witnesses to the ends of the earth, starting from where we are now. In your name we pray. **Amen.**

▶ **17.66** FOR STRENGTH TO WITNESS
From 'A New Zealand Prayer Book'

Almighty Father, grant that we your children may never be ashamed
to confess the faith of Christ crucified, but continue his faithful
servants to our lives' end. **Amen.**

▶ **17.67** FOR COURAGE
Editor

Our heavenly Father,
your Son left his glory for the sorrow of our world:
grant us the strength
to leave behind our comfort and security,
to take up the cross of our Saviour
and follow where he leads;
for his name's sake. **Amen.**

▶ **17.68** TO BE READY
From 'A New Zealand Prayer Book'

Rouse our spirits, Lord Jesus,
that whenever you come to the door and knock
you may find us awake,
ready to admit and serve you. **Amen.**

17.69 FOR OUR WITNESS
From Isaiah 61†

O Sovereign Lord, you have anointed us with your Spirit and have
sent us to preach good news to the poor, to bind up the broken-
hearted, to announce freedom to the captives and release for the
prisoners of darkness; to proclaim God's grace and his judgement, to
provide for those who mourn. Bless all to whom we go; bestow on
them a crown of beauty instead of ashes, the oil of gladness instead
of mourning, and a garment of praise instead of despair; through us,
make them like trees you have planted, rooted in righteousness, that
they may display your splendour, through Jesus Christ our Lord.
Amen.

▶ **17.70** THANKSGIVING
Editors

Lord God, we thank you for our heritage of faith:

For the vision of apostles and evangelists who brought it to us,
gracious Lord,
we give you thanks and praise.

For the courage of martyrs and teachers who secured it for us,
gracious Lord,
we give you thanks and praise.

For the devotion of preachers and pastors who proclaimed it to us,
gracious Lord,
we give you thanks and praise.

For the love of families and friends who nourished it within us,
gracious Lord,
we give you thanks and praise.

For the freedom to speak of it in the world about us, and to share it
with our neighbours, gracious Lord,
we give you thanks and praise.

Lord God,
we thank you for our heritage of faith:
give us the will and the strength
to pass it on to others
for glory of your name;
through Jesus Christ our Lord. Amen.

▶ **17.71** DEDICATION
Editors

God our Father,
we dedicate ourselves to serve you faithfully
and to follow Christ:
send us out to work and to witness
freely, gratefully and hopefully,
in the power of the Holy Spirit,
and for the honour and glory of your Son,
Jesus Christ our Lord. Amen.

▶ **17.72** ASCRIPTION
From Revelation 4†

You are worthy, O Lord our God:
to receive glory and honour and power.

For you created all things:
**and by your will they existed
and were created.**

You are worthy, O Christ, for you were slain:
**and by your blood
you ransomed us for God.**

From every tribe and tongue and people and nation:
you made us a kingdom of priests to serve our God.

To him who sits upon the throne, and to the Lamb:
**be blessing and honour
and glory and might
for ever and ever. Amen.**

▶ **17.73** DEDICATION
Liturgical Commission

Send us to tell the world
the good news of your healing love;
Father, by your Spirit:
bring in your kingdom. Amen.

17.74 BLESSING
From Isaiah 61†

The Sovereign Lord anoint you with his blessing: preach good news
to the poor, go and bind up the broken-hearted, proclaim freedom
for the captives and release for those who are in darkness, declare
the Lord's favour and his judgement, comfort all who mourn; and
the blessing of God the Father, God the Son, and God the Holy Spirit
be with you always. **Amen.**

17.75 BLESSING
From Matthew 28†

At the word of Christ, and by the authority given to him in heaven and on earth, let us go and make disciples of all people in the name of the Father and of the Son and of the Holy Spirit; and the presence of Christ be with *you* always and through all ages. **Amen.**

17.76 BLESSING
From 'Still Waters, Deep Waters'

Go now in the peace and strength of God, ready to impart to others what you have first received from him: and may the presence and power of God, Father, Son and Holy Spirit, go with you. **Amen.**

17.77 DISMISSAL
From John 20†

Jesus said 'As the Father has sent me, I am sending you – receive the Holy Spirit'. Go in the name of Christ. **Amen.**

The Caring Church, Healing

▶ **18.1** GREETING
From 1 Peter 5†

Peace to all of you who are in Christ:
let us greet one another with love.

18.2 SENTENCE
1 John 4.16

God is love; those who live in love live in God, and God lives in them.

18.3 SENTENCE
Psalm 147.3

The Lord heals the broken-hearted and binds up their wounds.

18.4 SENTENCE
John 13.34

Jesus said 'A new commandment I give to you, that you love one another, as I have loved you'.

18.5 SENTENCE
Romans 13.8

Owe no-one anything, except to love one another, for he who loves his neighbour has fulfilled the law.

18.6 SENTENCE
Colossians 3.17

Whatever you do, in word or deed, do everything in the name of the Lord Jesus.

▶ **18.7**   RESPONSE
From Amos 5†

Let justice flow like a river:
and righteousness like a never-failing stream.

▶ **18.8**   RESPONSE
From Matthew 20†

The Son of Man did not come to be served, but to serve:
and to give his life as a ransom for many.

▶ **18.9**   RESPONSE
From Galations 2†

Help to carry one another's burdens:
and so obey the law of Christ. Amen.

▶ **18.10**   RESPONSE
From 1 John 4

Love one another,
for love is of God,
and whoever loves is born of God and knows God:
Spirit of God, search our hearts. Amen.

▶ **18.11**   FOR HEALING
Editors

O God of peace and Lord of love, help us to be quiet, relaxed and receptive today, accepting the inpouring of yourself, so that in the depths of our nature and being, your healing grace may take from us any anxious cares, any unworthy thoughts, and all ingratitude:
Forgive us, cleanse us, and renew us,
that our hearts may be at rest in you,
through Jesus Christ our Saviour. Amen.

18.12   APPROACH
Editors

Father God, we come to you rejoicing in all your goodness and mercy: you created the world and you continue to preserve it. The dependability of nature and time enables us to live; your faithfulness is everlasting. We greet each new morning, we share with you each day, and we rest at night in the sure knowledge of your care. You patiently deal with us, restraining us from self-destruction, forgiving our wilfulness and our sin. Through your Son our Saviour, Jesus Christ, you have broken down the barriers which separated us from yourself. In him we rediscover peace, harmony, beauty and unity. Help us to know the breadth, the length and the height of your love, that being enriched by your grace we may love you with all our heart and mind and will, and serve you for the good of others and for your glory for ever. **Amen.**

▶ **18.13** PRAISE
From Psalm 105†

Give thanks to the Lord, call on his name;
make his deeds known in the world around.

Sing to him, sing praise to him;
tell of the wonderful things he has done.

Glory in his holy name;
let those who seek the Lord rejoice! Amen.

▶ **18.14** CONFESSION
Editors

Father, the constancy of your caring love never ceases to amaze us. We confess that our lives are often careless and sometimes loveless. When our love for you is weak, forgive us:
O God, have mercy.

When our concern for those in need is inadequate, forgive us:
O God, have mercy.

When our giving is meagre and thoughtless, forgive us:
O God, have mercy.

We confess we are often self-centred, and sometimes heartless. When we distrust the generosity of others, or suspect their motives, forgive us:
O God, have mercy.

When we lack the vision and dedication to bring relief and care to the hungry, the homeless, the displaced person or the refugee, forgive us:
O God, have mercy.

Help us, O God,
to shoulder our responsibilities
in the strength of our risen saviour and Lord,
and by your grace to become agents of your transforming love,
for the glory of your name. Amen.

▶ **18.15** CONFESSION
Diocese of Sheffield, adapted

O God our Father, we ask your forgiveness, for we have failed you:
We have not cared enough for your world: in your great mercy:
forgive us, O God.

We have not cared enough for you: in your great mercy,
forgive us, O God.

We have been content with ourselves as we are: in your great mercy,
forgive us, O God.

**Give us the will and the power
to live in the spirit of Jesus,
now and always. Amen.**

▶ **18.16** CONFESSION
From 'A New Zealand Prayer Book'

In God there is forgiveness:
**Loving and all-seeing God,
forgive us where we have failed to support one another
and to be what we claim to be.
Forgive us where we have failed to serve you;
and where our thoughts and actions
    have been contrary to your word,
we ask your pardon. Amen.**

▶ **18.17** CONFESSION
Editor

We confess to you, our heavenly and holy Father, our faltering faith, our foolishness in not following our Lord Jesus Christ more closely, and our failure in Christian living. We have lost opportunities to help and to heal, to comfort and sustain. Give us your strength and pardon our continual mistakes:

Lord, have mercy on us:
forgive our sins,
and restore us in love
to the service of Jesus Christ our Lord. Amen.

18.18 ABSOLUTION
From 'A New Zealand Prayer Book'

God forgives you. Forgive others; forgive yourself. Through Christ, God has put away your sin: approach your God in peace, through Jesus your redeemer. **Amen.**

18.19 ABSOLUTION
From Psalm 103†

The Lord forgive *you* all your sin, and heal the disease of *your* soul; the Lord redeem *your* life from the grave, and bless *you* with his love and mercy (for his name's sake). **Amen.**

18.20 ABSOLUTION
From Isaiah 38†

The Lord restore *you*; the Lord bring *you* salvation and let *you* live; the Lord in his love keep *you* from the pit of destruction and put *your* sins behind his back for ever. **Amen.**

▶ 18.21 COLLECT
From 'The Gelasian Sacramentary'

O God,
you are the light of the minds that know you.
the life of the souls that love you,
and the strength of the wills that serve you:
help us so to know you that we may truly love you,
and so to love you that we may truly serve you;
whom to serve is perfect freedom;
through Jesus Christ our Lord. **Amen.**

▶ **18.22** COLLECT
For the Sick, ASB 1980

Creator and Father of all,
we pray for those who are ill.
Bless them, and those who serve their needs,
that they may put their whole trust in you
and be filled with your peace;
through Jesus Christ our Lord. **Amen.**

▶ **18.23** COLLECT
Maundy Thursday 2, ASB 1980

Almighty Father,
whose Son Jesus Christ has taught us
that what we do for the least of our brothers and sisters
we do also for him;
give us the will to be the servant of others
as he was the servant of all,
who gave up his life and died for us,
but is alive and reigns with you and the Holy Spirit,
one God, now and for ever. **Amen.**

▶ **18.24** PSALM
Psalm 103.1–22†

The congregation may divide at A *and* B

    Praise the Lord, my soul:
  A **all my being, praise his holy name!**

    Praise the Lord, my soul:
  B **and do not forget how generous he is.**

  A **He forgives all my sins**
  B **and heals all my diseases.**
  A **He keeps me from the grave:**
  B **and blesses me with love and mercy.**

    The Lord is gracious and compassionate:
  A **slow to become angry,**
  B **and full of constant love.**

    He does not keep on rebuking:

A **he is not angry for ever.**

He does not punish us as we deserve:
B **or repay us for our wrongs.**

As far as the east is from the west:
A **so far does he remove our sins from us.**

As kind as a Father to his children:
B **so kind is the Lord to those who honour him.**

Praise the Lord, all his creation:
ALL **praise the Lord, my soul! Amen.**

▶ **18.25** PSALM
Psalm 117.1–2†

The congregation may divide at A *and* B

Praise the Lord, all you nations:
A **praise him, all you people!**

Great is his love towards us:
B **his faithfulness shall last for ever.**

Praise the Lord:
ALL **Amen.**

18.26 READING: THE GOOD SAMARITAN
Luke 10.25–37

Cast: Narrator, Lawyer, Jesus, Samaritan

Narrator
A teacher of the Law came up and tried to trap Jesus.

Lawyer
Teacher, what must I do to receive eternal life?

[Narrator
Jesus answered him:]

Jesus
What do the Scriptures say? How do you interpret them?

Lawyer
'Love the Lord your God with all your heart, with all your soul, with all your strength, and with all your mind'; and 'Love your neighbour as you love yourself.'

Jesus

You are right; do this and you will live.

Narrator

But the teacher of the Law wanted to justify himself, so he asked Jesus:

Lawyer *(pertly)*

Who is my neighbour?

Jesus

There was once a man who was going down from Jerusalem to Jericho when robbers attacked him, stripped him, and beat him up, leaving him half dead. It so happened that a priest was going down that road; but when he saw the man, he walked on by, on the other side. In the same way a Levite also came along, went over and looked at the man, and then walked on by, on the other side. But a Samaritan who was travelling that way came upon the man, and when he saw him, his heart was filled with pity. He went over to him, poured oil and wine on his wounds and bandaged them; then he put the man on his own animal and took him to an inn, where he took care of him. The next day he took out two silver coins and gave them to the innkeeper.

Samaritan

Take care of him, and when I come back this way. I will pay you whatever else you spend on him.

Narrator

And Jesus concluded:

Jesus

In your opinion, which one of these three acted like a neighbour towards the man attacked by the robbers?

Narrator

The teacher of the Law answered:

Lawyer

The one who was kind to him.

Jesus

You go, then, and do the same.

Cast
  [This is] the word of the Lord.   OR   This is the Gospel of Christ/
                                                     This is the Gospel of the Lord.

All
  Thanks be to God.   **Praise to Christ our Lord/**
                                                     Praise to you, Lord Jesus Christ.

FURTHER BIBLE READINGS
Readings appropriate to this theme will be found listed in our companion volume. 'The Dramatised Bible' (published by HarperCollins) on index page 430.

▶ **18.27   CREED**
Diocese of London

Let us declare our faith and trust in God:

Do you believe and trust in God the Father, who made the world and loves it and sustains it?
We believe and trust in him.

Do you believe and trust in God the Son, who came into the world not to be served but to serve, and to give his life as a ransom for many?
We believe and trust in him.

Do you believe and trust in God the Holy Spirit, who fills all creation and who pours out his love in the hearts of those who seek him?
We believe and trust in him.

Will you then constantly ask for the grace of the Holy Spirit, that you may love and serve God, your neighbours and each other, after the example of Christ and in accordance with the Father's will?
By God's help we will. Amen.

▶ **18.28   FOR OUR NEIGHBOURS**
From 'A New Zealand Prayer Book'

Jesus Christ, you have taught us
that what we do to each other, we do to you;
make us quick to help and slow to hurt,
knowing that in our neighbour
it is you who receive our love or our neglect. **Amen.**

18.29   FOR THOSE WHO SUFFER
Editors

Heavenly Father of compassion, we pray for all those who feel trapped or afraid because of ill health. Please grant them special courage and quell their fears with the reality of your love. Thank you for Jesus our Saviour, who will always hold us fast, however weak our grip; in his precious name. **Amen.**

18.30   FOR THE ELDERLY
Editors

We thank you Lord that your care, which surrounds us all throughout our lives, is given especially to those who are worried, or feel they are losing their usefulness. We thank you for what we can learn from the experiences and the gathered insights of the elderly. Strengthen those who are frail and weak through age; help those who are fearful of illness or death; comfort those who are worried because of loss of independence or diminishing powers of control. Be near, we pray, to the housebound; and remind us of those who need us to visit them. Lord of every generation, age is no barrier to your love: help all older people to find hope and pleasure and peace in you; for Jesus' sake. **Amen.**

18.31   FOR ELDERLY PEOPLE IN POOR HOUSING
Editors

Lord Jesus, you came to heal the broken-hearted, to comfort the distressed and to care for the mishandled people in society: we pray for those among the elderly forced by their circumstances to live in poor quality housing; especially those confined to the loneliness of a single room, living a solitary life with few relatives and no callers. Help us to share your compassion; enable us to bring comfort and hope; inspire us to work and pray, that better and more secure housing, with adequate care, may be provided. We ask this in your name and for your sake. **Amen.**

18.32   FOR THE DEAF
Editors

We pray to you, O Lord, for those who are deaf and can no longer hear the birds singing, the music of stringed instruments and all the many voices of the world. We ask you to turn the colours of the world into singing for them, and the order of it to melodious harmony. Lord, deliver their silence from emptiness and grant that they may find these in the fulness of your love in Jesus Christ our Lord. **Amen.**

18.33   COMFORT FOR THE SERIOUSLY ILL
Editors

Lord Jesus, our great Physician and Friend, draw near to us in our need, for in your presence we have nothing to fear; in you we have complete security. Thank you for your promise never to leave us or forsake us. Thank you for the joy of knowing that nothing can separate us from your love which is indestructible, and everlasting: cover us with your grace, Lord, and bless us as we rest in the sweet refuge of your peace. **Amen.**

18.34   THOSE IN HOSPITAL
From 'Prayers for Use in Hospital'

O God, creator of us all, to whom alone is known the mystery of suffering, hear our prayers on behalf of those in hospital who are bearing the burden of illness or pain, or have to undergo an operation: in their weakness and anxiety draw near to them with your comfort and strength, and give them the assurance that, sharing their suffering, you will also share with them your peace, in Jesus Christ our Lord. **Amen.**

18.35   FOR THOSE ENTERING HOSPITAL,
AND FOR SURGEONS
Editors

Creator God, you have a variety of gifts for health and healing: we praise you for your gracious provision for scarred humanity. We pray for surgeons who, by their training and skill, are able to take the lives of others in their hands: give them wisdom, courage and dexterity; may those who enter hospital frightened and alarmed, find sympathy and understanding; and will you, Lord God, heal them; through Jesus Christ our Saviour. **Amen.**

18.36   FOR THE OPPRESSED
Editors

We thank you, our God, that your world is full of beautiful things: you are a holy Father who provides richly for our needs. It is your perfect will that we should enjoy the world and the life you have given to us.

Lord, hear us for those caught in the spirals of poverty, disease, unemployment, violence and deprivation. Help us not to misuse our privilege, or to rest content until we have done our utmost to help all who suffer. Your desire is life for all people: help us to forward that purpose today; through Jesus Christ our Lord. **Amen.**

18.37   FOR VICTIMS OF RACIAL INTOLERANCE
Editors

Lord God, forgive our human prejudice and pride. Forgive our blasphemies which breed bitterness, hatred and desperate corruption. Forgive us when we allow the colour of our skin to create barriers and shackles which disadvantages millions of your creatures whom you love. Cure this scourge by the power of your love. Restore our minds so that we may rejoice in human dignity and racial equality. Make us one in you, our Lord Jesus Christ. **Amen.**

18.38   FOR THE MENTALLY ILL
Elizabeth Goudge

O God of light and peace, give light and peace to those whose minds are troubled; grant them courage and patience, that they may seek for the causes of their ills; and give wisdom to those who help them to do so. And for those whose sufferings continue, we pray that they may be cared for in love and that none may add to their griefs. We ask this in the name of him who came to the help of the distressed, your Son, Jesus Christ our Lord. **Amen.**

18.39   FOR THE HEALING OF MINDS
Editors

O Lord, you know our deepest thoughts, our human griefs and anxieties. We bring to you those whose minds are troubled, whose bodies are in pain and who are disappointed in spirit; we pray for little children whose minds and emotions have been molested and tormented by the indiscipline of adults: give them confidence to share their problems and to recover hope and strength. We pray for those overwhelmed and consumed by habits they are powerless to break: bring them to admit their weakness, and to seek counsellors who have sympathy and understanding and can give them help. We pray for the callous and careless in the world who cause pain to others and create within their own lives a bitter spirit and an unpleasant atmosphere: reveal to them the tender love of our Saviour; and when we are the victims of unhelpful comment and unjust criticism, keep us from all resentment and all bitterness. Channel our energies into your service, secure us by your almighty strength, and help us to find our healing in you, for Jesus' sake. **Amen.**

▶ **18.40**   AT A SERVICE OF PRAYER FOR HEALING
Editors

Lord, hear us as we pray for N. We pray for *his* healing. May *he* trust in you and grow in strength and faith:
Jesus, in your mercy, come to heal us;
Jesus, in your mercy, take our pain;
Jesus, special friend of all who suffer,
bless us now, and make us whole again. Amen.

18.41   FOR THE ADDICTED
Editors

We pray for those whose lives are caught in a tangled web of despair, because they are addicts of unhealthy and dangerous habits. We ask that all who seek ways of escape from real life, may be kept from easy and evil solutions: give them courage and insight. Help them to seek truth, life and salvation, to find their weak wills reinforced by the power of God in Christ. Help us as Christians to recognise those who are desperate, lonely and overwhelmed, that we may offer sympathy and understanding, and enter into their feelings of despair – to share them and bring Christ's healing. Help us never to condemn or despise others, since we may not have walked their path nor have been consumed with the fierce desires that burn within their flesh and mind. O God, help us to stretch out to them our hands of help and healing. Support all who lift up the fallen, and cling to the overwhelmed; through Jesus Christ our Lord. **Amen.**

▶ **18.42**   FOR THOSE IN NEED
Christopher Idle

Remember, O merciful God, all those in need;
people with no good food or proper clothes,
no home of their own or no work to do,
no family or friends,
no knowledge of your love.
Move us to respond to their plight
and strengthen us to help them;
through Jesus Christ, our Lord. **Amen.**

18.43   FOR ALL WHO DO NOT FIT IN OUR SOCIETY
Michael Walker

God of the outcast and stranger, help us not to turn our face from the
plight of those who have fallen through all the safety-nets of home,
school and society: the drug addict with bruised arms and sunken
face and wild dreams; the winos, a fragile fellowship passing a bottle
from mouth to mouth; the homeless drifter asleep in a hostel bed or
huddled under a cardboard box in a sheltered doorway. Like the tax-
gatherers and others they do not fit easily into society; yet they fit
into your compassion. Be with them, and help us and them to
understand your grace of new life in Jesus our Lord. **Amen.**

18.44   FOR THE HOUSEBOUND
Editors

Father, God of all mercy, we bring before you our sisters and
brothers in Christ who would like to worship among us, but are now
unable to for one reason or another: bless them with your peace and
grant them courage and a firm faith. Bestow upon those who care for
them your gifts of grace and compassion. As members of one family
we pray for one another in the love of your Holy Spirit, and for the
sake of Jesus our Saviour. **Amen.**

18.45   FOR THOSE WHO FEEL ALONE IN CITIES
Editors

In our cities there are many thousands of visitors from overseas who
feel lonely: some here on business, others here to study, or to work.
There are many who feel that they are strangers in a strange place;

some desperately home-sick, longing to be back with parents and loved ones; others in lonely occupations. For these we pray:

O Lord, who accepted and blessed the stranger and the foreigner: help us not to shut them out of our lives or our homes, but rather to seek to understand them and their deep needs, and to allow your love and strength to overflow from us to them. This we ask for your name's sake, Lord Jesus Christ. **Amen.**

18.46 FOR DEPRIVED YOUNG PEOPLE
Eddie Neale

Over half the number of convicted criminals each year are under seventeen. The average age is fourteen-and-a-half! Many of them are brought up in areas where they are herded together with little else to do and crime is an accepted part of life. For these we pray:

Father of purity and light, goodness and love, with whom there are no shades of grey or passing shadows: we bring before you many young people who by accident of birth live often in the shadows; some without a father, some with parents who are mentally ill, some bursting with stifled intelligence, some innocently caught up with a bad gang; those in detention or those who are slaves to drink or drugs from an early age. Father of light, allow that great light to shine through us on the people who walk in darkness; through the Light of the World, Jesus Christ our Lord. **Amen.**

▶ 18.47 FOR OFFENDERS
From 'New Every Morning', adapted

Christ our Lord,
friend of outcasts and sinners:
grant your gift of repentance
to all offenders against the law;
and the knowledge of your forgiveness
to the penitent;
so renew a right spirit within them
that they may find true joy and freedom
in your service. **Amen.**

18.48 FOR YOUNG PRISONERS
Elizabeth Goudge

Jesus Christ, yourself a prisoner for our sakes and sinless in your captivity, we bring to your great love and unending compassion all prisoners who are young, and all who are first offenders, those who have come where they are through misfortune or sudden temptation, and are afraid and bewildered. Lord, uphold them in their shame and confusion, protect them from evil and bring to their help those who will steady and comfort them. We beseech you, let the days pass hopefully for them, let them come to no harm and let them find their true freedom in you, Jesus our Lord. **Amen.**

18.49 FOR PRISONS
Elizabeth Goudge

Grant your grace, O God, to those who have the care of prisoners: the police and warders, the prison governors, chaplains and doctors, the prison visitors, and those working for discharged prisoners; grant to them your gifts of wisdom, courage and patience in all their difficulties. When their work is dangerous and unrewarding, grant your special grace, that they may be saved from attitudes of cruelty and indifference. Let your love be always present with them and let your mercy guide them, through Jesus Christ our Lord. **Amen.**

18.50 FOR THE DISRUPTIVE
Editors

Lord Jesus, we see in your life among us a wonderful expression of joyful fulfilment. You never seemed to be crushed by the pressures of every day; you lived in a brutal world, yet you faced persecution with grace. For the whole of your human life you saw hardness and repression, arrogance, hardship and poverty. There were always too many to hold and heal, yet you never allowed these pressures to conquer you.

We pray that we may face hardship with the courage and the strength you can give us. We pray for others, young and old, who live in difficult circumstances and react with senseless destruction. We pray for vandals who uproot flowers and shrubs, who wreck property and create tension, anger and suffering. We pray for those in bondage to drugs or drink who commit crime to pay for their addiction.

Help us, forgive us, and cause your people who are called by your name, to pray and work that human spirits may be transformed by your Holy Spirit to your glory and praise. **Amen.**

▶ **18.51**   HEALING
Editors

Lord, we bring to you . . . :
surround *him* with your love. Amen.

▶ **18.52**   FOR THOSE WHO HURT AND THOSE WHO HEAL
Editors

Lord Jesus, we remember those who suffer pain: some physically ill and weary, some nervous, tense and distressed, some with burdens they cannot share with others. All have need of you; we bring their needs before you:
Lord, in your love and mercy, heal and comfort them.

Lord Jesus, we remember before you those who are disappointed in life: some feeling that life has passed them by, some unwanted and unloved, some unemployed and frustrated, some never having realised their potential. All have need of you; we bring their needs before you:
Lord, in your love and mercy, restore and encourage them.

Lord Jesus, we pray for those who seek to relieve pain and disappointment: doctors, nurses, and hospice staff; research workers, counsellors, and all who minister to us when we are in need:
grant them wisdom, strength, and good success;
so bless your people
to the glory of God the Father. Amen.

18.53   FOR THOSE WHO BRING COMFORT
Editors

In this rough and tumble world, dear Lord, we get hurt and disappointed, distressed and afraid. Receive our thanksgiving for those who comfort our lives when we are emotionally wounded and struggling in our minds. We pray for those who give us careful advice in our difficulties, who share our burdens and our perplexities without condemning us. We thank you for all who encourage us in our successes without envy and malice. Give us grace to help when friends turn to us in their need, and when they wish us to share their burdens. Help us to rejoice with those that rejoice and weep with those who weep; and so continue the service of Christ. We ask this for his compassion's sake, and to his glory. **Amen.**

▶ **18.54**   FOR HEALING
From Jeremiah 17†

O Lord, heal us,
and we shall be healed,
save us,
and we shall be saved:
and the praise shall be yours alone. **Amen.**

▶ **18.55**   FOR HEALING
St Michael-le-Belfrey, York

Merciful Father,
help all who suffer pain of body or grief of heart,
to find in you their help;
and, as Jesus suffered pain in his body
and healed it in others,
help them to find their peace and healing in him;
for his sake. **Amen.**

18.56   FOR THE MINISTRY OF HEALING
Patricia Mitchell

Lord God, we thank you for all those who stretch out their hands to heal: for scientists who, by research and experiment, stretch out their hands to heal; for all doctors and nurses, physiotherapists and social workers, administrators and clergy, who stretch out their hands to heal. And we pray especially for those who stretch out their hands to heal where hospitals are few and resources are scarce. We thank you that through our gifts of prayer and money we too are able to stretch out our hands and heal; through Jesus Christ our Lord. **Amen.**

18.57 FOR ALL WHO ARE ILL AND ALL WHO HELP
Editors

O God our Father, you are the Lord of all that is good in life, your strong and loving hands hold us. And you call us to be fellow-workers with you in the issues of life and death. We bring to you those who are in distress of body or of mind. We believe your perfect will for each one is health. Show us how to co-operate with you to bring health to people in great need; reveal to scientists new avenues in medical research, and grant faith to pursue fresh insights, so that dedicated knowledge and consecrated love may be used by you in healing and consoling work. And when we grope in darkness and cannot help; when your children must suffer and those who love can only look on, save both, we pray, from rebellion and unbelief. Show us that for those who trust you, no distress can be in vain, that all things find a place in your purposes at last. So we ask for them patience and endurance and a quiet mind, until pain vanishes or all is made plain. We ask this in the strong name of the greatest physician, Jesus our Lord. **Amen.**

18.58 FOR MEDICAL RESEARCH
Editors

O God the creator of our bodies, and of all that exists: we thank you for the knowledge and the skill of scientists, surgeons and doctors, and for the advances that have been made in combating disease. We pray that all those in the forefront of medical research may be guided both in the practical and ethical aspects of their work; let the good of the patients never be sacrificed for the sake of prestige, or of any other unworthy cause; may the side-effects and complications induced by new treatments be foreseen and overcome. Let all be done in the spirit of him who went about healing all kinds of sickness and disease among the people, your Son, Jesus Christ our Lord. **Amen.**

▶ **18.59** FOR THOSE WHO BRING HEALTH
Editors

We are so grateful, our God, that you have placed us together in life to serve and help one another. We give thanks to you and pray for all who care for the health of our people.

For doctors and surgeons, nurses, technicians and all who combine their skills to help us when we are unwell, Lord, we ask your help:
strengthen and encourage them.

For scientists and researchers who seek new ways and means of combating disease, Lord, we ask your help:
strengthen and encourage them.

For all who play a supportive role in our health services – ambulance crews, administrators, chaplains, catering staff, and all voluntary workers – for these, Lord, we ask your help:
strengthen and encourage them.

For all who bear witness to you as the ultimate healer – for prophets, pastors and preachers, and for individual believers filled with the Father's love, the Saviour's compassion and the Spirit's energy:
through us, Lord,
work out your great redemption
for the glory of your name. Amen.

18.60 FOR THE CHURCH'S CARING MISSION
Dick Williams

Thank you, Lord Jesus, for stopping to listen to every sick person who called out to you; thank you for healing every kind of sickness there is, for feeding the hungry, for setting people free and for raising the dead. Bless all the people all over the world who are trying to follow your example; bless those who are taking food to the hungry, medicine to the ill, compassionate government to nations which do not have real freedom, and your holy gospel to those whose love for others is dead. Bless them all, and the sick, the sad and the lonely to whom they go, for your dear name's sake. **Amen**

▶ **18.61** FOR VISION AND STRENGTH
Editors

O God our Father, who in Jesus came to bring good news to the poor, sight to the blind, freedom to the oppressed, and salvation to your people:

Inspire us to care for each other like brothers and like sisters: Father, by your grace,
help us to love one another.

Send us out to relieve the poor and rescue the oppressed: Father, by your grace.
help us to love one another.

Prepare us to tell the world the good news of your saving love: Father, by your grace,
help us to love one another.

O God, make us one in heart and mind,
in the spirit of service,
and in the faith of Jesus Christ our Lord. Amen.

▶ **18.62** FOR GRACE
Franciscan prayer

Lord, make us instruments of your peace:

Where there is hatred,
let us bring love.

Where there is injury,
let us bring pardon.

Where there is doubt,
let us bring faith.

Where there is despair,
let us bring hope.

Where there is sadness,
let us bring joy.

Where there is darkness,
let us bring light.

O Divine Master, let us seek not so much to be comforted as to comfort, to be understood as to understand, to be loved as to love:
for it is only in giving that we receive,
in forgetting ourselves that we find,
in pardoning that we are pardoned,
in dying that we rise to eternal life;
through Jesus Christ our Lord. Amen.

▶ **18.63** FOR A SPIRIT OF CARING
St Michael-le-Belfrey, York

O God our Father,
we praise you
that through Jesus Christ your only Son,
you have adopted us into your family the Church
and made us your children:
help us to show our love and thanks to you
by care and concern for one another;
use us to spread your love in all the world
by the power of your Holy Spirit,
and to the honour of your name. **Amen.**

18.64 FOR WHOLENESS
Editors

Lord God, so often in life we want to hide our true selves from you
and from others: we shrink from self-knowledge, we lack courage to
put our trust in you; we often feel insecure and vulnerable. Ours is a
restless world so fiercely competitive that human people are
damaged and destroyed: forgive us when we are indifferent to the
weariness and pain of other travellers on life's pilgrimage. Help us
not to be immobilised by guilt or by the seeming hugeness of our
social problems. Relieve us from the paralysis of apathy, and help us
to serve and bring wholeness to our community in the name of Jesus
Christ our Lord. **Amen.**

18.65 FOR DELIVERANCE FROM ARROGANCE AND PRIDE
Editors

Good Lord who sent your Son to be the servant of all, save us from
the arrogance and pride which make us contemptuous of people
with whom we live and work; grant that stubbornness and all
intolerance may daily be crucified in us, that seeds of acceptance,
understanding and sympathy may be sown and produce lives which
bring harmony and peace, rich in your love.

So may we learn to bring healing to others, and peace to the
communities in which we live; through Jesus Christ our Lord.
Amen.

18.66 FOR OUR SOCIAL RESPONSIBILITY
Susan Williams

'Let justice roll on like a river, righteousness like a never-failing stream'. *Amos 5.24*

O God of love, you have always required that people and actions should be just: forgive our complacency and lack of care; forgive us for burying our heads in the Welfare State and believing that all is well with the poor, the hungry and the handicapped. Lest those who shout loudest be best rewarded, open our eyes to the injustice around us and help us to give our energy, our time and our money to the service of others and of yourself; through Jesus Christ our Lord. **Amen.**

▶ **18.67** FOR INSPIRATION TO CARE
From 'A New Zealand Prayer Book'

Save us, Lord, from hurrying away,
because we do not wish to help,
because we know not how to help,
because we dare not.
Inspire us to use our lives
serving others;
through Jesus Christ our Lord. **Amen.**

▶ **18.68** FOR HEALING AND LIBERTY
From 'A New Zealand Prayer Book'

We need your healing, merciful God:
give us true repentance.
Some sins are plain to us;
some escape us,
some we cannot face.
Forgive us;
set us free to hear your word to us;
set us free to serve you. **Amen.**

18.69   THE LAYING ON OF HANDS
From 'A New Zealand Prayer Book'

In the name of God most high we lay our hands upon you. Receive Christ's healing touch to make you whole in body, mind and spirit. The power of God strengthen you, the love of God dwell in you and give you peace. **Amen.**

▶ **18.70**   FOR GOD'S HELP (MORNING)
From 'A New Zealand Prayer Book'

Loving God, thank you for this new day:
thank you for your love and care for us,
thank you for making each of us special;
help us today to be kind to each other. **Amen.**

▶ **18.71**   THANKSGIVING
From 'More Prayers for Today's Church'

We thank you, Father, for your gift of perfect love – for our Saviour Jesus Christ. We thank you for all who loyally serve him, through whom your light shines on your world:

For those who in the name of Christ seek to improve the plight of the homeless and the badly housed:
Father, we thank you.

For young people who share their learning and energy freely through voluntary service at home and abroad:
Father, we thank you.

For all organisations which help to relieve suffering and distress in stricken lands:
Father, we thank you.

For missionaries living out your message in the midst of ignorance, fear and disease:
Father, we thank you.

For all those who freely give time and energy and money to bring comfort, hope and help to those with needs:
Father, we thank you.

Your light shines in the darkness,
and the darkness has not overcome it:
thank you, Father, for your light
in Jesus Christ our Lord. Amen.

▶ **18.72**   THANKSGIVING AND DEDICATION
Editor

Almighty God,
we thank you for your mercy and your grace:
you are our light in darkness,
our strength in weakness,
and our comfort in sorrow.
You heal our bodies and our minds;
you ease our pain,
you lift our anxieties
and give us hope.
So fill us with your Spirit's power
that we may take your healing love
to a world in need,
and bring glory to your name:
through Jesus Christ our Lord. **Amen.**

▶ **18.73**   THANKSGIVING AND DEDICATION
Editors

We thank God for our mission in Christ, and pledge the service of
our lives:

For the vision, courage and enterprise of your servants in past days
and for their acts of kindness and compassion:
thank you, O God.

For what is being achieved through the churches in our day, to the
relief of suffering and the betterment of human life:
thank you, O God.

To support the oppressed:
we dedicate ourselves.

To work for justice:
we dedicate ourselves.

To share in Christ's mission and make him known as the Way the
Truth and the Life:
we dedicate ourselves.

O God of mercy:
let your kingdom come today. Amen.

18.74   DEDICATION TO SERVICE
Alan Gaunt

Living God, you have taught us that faith without works is dead: so temper our faith with love and hope that we may follow Christ and give ourselves freely to others in their need; let the lives we live and the good we accomplish prove our faith and honour you for ever. **Amen.**

▶ **18.75**   DEDICATION TO MISSION
Liturgical Commission

Send us to tell the world the good news of your healing love:
Father, by your Spirit bring in your kingdom. Amen.

18.76   GLORIA
From Romans 11†

O Lord our God, your judgements are unsearchable and your paths beyond tracing out; from you, and through you, and to you are all things: to you be the glory for ever! **Amen.**

▶ **18.77**   ASCRIPTION
From 1 Timothy 1†

Now to the king eternal, immortal, invisible, the only God,
be honour and glory for ever and ever. **Amen.**

18.78   BLESSING
From 1 Thessalonians 3†

The Lord make *your* love increase and overflow for each other and for everyone else; the Lord strengthen *your* hearts so that *you will* be blameless and holy in the presence of our God and Father; and the blessing of God the Father, the Son and the Holy Spirit remain with *you* always. **Amen.**

18.79   BLESSING
From Isaiah 57†

The Lord guide you and restore his comfort to you; the Lord bring praise to your lips; the Lord send you peace wherever you go; the Lord in his mercy heal you: and the blessing of God almighty, the Father, the Son and the Holy Spirit, be with you now and always. **Amen.**

18.80   BLESSING
From Isaiah 57†

The Lord look upon *your* need and heal *you*; the Lord guide *you* and restore comfort to *you*; the Lord give *you* his peace; through Jesus Christ our Lord. **Amen.**

18.81   BLESSING
From Colossians 3†

Let the peace of Christ rule your hearts, let the word of Christ dwell in you richly; whatever you do in word or deed, do it all in the name of the Lord Jesus: and the blessing of God the Father, God the Son and God the Holy Spirit be upon you. **Amen.**

18.82   BLESSING
From 2 Thessalonians 2†

The Lord Jesus Christ, who loved us, and by his grace gave us eternal encouragement and good hope: confirm *your* hearts, and strengthen *you* in every good deed and word; and the blessing of God almighty, Father, Son and Holy Spirit, be with *you* always. **Amen.**

18.83   BLESSING
From 'Still Waters, Deep Waters'

Stand tall now, knowing that you have been healed and made whole deep within your being, and the compassion of the Father, the tenderness of the Holy Spirit, and the guiding hand of Jesus be with you now and always. **Amen.**

God's Gifts to the Church, Renewal

▶ **19.1** GREETING
From Philippians 4 and Philemon†

The grace of the Lord Jesus Christ be with your spirit. **Amen.**

19.2 SENTENCE
John 20. 22,23

Jesus said 'Receive the Holy Spirit. If you forgive anyone their sins they are forgiven, if you do not forgive them, they are not forgiven!'

19.3 SENTENCE
Galatians 5. 22,23

The fruit of the Spirit is love, joy, peace, patience, kindness, goodness, faithfulness, gentleness and self-control.

19.4 SENTENCE
Romans 8.16

The Spirit himself testifies with our spirit that we are God's children.

19.5 SENTENCE
2 Corinthians 3.18

In our faces we reflect the glory which comes from the Lord, who is the Spirit.

19.6 SENTENCE
2 Corinthians 3.17

The Lord is the Spirit, and where the Spirit of the Lord is, there is freedom.

19.7 SENTENCE
Revelation 2.7 etc.

If you have ears to hear, listen to what the Spirit is saying to the churches.

19.8   SENTENCE
Romans 14.17

The kingdom of God is righteousness, peace and joy in the Holy Spirit.

19.9   SENTENCE
2 Timothy 1.6

Fan into flame the gift of God which is in you through the Spirit.

19.10   SENTENCE
2 Timothy 1.7

God has not given us a Spirit of timidity, but a Spirit of power and love and self-control.

19.11   SENTENCE
1 Corinthians 3.16

Do you not know that you are God's temple and that God's Spirit dwells in you?

19.12   SENTENCE
Colossians 2.10

You have been given fulness in Christ.

▶ **19.13**   RESPONSE
From Romans 12†

In Christ we who are many form one body and each member belongs to all the others:
we have different gifts, according to the grace given us.

▶ **19.14**   RESPONSES
From 1 Corinthians 12†

There are differing kinds of gifts:
but the same Spirit.

There are differing kinds of service:
but the same Lord.

There are differing ways of working:
but it is God who works in all.

▶ **19.15**   RESPONSE
From 2 Corinthians 1†

All God's promises are 'Yes!' in Christ, and through him we reply 'Amen', to the glory of God:
Amen.

▶ **19.16**   RESPONSE
From 2 Corinthians 5†

In Christ you are a new creation:
the old has gone,
the new has come. Amen.

▶ **19.17**   RESPONSE
From 1 Corinthians 6†

Now you are washed, you are sanctified, you are justified:
in the name of the Lord Jesus Christ
and by the Spirit of our God. Amen.

▶ **19.18**   RESPONSE
From Ezekiel 47†

I saw water flowing from the temple . . . it brought God's life and his salvation. The people sang in joyful praise:
Alleluia, alleluia! Amen.

▶ **19.19**   RESPONSE FOR CHOIR/MINISTERS
From Psalm 135†

Praise the Lord:
praise the name of the Lord.

Praise him, you servants of the Lord who lead the worship of his house. Here in the house of our God, praise the Lord:
praise the Lord, for the Lord is good.

Sing praises to his name, for he loves to hear them:
praise the Lord. Amen.

19.20 APPROACH
Unknown

The three prayers 19.20–19.22 can be used as one by omitting the words in square brackets

Lord, we want to worship you with our eyes, because they can see
the wonderful world you have made; Lord, we want to worship you
with our ears, because they can hear your words, and the sounds
of your world; Lord, we want to worship you with our voices,
because they can shout your praise; Lord, we want to worship you
with our hands, because they can help other people; Lord, we want
to worship you with everything, because you have made us your
children; [through Jesus Christ our Lord. **Amen.**]

19.21 APPROACH
Editors

[Lord,] help us to sense your presence as we become alive in your
Spirit; help us to turn ourselves to you in worship today, as in your
sight we sense colour, variety and beauty. Set our tongues on fire
with praise, our emotions overflowing with love. Let our minds be
strengthened and stimulated. Save us from limiting you by small-
mindedness, quenching your Spirit by insistence on tidiness. Help us
now to perceive your ministry to our whole personality. [We ask you
this for your glory and our good; through Jesus Christ our Lord.
Amen.]

19.22 APPROACH
Editors

Grant, O Lord, that through our worship we may be awakened to
the wonder of your love for us; that familiar words may shine with
new meaning and that the habit of worship may be cleansed of all
undue formality and mere ceremonial observance. Open our eyes to
see your loveliness, and warm our hearts as you speak your word to
us. May we know ourselves forgiven; energised with new life and
throbbing with new vitality and power through your Holy Spirit; for
the sake of Jesus Christ our Lord. **Amen.**

19.23   APPROACH
Alan Gaunt

God, take hold of us in this act of worship; force our hands apart and make us let go of the sins and fears we hug to ourselves. Make us wide open to receive you: shake us, disturb us – but give us peace, such as none but you can give; through Jesus our Saviour. **Amen.**

19.24   APPROACH
Editors

Lord, today we want to hear the music of heaven – to find new impulses of love, new outlets for our charity, a new warmth in our hearts and a new sense of your presence. Lord, speak to us; commune with us as we worship that we shall be filled with yourself. To you be praise and glory for ever and ever. **Amen.**

▶ **19.25**   APPROACH
Alan Gaunt, adapted

This is the place and this the time; here and now God waits to break into our experience: here and now,
let us praise him!
God waits to change our minds, to change our lives, to change our ways: here and now,
let us praise him!
God waits to make us see the world and the whole of life in a new light: here and now,
let us praise him!
God waits to fill us with hope, joy and certainty for the future: here and now,
let us praise him!
This is the place as are all places;
this is the time as are all times:
here and now,
let us praise him! Amen.

▶ **19.26** PRAISE
From Psalm 66†

Shout with joy to God, all the earth;
sing to the glory of his name!

Come and see what God has done:
how awesome are his works!

Praise our God, all you people;
sound aloud his praise: Amen.

▶ **19.27** CONFESSION
Unknown

O God, we come to you in repentance, conscious of our sins:

When we are self-satisfied, you expose our failure. Lord, forgive us:
save us and help us.

When we are self-assertive you challenge our pride. Lord, forgive us:
save us and help us.

When we are self-opinionated, you show us we do not know
everything. Lord, forgive us:
save us and help us.

When we are self-indulgent, you condemn our greed. Lord, forgive
us:
save us and help us.

When we are self-centred, you take our peace away. Lord, forgive us:
save us and help us.

Give us a new vision of your holiness,
make us worthy to be your people,
and help us to live up to our calling
in Jesus Christ our Lord. Amen.

▶ **19.28** CONFESSION
From Psalm 143†

O Lord,
hear our prayer as we cry for your mercy;
come to help us
in your faithfulness and righteousness.
Do not bring us to judgement,

for no-one is innocent before you.
Answer us now, Lord;
do not hide yourself from us,
show us the way we should go,
rescue us from the enemy.
Teach us to do your will,
and by your good Spirit
lead us in a safe path,
for your name's sake. Amen.

▶ **19.29**   CONFESSION
Editors

Most loving saviour, Jesus,
have mercy on us, for we have sinned
and this has caused you grief.
We confess to you now,
not because you do not already know all about us,
but because we are deeply ashamed
and need to admit our wrong-doing to you.
Have pity and forgive us, dear saviour,
cleanse and refresh us with your living water;
for our true desire is to be clean and whole,
walking in your paths of righteousness always,
for your name's sake. Amen.

▶ **19.30**   A PERSONAL PRAYER OF CONFESSION
Editors

Holy Spirit, help me to take an honest look at myself and ask myself
some questions: do I love God with all my heart and soul and
strength? Do I reflect the love of Christ in my daily living? Do I
gladly give myself to the service of others? Is my main desire to
abide always in the love of God?

Holy Spirit,
I admit that I have not always obeyed your voice:
please forgive me,
and lift me into your light
where I may yield your fruit –
to the glory of God's Kingdom;
through Jesus my Saviour. Amen.

▶ **19.31** CONFESSION
Alan Gaunt

For all our confessions of faith which have led to nothing, Lord,
forgive us:
forgive us and help us.

For all our protestations of love to each other and to you which have
come to nothing Lord, forgive us:
forgive us and help us.

For all our chasing after dreams and striving after schemes which
have achieved nothing, Lord, forgive us:
forgive us and help us.

**Teach us to put our faith in you
rather than in ourselves;
so that loving you
we may love each other
with transforming, creative love
like that of Jesus Christ our Lord. Amen.**

▶ **19.32** CONFESSION
From Jonah 2†

**O Lord our God,
in distress we call to you;
from the depths we cry for help –
the storm swirls around us,
our troubles threaten to engulf us.
We feel we have been banished from your sight,
but we look again towards your loving peace.
We have clung to worthless things
and forfeited the grace that
could have been ours.
We are trapped under a weight of sin,
and our life in you is ebbing away.
O Lord, we call to you:
forgive us and restore us,
through Jesus our redeemer. Amen.**

19.33   ABSOLUTION
From Jonah 1†

Because you have remembered the Lord your God he listens to your prayer, he hears your cry and he answers you; he brings up your life from the depths, he forgives all your sin: praise him with a song of thanksgiving, make good your promises to him. Salvation comes from the Lord! **Amen.**

19.34   ABSOLUTION
From Psalm 142†

The Lord hears your cry and gives you his mercy; he watches over you and sees your trouble; he is your refuge and the hope of your life – he knows your need; in Jesus Christ he sets you free, so that you may praise his name. **Amen.**

19.35   ABSOLUTION
From Isaiah 25†

The faithful Lord, the sovereign Lord, wipe away your tears and remove your disgrace from you. The Lord has spoken. He is your God: trust him, and he will save you. Rejoice and be glad in his redemption; through Jesus Christ. **Amen.**

▶ **19.36**   COLLECT
Pentecost 6, ASB 1980

Almighty God,
without you we are not able to please you.
Mercifully grant that your Holy Spirit
may in all things direct and rule our hearts;
through Jesus Christ our Lord. **Amen.**

▶ **19.37**   PSALM
Psalm 143.6–10, and Psalm 51.6–12†

Psalms 143 and 51 have been grouped together to provide for an occasion when the person and work of the Holy Spirit is being considered

O Lord, I spread my hands out to you:
I thirst for you like dry ground.

332

Teach me to do your will, for you are my God:
let your good Spirit lead me in safety.

You require sincerity and truth in me:
fill my mind with your wisdom.

Create in me a pure heart, O God:
and renew a faithful spirit in me.

Do not cast me from your presence:
or take your Holy Spirit from me.

Give me again the joy of your salvation:
and make me willing to obey. Amen.

▶ **19.38** PSALM
Psalm 150. 1–6†

The congregation may divide at A *and* B

Praise the Lord!
Praise God in his sanctuary:
praise his strength beyond the skies!

Praise him for his acts of power:
A **praise him for his surpassing greatness.**

Praise him with the sounding of the trumpet:
B **praise him with the harp and lyre.**

Praise him with tambourine and dancing:
A **praise him with the strings and flute.**

Praise him with the clash of cymbals:
B **praise him with resounding cymbals.**

Let everything that has breath praise the Lord:
ALL **Praise the Lord! Amen.**

19.39 READING: ONE BODY WITH MANY PARTS
From 1 Corinthians 12.12–27

Cast: Paul, Foot, Ear, Eye, Head

Paul

Christ is like a single body, which has many parts; it is still one
body, even though it is made up of different parts. In the same
way, all of us, whether Jews or Gentiles, whether slaves or free,

have been baptized into the one body by the same Spirit, and we have all been given the one Spirit to drink.

For the body itself is not made up of only one part, but of many parts. If the foot were to say:

Foot
Because I am not a hand, I don't belong to the body.

Paul
That would not keep it from being a part of the body. And if the ear were to say:

Ear
Because I am not an eye, I don't belong to the body.

Paul
That would not keep it from being a part of the body. If the whole body were just an eye, how could it hear? And if it were only an ear, how could it smell? As it is, however, God put every different part in the body just as he wanted it to be. There would not be a body if it were all only one part! As it is, there are many parts but one body.

So then, the eye cannot say to the hand:

Eye
I don't need you!

Paul
Nor can the head say to the feet:

Head
Well, I don't need *you!*

Paul
On the contrary, we cannot do without the parts of the body that seem to be weaker.

Cast
All of you are Christ's body, and each one is a part of it.

Cast
[This is] the word of the Lord.

All
Thanks be to God.

FURTHER BIBLE READINGS
Reading appropriate to this theme will be found listed in our companion volume, 'The Dramatised Bible' (published by HarperCollins) on index pages 430–431.

▶ **19.40**   RESPONSE AFTER READING
From Revelation 2 and 3†

Hear what the Spirit is saying to the Church:
Thanks be to God. Amen.

▶ **19.41**   CREED
From 1 Corinthians 12†

Let us affirm our faith in the unity and the diversity of God:

**We believe in the one Holy Spirit
giver of gifts of various kinds.**

**We believe in one Jesus Christ
Lord of various kinds of service.**

**We believe in one almighty Father
working in various ways.**

**We believe in one God
Father, Son and Holy Spirit. Amen.**

19.42   FOR THE NEW DAY
Editors

Creator God, we praise you in the morning of this new day. For the restfulness of the night and strengthening sleep, we praise you. For the problems and possibilities of each hour, we praise you. Take our lives, our abilities and our gifts and show us how you wish us to use them for your glory. Make our actions, our words and our attitudes reflect the power of your indwelling perfect love. It is in the name of our Lord Jesus Christ that we pray, and for his sake. **Amen.**

▶ **19.43**   PRAISING THE LORD
Editors

Lord God, our loving heavenly Father, we speak your praise, for you are ever faithful. Your mercy is from eternity to eternity.

For your love, which never wearies or grows old or becomes indifferent, but is fresh with each new day, we praise you:
Alleluia! Amen.

You have made all things by your power, you rule all things in your wisdom. For the richness of creation and for the mercy and grace which sustains and strengthens us, we thank you:
Alleluia! Amen.

You are always bringing order and beauty out of chaos and confusion. For taking the broken fragments of our lives and knitting them together into renewed wholeness, we praise you:
Alleluia! Amen.

For your continuing grace of forgiveness, and for the constant enrichment of your Holy Spirit, we thank you:
Alleluia! Amen.

We can never restrict your gifts of music, beauty, art or love, or imprison your enriching spiritual gifts – to limit them is to lose your power, to use them selfishly brings spiritual impoverishment. For all these your gifts we praise you:
Alleluia! Amen.

We come to you today full of expectation of your continuing mercy, love and provision:
**For yours is the kingdom,
the power and the glory for ever.**

**Receive our praises,
hear our prayers,
be present through your Spirit
in the name of Jesus Christ our Lord. Amen.**

▶ **19.44**   FOR MERCY
From Psalm 143†

O Lord,
hear our prayer as we cry for your mercy;
in your faithfulness and righteousness
come to help us.

Do not bring us to judgement,
for no-one is innocent before you.

We remember days gone by,
and think about all you have done for us;
we lift our hands to you in prayer
and our souls thirst for you.
Answer us now, Lord,
don't hide yourself from us;
remind us each morning of your constant love,
for we put our trust in you.

We pray to you:
show us the way we should go;
rescue us from the enemy,
teach us to do your will,
by your good spirit
lead us in the right path,
for your name's sake. **Amen.**

▶ **19.45** THANKSGIVING (MUSICAL SERVICE)
From Psalm 150†

*Here the instruments being used in the service may be named

O God, we praise you:

We praise you in your sanctuary:
we praise you in your mighty heaven.

We praise you for your acts of power:
we praise you for your surpassing greatness.

With . . . *, we praise you:
with every breath your people praise you.

We praise you, O God:
Amen. Amen.

▶ **19.46** INVOCATION
From 'A New Zealand Prayer Book'

Come, Holy Spirit, with the new fire;
when our prayer seems to fail,
when we hear no voice nor any answer,
rouse us and light our way. **Amen.**

19.47   FOR THE CHURCH
Editors

Lord Jesus, you are the good shepherd; you feed us with your truth and lead us on to understand your will: give to your church today a new vision, a deepening commitment, a serving love, and a spiritual unity. Let the eternal message of hope and salvation, unimpeded by weight of tradition, and unobscured by the trappings of practice, come as good news to the people of this age. You have promised to make all things new: renew your church with brightness and clarity; through Jesus Christ our Lord. **Amen.**

19.48   FOR THE CHURCH
Michael Saward

Lord of the Church, enable your people to *be* the Church – a redeemed people, a holy people, a united people, a missionary people, and in all things a people gladly submissive to the truth you have shown us in yourself, Jesus Christ our Lord. **Amen.**

19.49   FOR THE CHURCH'S RENEWAL
William Laud

Gracious Father, we beseech you for your church: Fill it with all truth and in all truth with all peace; where it is corrupt, purge it; where it is in error, direct it; where it is superstitious, rectify it; where it is amiss, reform it; where it is right, strengthen and confirm it; where it is in need, furnish it; where it is divided and torn, heal it. Hear us, O Holy One of Israel, for the sake of Jesus Christ our Lord and Saviour. **Amen.**

19.50   FOR OUR CHURCHES
Alan Gaunt

We pray for a renewal of faith in the church; faith which is not afraid of criticism or doubt, faith which is honest and open – never evasive, faith which faces every challenge with humility and meets every need with loving generosity, faith which is always at the spring and always blossoming into the full bloom of thought, to set others thinking, singing, writing, painting, to your glory; through Jesus Christ our Lord. **Amen.**

19.51   FOR THE CHURCH'S RENEWAL
Edinburgh House Press, adapted

Spirit of promise, Spirit of unity, we thank you that you are also the Spirit of renewal. Renew in the whole church, we pray, that passionate desire for the coming of Christ's kingdom which will unite all Christians in one mission to the world. May we all grow up together into him who is our head, the Saviour of the world, Jesus Christ our Lord. **Amen.**

19.52   FOR THE CHURCH'S RENEWAL
Percy Dearmer

O God, our Shepherd, give to the Church a new vision and a new charity, new wisdom and fresh understanding, the revival of her brightness and the renewal of her unity; that the eternal message of your Son, unfettered by our human traditions, may be hailed as the good news of the coming age; through him who makes all things new, Jesus Christ our Lord. **Amen.**

▶ ## 19.53   FOR LIBERTY IN GOD'S FAMILY
From 'A New Zealand Prayer Book'

Loving God,
in Jesus you gather us into your family;
confidently we call you Father:
may your Spirit bring us to share
the glorious liberty of your children,
now and for ever. **Amen.**

19.54   FOR MUSIC AND MUSICIANS
From 'New Every Morning'

Eternal Lord God, source of all beauty and harmony, we praise you for the gift of music; for the inspiration given to those who compose it, for the skill and devotion of those who perform it, for the faculties and powers which enable us to enjoy it; and we pray that as by this gift our lives are enriched and renewed, so we may glorify you in a fuller dedication of ourselves, giving thanks always for all things in the name of our Lord Jesus Christ. **Amen.**

▶ **19.55**   AT A MUSICAL OCCASION
Editors

God, our creator:
thank you for music and musicians,
thank you for the creation of new songs and hymns,
thank you for your Holy Spirit,
who fills our hearts with joy
    when we sing melodies of praise to you;
in Jesus' name. **Amen.**

19.56   AT A CONVENTION/CONFERENCE
Editors

We give you thanks, our God for these days of convention
/*conference*: for the mingling of minds and personality, for the clash
of provocative thought and expression, for the great variety of skills,
talents and gifts represented here. Let your Holy Spirit flow into our
lives, that all these abilities may be used to fulfil your purposes and
extend the kingdom of our Lord Jesus Christ. **Amen.**

▶ **19.57**   FOR THE BODY OF CHRIST
Editors

O God our Father, you grant your people gifts, that we may work
together in the service of your Son:

Bless those who lead, that they may be strong and true, yet be
humble before you: Lord, through your Spirit,
answer our prayer.

Bless those who teach, that they may enlighten our understanding,
yet be taught by your wisdom: Lord, through your Spirit,
answer our prayer.

Bless those who offer healing, that they may extend your touch of
grace, yet always know your healing presence: Lord, through your
Spirit,
answer our prayer.

Bless those through whom you speak, that they may proclaim your
word in power, yet have their ears open to your gentle whisper:
Lord, through your Spirit,
answer our prayer.

Bless those who administer, help, and organise, that they may be diligent in their duty, yet seek your kingdom first: Lord, through your Spirit,
answer our prayer.

Grant that as one Body
we may grow up into him
who is the head of the Church,
even Jesus Christ our Lord. Amen.

▶ **19.58** FOR CHURCH FAMILY LIFE
Unknown

Look upon us, O Lord,
and grant us the grace of your Holy Spirit:
where there is weakness, give us strength;
where there is disagreement, give us tolerance;
where there is misunderstanding, give us patience,
and where there is hurt, give us the courage to forgive
and the grace to accept forgiveness;
through Jesus Christ our Lord. **Amen.**

19.59 FOR RELEASE FROM SELFISH CONCERN
Editors

O Lord, you have given us the ability to absorb beauty; you have given us power in the Spirit to breathe clean fresh moral air; you give us thoughts that range through eternity.

Release us this day, O Lord, from the ugliness and sordidness of our selfish concerns for prestige and prosperity. Give us a sense of the vastness of your love – save us from fear; wrap your eternal arms around us. Let us rejoice in you alone for you are our God, the Lord of all goodness; the King of glory, for ever and ever. **Amen.**

19.60 FOR WILLINGNESS TO CHANGE
Alan Gaunt

God, make us aware, sensitive, ready to be changed, ready for complete commitment to the shocking Christ who shook a nation's faith, took death by surprise, and still comes to give new meanings to old truths. Forgive our rigidity, our fixed ideas, our meagre sense of right and wrong, our feeble grasp of joy and sorrow; forgive the paltriness of our convictions, so right and yet so narrow and divisive. Give us long, whole, simple vision, that can bear the shame of the cross for the sake of the future. Rule in our hearts, Lord Christ, living Word of God; give meaning to our joy and sorrow, our happiness and sadness, our success and failure; put your Spirit in our hands to work new miracles of love and truth, for the sake of all humankind, in the name of Jesus Christ our Lord. **Amen.**

▶ **19.61**   FOR OUR RENEWAL
Epiphany 4, ASB 1980

Almighty God,
in Christ you make all things new:
transform the poverty of our nature
by the riches of your grace;
and in the renewal of our lives
make known your heavenly glory;
through Jesus Christ our Lord. **Amen.**

19.62   FOR RENEWAL
Alan Gaunt

Make us good wine, exciting, sparkling, full of promise for all the people to whom we must be the sign of your continuing presence, the full weight of your glory; we ask these things in Jesus Christ our Lord. **Amen.**

▶ **19.63**   FOR RENEWAL OF HEART AND MIND
From Psalm 51†

Lord, you require in us
sincerity and truth:
fill our minds with your wisdom,
make us happy in your service;
create in us a new heart
and put a loyal spirit in us.
Do not banish us from your presence,
or take your holy spirit from us;
give us the joy that comes from your salvation,
and make us willing to obey you
through Jesus Christ our Lord. **Amen.**

▶ **19.64** RENEWAL: A PERSONAL PRAYER
Editors

Lord, help me to forget myself,
but never let me forget you;
save me from self-pity,
but give me true compassion for others;
deliver me from self-seeking,
but instil in me the desire to find you;
keep me from being self-willed,
but make me always keen to obey your will.
Christ, King of Love, live in me. **Amen.**

19.65 FOR PERSONAL RENEWAL
Editors

Lord God, my God, cleanse me, strengthen me, renew me and
confirm me as your disciple; make me your trusted witness and send
me where you will with your joyful message of new life in Christ.
Fill my heart with love, and compel me to bind up the wounds of my
sisters and brothers in this broken world; guide me to anyone in pain
or turmoil or darkness, and let your Holy Spirit work through me to
minister the love of Christ, the peace of Christ, the light of Christ.
Help me to serve with sympathetic action as well as kindly speech;
grant me inner mercy as well as outward willingness. And help me
to remember, Lord, that you are my true Companion all along the
way. **Amen.**

▶ **19.66** RENEWAL: FOR MISSION
Editors

Lord, call us from the world
to cleanse, teach and equip us.
Then send us back again
to love, serve, and tell the good news
    that you are the Christ,
the sacrificial Lamb of God,
the Resurrection and the Life,
the Holy One, the Almighty,
the Alpha and Omega. **Amen.**

▶ **19.67**   FOR A DEEPER LIFE IN THE SPIRIT
Editors

Holy Spirit of God, you are continually transforming life and always giving us grace to follow the Lord Jesus Christ.

We pray for the blessing of faith which expects new truth to break into our minds:
Lord, give us faith.

We pray for the blessing of strength to explore the new life which we have received in Christ Jesus:
Lord, give us strength.

We pray for the blessing of hope, that we may conquer our doubts and believe in the power of your good news:
Lord, give us hope.

We pray for the blessing of love that is patient and kind: break down our self-seeking and unforgiving spirit. Help us to delight in the happiness of others and to rejoice in another's success as much as in our own:
Lord, give us love.

O Holy Spirit of God,
deepen our experience of your transforming power
through Jesus Christ our Lord. Amen.

▶ **19.68**   FOR RENEWAL IN THE SPIRIT
From Ephesians 4 and Colossians 3, Editors

Lord, our God, by the power of your Holy Spirit cleanse us and strengthen us; help us to put off the old and put on the new.

Help us to put off deception and put on truth,
by the power of your Holy Spirit.

Help us to put off impurity and put on holiness,
by the power of your Holy Spirit.

Help us to put off malice and put on forgiveness,
by the power of your Holy Spirit.

Help us to put off anger and put on peace,
by the power of your Holy Spirit.

Help us to put off coldness and put on compassion,
by the power of your Holy Spirit.

Help us to put off greed and put on generosity,
by the power of your Holy Spirit.

Help us to put off doubt and put on faith,
by the power of your Holy Spirit.

Help us to put off darkness and put on Light,
by the power of your Holy Spirit.

In the name of Christ who shines upon us.
Amen.

19.69 FOR THE FRUITS OF THE SPIRIT
Editors

Lord Jesus Christ, your name is above all names: Wonderful, Perfect, Holy – and we believe you can do great things for us. Grant us the courage to receive your love and act on it. Fill our hearts with pure praise to you, and let our lives bring forth the fruit of your Spirit, which is . . love . . joy . . peace . . patience . . kindness . . goodness . . faithfulness . . gentleness . . and self-control. Make us your witnesses on earth, until your purpose is fulfilled and you call us home to your glory for ever. **Amen.**

19.70 ABOUT BEING OPEN TO EACH OTHER
Alan Gaunt

God, you are no idol of our making, but the living God, coming, going, revealed or hidden – as you decide: give us the capacity to be surprised into new understanding. Break through our traditions and set phrases, and show yourself alive – the strength of our present and the promise of our future. Give us the capacity to be surprised by each other: to recognise truth in words spoken, movements made and glances given; seeing new dimensions in each other. Help us to be startled by grace where we could see no virtue, by kindness where we could see only coldness, by the need of love where we could see only arrogance and ingratitude, by the need of generous aid where we could see only dirt, squalor and laziness. Meet us, Lord, in unexpected places; speak to us through unexpected voices;

and do not let us refuse to see or hear you anywhere. Help us of our own free will to love and cherish one another and all people, everywhere, until every man, woman and child becomes aware of being loved, cherished, forgiven and accepted by you, and the universe rings with loud and joyful praise to the glory of your name. **Amen.**

19.71   FOR RENEWED HEARTS AND LIVES
Editors

Everlasting Father of love, we worship you: breathe on us, and waken us to the power of your Holy Spirit, cleanse us and grant us a renewed faith and a new desire to pray. Help us to forget our own selfish ambitions, and let our aim be to hear your call and obey you; draw us into your light, so that we see clearly and walk in the path you have set before us. Let us find Christ in ourselves and in each other as we respond to the all-embracing love of your Spirit. **Amen.**

19.72   ABOUT OUR WEAKNESS
From 2 Corinthians 12†

God our redeemer, you have taught us (through St Paul) that your grace is sufficient for us and your power is made perfect in weakness: help us to acknowledge our weaknesses so that Christ's power may rest upon us; to delight in hardships, persecutions and difficulties, and to know that when we are weak, then we are strong; through Jesus Christ our Lord. **Amen.**

▶ 19.73   FOR HEALING AND LIBERTY
From 'A New Zealand Prayer Book'

We need your healing, merciful God:
give us true repentance.
Some sins are plain to us;
some escape us,
some we cannot face.
Forgive us;
set us free to hear your word to us;
set us free to serve you. **Amen.**

▶ **19.74**   FOR HEALING: A PERSONAL PRAYER
Editors

Lord Christ, Son of God:
come to me and cleanse me from my sin,
come to me and heal me by the power of your Spirit,
come to me and liberate me with your love.
So, through your grace
may I bring comfort to my sisters and brothers
and lead them into the security
  of your glorious light. **Amen.**

19.75   THANKSGIVING
Editors

Gracious God, we rejoice in your creative and energising Holy Spirit.
At creation your Spirit brought order out of chaos: we praise you for
the work of your Spirit in the church and in the world, constantly
redeeming and renewing your creation and imparting gifts to your
church – power to proclaim your word, conviction of sin, strength
for repentance, and certainty of your love through Christ's death,
Resurrection and Ascension. We praise you that your Spirit is giving
us faith to displace unbelief, love instead of insecurity, hope where
once was despair. Continually fill us with your Spirit that we may
enter more fully into the immeasurable riches of your grace in Christ
Jesus our Lord, to his praise and glory. **Amen.**

▶ **19.76**   THANKSGIVING
Emmanuel Church, Northwood

We give thanks to God for all his gifts to us:

For birth and life and strength of body, for safety and shelter and
food: we give you thanks, O God,
and praise your holy name.

For sight and hearing and the beauty of nature, for words and music
and the power of thought: we give you thanks, O God,
and praise your holy name.

For work and leisure and the joy of achieving, for conscience and
will and depth of feeling: we give you thanks, O God,
and praise your holy name.

For grace and truth in Jesus Christ, for the gifts of the Spirit and the hope of heaven: we give you thanks, O God,
and praise your holy name.

**We shall not forget
that you are our God,
and we are your people,
in Jesus Christ our Lord. Amen.**

▶ **19.77** THANKSGIVING: A PERSONAL PRAYER
Editors

Lord Jesus Christ,
you are the Alpha and the Omega,
the bright morning star,
the resurrection and the life,
the Light of the world –
and yet you know me.
Thank you, Lord;
thank you for touching my heart with your love. **Amen.**

19.78 CONCLUDING PRAYER
Editors

We came to praise you this morning, our God. You stirred us, wakened us to a new day – a day we set apart to give more time to you and each other.

You, Lord, have poured upon us so many blessings and benefits: gifts spiritual and temporal come in richness and quantity. We have lived with a constant sense of your great goodness; now we have tasted again that you are good – we have touched a little more of eternity, we have discovered afresh the dimensions of your grace. Therefore take from our lives anything that mars your beauty in us; deliver us from all meanness, falseness and unhealthy fear, correct our ignorance, open our minds to truth, our ears to hear your words, release our tongues to sing your praise, expand our capacity for you, so that more love may be poured in by the Holy Spirit. Let every day be marked by the unfailing inspiration of our risen Lord and Master.

Lord, we are never safer, sweeter or saner than when we are praising: so keep us joyfully praising you as we enter another working week – with joy and gladness in our hearts and on our lips the name of Jesus Christ our Lord. **Amen.**

▶ **19.79** DEDICATION
Editors

Lord Christ, our Master,
purify us by the kindling of your Holy Spirit,
and let the unquenchable flame of your love
burn within us every day,
so that we never forget you. **Amen.**

▶ **19.80** DEDICATION: A PERSONAL PRAYER
Editors

Lord Jesus Christ, I am healed through the prayer of faith, accepted
by you and drawn to your open arms, and so I come to you now in
deep thankfulness. I receive your gift of Salvation and new life, and I
resolve to live for you in the power of your Spirit. Thank you for the
new peace in my heart and for the joy of knowing that one day I
shall see you in all your heavenly splendour. **Amen.**

19.81 BLESSING
From 2 Corinthians 6†

Purify yourselves from everything that makes the body or soul
unclean, and be completely holy by living in awe of God; and
blessing from God the Father, the Son and the Holy Spirit be upon
you always. **Amen.**

19.82 BLESSING
From 2 Corinthians 6†

Show yourselves to be God's servants through the Holy Spirit – by
your purity, knowledge, patience and kindness; by your true love, by
your message of truth and by the power of God; and the blessing of
God the Father, and the Son and God the Holy Spirit be with you
always. **Amen.**

19.83 BLESSING
From Ephesians 3†

God, from the wealth of his glory give you power through his Spirit
to be inwardly strong; Christ make his home in your hearts through
faith, that you may come to know how broad, long, high and deep is

his love and be filled with the very nature of God – Father, Son and Holy Spirit. **Amen.**

19.84 BLESSING
From Ephesians 5†

Be filled with the Spirit; speak to one another with psalms, hymns and spiritual songs; sing and make music in your hearts to the Lord; and the blessing of God almighty, the Father, the Son and the Holy Spirit be with you always. **Amen.**

19.85 BLESSING
1 Thessalonians 5. 23†

God who gives us peace, make you holy in every way: keep your whole being, spirit, soul and body, free from every fault at the coming of our Lord Jesus Christ; and the blessing of God who is faithful, Father, Son and Holy Spirit be with you always. **Amen.**

19.86 BLESSING
From 2 Corinthians 3†

Fix your gaze with faces unveiled upon the glory of the Lord, and be transfigured into his likeness from one degree of glory to another: the Spirit of the Lord work this miracle in you; and the blessing of God almighty, Father, Son and Holy Spirit be with you always. **Amen.**

The Local Church:
Anniversary, Commitment, Giving

▶ **20.1** GREETING
From 1 Corinthians 1†

*Here the local name is supplied.

To the church of God in . . . *, to those sanctified in Christ Jesus and called to be holy, to all those everywhere who call on the name of our Lord Jesus Christ – their Lord and ours: grace and peace to you from God our Father and the Lord Jesus Christ. **Amen.**

▶ **20.2** GREETING (EVENING)
From Psalm 134†

All of you who serve the Lord; you who come in the evening of the day to worship in his house, you who lift up your hands in his holy place and praise the Lord: (may) the Lord, the maker of heaven and earth, bless you! **Amen.**

20.3 SENTENCE
1 Peter 2. 4,5

Come to the Lord, the living stone, rejected by man as worthless but chosen by God as valuable. Come as living stones and let yourselves be used in building the spiritual temple.

20.4 SENTENCE
Ephesians 2. 19,20

You are no longer strangers and sojourners, but you are fellow-citizens with the saints and members of the household of God, Christ Jesus himself being the chief corner-stone.

20.5 SENTENCE
Ephesians 4. 15,16

Speaking the truth in love, we will in all things grow up into him who is the head that is Christ. From him the whole body, joined and held together by every supporting ligament grows and builds itself up in love as each part does its work.

20.6 SENTENCE
Ephesians 1. 22,23

God has appointed Christ to be head over everything for the Church, which is his body, the fulness of him who fills everything in every way.

20.7 SENTENCE
Genesis 33.11

God has been kind to me, and given me everything I need.

20.8 SENTENCE
2 Corinthians 8.9

You know the grace of our Lord Jesus Christ, that though he was rich, yet for your sakes he became poor, so that you through his poverty might become rich.

20.9 SENTENCE
1 Corinthians 6.20

You are not your own: you are bought with a price.

20.10 SENTENCE
2 Corinthians 8.7

St Paul says, 'Just as you excel in everything – in faith, in speech, in knowledge, in complete earnestness and in your love for us – see that you also excel in this grace of giving'.

20.11 SENTENCE
1 Corinthians 15.58

St Paul says, 'On the first day of every week, each one of you should set aside a sum of money in keeping with your income'.

20.12 SENTENCE
Deuteronomy 16.17

We read in Deuteronomy, 'Each of you must bring a gift in proportion to the way the Lord your God has blessed you'.

20.13 SENTENCE
2 Corinthians 9.6

St Paul says, 'Each one should give as he has decided, not with regret or out of a sense of duty; for God loves the one who gives gladly'.

▶ **20.14** RESPONSE
From Psalm 30†

Sing praise to the Lord, all his faithful people:
Remember what the Holy One has done,
and give him thanks! Amen.

▶ **20.15** RESPONSE
From Revelation 1†

Jesus has made us a kingdom of priests to serve his God and Father:
to him be glory and power
for ever and ever. Amen.

▶ **20.16** RESPONSE
From Ephesians 2†

Jesus Christ is the chief cornerstone:
in him we are being built together into a temple
in which God lives by his Spirit. Amen.

▶ **20.17** RESPONSE
From Hebrews 12†

Let us thank God because we have received a kingdom which cannot be shaken:
let us be grateful,
and worship him
in a way that will please him –
with reverence and awe. Amen.

▶ **20.18**   RESPONSE
From 2 Corinthians 1†

As surely as God is faithful, no matter how many promises he has
made they are 'yes' in Christ:
to the glory of God. Amen.

▶ **20.19**   RESPONSE
From Ezekiel 47

I saw water flowing from the temple . . . it brought God's life and his
salvation. The people sang in joyful praise:
Alleluia, alleluia! Amen.

▶ **20.20**   EVENING EXHORTATION/WELCOME
From Psalm 134†

All of you who serve the Lord:
praise the Lord.

You who come in the evening of the day to worship in his house:
praise the Lord.

Lift up your hands in his holy place:
praise the Lord.

May the Lord, the maker of heaven and earth, bless you here;
through our Saviour, Jesus Christ. **Amen.**

20.21   APPROACH
From Deuteronomy 12†

Lord, our God, this is the place where we may worship you; you
have set your name here. Here in your presence our families shall
rejoice, because you have blessed us; here we present to you the
offering of our lives; here we pledge our obedience to your laws;
here we pray for our children, that we and they may do what is right
in your sight; through Jesus our Redeemer. **Amen.**

20.22 APPROACH
From 1 Kings 8†

O Lord our God, there is no God like you in heaven above or on earth below; you keep your covenant of love with your servants who continue in your way with all their heart. You have kept your promise to our forbears – with your mouth you promised, with your hand you performed it! But will you really dwell on earth? The heaven, even the highest heaven, cannot contain you. How much less this house of prayer we have built; in which we worship you. Yet give attention to your servants' prayer and our plea for mercy, O Lord God; hear the cry and the prayer that your servants are praying in your presence this day: may your eyes be open toward this place which is dedicated/*we now dedicate* to your name. Hear the supplication of your people when they pray in this place; hear from heaven and, when you hear, forgive; through Jesus Christ our Lord. **Amen.**

20.23 APPROACH
Editors

Eternal God, praised for ever, you do not dwell in temples made with hands, but you desire to make the humble, penitent, and obedient heart your dwelling; come to our hearts this day, and bring every one of our thoughts into captivity through Christ, that we may worship you in Spirit and in truth. Deliver us from the distraction of this world – its business and its noise – and make us live close to you in quietness and peace. Give us renewed energies, greater capacity for life, and true direction of purpose; that your name may be honoured through Jesus, our Lord. **Amen.**

▶ **20.24** PRAISE
From Psalm 150†

Praise God in his sanctuary;
praise him in his mighty heavens.

Praise him for his acts of power;
praise him for his surpassing greatness

Let everything that has breath praise the Lord:
praise the Lord! Amen!

355

20.25 CONFESSION
Editors

Our loving and forgiving Father, we now confess that our lives do not measure up to the pure ideals and teaching of our Lord Jesus Christ. We are conscious that no part of our life is worthy of your holy presence. We confess that often we have been forgetful of you, careless of others and have followed our own selfish ways. We are aware that we have not reflected the love and concern of the Lord Jesus in the world. Our Father in heaven, we know we are sinners: but help us here and now to accept your forgiveness and the freedom from guilt which you offer. We ask this in the name of your Son, our saviour, Jesus Christ. **Amen.**

▶ **20.26** CONFESSION
From 1 Corinthians 13†

Let us confess our lack of love, and our need of grace:

**When we lose patience,
when we are unkind,
when we are envious,
when we are rude or proud,
when we are selfish or irritable,
and when we will not forgive:
have mercy on us, O God.**

**Help us not to delight in evil,
but to rejoice in the truth;
help us always to protect, to trust,
to hope and to presevere
so that we may see you face to face,
and learn to love as you love us
in Jesus Christ our Lord. Amen.**

▶ **20.27** CONFESSION
From 'The Promise of His Glory'

**Most merciful God,
we confess that we have sinned against you
in thought, and word, and deed.
We are truly sorry for our pride,
and for our lack of faith,**

of understanding and of love;
We repent of our narrow-mindedness,
of our bitterness and our prejudices.
Pardon and forgive us,
save us and renew us,
that we may delight in your will
and walk in your ways;
through Jesus Christ our Lord. Amen.

20.28 ABSOLUTION
From Psalm 31†

The Lord have mercy upon *you* in *your* distress; the Lord deliver *you* in all temptation; the Lord make his face to shine upon *you* and save *you* in his unfailing love; for his name's sake. **Amen.**

▶ ## 20.29 COLLECT
Dedication/Consecration of a Church, ASB 1980

Almighty God,
to whose glory we celebrate
the *dedication/consecration* of this house of prayer:
we praise you for the many blessings
you have given to those who worship here;
and we pray
that all who seek you in this place
may find you,
and being filled with the Holy Spirit
may become a living temple
acceptable to you;
through Jesus Christ our Lord. **Amen.**

▶ ## 20.30 COLLECT
For a Synod, ASB 1980

Almighty God,
you have given your Holy Spirit to the church
that he may lead us into all truth.
Bless with his grace and presence
the leaders of this church;
keep them steadfast in faith and united in love,

that they may reveal your glory
and prepare the way of your kingdom;
through Jesus Christ our Lord. **Amen.**

▶ **20.31** PSALM
Psalm 100.1–5†

Rejoice in the Lord, all the earth:
worship the Lord with gladness.

Remember the Lord is our God:
we are his flock and he made us.

Come to his temple with praise:
enter his gates with thanksgiving.

The love of the Lord will not fail:
God will be faithful for ever. Amen.

▶ **20.32** PSALM
Psalm 118.1–29†

M – *minister*, W – *worshipper, from doorway, then moving through congregation*, C– *choir/chorus*, D – *director, in matter-of-fact tone.*

M Give thanks to the Lord, for he is good:
his love endures for ever.

M All those who fear the Lord shall say:
His love endures for ever.

W Open for me the gates of the Temple; I will go in and give
thanks to the Lord.

M This is the gate of the Lord, only the righteous
can come in.

W I will give thanks because you heard me; you have become my
salvation.

C **The stone which the builders rejected as worthless
turned out to be the most important of all:
The Lord has done this – what a wonderful sight it is!**

W This is the day of the Lord's victory – let us be happy, let us
celebrate:
O Lord save us – O Lord, grant us success.

M May God bless the one who comes in the name of the Lord:

358

The Lord is God – he has been good to us!

c From the Temple of the Lord, we bless you.

d With branches in your hands, start the procession and march round the altar:

w You are my God and I will give you thanks:
You are my God, and I will exalt you.

m Give thanks to the Lord, for he is good:
His love endures for ever. Amen.

▶ **20.33** PSALM
Psalm 134.1–3†

You servants of the Lord, who stand in his temple at night:
praise the Lord!

Lift your hands in prayer to the Lord:
in his sanctuary, praise the Lord!

May the Lord who made the heaven and earth bless you from Zion:
Amen!

20.34 READING: SOLOMON'S PRAYER
2 Chronicles 6.12–21

Cast: Chronicler, [Commentator], Solomon

Chronicler
In the presence of the people Solomon went and stood in front of the altar and raised his arms in prayer.

[Commentator]
Solomon had made a bronze platform and put it in the middle of the courtyard. It was 2.2 metres square and 1.3 metres high. He mounted this platform, knelt down where everyone could see him, and raised his hands towards heaven.

Chronicler
Solomon prayed:

Solomon
Lord God of Israel, in all heaven and earth there is no god like you. You keep your covenant with your people and show them your love when they live in wholehearted obedience to you. You

have kept the promise you made to my father David; today every word has been fulfilled. Now, Lord God of Israel, keep the other promise you made to my father when you told him that there would always be one of his descendants ruling as king of Israel, provided that they carefully obeyed your Law just as he did. So now, Lord God of Israel, let everything come true that you promised to your servant David.

But can you, O God, really live on earth among men and women? Not even all heaven is large enough to hold you, so how can this Temple that I have built be large enough? Lord my God, I am your servant. Listen to my prayer and grant the requests I make to you. Watch over this Temple day and night. You have promised that this is where you will be worshipped, so hear me when I face this Temple and pray. Hear my prayers and the prayers of your people Israel when they face this place and pray. In your home in heaven hear us and forgive us.

Cast
[This is] the word of the Lord.

All
Thanks be to God.

20.35   READING: A CALL TO HOLY LIVING
1 Peter 1.13–25

Cast: Voice 1, Voice 2, Scripture

Voice 1
Have your minds ready for action.

Voice 2
Keep alert and set your hope completely on the blessing which will be given you when Jesus Christ is revealed.

Voice 1
Be obedient to God, and do not allow your lives to be shaped by those desires you had when you were still ignorant.

Voice 2
Instead, be holy in all that you do, just as God who called you is holy. The scripture says:

Scripture
Be holy because I am holy.

Voice 1

You call him Father, when you pray to God, who judges all people by the same standard, according to what each one has done; so then, spend the rest of your lives here on earth in reverence for him.

Voice 2

For you know what was paid to set you free from the worthless manner of life handed down by your ancestors. It was not something that can be destroyed, such as silver or gold; it was the costly sacrifice of Christ, who was like a lamb without defect or flaw.

Voice 1

He had been chosen by God before the creation of the world and was revealed in these last days for your sake.

Voice 2

Through him you believe in God, who raised him from death and gave him glory; and so your faith and hope are fixed on God. (PAUSE)

Voice 1

Now that by your obedience to the truth you have purified yourselves and have come to have a sincere love for your fellow-believers, love one another earnestly with all your heart. For through the living and eternal word of God you have been born again as the children of a parent who is immortal, not mortal. As the scripture says:

Scripture

All mankind are like grass,
and all their glory is like wild flowers.
The grass withers, and the flowers fall,
but the word of the Lord remains for ever.

Voices 1 and 2

This word is the Good News that was proclaimed to you.

Cast

[This is] the word of the Lord.

All

Thanks be to God.

20.36 READING: LIVING STONE, HOLY NATION
1 Peter 2. 1–10

Cast: Peter, Psalmist, Isaiah

Peter
Rid yourselves, then, of all evil; no more lying or hypocrisy or jealousy or insulting language. Be like new-born babies, always thirsty for the pure spiritual milk, so that by drinking it you may grow up and be saved. As the scripture says:

Psalmist
You have found out for yourselves how kind the Lord is.

Peter
Come to the Lord, the living stone rejected by man as worthless but chosen by God as valuable. Come as living stones, and let yourselves be used in building the spiritual temple, where you will serve as holy priests to offer spiritual and acceptable sacrifices to God through Jesus Christ. For the scripture says:

Isaiah
I chose a valuable stone, which I am placing as the cornerstone in Zion; and whoever believes in him will never be disappointed.

Peter
This stone is of great value for you that believe; but for those who do not believe:

Psalmist
The stone which the builders rejected as worthless turned out to be the most important of all.

Peter
And another scripture says:

Isaiah
This is the stone that will make people stumble, the rock that will make them fall.

Peter
They stumbled because they did not believe in the word; such was God's will for them. But you are the chosen race, the King's priests, the holy nation, God's own people, chosen to proclaim the wonderful acts of God, who called you out of darkness into his own marvellous light. At one time you were not God's people, but now you are his people; at one time you did not know God's mercy, but now you have received his mercy.

Cast
[This is] the word of the Lord.

All
Thanks be to God.

FURTHER BIBLE READINGS
Reading appropriate to this theme will be found listed in our companion volume, 'The Dramatised Bible' (published by HarperCollins) on index pages 431–432.

▶ **20.37** CREED
From Colossians 1†

Let us confess our faith in the Son of God:

Christ is the image of the invisible God,
the firstborn over all creation.
By him all things were created:
things in heaven and on earth,
visible and invisible,
thrones, powers, rulers, and authorities;
all things were created by him and for him.

He is before all things
and in him all things hold together.

He is the head of the body, the Church;
he is the beginning
and the firstborn from the dead. Amen.

▶ **20.38** CREED
From Revelation 1†

We believe in God almighty,
the Lord, the first and the last,
who is, who was and who is to come.

We believe in Jesus Christ,
the faithful witness,
the first to be raised from death,
the ruler of the kings of the earth:
he loves us,
and by his sacrificial death
he has freed us from our sins

**and made us a kingdom of priests
to serve our God and Father. Amen.**

▶ **20.39** ACT OF PRAISE
Editors

For your living church, that world-wide concourse of people whom
you have graciously called to be your own; this day, O God:
we adore you and praise your holy name.

That you are enthroned in heaven, and that your rule extends
through all creation; this day, O God:
we adore you and praise your holy name.

For your consistent goodness and gentleness and for your constant
love and kindness to us and to everyone; this day, O God:
we adore you and praise your holy name.

That in Christ you freely forgive those who are penitent, and offer
your pardon to sinners; this day, O God:
we adore you and praise your holy name.

That Jesus lived, died and rose again to redeem us and make us your
own people; this day, O God:
we adore you and praise your holy name.

We rejoice this day in your promises fulfilled in us, and for the hope
of life everlasting.
May your will be done on earth, as it is in heaven. Amen.

▶ **20.40** FOR THE CHURCH OF CHRIST
From BCP, Episcopal Church USA

For the holy Church of God, that it may be filled with truth and love,
and be found without fault at the day of his coming, let us pray to
the Lord:
Lord, have mercy. Amen.

20.41   AT A LOCAL CHURCH ANNIVERSARY
Editors

*Here the various offices held by members of the church may be listed, or the office-holders named

Our God, on this special occasion in the life of your gathered people in this place, we give you thanks for the fellowship of kindred minds, for the warmth of our common inheritance in worship, for our forbears who nobly strove to establish this cause for your glory. And, in our generation, we thank you for all who give time, thought and energy to the work; for the officers of the Church . . . *; and for this quiet house where prayer is offered for strength and inspiration, and intercession made for others and for your kingdom to come; through Jesus Christ our Lord. **Amen.**

20.42   FOR THIS HOUSE OF PRAYER
Unknown

O God, make the doorway of this house wide enough to receive all who need human love and fellowship; narrow enough to shut out all envy, pride and strife. Make its threshold smooth enough to be no stumbling-block to children, or barrier to the elderly and disabled. Let its door be rugged and strong to turn back the tempter's power, but open and inviting to those who are your guests: God, make this house the doorway to your eternal kingdom; through Jesus Christ our Lord. **Amen.**

20.43   FOR YOUNG AND OLD
Editors

Creator God, you grant youth to see visions and age to dream dreams: help both young and old to understand each other. Let the young be courteous to the aged – neither resenting the lessons of experience nor the restraints of discipline; let those who are older look with sympathy at new ideas. Let age grant to youth this inheritance: the love that encourages and not the fear that represses. So may we all work together for your kingdom; for the sake of Jesus Christ our Lord. **Amen.**

▶ **20.44**   FOR PATIENCE
Christopher Idle

Grant, our Father,
that in this church
the younger may respect the traditions
   of the older,
and the older may understand
   the impatience of the younger;
so that young and old
may share together in your service,
and gladly recognise
that all are one in Jesus Christ. **Amen.**

▶ **20.45**   ABOUT OUR STEWARDSHIP
Michael Botting

Lord Jesus Christ,
you have taught us
that we cannot love both God and money,
and that all our possessions
are a trust from you:
teach us to be faithful stewards
of our time, our talents, and our money,
that we may help others extend your kingdom;
for your name's sake. **Amen.**

20.46   ABOUT OUR POSSESSIONS
Unknown

O Lord, you told us not to store up possessions for ourselves on
earth: help us to understand that everything we possess is a gift from
you – which you have given to us to enjoy, but not to cling to. So
help us to detach ourselves from our possessions, that we shall be
free to use them in the way that you want, through Jesus Christ our
Lord. **Amen.**

▶ **20.47** PROMISES/THANKSGIVING
From Revelations 2†

Hear the promises of Jesus, the first and the last, the living one, who was dead but now is alive for ever and ever, who has authority over death and the world of the dead:

Those who win the victory will eat from the tree of life:
thank you, Lord Jesus.

Those who win the victory will not be hurt by the second death:
thank you, Lord Jesus.

Those who win the victory will receive a new name:
thank you, Lord Jesus.

Those who win the victory will receive authority from the Father:
thank you, Lord Jesus.

Those who win the victory will be clothed in white, and their names not removed from the book of the living:
thank you, Lord Jesus. Amen.

▶ **20.48** DEDICATION
Liturgical Commission

God and Father,
whose Son our Lord Jesus Christ was rich
yet became poor for our sake,
to make us rich out of his poverty;
by your grace let our lives overflow
in a wealth of generous service
to you and to our neighbour;
through the same Jesus Christ our Lord. **Amen.**

▶ **20.49** AFTER INTERCESSION
From 'A New Zealand Prayer Book'

Those things, good Lord,
that your servants have prayed for,
give us grace to work for;
and in the purpose of your love
answer our prayers and fulfil our hopes
for Jesus' sake. **Amen.**

▶ **20.50** THANKSGIVING FOR OUR HERITAGE
Editors

We thank God for every gracious influence of godly people:

For parents who were examples of the spiritual truths they believed:
with grateful hearts,
our God, we bring you thanks.

For teachers who loved, taught and trained us: with grateful hearts,
our God, we bring you thanks.

For patterns of worship, in music, word and action: with grateful
hearts,
our God, we bring you thanks.

For customs of practice and ministry: with grateful hearts.
our God, we bring you thanks.

Help us not to deny our heritage,
remind us that
you are the giver of every good and perfect gift,
and strengthen us
that we may offer ourselves for your service,
to the glory of your name. Amen.

▶ **20.51** THANKSGIVING: CONCLUSION
From Ephesians 5

We give thanks for everything to God the Father in the name of our
Lord Jesus Christ. **Amen.**

▶ **20.52** ACT OF DEDICATION
Editors

Lord God, holy Father, since you have called us through Christ to
share in a gracious Covenant, we take upon ourselves afresh the
yoke of obedience. And, for love of you, we engage ourselves in the
task of witness to our neighbours and service to them in your name;
each of us saying:

I am no longer my own, but yours –
send me where you will,
rank me with whom you will;
let me be employed for you,
or laid aside for you;

exalted for you,
or brought low for you;
let me be full, let me be empty;
let me have all things,
let me have nothing.

Freely and wholeheartedly
I yield my life and all I possess
to your pleasure and disposal. Amen.

▶ **20.53** PRAYER OF DEDICATION
Editors

We offer to God our skills and our service, our lives and our
worship:

O God, you have given us life and health and strength, and in Jesus
Christ you have given us a saviour and a friend.

For the love that made you enter our world in Jesus to share our joys
and sorrows and to die for our sin: Father,
receive the gift of our love.

For the forgiveness you promise to all who confess their sins and
trust in his sacrifice on the cross: Father,
receive the gift of our penitence.

For the hope of eternal life we have in Christ because you raised him
from the dead: Father,
receive the gift of our lives.

For the blessing of friendship and the satisfaction of working
together, for the stretching of mind and the exercise of body: Father,
receive the gift of our service.

Because you are the Lord of all, yet your ears are open to our cry;
and because we delight to praise you: Father,
receive the gift of our worship.

Holy, holy, holy Lord,
God of power and might
heaven and earth
are full of your glory.
Hosanna in the highest. Amen.

20.54   COMMITMENT
Editors

Lord God, our Father, in your gracious love, draw near to us as we reach out to you; wash all sin from us, and sanctify us to be a part of your great work. We acknowledge that we are completely dependent on you, and so we pray that you will revive us by the power of your Holy Spirit and lead us into a deeper relationship with you.

We want to trust you in all things, Lord; strengthen our faith and make us sensitive to your gentle prompting; guide us each day into your path of truth and obedience. Help us to be willing to accept change – and to change ourselves if you so direct; may we always obey you – humbly and without question. Open our eyes to the needs of others, and inspire us to show the love of Christ and to share with them the treasure of his Gospel of peace.

We offer ourselves to you, Father: make us fit for your service, for the sake of our precious Saviour, Jesus Christ. **Amen.**

▶ 20.55   FOR OBEDIENCE
Liturgical Commission

Lord Jesus Christ,
Son of the living God;
teach us to walk in your way more trustfully,
to accept your truth more faithfully,
to share your life more lovingly;
so that we may come
by the power of the Holy Spirit
as one family
to the kingdom of the Father
where you live for ever and ever. **Amen.**

▶ 20.56   OFFERTORY PRAYER
Stanley Pritchard

Heavenly Father,
let these gifts go where we cannot go,
and help those whom we cannot reach;
through them
let the unlearned be taught,
the hungry fed,

the sick healed,
and the lost found;
for Jesus' sake. **Amen.**

▶ **20.57**   GOING OUT FROM WORSHIP
Michael Botting, adapted

Be with us, O God, as we go out in your name:
may the lips that have sung your praises
always speak the truth;
may the ears which have heard your word
listen only to what is good;
and may our lives as well as our worship
be always pleasing to you,
for the glory of Jesus Christ our Lord. **Amen.**

▶ **20.58**   DEDICATION
Editors

Father, we dedicate ourselves
to serve you faithfully
and to follow Christ,
to face the future with him,
seeking his special purpose for our lives.
Send us out now to work and to witness
freely, gratefully and hopefully,
in the power of the Holy Spirit,
and for the honour and glory of your Son,
Jesus Christ our Lord. **Amen.**

▶ **20.59**   DEDICATION
Traditional

O God,
strengthen your servants with your heavenly grace,
that we may continue yours for ever,
and daily increase in your Holy Spirit more and more,
until we come to your everlasting kingdom. **Amen.**

▶ **20.60** DEDICATION
Sarum Primer, 1527

God be in my head and in my understanding,
God be in my eyes and in my looking,
God be in my mouth and in my speaking,
God be in my heart and in my thinking,
God be at my end and at my departing. **Amen.**

▶ **20.61** ASCRIPTION
From Ephesians 3†

Now to God the Father
who is able to do immeasurably more than all we ask or think
because the Spirit's power is at work in us:
to him be glory in the Church and in Christ Jesus
throughout all generations
for ever and ever! **Amen.**

▶ **20.62** BLESSING
From Psalm 128†

The blessing of the Lord be upon *you:*
we bless you in the name of the Lord. Amen.

20.63 BLESSING
From Ephesians 6.23†

Peace be to *you* and love with faith, from God the Father and the
Lord Jesus Christ; grace be with all those who love our Lord Jesus
Christ in sincerity; and the blessing of God – Father, Son and Holy
Spirit, be with *you* always. **Amen.**

20.64 BLESSING
From Jude†

Build yourselves up in your most holy faith, pray in the Holy Spirit,
keep yourselves in the love of God, wait for the mercy of our Lord
Jesus Christ to bring you to eternal life; and the blessing of God
almighty, the Father, the Son and the Holy Spirit, be with you
always. **Amen.**

20.65 EVENING BLESSING
From Psalm 134†

Praise the Lord, all you his servants who worship in his house in the evening of the day, who lift up your hands in his presence and praise the Lord. The Lord, the maker of heaven and earth, bless *you* from his holy place; (may) the Father, the Son and the Holy Spirit go with *you*. **Amen.**

Harvest Thanksgiving

▶ **21.1** GREETING
From Philemon 1†

Grace to you and peace from God our Father and the Lord Jesus
Christ. **Amen.**

21.2 SENTENCE
Psalm 50.23

The mighty One, God the Lord says, 'Giving thanks is the sacrifice
that honours me, and I will surely save all who obey me.'

21.3 SENTENCE
Genesis 8.22

As long as the earth endures, seedtime and harvest, cold and heat,
summer and winter, day and night will never cease.

21.4 SENTENCE
Genesis 33.11

God has been kind to us, and given us everything we need.

21.5 SENTENCE
Deuteronomy 16.15

The Lord your God will bless you in your harvest, and in all the
work of your hands, and your joy will be complete.

21.6 SENTENCE
Luke 6.38

(Jesus said:) Give, and it will be given to you. A good measure,
pressed down, shaken together and running over, will be poured
into your lap. For with the measure you use, it will be measured to
you.

21.7 SENTENCE
Hosea 10.12

God said, 'Plough new ground for yourselves, plant righteousness, and reap the blessings that your devotion to me will produce. It is time for you to turn to me, your Lord, and I will come and pour out blessings upon you.'

▶ **21.8** RESPONSE
From Psalm 67†

The land has yielded its harvest:
God, our God, has blessed us.

God *has* blessed us:
let everyone everywhere honour him! Amen.

▶ **21.9** RESPONSE
From Joel 2†

We have plenty to eat and are satisfied:
Praise the Lord our God
who has done wonderful things. Amen.

▶ **21.10** APPROACH
Editors

Our Heavenly Father, we rejoice this day that you have again fulfilled your promise that 'seed–time and harvest will not cease'. We thank you for the seasonal miracle which sustains human life; we have buried the dust-like seed in the dark soil, you have brought it to birth and fulness of life. So, you supply the needs of our bodies; you provide in abundance, and we are satisfied with good things.

For the ever-changing seasons of the year, for all the beauty of your creation, for the sheer loveliness of the earth as the bursting ears of corn sway in a gentle breeze: today, O Lord, we thank you
and rejoice together in your love.

For the astonishing beauty of the structure of matter, of flower and of fruit, for the energising sun beaming its life-giving rays upon the earth, summoning seed to grow in the warmed and fruitful soil, for the soft sweetness of the gentle rain and its life-giving moisture: today, O Lord, we thank you
and rejoice together in your love.

For those who have laboured on the land, for their skill and handed-down wisdom, for their diligence, dexterity and courage in days of difficulty and disappointment: today, O Lord, we thank you
and rejoice together in your love.

Most of all we praise you that you are at work in us; that through the energy of your Holy Spirit we may know the power of your everlasting love for us revealed in Jesus. For the miracle of spiritual rebirth in human lives; for your presence generating in us the grace and beauty of our Saviour: today, O Lord, we thank you
and rejoice together in your love.

In response to all these,
your many and rich blessings:
today, we celebrate your faithfulness
and honour you with our harvest thanksgiving. Amen.

▶ **21.11** PRAISE
From Psalm 103†

Praise the Lord, O my soul
and do not forget his blessings.

He crowns us with his love
and satisfies our need.

▶ **21.12** CONFESSION
Editor

O God our Father, we confess that we have often used your gifts carelessly, and acted as though we were not grateful. Hear our prayer, and in your mercy forgive us and help us:

When we enjoy the fruits of the harvest, but forget they come from you – then, Father, in your mercy,
forgive us and help us.

When we are full and satisfied, but ignore the cry of the hungry and those in need – then, Father, in your mercy,
forgive us and help us.

When we are thoughtless, and do not treat with respect or care the wonderful world you have made – then, Father, in your mercy,
forgive us and help us.

When we store up goods for ourselves alone, as if there were no God
and no heaven – then, Father, in your mercy,
forgive us and help us.

Grant us thankful hearts
and a loving concern for all people;
through Jesus Christ our Lord. Amen.

▶ **21.13**   CONFESSION
Editors

Lord God, forgive us that though we live in a rich world of plenty,
we so often tolerate poverty.

Children die through our indifference:
forgive us, good Lord.

Young people are deprived because of inherited selfishness:
forgive us, good Lord.

Men and women are embittered by injustice or poverty:
forgive us, good Lord.

Stir us to consider our priorities,
strengthen our wills to examine the way we live,
guide all who make political decisions which affect the poor:
in the name of him
who, though he was rich,
yet for our sakes became poor
that we, through his poverty,
might become rich;
Jesus Christ, our Lord. Amen.

▶ **21.14**   CONFESSION
From Isaiah 43†

O Lord our God,
we confess that we have not called upon you,
nor have we tried hard to serve you;
we have not given to you from our wealth,
nor have we honoured you
with the work of our hands;
but we have burdened you with our sins,
and wearied you with our wrongdoing:

**blot out our transgressions
and remember our sin no more,
for your name's sake. Amen.**

21.15 ABSOLUTION
From Isaiah 49†

Hear the assurance of God's forgiveness:

In the time of his favour the Lord answers you; in the day of salvation he helps you; the Lord comforts you, he has compassion upon you; he has not forsaken you, nor has he forgotten you. Lift up your eyes and look around: the Lord is your saviour and your redeemer: in Christ you are forgiven. **Amen.**

▶ 21.16 COLLECT
Harvest, ASB 1980

Almighty and everlasting God,
we offer you our hearty thanks
for your fatherly goodness and care
in giving us the fruits of the earth in their seasons.
Give us grace to use them rightly,
    to your glory,
    for our own well-being,
    and for the relief of those in need;
through Jesus Christ our Lord. **Amen.**

▶ 21.17 COLLECT
Rogation Days, ASB 1980

Almighty God,
you have provided
the resources of the world
to maintain the life of your children,
and have so ordered our life
that we are dependent upon each other.
Bless us all in our daily work
and, as you have given us
    the knowledge to produce plenty

so give us the will
to bring it within reach of all;
through Jesus Christ our Lord. **Amen.**

▶ **21.18** PSALM
Psalm 65.1–13†

The congregation may divide at A *and* B

O God, it is right for us to praise you, because you answer our prayers:

You care for the land and water it:
A **and make it rich and fertile.**

You fill the running streams with water:
B **and irrigate the land.**

You soften the ground with showers:
A **and make the young crops grow.**

You crown the year with goodness:
B **and give us a plentiful harvest.**

The pastures are filled with flocks:
A **the hillsides are clothed with joy.**

The fields are covered with grain:
ALL **they shout for joy and sing. Amen.**

21.19 READING: LAWS ABOUT HARVEST
From Deuteronomy 14.22–29, 16.9–12; Leviticus 23.15–21, 22

Cast: Leviticus, Deuteronomy

Leviticus
Count seven full weeks from the day after the Sabbath on which you bring your sheaf of corn to present to the Lord. On the fiftieth day, the day after the seventh Sabbath, present to the Lord another new offering of corn. Each family is to bring two loaves of bread and present them to the Lord as a special gift. Each loaf shall be made of two kilogrammes of flour baked with yeast and shall be presented to the Lord as an offering of the first corn to be harvested . . . On that day do none of your daily work, but gather for worship. Your descendants are to observe this regulation for all time to come, no matter where they live.

Deuteronomy

Set aside a tithe – a tenth of all that your fields produce each year. Then go to the one place where the Lord your God has chosen to be worshipped; and there in his presence eat the tithes of your corn, wine, and olive-oil, and the first-born of your cattle and sheep. Do this so that you may learn to honour the Lord your God always . . . Do not neglect the Levites who live in your towns; they have no property of their own. At the end of every third year bring the tithe of all your crops and store it in your towns. This food is for the Levites, since they own no property, and for the foreigners, orphans, and widows who live in your towns. They are to come and get all they need. Do this, and the Lord your God will bless you in everything you do.

Leviticus

When you harvest your fields, do not cut the corn at the edges of the fields, and do not go back to cut the ears of corn that were left; leave them for poor people and foreigners. The Lord is your God.

Deuteronomy

Count seven weeks from the time that you begin to harvest the corn, and then celebrate the Harvest Festival, to honour the Lord your God, by bringing him a freewill offering in proportion to the blessing he has given you. Be joyful in the Lord's presence, together with your children, your servants, and the Levites, foreigners, orphans, and widows who live in your towns. Do this at the one place of worship. Be sure that you obey these commands; do not forget that you were slaves in Egypt.

Cast
   [This is] the word of the Lord.

All
   Thanks be to God.

21.20   READING: HARVEST OFFERINGS
Deuteronomy 26.1–15

Cast: Moses, Worshipper

Moses

After you have occupied the land that the Lord your God is giving you and have settled there, each of you must place in a basket the first part of each crop that you harvest and you must take it with you to the one place of worship. Go to the priest in charge at that time and say to him:

Worshipper

I now acknowledge to the Lord my God that I have entered the land that he promised our ancestors to give us.

Moses

The priest will take the basket from you and place it before the altar of the Lord your God. Then, in the Lord's presence you will recite these words:

Worshipper

My ancestor was a wandering Aramean, who took his family to Egypt to live. They were few in number when they went there, but they became a large and powerful nation. The Egyptians treated us harshly and forced us to work as slaves. Then we cried out for help to the Lord, the God of our ancestors. He heard us and saw our suffering, hardship, and misery. By his great power and strength he rescued us from Egypt. He worked miracles and wonders, and caused terrifying things to happen. He brought us here and gave us this rich and fertile land. So now I bring to the Lord the first part of the harvest that he has given me.

Moses

Then set the basket down in the Lord's presence and worship there. Be grateful for the good things that the Lord your God has given you and your family; and let the Levites and the foreigners who live among you join in the celebration. Every third year give the tithe – a tenth of your crops – to the Levites, the foreigners, the orphans, and the widows, so that in every community they will have all they need to eat. When you have done this, say to the Lord:

Worshipper

None of the sacred tithe is left in my house; I have given it to the Levites, the foreigners, the orphans, and the widows, as you commanded me to do. I have not disobeyed or forgotten any of your commands concerning the tithe. I have not eaten any of it when I was mourning; I have not taken any of it out of my house when I was ritually unclean; and I have not given any of it as an offering for the dead. I have obeyed you, O Lord; I have done everything you commanded concerning the tithe. Look down from your holy place in heaven and bless your people Israel; bless also the rich and fertile land that you have given us, as you promised our ancestors.

Cast
[This is] the word of the Lord.

All
Thanks be to God.

21.21   READING: THE RICH MAN (*LONGER VERSION*)
Luke 12.13–21

Cast: Narrator, Man, Jesus, Rich Man, God

Narrator
A man in the crowd said to Jesus:

Man (*angrily*)
Teacher, tell my brother to divide with me the property our father left us.

[Narrator
Jesus answered him:]

Jesus (*to the Man*)
My friend, who gave me the right to judge or to divide the property between you two?

Narrator
And he went on to say to them all:

Jesus (*to everyone*)
Watch out and guard yourselves from every kind of greed; because a person's true life is not made up of the things he owns, no matter how rich he may be.

Narrator
Then Jesus told them this parable:

Jesus
There was once a rich man who had land which bore good crops. He began to think to himself:

Rich man
I haven't anywhere to keep all my crops. What can I do? (PAUSE TO THINK)

This is what I will do; I will tear down my barns and build bigger ones, where I will store my corn and all my other goods. Then I will say to myself, 'Lucky man! You have all the good things you need for many years. Take life easy, eat, drink, and enjoy yourself!'

Jesus

But God said to him:

God

You fool! This very night you will have to give up your life; then who will get all these things you have kept for yourself?

Narrator

And Jesus concluded:

Jesus

This is how it is with those who pile up riches for themselves but are not rich in God's sight.

Cast

[This is] the word of the Lord.   OR   This is the Gospel of Christ/
                                                              This is the Gospel of the Lord.

All

    Thanks be to God.   **Praise to Christ our Lord/
                                                              Praise to you, Lord Jesus Christ.**

21.22   READING: THE RICH MAN (*SHORTER VERSION*)
Luke 12.16–21

Cast: Jesus, Rich man, God

Jesus

There was once a rich man who had land which bore good crop. He began to think to himself:

Rich man

I haven't anywhere to keep all my crops. What can I do?

Jesus

He told himself:

Rich man

This is what I will do; I will tear down my barns and build bigger ones, where I will store my corn and all my other goods. Then will say to myself, 'Lucky man! You have all the good things you need for many years. Take life easy, eat, drink, and enjoy yourself!'

Jesus
But God said to him:

God
You fool! This very night you will have to give up your life; then who will get all these things you have kept for yourself?

Jesus
This is how it is with those who pile up riches for themselves but are not rich in God's sight.

Cast
[This is] the word of the Lord.   OR   This is the Gospel of Christ/
This is the Gospel of the Lord.

All
Thanks be to God.   **Praise to Christ our Lord/**
Praise to you, Lord Jesus Christ.

FURTHER BIBLE READINGS
Readings appropriate to this theme will be found listed in our companion volume. 'The Dramatised Bible' (published by HarperCollins) on index page 432.

▶ **21.23**   CREED
Alternative Service Book 1980, adapted

**We believe and trust in God the Father
who made the world.**

**We believe and trust in his Son Jesus Christ,
who redeemed mankind.**

**We believe and trust in his Holy Spirit,
who gives life to the people of God.**

**We believe and trust in one God:
Father, Son, and Holy Spirit. Amen.**

▶ **21.24**   A HARVEST CREED
From Psalm 65†

We believe in one God who answers our prayers:

Has he given us victory, and done wonderful things to save us?
He has!

384

Did he set the mountains in place by his strength, and calm the roar of the seas?
He did!

Do his deeds bring shouts of joy from one end of the earth to the other?
They do!

Does he make the land rich and fertile; does he fill the streams with water, and provide the earth with crops; does he send rain on the fields, and soften the soil with showers, and make the young plants grow; does he fill the pastures with herds; does he cover the hills with sheep, and the valleys with golden wheat?
He does!

Do his people shout and sing for joy?
We do! Amen.

▶ **21.25**   OFFERING AT 'LAMMAS'/HARVEST
D. L. Couper, adapted

In the name of the farmers and farmworkers of . . . , we come to offer our gifts to God in thanksgiving for his blessing [and to pray for our harvest].

We bring before you, O Lord, this sheaf, the first-fruits of our harvest, in token of the gratitude in our hearts.
Blest be God for ever.

We bring before you, O Lord, this loaf, made from the first ears of the ripe corn, in humble acknowledgement of our dependence on all your gifts.
Blest be God for ever.

We bring before you Lord this token of the wealth that you have given us, and with it we offer the love of our hearts and the service of our lives.
Yours, Lord, is the greatness, the power,
the glory, the splendour, and the majesty;
for everything in heaven and on earth is yours.
All things come from you,
and of your own do we give you. Amen.

▶ **21.26** OFFERING AT HARVEST
From Genesis 33†

Spoken by a member of the congregation to the Minister of the church

M, please accept these gifts which we have brought:
God has been kind to us
and given us everything we need. **Amen.**

OR

21.27 OFFERING PRAYER
From Genesis 33†

Lord, please accept these gifts which we have brought: you have
been kind to us and given us everything we need. **Amen.**

21.28 FOR THE HUNGRY
From 'New Every Morning'

We thank you, Lord and Creator of all things, for the blessings of this
life and the abundant variety of your gifts; for the food we eat and
the pleasure it gives us. But we know that millions have less than
enough while others eat to excess; food is wasted while many starve,
nature's resources are misused to bring profit to the already rich.
Forgive us, Lord, our selfishness, and open our hearts to the needs of
the hungry wherever they may be, for the sake of our Lord Jesus
Christ. **Amen.**

21.29 FOR HEALING IN THE WORLD
Dick Williams

Thank you, Lord Jesus, for stopping to listen to every sick person
who called out to you; thank you for healing every kind of sickness
there is, for feeding the hungry, for setting people free and for raising
the dead. Bless all throughout the world who are trying to follow
your example; bless those who are taking food to the hungry people,
medicine to sick people, proper forms of government to nations
which do not have real freedom, and your holy gospel to those
whose love for other people is dead. Bless them all, and bless all the
sick, sad and lonely people to whom they go, for your dear name's
sake. **Amen.**

21.30 FOR THE UNDER-PRIVILEGED
George Appleton

O merciful and loving Father of all, look down, we pray, on the hungry millions in the world today who are at the mercy of disease. Grant that we who live so comfortably and gently may have true sympathy with them, and do all in our power to help them to that full life which is your will: through Jesus Christ our Lord. **Amen.**

21.31 FOR REFUGEES
Editors

Loving Father, we pray for millions of silent people today – refugees, displaced persons, forced to live in tents or shacks, often in camps herded together; we pray for people whose harvest has failed for years, who must listen to the sobs of children with daily hunger pains. Forgive us that we see such pictures and hear such stories so often that we almost cease to notice or care; strengthen every missionary, every church organisation, every national fund seeking to rescue the forgotten millions; and show us how we can best help these our neighbours in need. Hear our prayer and enliven our response for Jesus' sake. **Amen.**

21.32 FOR ALL WHO NEED OUR AID
C. S .Woodward

Our Father in heaven, help us, we pray, to give to all the peoples of the earth the food and warmth and clothing which they need; have mercy upon those who are cold and hungry, and give your people no rest until poverty and famine have been driven from your world; in the name of our saviour, Jesus Christ. **Amen.**

21.33 FOR RELIEF WORKERS
Rita Snowden

Bless, O God, all who dedicate their powers today to the making of peace in the world; bless all who give their training and experience to feed, clothe and house the destitute; bless all who lend their energies and skills to teach impoverished people to till their land, to water it, and harvest it. Give us all a lively concern for the underprivileged, and show us practical ways of helping; for Christ's sake. **Amen.**

▶ **21.34** THANKSGIVING
D. L. Couper

For the rich soil of the countryside, for good seed, and for the green corn springing out of the earth, we thank you O God,
and praise your holy name.

For the warm sweetness of the fertile rain, for the hot days of ripening sun, and for the harvest, we thank you O God,
and praise your holy name.

For the yield of the forests, the earth and the sea, we thank you O God,
and praise your holy name.

For all who work on the land, in the mines, or on the waters, and for their courage in days of difficulty and disappointment, we thank you O God,
and praise your holy name.

For those who work in office, shop, factory or in transport, to meet our needs, we thank you O God,
and praise your holy name.

For these and all your blessings we make our harvest thanksgiving and give you all the glory:

Glory to the Father, and to the Son,
and to the Holy Spirit,
as it was in the beginning, is now,
and shall be for ever. Amen.

▶ **21.35** THANKSGIVING FOR THE HARVEST
Christopher Idle

We thank you, God,
for the harvest of all good things:
for making plants to grow in the earth,
for giving farmers strength to work,
for supplying the food we have each day.
Teach us to use your gifts fairly and generously
and to remember that *you* gave them to us;
through Jesus Christ our Lord. **Amen.**

▶ **21.36**   THANKSGIVING FOR THE HARVEST
Jamie Wallace

Thank you, God, for the harvest:

For farmers ploughing and digging, tending and reaping the crops, breeding flocks and herds: God, we give you thanks,
and bring you our praise.

For fishermen, miners and oilmen who live dangerously to feed and warm us: God, we give you thanks,
and bring you our praise.

For businessmen and women, sailors and airmen, and those who drive lorries and trains bringing the food to our shops: God, we give you thanks,
and bring you our praise.

For shopkeepers, check-out staff and roundspeople; for those who cook meals and lay tables and do the washing up: God, we give you thanks,
and bring you our praise.

All this work that people do – and your miraculous gifts of soil and frost, sunshine and rain, and the mystery of growth and ripening!
Forgive us, heavenly Father,
for taking it so much for granted.

Forgive us also for the times we have been selfish with the things that you have given.
Help us to see the wonder of it all;
show us how to help hungry people
to have their fair share
for Jesus' sake. Amen.

▶ **21.37**   THANKSGIVING FOR THE HARVEST
Dick Williams, adapted

Lord of all creation, we gratefully acknowledge our dependence on you for all the good things we enjoy.

For the fruits of the earth, O Lord:
we give you thanks and praise.

For the harvest of the sea, O Lord:
we give you thanks and praise.

For the wealth of the mines, O Lord:
we give you thanks and praise.

For all the beauty of the world in which we live, O Lord:
we give you thanks and praise.

Accept our thanksgiving,
and fill our hearts with praise;
through Jesus Christ our Lord. Amen.

▶ **21.38**   WE GIVE THANKS FOR GOD'S PROVISION
Frank Colquhoun, adapted

Almighty God, we are taught by you that for our daily needs we are dependent not only on the work of our hands but also on your providence and care.

For your gifts to us in nature by which the earth is enriched and made fruitful: with thankful hearts,
we praise and adore you.

For the labours of those by whom the harvest is gathered in: with thankful hearts,
we praise and adore you.

For all that we receive at your hands: with thankful hearts,
we praise and adore you.

O God, teach us
that in the whole of life
we are workers together with you,
the author and giver of all good things;
through Jesus Christ our Lord. Amen.

▶ **21.39**   FOR GRATEFUL HEARTS
From 'New Every Morning'

Heavenly Father, giver of all things:
make us more thankful for what we have received,
make us more content with what we have,
make us more mindful of people in need,
and make us more ready to help and serve them
    in whatever way we can,
as servants of Jesus Christ our Lord. **Amen.**

▶ **21.40** ABOUT OUR POSSESSIONS
Michael Botting

Lord Jesus Christ,
you have taught us
that we cannot love both God and money,
and that all our possessions
are a trust from you:
teach us to be faithful stewards
of our time, our talents, and our money,
that we may help others extend your kingdom;
for your name's sake. **Amen.**

21.41 BLESSING
From Numbers 6†

The Lord bless *you* and take care of *you*; the Lord be kind and
gracious to *you*; the Lord look on *you* with favour and give *you* peace.
Amen.

21.42 BLESSING
From Psalm 37

Trust the Lord and do right, find him in your happiness and your
heart's desire, give yourself to him, wait patiently for him; and the
Lord God almighty bring you prosperity and peace. **Amen.**

Christian Character and Conflict,
Our Work, Schools

▶ **22.1** GREETING
From Revelation 1†

Grace and peace to you from Jesus Christ, who is the faithful witness, the firstborn from the dead. **Amen.**

22.2 SENTENCE
1 Corinthians 15.58

Stand firm. Let nothing move you. Always give yourselves fully to the work of the Lord, because you know that your labour in the Lord is not in vain.

22.3 SENTENCE
Philippians 1.29

It has been granted to us that for the sake of Christ we should not only believe in him, but also suffer for his sake.

22.4 SENTENCE
2 Timothy 2. 11,13

Here is a trustworthy saying: If we died with him we will also live with him; if we endure, we will also reign with him. If we disown him, he will also disown us; if we are faithless, he will remain faithful, for he cannot disown himself.

22.5 SENTENCE
Hebrews 12. 22–24

We have come to Mount Zion, to the city of the living God, the heavenly Jerusalem with its thousands of angels; we have come to the joyful gathering of God's first-born, whose names are written in heaven; we have come to God who is the judge of all the world; we have come to him who sealed the new covenant in his own blood, Jesus Christ our Lord.

▶ **22.6** RESPONSE
From 1 Peter 5†

The God of all grace who calls you in Christ will himself make you strong, firm, and steadfast:
to him be the power for ever and ever. Amen.

▶ **22.7** RESPONSE
From Revelation 7†

Salvation belongs to our God, who sits on the throne, and to the Lamb:
Amen!

Praise and glory
and wisdom and thanks and honour
and power and strength
be to our God for ever and ever. Amen.

22.8 APPROACH
Editors

Our God, your eyes are open day and night watching your children, your ears are always ready to listen to their prayer: we have come to worship you. We come as sinners, in need of your forgiveness; we come tired from our work, in need of refreshment and recreation; we come with worries, in need of your guidance. But first, lift us out of our pre-occupation with our own needs; allow us to see you with the eyes of faith, and to hear with understanding what you say to us; make us thankful for all the good we have received from you; awaken in us a longing to do what is right, and make us aware of the great company, past, present and to come, with whom we join to worship you in the name of Jesus our Lord. **Amen.**

▶ **22.9** PRAISE
From Psalm 117†

Praise the Lord, all you nations;
extol him all you peoples!

For his love protecting us is strong;
his faithfulness endures for ever!

▶ **22.10** PRAISE
Psalm 117. 1–2†

Praise the Lord, all you nations:
praise him, all you people!

Great is his love towards us:
his faithfulness shall last for ever.

Praise the Lord:
Amen.

▶ **22.11** CONFESSION
Guy King

Heavenly Father,
we are here to worship you,
but first we ask you
to forgive us all our sins:
so many wrong things
we ought not to have done,
we have done;
so many right things we ought to have done
we have not done.
In your mercy forgive us –
help us to do right,
and to reject what is wrong;
through Jesus Christ our Lord. Amen.

▶ **22.12** CONFESSION
Editors

Father,
we are truly sorry for causing you grief
and we repent.
Please forgive us
and cast away all shadows of guilt.
Cleanse us, release us, bless us, refresh us.
And bring us once again into your glorious light,
so that we may receive your comfort
and rejoice in your love;
through Jesus our redeemer. Amen.

22.13 ABSOLUTION
From Isaiah 41†

Receive forgiveness in the name of our God, the first and the last:
you are his servant, he has chosen you and has not rejected you – do
not fear for he is with you; do not be dismayed for he is your God –
he will strengthen you and help you; he will uphold you with his
righteous right hand; through Jesus Christ our Lord. **Amen.**

▶ **22.14** COLLECT
Pentecost 9, ASB 1980

Almighty God,
you call us to your service:
give us strength to put on the armour you provide
that we may resist the assaults of the devil,
and ever trust in the salvation
which you have promised us
in Jesus Christ our Lord. **Amen.**

▶ **22.15** PSALM
Psalm 46.1–11†

The congregation may divide at A *and* B; V *can be a distant voice, or said by
the minister.*

God is our refuge and strength:
an ever-present help in trouble.

Therefore we will not fear:
A **though the earth should shake,**
B **though the mountains fall into the sea,**
A **though the waters surge and foam,**
B **though the mountains shake and roar.**

The Lord almighty is with us:
ALL **the God of Jacob is our fortress.**

There is a river whose streams make glad the city of God, the
holy place where the Most High dwells.
A **God is within her, she will not fall:**
B **God will help her at break of day.**

Nations are in uproar, kingdoms fall:
A **God lifts his voice –**
B **the earth melts away.**

The Lord Almighty is with us:
ALL **the God of Jacob is our fortress.**

Come and see what God has done:
ALL **his devastation on the earth!**
He stops the wars throughout the world:

A **he breaks the bow and shatters the spear –**
B **he sets the shield on fire.**

V Be still, and know that I am God: I will be exalted over the nations, I will be exalted over the earth.

The Lord Almighty is with us:
ALL **the God of Jacob is our fortress. Amen.**

▶ **22.16** PSALM
Psalm 66.1–20†

The congregation may divide at A, B, *and* C

Praise your God with shouts of joy:
all the earth, sing praise to him.

Sing the glory of his name:
A **offer him your highest praise.**

Say to him: How great you are:
B **wonderful the things you do!**

All your enemies bow down:
C **all the earth sings praise to you.**

Come and see what God has done:
A **causing mortal men to fear –**
B **for he turned the sea to land,**
C **let his people safely through.**

We rejoice at what he does –
A **ruling through eternity,**
B **watching over all the world,**
C **keeping every rebel down.**

Praise our God, you nations, praise:
A **let the sound of praise be heard!**
B **God sustains our very lives:**
C **keeps our feet upon the way.**

Once, you tested us, O God –
A **silver purified by fire –**

Let us fall into a trap,
B **placed hard burdens on our backs –**

Sent us through the flame and flood:
C **now you bring us safely home.**

I will come to worship you:
A **bring to you my offering,**
B **give you what I said I would,**
C **when the troubles threatened me.**

All who love and honour God:
A **come and listen, while I tell**
B **what great things he did for me**
C **when I cried to him for help,**
A **when I praised him with my songs.**

B **When my heart was free from sin,**
C **then he listened to my prayer.**

Praise the Lord who heard my cry:
ALL **God has shown his love to me! Amen.**

22.17 READING: DAVID DEFEATS GOLIATH
From 1 Samuel 17.40–50

Cast: Narrator, Goliath, David

Narrator
David took his shepherd's stick and then picked up five smooth stones from the stream and put them in his bag. With his catapult ready, he went out to meet Goliath. The Philistine started walking towards David, with his shield-bearer walking in front of him. He kept coming closer, and when he got a good look at David, he was filled with scorn for him because he was just a nice, good-looking boy. [He said to David:]

Goliath
What's that stick for? Do you think I'm a dog?

Narrator

He called down curses from his god on David. He challenged David:

Goliath

Come on, I will give your body to the birds and animals to eat.

Narrator

[David answered:]

David

You are coming against me with sword, spear, and javelin, but I come against you in the name of the Lord Almighty, the God of the Israelite armies, which you have defied. This very day the Lord will put you in my power; I will defeat you and cut off your head. And I will give the bodies of the Philistine soldiers to the birds and animals to eat. Then the whole world will know that Israel has a God, and everyone here will see that the Lord does not need swords or spears to save his people. He is victorious in battle, and he will put all of you in our power.

Narrator

Goliath started walking towards David again, and David ran quickly towards the Philistine battle line to fight him. He put his hand into his bag and took out a stone, which he slung at Goliath. It hit him on the forehead and broke his skull, and Goliath fell face downwards on the ground. And so, without a sword, David defeated and killed Goliath – with a catapult and a stone!

Cast

[This is] the word of the Lord.

All

Thanks be to God.

22.18   READING: SOLOMON'S PRAYER
2 Chronicles 6.22–31

Cast: Voice 1, Voice 2

Voice 1

When a person is accused of wronging another and is brought to your altar in this Temple to take an oath that he is innocent –

Voice 2

O Lord, listen in heaven and judge your servants. Punish the guilty one as he deserves and acquit the one who is innocent.

Voice 1

When your people Israel are defeated by their enemies because they have sinned against you and then they turn to you and come to this Temple, humbly praying to you for forgiveness –

Voice 2

Listen to them in heaven. Forgive the sins of your people and bring them back to the land which you gave to them and to their ancestors.

Voice 1

When you hold back the rain because your people have sinned against you and then when they repent and face this Temple, humbly praying to you –

Voice 2

O Lord, listen to them in heaven and forgive the sins of your servants, the people of Israel, and teach them to do what is right. Then, O Lord, send rain on this land of yours, which you gave to your people as a permanent possession.

Voice 1

When there is famine in the land or an epidemic or the crops are destroyed by scorching winds or swarms of locusts, or when your people are attacked by their enemies, or when there is disease or sickness among them –

Voice 2

Listen to their prayers.

Voice 1

If any of your people Israel, out of heartfelt sorrow, stretch out their hands in prayer towards this Temple –

Voice 2

Hear their prayer. Listen to them in your home in heaven and forgive them. You alone know the thoughts of the human heart. Deal with each person as he deserves, so that your people may honour you and obey you all the time they live in the land which you gave to our ancestors.

Cast

[This is] the word of the Lord.

All

Thanks be to God.

22.19 READING: THE WHOLE ARMOUR OF GOD
Ephesians 6.10–18

Cast: Voice 1, Voice 2 [urgent], Voice 3 [can be the same as Voice 1]

Voice 1
Build up your strength in union with the Lord and by means of his mighty power.

Voice 2
Put on all the armour that God gives you, so that you will be able to stand up against the Devil's evil tricks.

Voice 1
For we are not fighting against human beings but against the wicked spiritual forces in the heavenly world, the rulers, authorities, and cosmic powers of this dark age.

Voice 2
So put on God's armour now!

Voice 1
Then when the evil day comes, you will be able to resist the enemy's attacks; and after fighting to the end, you will still hold your ground.

Voice 2
So stand ready –

Voice 3
With truth as a belt tight round your waist.

Voice 2
With righteousness as your breastplate.

Voice 3
And as your shoes, the readiness to announce the Good News of peace.

Voice 2
At all times carry faith as a shield; for with it you will be able to put out all the burning arrows shot by the Evil One.

Voice 3
And accept salvation as a helmet –

Voice 2
And the word of God as the sword which the Spirit gives you.

Voice 1
Do all this in prayer, asking for God's help. Pray on every occasion, as the Spirit leads. For this reason keep alert and never give up.

Cast
[This is] the word of the Lord.

All
Thanks be to God.

FURTHER BIBLE READINGS
Readings appropriate to this theme will be found listed in our companion volume, 'The Dramatised Bible' (published by HarperCollins) on index pages 432–434.

▶ **22.20** CREED
Hebrews 4.16†

Let us hold firmly to the faith we profess:

**We have a great High Priest
who has gone into the very presence of God;
one who can feel sympathy for our weakness,
who was tempted in every way that we are
but did not sin –
Jesus, the Son of God.**

Let us have confidence and approach God's throne, where we will receive mercy and grace to help us when we need it. **Amen.**

▶ **22.21** CREED
From 1 Timothy 3 and 2 Timothy 2†

Let us proclaim the mystery of our faith:

**We believe in one Lord Jesus Christ:
he was revealed in the flesh,
attested by the Spirit,
seen by angels,
proclaimed to the nations,
believed in throughout the world,
and taken up to glory. Amen.**

If we died with him,
we shall live with him.

If we endure,
we shall reign with him. Amen.

▶ **22.22**   CREED
From Revelation 1†

We believe in God almighty,
the Lord, the first and the last,
who is, who was and who is to come.

We believe in Jesus Christ,
the faithful witness,
the first to be raised from death,
the ruler of the kings of earth:
he loves us,
and by his sacrificial death
he has freed us from our sins
and made us a kingdom of priests
to serve our God and Father. Amen.

22.23   FOR WORKERS IN INDUSTRY
William Hampson

Almighty and everlasting God, we pray for all who work in industry. Bless meetings between employers and employees; remove all bitterness, distrust and prejudice from their deliberations. Give them your spirit of tolerance, and the earnest desire to seek for justice and truth; that they may work together for the common good, through Jesus Christ our Lord. **Amen.**

22.24   FOR THOSE WHO WORK IN SPORT
Dick Williams

We pray, Lord, for all engaged in professional sport as players or administrators. Help them to see their work as part of a wider life, and to remember that all life comes from you. Strengthen them to set for themselves the highest standards of personal and professional behaviour, both on and off the field; and for those who follow their fortunes may they provide an example to help make the heart of this great nation sound; through Jesus Christ our Lord. **Amen.**

22.25   FOR INDUSTRIAL PEACE
Editors

Lord of love and reconciliation, your desires for your created people are for peace and unity. We ask that your Holy Spirit may move upon our communities and industries to bring order out of confusion and agreement where there has been strife and resentment. Give to those who are engaged in conciliation your wisdom. Allow those who have deep grievances to think through their positions and to see each other's points of view. Give them the ability to discuss without acrimony and to listen without prejudice. Let a new spirit emerge which seeks the interest of all and the welfare of our common society; through Jesus Christ our Lord. **Amen.**

22.26   FOR REPRESENTATIVES IN THE WORKPLACE
William Hampson

Lord Jesus, you once worked with your hands at the carpenter's bench, and you know the difficulties of a working day: bless those who represent their fellow-workers' needs and meet with their employers in their name; may they see the problems clearly and try to solve them in the spirit you have shown us, for your truth and mercy's sake. **Amen.**

22.27   FOR TRADES UNIONS
Peter Markby

God our Father, we thank you for the trades unions and for all that they have achieved in the past to improve the wages and conditions of workers. We ask you to bless all union leaders that they may use the powers they possess wisely and well, and contribute to that justice in industrial relations which is essential to the wellbeing of all. And to all Christians with positions of responsibility in the unions give your guidance, that they may bring glory to your name, through Jesus Christ our Lord. **Amen.**

22.28 FOR THOSE MADE REDUNDANT
Editors

Bless, O Lord, all those who at the height of their powers have been deprived of their jobs. Help them and their families to adjust to this demand and deprivation, and enable them in their crisis to work together as a loving and courageous team. Grant that all who lose security of employment may find an inner security in Christ and, always being active in his service, may be led to full employment once again. We pray that governments and industry may plan humanely and well, choosing the right path and serving the justice of God; through Jesus Christ our Lord. **Amen.**

22.29 FOR THE UNEMPLOYED
Editors

Our gracious Heavenly Father, we are so grateful that your Son, our Saviour, worked with wood and tools earning his living by the labour of his hands: may we know, as he did, the sense of fulfilment that comes through work completed and well done; and enjoy the satisfaction and self-respect that work provides. Hear us as we pray for those who are unemployed: save them from despair and bitterness. Strengthen those who are discouraged, aid those with dependent families, ease the stress that lack of work brings. Lift from their spirits the anxiety of debt, the sense of uselessness, the fear of losing long-practised skills. Help us to care for these our neighbours, and encourage all who are able to employ others. Give wisdom to our politicians, that they may ever consider human need above party advantage. This we ask in the name of Jesus Christ our Lord. **Amen.**

22.30 FOR OUR WORK
Editors

In our daily work, O Lord, make us diligent in business, fervent in spirit serving the Lord. Help us to work not simply for wages, advancement or power, but primarily for your glory. Help us not to be clock-watchers, people-pleasers; but to know the privilege of working. If our job is uninviting, undemanding, or purely routine, sustain our interest and help us to see it as only a part of life. Help us to do your will whatever our outward circumstances, and to serve you above all in this world, for your glory's sake. **Amen.**

22.31   FOR OUR WORK
Christopher Idle

Thank you, Lord, for the gift of work, and for the strength in which
to do it. Thank you for our brains and our senses, and the strength in
our limbs and bodies; help us to use them well for you; to work well
with other people; and to make the place where we work a happier
place. Help us to make the work of others easier and more pleasant.
Be with all who find work difficult or dull or full of arguments. Bless
those for whom we work, and those who work for us; in the name of
Jesus, the carpenter, and the Saviour. **Amen.**

22.32   FOR GOD'S PRESENCE AT WORK
Editors

You have promised, Lord Jesus, to be near us at every turn and twist
of life. To seek you is to find you: help us in the business of these
days to be inwardly aware of your presence. When the tensions and
crises of life crush in upon us, enable us to know you are sharing our
burdens with us. As we contemplate decisions, make us aware of the
Holy Spirit alerting our minds, bringing clarity of thought, inspiring
confidence. Give us the joy of your companionship in our duties,
and your presence in every aspect of our lives. We ask this in your
name, for the Father's glory. **Amen.**

22.33   FOR SCHOOLS
Editors

Lord God, our loving Father, we thank you for all the children in our
schools and for all the staff who care for them: bless our schools,
Lord, and let *them* be *places* where we all gain wisdom and
knowledge and learn to value goodness and kindness. If anyone is
unhappy there, show us how to help; if anyone feels lonely there,
show us how to be a true friend; if anyone has a special need, show
us how to share our talents and skills. Above all, Lord, show us how
we may serve you and be a blessing in your world. **Amen.**

22.34   FOR A PARTICULAR SCHOOL
Timothy Dudley-Smith

Father, we hold before you in prayer our life together in this school: help us to give to it of our best, and to receive in turn the best it has to give. Teach us to know the joys of discovery, the warmth of friendship, the satisfaction of attempting and achieving, and the demands of truth. Open for us week by week new windows on our world; increase our understanding of ourselves and others. Let teachers and taught alike seek first your kingdom, for the good of this school and to the glory of your name, through Jesus Christ our Lord. **Amen.**

22.35   FOR OUR YOUNG PEOPLE
Editors

Lord Jesus Christ, we pray for the young people of our land. Help them to find that spiritual discipline by which alone life can be successfully lived and Christian character achieved. Give grace to discipline youthful energies, which can only be effective when controlled; protect them physically with your presence; be their teacher; be their guide, send into their lives the specially chosen companions and friends you want them to have; guard them from any costly blunder that would haunt them down the years; save them from instant temptations which inflame the mind and tantalise the passions; give to them that joy and happiness that enables us to go out to meet life in your strength. For their well-being and for your glory we ask this. **Amen.**

22.36   FOR TEACHERS
From 'New Every Morning'

Lord Jesus Christ, you showed on earth your love for children, and welcomed those who were brought to you: we ask you to guide with your Spirit those who are called to be teachers in the schools of this land; that nothing may hinder our children from growing in faith and in the knowledge of your love, and that your name may be honoured in the life of our nation. **Amen.**

22.37   FOR ALL IN COLLEGES AND SCHOOLS
Michael Botting

Lord Jesus Christ, the source of all knowledge and truth, give to all who teach, the spirit of wisdom and understanding, and grant that all who learn may have a true judgement in all things, that we may be an upright and God-fearing people; for your sake. **Amen.**

▶ **22.38**   FOR THOSE IN SCHOOLS
St Michael-le-Belfrey, York

Heavenly Father,
we pray for every boy and girl among us
who goes to school,
and for every adult who is a teacher:
let our schools teach what is true,
and make each one of us
willing to learn;
for Jesus' sake. **Amen.**

22.39   FOR CHILDREN AT SCHOOL
Frank Colquhoun, adapted

O God our Father, we pray for the children growing up in our schools: bless them in their work and play, now and as they prepare for their lives ahead; teach them wisdom as well as knowledge, to be strong in spirit and to do your will; through Jesus Christ our Lord. **Amen.**

▶ **22.40**   FOR TEACHERS
Liturgical Commission

Bless those who teach,
that they may increase our understanding,
and be open to your word for them:

Jesus, Lord of your Church,
in your mercy hear us. Amen.

22.41   FOR TEACHERS AND EDUCATORS
From 'A New Zealand Prayer Book'

God the source of all our inspiration, help us to understand ourselves, our world and you; and grant to those who teach us and our children respect for others' inventiveness and questioning, and for themselves commitment to truth. **Amen.**

22.42   FOR EDUCATIONAL INSTITUTIONS
From 'A New Zealand Prayer Book'

O Eternal God, bless all schools, colleges and universities (especially . . .), that they may be lively centres for sound learning, new discovery and the pursuit of wisdom; grant that those who teach and those who learn may find you to be the source of all truth. **Amen.**

▶ **22.43**   FOR OUR HOMES AND FAMILIES
St Michael-le-Belfrey, York

Heavenly Father,
we thank you for our homes,
for our food and clothing,
our families and our fellowship,
and for all the happiness we share together;
we ask that your love will surround us,
your care protect us,
and that we shall know your peace at all times;
for Jesus' sake. **Amen.**

22.44   FOR OUR LIVES THIS WEEK
Stephen Winward

Lord God of all power and might, preserver of all your creatures; keep us this week in health of body and soundness of mind, in purity of heart and cheerfulness of spirit, in contentment with our lot and charity with our neighbours; and further all our lawful undertakings with your blessing. In our work strengthen us, in our pleasures purify us, in our difficulties direct us, in our perils defend us, in our troubles comfort us; and supply all our needs according to the riches of your grace in Christ Jesus our Lord. **Amen.**

22.45 FOR POWER OVER TEMPTATION
Harold Evans

O Lord Jesus Christ, as man you knew the weakness of our nature and the power of temptation, but overcame all things by the grace of God: so breathe into our hearts the strength of your Spirit and clothe us with heavenly armour, that we may conquer all that wars against our souls and be kept your faithful soldiers and servants to the end. **Amen.**

22.46 FOR COURAGE
Editors

Lord God, thank you for the gift of a new day. Please help us to live it your way, in truth and light and love. We do not know what this day holds, but we believe you will help us in every situation. Your strength will be our courage; and when darkness falls we shall not be afraid, for perfect love casts out fear. Thank you, Lord, for your promise never to leave us or forsake us. **Amen.**

22.47 FOR STRENGTH
William Hampson

O Eternal God, help us always to remember the great unseen cloud of witnesses who are round about us. When in danger give us courage like theirs, and when in difficulty, perseverance like theirs; so that we too may be faithful. Then shall we rejoice with all the saints in your eternal kingdom; through Jesus Christ our Lord. **Amen.**

22.48 FOR COURAGE
Editors

Lord Jesus, it is so easy to take the short cuts in life, to avoid real situations and refuse to face the unpleasant issues. Reinforce our will and allow us to possess your mind more fully. So may we fulfil your purpose and be at peace in our work and recreation. Hear us and answer us, O Lord, for your glory. **Amen.**

▶ **22.49** FOR RIGHT BEHAVIOUR
From Psalm 141†

O Lord, we call to you:
come quickly in answer to our prayer.
We lift our hearts and our hands to you:
set a guard over our mouths,
a sentry at the door of our lips;
keep us from wanting to do wrong
or joining in evil deeds.
Help us to accept correction
    given to us in kindness from good people,
Strengthen us to pray for the wicked,
but to reject their enticing ways;
for the glory of your name. **Amen.**

22.50 FOR OUR ATTITUDES
Editors

Save us, Good Lord, from attitudes and actions which divide and
impoverish life; deliver us from the arrogance and pride which make
us contemptuous of people with whom we live and work; grant that
stubbornness and all intolerance may daily be crucified in our lives.
Let seeds of understanding and sympathy be sown; let your love in
us yield harmony and peace, to bring healing and peace to our
communities and countries, through our Saviour Jesus Christ.
Amen.

▶ **22.51** FOR HUMILITY
From Psalm 131†

O Lord God,
keep our hearts from pride,
keep our eyes from haughty looks,
keep our minds from arrogance,
keep our spirit calm
    in childlike dependence upon you:
for you are our hope
both now and for evermore. **Amen.**

▶ **22.52** AGAINST TEMPTATION
From Psalm 141†

O sovereign Lord,
when the enemy seeks to tempt and ensnare us,
fix our eyes on you
that we may pass by in safety:
then yours shall be the glory. **Amen.**

22.53 FOR KNOWLEDGE OF GOD'S WAY
Editors

God our Redeemer, we give you thanks for all in whose lives we
have caught some hint of the truth, a glimpse of your light; and in
whom we have seen something of your love. God our Saviour, who
comes to us in Christ, save us from the deception of merely listening
to the truth, yet not doing it; of giving faint praise, or of criticising
others when they look for our help; of professing more than we
believe to be true or, of distorting what we know to be the truth and
living a lie. Let us in word and deed be witness to the truth we have
seen in Jesus Christ our Lord. **Amen.**

▶ **22.54** PRAISE AND ADORATION
Editors

Our God and Father, we rejoice today and give you thanks for
everything in life that leads to wholeness and fulfilment:

For strength of body, mind and Spirit, for healing and health, for
powers to think and apply knowledge, for craft, design and art: we
praise you –
we give you thanks, our God.

For life's pleasures and creative gifts, for the uplifting notes of music,
for the expressive words of prose and poetry, for the satisfaction
found in our enjoyment of gardens and homes: we praise you –
we give you thanks, our God.

For knowledge of all that is true, noble, right, pure, lovely and
honourable, for moments of grace and spiritual awakening, for
sensitive awareness of others in need: we praise you –
we give you thanks, our God.

For your living church, the body of Christ on earth, for the mystery of your grace which reaches into our sinful lives, for the wonder of redemption in Jesus Christ, for the indwelling of the Holy Spirit, who enables us to live to your glory: we praise you –
we give you thanks, our God.

**Our God and Father,
hear and accept our thanksgiving
for your love's sake. Amen.**

▶ **22.55** DEDICATION
Editors

Jesus, Son of God,
let your love shine through our eyes,
your Spirit inspire our words,
your wisdom fill our minds,
your mercy control our hands,
your will capture our hearts,
your joy pervade our being;
until we are changed into your likeness
from glory to glory. **Amen.**

▶ **22.56** GLORIA
Liturgical Commission

In a world of change and hope,
of fear and adventure:
faithful God,
glorify your name. **Amen.**

22.57 BLESSING
Alan Gaunt

May the strength of God support you through the coming days, and his Holy Spirit keep you steadfast on your way, bringing you at last to overwhelming victory by the power of him who loved us, Jesus Christ our Lord. **Amen.**

22.58 BLESSING
From 2 Thessalonians 2†

Our Lord Jesus Christ himself and God our Father, who loved us and in his grace gave us an unfailing courage and a firm hope, encourage you and strengthen you always to do and always to say what is good; and the blessing of God the Father, God the Son, and God the Holy Spirit be with you. **Amen.**

22.59 BLESSING
From 2 Thessalonians 3†

The Lord, who is faithful, strengthen *you*, protect *you* from the evil one and lead *your* hearts in the love of God and the endurance of Jesus Christ our Lord. **Amen.**

22.60 BLESSING
From Joshua 1†

Be strong and courageous, be careful to obey God's commandments – remember them, speak of them, obey them; do not be fearful, do not be discouraged; and the Lord your God be with you wherever you go. **Amen.**

22.61 BLESSING
From 1 Corinthians 16†

Be on your guard, stand firm in the faith, be people of courage, be strong, do everything in love; and the grace of the Lord Jesus be with you. **Amen.**

22.62 BLESSING
From 'St Patrick's Breastplate'

Christ be with *you*, Christ within *you*, Christ behind *you*, Christ before *you*, Christ beside *you*, Christ to win *you*, Christ to comfort and restore *you*, Christ beneath *you*, Christ above *you*, Christ in hearts of all that love *you*: now and always. **Amen.**

22.63 BLESSING
From 'A New Zealand Prayer Book'

Christ be within *you* to keep *you*, beside *you* to guard, before *you* to
lead, behind *you* to protect, beneath *you* to support, above *you* to
bless. **Amen.**

22.64 BLESSING
Book of Common Prayer, adapted

God our Father who knows that we are surrounded by many and
great dangers, and that we cannot always stand upright because of
the weakness of our human nature: grant *you* strength and
protection to support *you* in all danger and carry *you* through all
temptation; and the blessing of God – Father, Son and Holy Spirit –
be with *you* always. **Amen.**

22.65 BLESSING
From Hebrews 12†

Fix your eyes on Jesus, the author and finisher of our faith, who for
the joy set before him endured the cross, scorning its shame, and sat
down at the right hand of the throne on high; and the blessing of
God the Father, God the Son and God the Holy Spirit be with you
always. **Amen.**

22.66 BLESSING
From Hebrews 12†

Fix your eyes on Jesus, the author and finisher of our faith, who for
the joy set before him endured the cross, scorning its shame, and has
sat down at the right hand of the throne of God; consider him who
endured such opposition from sinful men, so that you will not grow
weary and lose heart; and the blessing of almighty God, Father, Son
and Holy Spirit (shall) be with you always. **Amen.**

▶ **22.67**   BLESSING
From 1 Peter 5†

The God of all grace who called *you* to his eternal glory in Christ, make *you* strong, firm and steadfast:
to him be the power for ever and ever. Amen.

22.68   BLESSING
From Colossians 1†

The Lord God fill you with the knowledge of his will; his Spirit give you wisdom and understanding; Christ strengthen you with his glorious power so that you may be able to endure, to be patient and to give thanks to the Father with joy in your hearts; and the blessing of God almighty, the Father, the Son, and the Holy Spirit, be with you always. **Amen**

22.69   BLESSING
From 2 Corinthians 4†

Never be discouraged even though your world decays; be renewed in your spirit day after day, look forward to tremendous and eternal glory, fix your heart on your unseen home which will last for ever; and the blessing of God who has created us for heaven and in token has given us his Spirit be upon you now and always. **Amen.**

22.70   BLESSING
From 2 Timothy 2†

Be strong through the grace that is ours in union with Christ Jesus; take your part in suffering, as his loyal soldier: and the blessing of God almighty, the Father, the Son and the Holy Spirit be with you always. **Amen.**

22.71   BLESSING
From 2 Timothy 4†

Run the good race to the end, keep the faith, receive the crown of righteousness which God the righteous judge will give on that day to us who have loved him and long to see him: and the blessing of God – Father, Son and Holy Spirit – be with you always. **Amen.**

22.72 BLESSING
From 2 Timothy 4†

In the presence of God and of Christ Jesus who will judge the living and the dead, and because he comes as King: preach the word, be prepared at all times whether people will listen or not; practise self-control, endure suffering, share the good news of Christ, do the task that God has given you: and the blessing of God almighty, the Father the Son and the Holy Spirit be with you always. **Amen.**

Heaven, God's Peace, Encouragement

▶ **23.1**   GREETING
From 2 Corinthians 13†

The God of love and peace be with you. **Amen.**

23.2   SENTENCE
2 Corinthians 5.5

We have an eternal home in heaven. God has made us for this very purpose, and has given us his Spirit as a pledge.

23.3   SENTENCE
Philippians 3.30

Our homeland is in heaven and from heaven comes the Saviour we are waiting for, the Lord Jesus Christ.

23.4   SENTENCE
2 Corinthians 4.14

We know that God who raised the Lord Jesus from the dead will also raise us with Jesus, therefore we do not lose heart.

23.5   SENTENCE
1 John 3.2

When Christ is revealed, we shall be like him; for we shall see him as he is.

23.6   SENTENCE
Isaiah 64.4 and 1 Corinthians 2.9

No eye has seen, no ear has heard, no mind has conceived what God has prepared for those who love him.

23.7 SENTENCE
1 Peter 1.8

Without having seen Christ you love him; though you do not now see him, you believe in him and rejoice with unutterable and exalted joy.

23.8 SENTENCE
Revelation 11.5

The kingdom of this world has become the Kingdom of our Lord and of his Christ, and he will reign for ever and ever.

23.9 SENTENCE
Romans 5.1

Since we have been justified by faith we have peace with God through our Lord Jesus Christ.

23.10 SENTENCE
John 12.24

Unless a grain of wheat falls on the ground and dies, it remains a single grain: but, if it dies, it yields a rich harvest.

▶ 23.11 RESPONSE
From 1 Corinthians 15†

When the perishable has been clothed with the imperishable, and the mortal with immortality, then the saying that is written will come true:
Death has been swallowed up in victory. Amen.

▶ 23.12 RESPONSE
From 1 Corinthians 15†

The sting of death is sin, and the power of sin is the law!
But thanks be to God!
He gives us the victory
through our Lord Jesus Christ. Amen.

23.13 APPROACH
Editors

We proclaim your greatness, O God of heaven and earth. We praise you, Lord Jesus Christ, for you have come to destroy the enemy death. By the victory of your cross and resurrection, you have opened the kingdom of heaven to all who believe in you. Your grace is unending, your power is infinite, your love is unlimited. We celebrate the indwelling of the Holy Spirit, confirming your presence in us, and giving us grace to embrace your promise of eternal life; through Jesus Christ our Lord, who lives and reigns with you and the Holy Spirit, one God, now and for ever. **Amen.**

23.14 APPROACH
Editors

We thank you, our loving Father, that you are concerned both about the ordering of the stars in their orbits and also for the tiny sparrow who falls to the ground. Your concern encourages us when we are surrounded by doubts and perplexities. We recognise our own weakness in that we often seek to run our lives without any reference to your purposes and plan. We grow weary of life's demands; and we so often blunder on, trying to control our destiny. We ask this day that you will give us a clear sense of your presence, an insight into your design, an awareness of the unseen. We pray that you will help us to see your light upon our own troubled pathway and so find clearer direction. Give us courage; drive away our fears, make us brave again and restore to us the joy of heaven; through Jesus our Lord. **Amen.**

23.15 APPROACH (FUNERAL/MEMORIAL)
Alan Gaunt

Living God, we praise you: your presence still joins us to the one we mourn/*honour* who is your possession as are we all. While we live, *his* name will not die on earth; while you remain our Father, *his* name and our names will never die. Humbled by pain and death, as was Jesus Christ himself, we come to you with him whose name is above all names, to receive the Kingdom, the power and the glory, which are yours and ours for ever. **Amen.**

▶ **23.16**   PRAISE
From Psalm 86†

O Lord our God,
we will praise you with all our heart.

O Lord our God,
we will proclaim your greatness for ever.

Great is your constant love for us;
you have saved us from the grave itself! Amen.

▶ **23.17**   CONFESSION
Editor

O God, our Father in heaven, we confess to you our failure to live as
children of your grace and heirs of your promises:

When we make this world's goods our treasure, and are mindless of
your kingdom and your reward: in your mercy,
Father, forgive us and help us.

When we forget that here we have no enduring city, and fail to look
for the city which is to come: in your mercy,
Father, forgive us and help us.

When we measure worth by the standards of this passing age and
reject your eternal truth: in your mercy,
Father, forgive us and help us.

When we lose the vision of Christ and no longer run to win the prize
of your call to heaven: in your mercy,
Father, forgive us and help us.

Father,
you have raised us
together with Christ:
set our hearts and minds
on things above,
where he is seated in glory
at your right hand for evermore. Amen.

▶ **23.18** CONFESSION
Editors

Father God, you know just how much we need your mercy and continuing forgiveness.

When we are caught up with the trivialities and distractions of life, which blind us to the essential and eternal issues, in your mercy,
Lord God, forgive us and help us.

When we see glimpses of your glory and of the reality of heaven and we do not allow that vision to transform the way we live on earth, in your mercy,
Lord God, forgive us and help us.

When we concentrate almost exclusively on building treasure on earth, and we become mindless of your kingdom and careless of our reward, in your mercy,
Lord God, forgive us and help us.

When we lose the vision of Christ, and fail to strive after the abundant life which you offer us, in your mercy,
Lord God, forgive us and help us.

Father,
you have raised us together with Christ:
set our hearts and minds on things above
where he is seated in glory
at your right hand for evermore. Amen.

▶ **23.19** CONFESSION
From Psalm 109†

O Lord, we need you:
our hearts are wounded,
our days fade like evening shadows,
we are weak and despise ourselves;
for we have sinned against you.
Forgive us, O Lord,
and in your constant love save us;
through Jesus our redeemer. Amen.

23.20   ABSOLUTION
From Psalm 103†

The Lord, who is merciful and gracious, slow to anger and full of
love; who will not accuse us for ever, nor be angry with us always;
who does not treat us as we deserve or repay us according to our
wrongdoing: have compassion on *you*, as a father has compassion on
his children, and forgive *you your* sins; through Jesus Christ our
Lord. **Amen.**

▶ **23.21**   COLLECT
Last Sunday after Pentecost, ASB 1980

Merciful God,
you have prepared for those who love you
such good things as pass our understanding.
Pour into our hearts such love towards you
that we, loving you above all things,
may obtain your promises,
which exceed all that we can desire;
through Jesus Christ our Lord. **Amen.**

▶ **23.22**   COLLECT
Funeral Service, ASB 1980

Heavenly Father,
in your Son Jesus Christ
you have given us a true faith and a sure hope.
Strengthen this faith and hope in us all our days,
that we may live as those who believe
in the communion of saints,
the forgiveness of sins,
and the resurrection to eternal life;
through your Son Jesus Christ our Lord. **Amen.**

► **23.23** PSALM
Psalm 33.1–22†

The congregation – and ministers – may divide at A *and* B

    Sing joyfully to the Lord, you righteous:
    it is right that his people should praise him.

    Praise the Lord with the harp:
A **make music to him on the strings.**

    Sing to the Lord a new song:
B **play skilfully, and shout for joy.**

    For the word of the Lord is right and true:
ALL **and all his work is faithfulness.**

    The Lord loves righteousness and justice:
A **his endless love fills the earth.**

    By the word of the Lord the skies were formed:
B **his breath created moon and stars.**

    Let all the earth fear the Lord:
ALL **the people of the world revere him.**

    For he spoke, and it came to be:
A **he commanded, and all was made.**

    The Lord holds back the nations:
B **he thwarts their evil intent.**

    God's purposes are sure:
ALL **his plans endure for ever.**

    Happy is the nation whose God is the Lord:
A **happy the people he makes his own.**

    The eyes of the Lord are on those who fear him:
B **who trust in his unfailing love.**

    We wait in hope for the Lord:
A **he is our help and shield.**

    In him our hearts rejoice:
B **we trust his holy name.**

    May your constant love be with us, Lord:
ALL **as we put our hope in you. Amen.**

23.24   READING: JESUS TALKS TO HIS DISCIPLES
From John 14. 1–26 [27–31]

Cast: Jesus, Thomas, Philip, Judas – Thomas, Philip and Judas can all be the same

Jesus

Believe in God and believe also in me. There are many rooms in my Father's house, and I am going to prepare a place for you. I would not tell you this if it were not so. And after I go and prepare a place for you, I will come back and take you to myself, so that you will be where I am. You know the way that leads to the place where I am going.

Thomas

Lord, we do not know where you are going; so how can we know the way to get there?

Jesus

I am the way, the truth, and the life; no one goes to the Father except by me. Now that you have known me, you will know my Father also, and from now on you do know him and you have seen him.

Philip

Lord, show us the Father; that is all we need.

Jesus

For a long time I have been with you all; yet you do not know me, Philip? Whoever has seen me has seen the Father. Why, then, do you say, 'Show us the Father'? Do you not believe, Philip, that I am in the Father and the Father is in me? The words that I have spoken to you do not come from me. The Father, who remains in me, does his own work. Believe me when I say that I am in the Father and the Father is in me. And I will do whatever you ask for in my name, so that the Father's glory will be shown through the Son. If you ask me for anything in my name, I will do it.

I will ask the Father, and he will give you another Helper, who will stay with you for ever. He is the Spirit who reveals the truth about God. When I go, you will not be left all alone; I will come back to you. When that day comes, you will know that I am in my Father and that you are in me, just as I am in you.

My Father will love whoever loves me; I too will love him and reveal myself to him.

Judas

Lord, how can it be that you will reveal yourself to us and not to the world?

Jesus

Whoever loves me will obey my teaching. My Father will love him, and my Father and I will come to him and live with him.

I have told you this while I am still with you. The Helper, the Holy Spirit, whom the Father will send in my name, will teach you everything and make you remember all that I have told you.

[Peace is what I leave with you; it is my own peace that I give you. I do not give it as the world does. Do not be worried and upset; do not be afraid. You heard me say to you, 'I am leaving, but I will come back to you.' If you loved me, you would be glad that I am going to the Father; for he is greater than I. I have told you this now before it all happens, so that when it does happen, you will believe. I cannot talk with you much longer, because the ruler of this world is coming. He has no power over me, but the world must know that I love the Father; that is why I do everything he commands me.

Come, let us go from this place.]

Cast

[This is] the word of the Lord.   OR   This is the Gospel of Christ/
                                                              This is the Gospel of the Lord.

All

Thanks be to God.   **Praise to Christ our Lord/
                                                              Praise to you, Lord Jesus Christ.**

23.25   READING: THE NEW HEAVEN AND THE NEW EARTH
Revelation 21. 1–7 [8]

Cast: John, Voice, God

John

Then I saw a new heaven and a new earth. The first heaven and the first earth disappeared, and the sea vanished. And I saw the Holy City, the new Jerusalem, coming down out of heaven from God, prepared and ready, like a bride dressed to meet her husband. I heard a loud voice speaking from the throne:

Voice
> Now God's home is with mankind! He will live with them, and they shall be his people. God himself will be with them, and he will be their God. He will wipe away all tears from their eyes. There will be no more death, no more grief or crying or pain. The old things have disappeared.

John
> Then the one who sits on the throne said:

God
> And now I make all things new!

John
> He also said to me:

God
> Write this, because these words are true and can be trusted.

John
> And he said:

God (*slowly and deliberately*)
> It is done! I am the first and the last, the beginning and the end. To anyone who is thirsty I will give the right to drink from the spring of the water of life without paying for it. Whoever wins the victory will receive this from me: I will be his God, and he will be my son.

Cast
> [This is] the word of the Lord.

All
> **Thanks be to God.**

FURTHER BIBLE READINGS

Readings appropriate to this theme will be found listed in our companion volume, 'The Dramatised Bible' (published by HarperCollins) on index page 434.

▶ **23.26** CREED
From 2 Corinthians 4†

We speak because we believe:

God, who raised the Lord Jesus Christ to life,
will also raise us up with Jesus

and take us together into his presence.
Though outwardly we are wasting away,
inwardly we are being renewed day by day;
we live by faith, and not by sight. Amen.

▶ **23.27** CREED
From Revelation 2†

We believe in Jesus Christ
before whom we fall down and worship
but need not be afraid:
he is the first and the last,
the living one;
he has authority over death
and the world of the dead,
for he was dead, but now is alive
    for ever and ever. Amen.

▶ **23.28** CREED
From 2 Thessalonians 2 and 3†

Let us affirm the teaching to which we hold:

We believe in God the Father
who loved us,
and by his grace gave us
eternal encouragement and good hope.

We believe in God the Son
who encourages our hearts
and strengthens us in every good deed and word;
whose grace shall be with us all.

We believe in God the Holy Spirit,
the Lord of peace
who gives us peace at all times
and in every way.

We believe in one God:
Father, Son and Holy Spirit. Amen.

23.29   FOR THOSE IN NEED
Roger Pickering

To your keeping, O Lord God, we commend all whose enjoyment of life has been impaired by sickness, by tragedy, or by human sin. May your love sustain them in their suffering, and may your people care for them in the name of Jesus Christ our Lord. **Amen.**

23.30   FOR THE SUFFERING
Editors

Lord of the weary and care-worn: in love and with desire for their wholeness we bring to you those who are ill, and in great pain, and others for whom the journey back to health is along a difficult and tedious pathway. For the poor, lonely and the sorrow-filled give us compassion of heart that we may reach out and help them in their need and so fulfil his law of love, who is our saviour and our constant friend, Jesus Christ. **Amen.**

23.31   FOR THOSE WHOSE CIRCUMSTANCES HAVE
              CHANGED
Editors

O Lord, we pray for those who have experienced a sudden change in their lives and are frightened by it. Please help them to cope: you alone understand their fears. Ease their pain, Lord, and bless them with your peace: for it is you alone who can sustain them through the days ahead; your eternal love is their earthly strength, and you shall be their trust and joy for ever and ever. **Amen.**

▶ **23.32**   FOR THE BROKEN-HEARTED
Editors

The Lord is near to the broken-hearted and saves the crushed in spirit. (*Psalm 34*)

Let us pray for broken homes, for teenagers torn by doubts and disillusionment, for old people bewildered by infirmities and lack of contact, for sick people fearful of the future, and for those who mourn:

O God our redeemer,
on behalf of all people in distress,

especially those known to us,
we claim your promise to be near the broken-hearted,
and to save the crushed in spirit:
use us as channels of your healing power;
through Jesus Christ our Lord. Amen.

23.33 FOR THE LONELY
Editors

Lord of every generation, we pray for those who are lonely because they are old. We are concerned that many in this world have few friends, some have none; and that some older people feel unloved and unwanted. We pray that you will meet their needs and, if we can help them as your children, that you will show us how we might contact them and bring your joy and peace into their lives, for Jesus' sake. **Amen.**

23.34 FOR THOSE FEELING UNWANTED IN OLD AGE
Leslie Weatherhead, adapted

Lord, we lift to you those who are aged and who feel unwanted, unloved and in the way. Help them to try – by humour and patience, by resolutely refusing to grumble and complain, by seeking ever to minister where they can to those with whom they live – to become assets to the life of the home, beloved and admired as those are who seek to love more than to be loved and to serve rather than to be served. To all these reveal yourself as one who understands and cares, as one who guides and sustains, who shares every burden, who helps us back to humour and to inward peace. Remove fear and bitterness and self-pity from all our hearts and grant us your peace in Jesus our Lord. **Amen.**

23.35 FOR THOSE WHO ARE DYING
Michael Walker

Lord, let those who are dying know that you are very close.

Be with those whose minds are clear and whose senses are still alert. Let the presence of those they love, and the beauty and joy of the world glimpsed through the windows, all be signs of that peace and glory that awaits us in paradise.

429

Be with those who journey through a twilight world, seemingly beyond everything save our touch and the words we whisper in their ear. Let our touch be to them the strong grasp of Christ and our words an echo of his truth, now beyond all words.

Be present in the hour of death and grant a serene journey to all travellers to your eternal kingdom. Be with those who remain, for their grief is hard to bear. Comfort them in Jesus our redeemer; for his sake. **Amen.**

23.36 FOR THE BEREAVED
Dick Williams

We remember, Lord, the slenderness of the thread which separates life from death, and the suddenness with which it can be broken. Help us also to remember that on both sides of that divide we are surrounded by your love. Persuade our hearts that when our dear ones die neither we nor they are parted from you. Let us find our peace in you, and in you be united with them in the glorious body of Christ; for you have conquered death, and are alive – our saviour and theirs – for ever and ever. **Amen.**

23.37 TRUSTING FOR OTHERS
George Appleton

Dear Lord, we are learning to trust you not for ourselves alone, but for those also whom we love and who seem hidden by the shadow of death: that, as we know your power to have raised our Lord Jesus Christ from the dead, so we may trust your love to give eternal life to all who believe in him; through the same Jesus Christ our Lord. **Amen.**

23.38 COMMEMORATION
Christopher Idle

God of the living, and Father of our risen Lord, we are glad in your presence today as we remember those who have gone before us believing in your promises and trusting in your mercy. Help us to follow them, as they have followed Christ, and with all your people on earth and in heaven to give you the glory and the praise that is your due: through Jesus Christ our Lord. **Amen.**

23.39   FOR THE VICTIMS OF VANDALISM AND CRIME
Susan Williams

In this world, O Lord, where the violence of a few strikes random victims among the many, we pray to you for all who have been physically hurt, all who have been robbed of personal treasures, all who suffer reactions of bitterness and fear. O Lord Jesus Christ, your perfect life met death by violence and was not extinguished: so enter the hearts and minds of all victims that frailty may give way to your strength, loss to your gain, bitterness to your total and victorious love; for your name's sake. **Amen.**

23.40   WHEN WE LACK VISION
Editors

Lord, often we feel we have nothing to give you: We are drained of our enthusiasm, we lose confidence in our ability; somehow insights become less frequent. Show us at such times the richness of creation, the wonders of your grace, the joy of ordinary people; help us to see the good in others, help us to understand that the human flesh is weak – but that your Spirit can bring life to our mortal bodies and stability to our confused minds; through the healing name of Jesus our Lord. **Amen.**

23.41   FOR DAILY PROTECTION
Editors

Lord God, you are our protector, you are our complete saviour. We see the love you have for us in the mighty acts of Jesus Christ. There are times when we are harrassed, overwhelmed, when we feel that our pilgrim path of life is full of thorns and briars, and we are having to walk on in blindness with bare feet. Help us to know your comfort; let us ever be sure that if we have pain, you share it. If the path is difficult, you are there with us in all we experience; so with you we are safe and the wounds are only temporary. We ask these things so that we may know you rule in our lives. **Amen.**

▶ **23.42**   IN TROUBLE OR DIFFICULTY
From 'New Every Morning'

Father, give to us, and to all your people,
in times of anxiety, serenity;
in times of hardship, courage;
in times of uncertainty, patience;
and, at all times,
a quiet trust in your wisdom and love;
through Jesus Christ our Lord. **Amen.**

23.43   FOR PEACE AND REST
Michael Hollings and Etta Gullick, adapted

Teach us stillness, Lord, and confident peace in your perfect will –
deep calm of soul and content in what you will do with these lives
you have given; teach us to wait and be still, to rest in you, to hush
this clamorous anxiety, to lay in your arms all this wealth you have
given. You love us, with a love as far surpassing our own as the
glory of the moon surpasses the gleam of a candle. Therefore will we
be still and trust in you. **Amen.**

23.44   FOR THE ABILITY TO COPE WITH LIFE
Eileen Wheeler

O God who inspires, leads and sustains, help us at all times to do the
things that we ought to do: give us clear sight that we may know
what to do, courage to embark upon it, skill to find a way through
all its problems, perseverance to bring it to its appointed end, and
strength to resist all the temptations which would seek to lure us
aside; so help us to begin, to continue and to end all things in you,
through Jesus Christ our Lord. **Amen.**

23.45   FOR RELAXATION: A PERSONAL PRAYER
Unknown

Slow me down, Lord! Ease the pounding of my heart by the quieting
of my mind. Steady my hurried pace with a vision of the eternal
reach of time. Give me, amid the confusion of my day, the calmness
of the everlasting hills. Allow me to know the mystical restoring
power of sleep. Teach me the art of quiet reflection. Let me look up

into the branches of the towering oak and know that it grew great and strong because it grew slowly and well.

Slow me down, Lord, and inspire me to send my roots deep into the soil of life's enduring values that I may grow toward the stars of my greater destiny. **Amen.**

▶ **23.46** FOR STRENGTH AND SERENITY
From 2 Thessalonians 2†

O God our Father,
you loved us
and by your grace gave us
eternal courage and good hope:
encourage our hearts
and strengthen us in every good deed and word;
let the Spirit of peace give us peace
at all times and in every way;
and may the grace of the Lord Jesus Christ
be with us all. **Amen.**

▶ **23.47** FOR JESUS TO BE NEAR US
Editors

Lord Jesus,
when the unexpected happens
and we feel lost or afraid,
help us to remember that
    your peace is our comfort,
    your love is our strength,
    your presence is our joy.
Thank you, Lord for your light
when the way is dark. **Amen.**

▶ **23.48** FOR INWARD PEACE
Christina Rossetti

O Lord, your way is perfect:
help us, we pray,
always to trust in your goodness;
that walking with you in faith,
and following you in all simplicity,

we may possess quiet and contented minds,
and leave all our worries with you,
because you care for us;
for the sake of Jesus Christ our Lord. **Amen.**

23.49   RESTING IN GOD
Michael Hollings and Etta Gullick, adapted

Deep and silent and cool as a broad, still, tree-shaded river is the peace of your presence, and rest of our souls, O God. From the thousand problems of this our hurrying life we turn, with silent joy, to plunge into you, to steep our souls in your quiet depths where no clamour of earth disturbs our perfect content. You are our home and refuge, in you we are safe and at peace; ever in the din and hurry of the world we know that you are near. We know that close at hand – closer than our little life – flows that silent river of your presence and love; in a moment we may be with you and in you, in a moment be surrounded and soaked in your peace; in a moment, as this loud world clangs round us, we may rest secure in the bliss of your eternity. Thank you, God. **Amen.**

23.50   FOR THE COMING NIGHT
From 'The Leonine Sacramentary'

Be with us, merciful God, and protect us through the silent hours of this night, that we who are wearied by the changes and chances of this passing world, may rest in your eternal changelessness; through Jesus Christ our Lord. **Amen.**

23.51   IN TIMES OF DOUBT REGARDING BELIEF
Michael Hollings and Etta Gullick, adapted

In times of doubt and questioning, when our belief is perplexed by new learning, new teaching, new thought, when our faith is strained by creeds, by doctrines, by mysteries beyond our understanding, give us the faithfulness of learners and courage of believers in you; give us boldness to examine, and faith to trust in, all truth; give us patience and insight to master difficulties, stability to hold fast our tradition with enlightened interpretation, openness to admit all fresh truth made known to us, courage to grasp new knowledge and to combine it loyally and honestly with the old; insight to refrain from stubborn rejection of new revelations, and humility not to believe that we are always wiser than our fathers. Save us and help us, we humbly pray, O Lord. **Amen.**

▶ **23.52** FOR FAITH
David Silk

Grant to us, Lord God,
to trust you not for ourselves alone,
but for those also whom we love
and who are hidden from us by the shadow of death;
that, as we believe your power to have raised
 our Lord Jesus Christ from the dead,
so we may trust your love to give eternal life
 to all who believe in him;
through Jesus Christ our Lord,
who is alive and reigns with you and the Holy Spirit,
one God, now and for ever. **Amen.**

23.53 IN LONELINESS: A PERSONAL PRAYER
Editors

Lord God, help me and all who feel alone not to despair. Give us inspiration to use these times creatively so that we do not dread our condition, but use it as a means of closer fellowship and dependence upon you. Thank you, Lord. **Amen.**

23.54 PAIN AND INCREASING WEAKNESS
Editors

Lord, when we are weak or in pain and feel depressed, when we are tired and things irritate us; then give us courage to face the truth, and faith to believe that you are beside us and will strengthen us. Make us vividly aware of your presence, and save us from self-pity, pride and rebellious fretfulness. To you be the glory. **Amen.**

23.55 A MORNING PRAYER
Editors

O heavenly Father, I praise and thank you for the peace of the night; I praise and thank you for this new day; I praise and thank you for all your goodness and faithfulness throughout my life. You have granted me many blessings: now let me also accept what is hard from your hand. You will place upon me no more than I can bear. O heavenly Father, I praise and thank you. **Amen.**

23.56 GOD'S PRESENCE
From 'A Lutheran Manual of Prayer', adapted

Lord, stay with us for it is nearly evening, the day is almost over: stay with us and your whole church, stay with us in the evening of the day, stay with us in the evening of life, stay with us in the evening of the world; stay with us in your strengthening grace and mercy, stay with us in your word and ordinances/*sacraments*, stay with us in your comforting presence, stay with us with your constant blessing, stay with us through the night of distress and fear, stay with us through the night of doubt and temptation, stay with us through the night of death. Living Lord, stay with us through time and in eternity; for your name's sake. **Amen.**

23.57 ABOUT OUR RESURRECTION
From 1 Corinthians 15†

God of the imperishable kingdom: sound the trumpet, wake us from our long sleep, raise us in Christ, clothe us with immortality, swallow up death in victory! O mighty God, receive the thanks of your redeemed people, to whom you give the victory through our Lord Jesus Christ. **Amen.**

23.58 THANKSGIVING
From Isaiah 63†

Our God, we thank you for your kindnesses; for many gracious deeds we praise you – for all the good things you have done for us. You have become our saviour: in all our distress you too were distressed; in your love and mercy your redeemed us, through Jesus Christ our Lord. **Amen.**

▶ **23.59** THANKSGIVING
St Boniface, adapted

O God,
we cannot measure your love,
nor ever count your blessings:
we thank you for all your goodness;
for in our weakness you make us strong,
in our darkness you give us light,
and in our sorrows you bring comfort and peace.
And from everlasting to everlasting
you are our God,
Father, Son, and Holy Spirit. **Amen.**

23.60 THANKSGIVING FOR OUR KNOWLEDGE OF GOD
Editors

O Lord our God, we thank you that you have put eternity in our
hearts. You have expanded our minds and lives and given us a
hunger and thirst for more of yourself – for that greater knowledge,
for that greater love with which you alone can satisfy us. Truly we
see now through a darkened glass; but one day face to face. Then
shall we know as you know us and praise your holy name. **Amen.**

▶ **23.61** FOR GOD'S HELP IN ALL CIRCUMSTANCES
From 'A New Zealand Prayer Book'

In darkness and in light,
in trouble and in joy,
help us, heavenly Father,
to trust your love,
to serve your purpose,
and to praise your name,
through Jesus Christ our Lord. **Amen.**

▶ **23.62** ASCRIPTION
From Philippians 4†

O God, let your peace
which passes all understanding,
keep our hearts and minds in Christ Jesus;
and to you be glory
for ever and ever. **Amen.**

▶ **23.63** ASCRIPTION
Martin Luther King

And now to him who is able to keep us from falling,
and lift us from the dark valley of despair
to the bright mountain of hope,
from the midnight of desperation
to the daybreak of joy;
to him be power and authority, for ever and ever. **Amen.**

▶ **23.64** DEDICATION
Roger Pickering

And now, O Father in heaven,
we entrust ourselves to you;
that joyful or sorrowing,
living or dying,
we may ever be with our Lord Jesus,
safe in your eternal care. **Amen.**

▶ **23.65** DEDICATION
Elizabeth Goudge

Eternal Light, shine in our hearts,
eternal Goodness, deliver us from evil,
eternal Power, be our support,
eternal Wisdom, scatter our darkness,
eternal Pity, have mercy upon us:
that with all our heart and mind
and soul and strength
we may seek your face,
and be brought by your infinite mercy
to your holy presence;
through Jesus Christ our Lord. **Amen.**

23.66 BLESSING
From 'Still Waters, Deep Waters'

The blessing of God almighty, whose plans for *you* do not end in
death; and of our Lord Jesus Christ who entered *your* world so that
you might enter his; and of the Holy Spirit, who is at work in *you*

constantly – preparing *you* for that great day, be upon *you* and remain with *you* until *you* meet him face to face. **Amen.**

23.67 BLESSING
From 'A New Zealand Prayer Book'

God be your comfort, your strength; God be your hope and support; God be your light and your way; and the blessing of God – Creator, Redeemer and Giver of life – remain with you now and for ever. **Amen.**

23.68 BLESSING
From Isaiah 26†

Trust in the Lord, your eternal Rock, and he will keep your mind in perfect peace. Keep faith, walk with him, wait for him, desire him; reach out to him in the night, seek him in the morning: and his blessing (shall) be upon you always. **Amen.**

23.69 BLESSING
From Philippians 4†

Rejoice in the Lord always, let everyone know your gentleness, do not be anxious, make your needs known to God; and the peace of God guard you in Christ Jesus. **Amen.**

23.70 BLESSING
From Romans 15†

The God of hope fill *you* with all joy and peace as *you* trust in him, so that *you* may overflow with hope by the power of the Holy Spirit. **Amen.**

23.71 BLESSING
From John 14†

Jesus said, 'Peace I leave with you: my peace I give to you. Do not let your heart be troubled or afraid'. The peace of God be upon *you* all; and the blessing of God – Father, Son and Holy Spirit – remain with *you* for ever. **Amen.**

23.72 BLESSING
From Isaiah 57†

The Lord look upon *your* need and heal *you;* the Lord guide *you* and restore comfort to *you;* the Lord give *you* his peace; through Jesus Christ our Lord. **Amen.**

23.73 BLESSING
From 1 Peter 5†

Humble yourselves under the mighty hand of God that in due time he may exalt you. Cast all your anxieties on him, because he cares about you: and the blessing of God almighty, the Father, the Son and the Holy Spirit be with you always. **Amen.**

23.74 BLESSING
From 2 Corinthians 1†

The God and Father of our Lord Jesus Christ, the Father of compassion and the God of all comfort, comfort you in all your troubles, so that you can comfort those in any trouble with the comfort you yourselves have received from God; and the blessing of God almighty, the Father, the Son and the Holy Spirit be with you and remain with you always. **Amen.**

23.75 BLESSING
From 2 Thessalonians 3†

The Lord of peace himself give you peace at all times, wherever you may be; and the blessing of God – Father, Son and Holy Spirit be upon you all. **Amen.**

23.76 BLESSING
From 2 Corinthians 4†

Never be discouraged even though your world decays; be renewed in your spirit day after day, look forward to tremendous and eternal glory, fix your heart on your unseen home which will last for ever; and the blessing of God who has created us for heaven and in token has given us his Spirit be upon you now and always. **Amen.**

Christ's Coming, Judgement

▶ **24.1** GREETING
From Revelation 1†

Grace and peace to you from him who is, and who was, and who is to come. **Amen.**

THE ADVENT WREATH
Jane Austin

▶ **24.2** ADVENT 1 – THE PATRIARCHS
Genesis 12.2,3; Genesis 26.24; Deuteronomy 18.15; 2 Samuel 23.3

As we light the candles in our Advent Wreath we remember the preparations which God our Father made for the coming of his Son into the world.

Today is the First Sunday in Advent: we remember how God spoke to Abraham, Isaac, Moses and David and told them of the Messiah who was to come.

Abraham was promised, that through his descendants all the world world be blessed.
Thank you, Father.

Isaac was told, 'Do not be afraid, for I am with you.'
Thank you, Father.

Moses looked forward to the One who would be raised up to take his place as the leader of the people.
Thank you, Father.

David knew that a king would follow him who would reign for ever.
Thank you, Father.

The first candle is lit (the centre candle remaining unlit until Christmas Day)

As we light this first candle we remember Abraham, Isaac, Moses and David and, like them, we look forward to the coming Messiah.
Amen.

▶ **24.3** ADVENT 2 – THE PROPHETS
Isaiah 9.6; Jeremiah 3.15; Ezekiel 20.41; Micah 5.2.

The previous Sunday's candle is lit

As we light the candles in our Advent Wreath we remember the preparations which God our Father made for the coming of his Son into the world. Our first candle reminds us of Abraham, Isaac, Moses and David who looked forward to the coming of Jesus.

Today is the Second Sunday in Advent: we remember how God our Father also spoke to people through his prophets and told *them* of the Christ who was to come.

Isaiah said, 'A child is born to us! A son is given to us! He will be called Wonderful Counsellor, Mighty God, Eternal Father, Prince of Peace.'
Praise you, Lord.

Jeremiah said, '"The Days are coming," says the Lord, "when I will choose as king a righteous descendant of David. This king will reign wisely and do what is just and right in the land. This is the name by which he will be called: The Lord our Salvation."'
Praise you, Lord.

Ezekiel said, 'I will show myself holy among you in the sight of the nations. Then you will know that I am the Lord.'
Praise you, Lord

Micah said, 'Out of Bethlehem will come for me one who will be ruler over Israel, whose origins are from of old, from ancient times.'
Praise you, Lord.

The second candle is lit

As we light this second candle we remember Isaiah, Jeremiah, Ezekiel and Micah, who prepared the way for the Messiah who was to come. **Amen.**

▶ **24.4** ADVENT 3 – THE FORERUNNER
John 1.29; John 1.34; Luke 3.16; Mark 1.10,11.

The previous Sunday's two candles are lit

As we light the candles in our Advent Wreath we remember the preparations which God our Father made for the coming of his Son into the world. Our first candle reminds us of Abraham, Isaac, Moses

442

and David who looked forward to the coming of Jesus. Our second candle reminds us of Isaiah, Jeremiah, Ezekiel and Micah who told of the coming Messiah.

Today is the Third Sunday in Advent: we remember how John the Baptist was sent to prepare the way for the Lord.

John testified, 'Look, the Lamb of God who takes away the sin of the world!'
Praise you, Lord.

John said, 'I have seen and I testify that this is the Son of God.'
Praise you, Lord.

John promised, 'He will baptise you with the Holy Spirit and with fire.'
Praise you, Lord.

John saw the Holy Spirit descend on Jesus like a dove. And a voice came from heaven, 'You are my Son, whom I love; with you I am well pleased.'
Praise you, Lord.

The third candle is lit

We light this third candle and remember John the Baptist, who came to prepare the way for the Lord. **Amen.**

▶ **24.5   ADVENT 4 – THE VIRGIN MARY**
Luke 1.30; Luke 1.35; Luke 1.49; Matthew 1.23.

The previous Sunday's three candles are lit

As we light the candles in our Advent Wreath we remember the preparations which God our Father made for the coming of his Son into the world. Our first candle reminds us of Abraham, Isaac, Moses and David who looked forward to the coming of Jesus. Our second candle reminds us of Isaiah, Jeremiah, Ezekiel and Micah who told of the coming Messiah. Our third candle reminds us of John the Baptist who came to prepare the way for the Lord.

Today is the Fourth Sunday in Advent: we remember how Jesus, the Son of God was born of a human mother so that he was truly both God and man.

The angel Gabriel said, 'Do not be afraid, Mary, you have found favour with God.'
Thank you, Father.

Gabriel said to Mary, 'The holy one to be born of you will be called the Son of God.'
Thank you, Father.

Mary said, 'The Mighty One has done great things for me – holy is his name.'
Thank you, Father.

They will call him Immanuel, which means, God with us.
Thank you, Father.

The fourth candle is lit

As we light this fourth candle, we remember Mary who was obedient and so became the mother of Jesus. **Amen.**

▶ **24.6** CHRISTMAS DAY – CHRIST THE LIGHT OF THE WORLD

All the Advent Sunday candles are lit, leaving the one in the centre

As we light the candles in our Advent Wreath we remember the preparations which God our Father made for the coming of his Son into the world. Our first candle reminds us of Abraham, Isaac, Moses and David who looked forward to the coming of Jesus. Our second candle reminds us of Isaiah, Jeremiah, Ezekiel and Micah who told of the coming Messiah. Our third candle reminds us of John the Baptist who came to prepare the way for the Lord. Our fourth candle reminds us of Mary who was obedient and became the mother of Jesus.

The centre candle is lit

Today is Christmas Day: on this special day we light the last candle and rejoice together:
Christ, the Light of the World has come! Amen.

24.7 SENTENCE
Mark 1.15

The kingdom of God is close at hand. Repent, and believe the gospel.

24.8 SENTENCE
Hebrews 10.37

He who is coming will come, and will not delay.

24.9 SENTENCE
Matthew 24.27

As lightening that comes out of the east is visible even in the west, so will be the coming of the Son of Man.

24.10 SENTENCE
2 Peter 3.10

The day of the Lord will come like a thief. The heavens will disappear with a roar; the elements will be destroyed by fire, and the earth and everything in it will be laid bare.

24.11 SENTENCE
Matthew 25. 31,32

When the Son of Man comes in his glory, and all the angels with him, he will sit on his throne in heavenly glory, and all the nations will be gathered before him.

24.12 SENTENCE
Matthew 25. 6,13

At midnight the cry rang out: 'Here's the bridegroom! Come out to meet him!' Keep watch, because you do not know the day or the hour.

24.13 SENTENCE
Matthew 24.44

So you must be ready, because the Son of Man will come at an hour when you do not expect him.

24.14 SENTENCE
Luke 21.36

Watch at all times, praying for strength to stand with confidence before the Son of Man.

24.15 SENTENCE
1 Corinthians 4.5

When the Lord comes, he will bring to light things now hidden in darkness, and will disclose the purposes of the heart.

24.16 SENTENCE
Hebrews 4.13

Everything is uncovered and laid bare before the eyes of him to whom we must give account.

24.17 SENTENCE
2 Peter 3.8,9

With the Lord, a day is like a thousand years. The Lord is not slow in keeping his promise; he is patient, not wanting anyone to perish, but everyone to come to repentance.

▶ **24.18** RESPONSE
From Romans 13†

Now is the time to wake from sleep:
our salvation is nearer
than when we first believed.

▶ **24.19** RESPONSE
From Isaiah 40†

The glory of the Lord shall be revealed:
and everyone
shall see it together!

▶ **24.20** RESPONSE
From Daniel 4†

We tell of the miraculous signs and wonders that the Most High God has performed for us:

How great are his signs:
how mighty are his wonders!

His kingdom is eternal:
his reign endures from generation to generation for ever! Amen.

▶ **24.21** RESPONSE
From Revelation 1†

Look, he is coming with the clouds:
and every eye will see him.
Even those who pierced him.

All the peoples of the earth shall mourn because of him.
So shall it be! Amen.

▶ **24.22** RESPONSE
From Revelation 1†

Look, he is coming on the clouds:
everyone will see him.

All people on earth will mourn over him:
so shall it be!

'I am the first and the last,' says the Lord God Almighty:
who is, who was, and who is to come. Amen.

▶ **24.23** RESPONSE
From Revelation 11†

The kingdom of this world has become the kingdom of our Lord and
of his Christ:
he will reign for ever and ever. Amen.

24.24 APPROACH
From Matthew 24†

Lord, we come to you, Alpha and Omega, the beginning and the
end. We wait for your return, keeping watch because we do not
know the day or the hour. We hear of wars and rumours of wars –
and we know that such things must happen; nation rises against
nation. There are famines and earthquakes, signs in the sun and the
moon – birth-pangs of the new age – all creation yearns for the
setting free of the children of God. Lord, false prophets appear and
we need your discernment; the love of many grows cold – help us to
stand firm in our salvation! Yet the gospel of the kingdom is being
preached to the whole world, as a testimony to all nations; the leaves
of the tree are sprouting and we know that summer is near. For this,
O Lord, we praise you. Heaven and earth will pass away, but your
word stands for ever and ever. **Amen.**

▶ **24.25** PRAISE
From Psalms 82 and 83†

Come, O God, and rule the earth:
every land belongs to you.

Let them know that you are king,
sovereign over all the world! Amen.

▶ **24.26** CONFESSION
Editors

We must give account of our stewardship: let us ask forgiveness for
our sin and failure.

Lord, we have not used your gifts wisely: forgive us for being
unprofitable; in your mercy,
hear us and help us.

Lord, we have not kept brightly burning the light you entrusted to
us: forgive us for being unprepared; in your mercy,
hear us and help us.

Lord, we have sometimes ended the day in anger or bitterness:
forgive us for being unrepentant: in your mercy,
hear us and help us.

Renew our vision,
restore our watchfulness,
make us faithful as you are faithful,
that when you come in glory
we may hear you say:
'Enter into the joy of your Lord.' Amen.

▶ **24.27** CONFESSION
Liturgical Commission

Lord God, we come to you
with sorrow for our sins;
and we ask for your help and strength.
Help us to know ourselves
and to accept our weakness.
Strengthen us with your forgiving love,
so that we may more courageously
   follow and obey your Son,
whose birth we are soon to celebrate. Amen.

▶ **24.28** CONFESSION
From Psalm 51†

O God, in your goodness have mercy on us,
wash us clean from our guilt:
and purify us from our sin.

We know our faults well:
and our sins hang heavy upon us.

Against you only have we sinned:
and done evil in your sight.

So you are right to judge us:
you are justified in condemning us.

Remove our sin and we will be clean:
wash us, and we will be whiter than snow.

Hide your face from our sins:
**and wipe out all our guilt
through Jesus Christ our Lord. Amen.**

▶ **24.29** CONFESSION
From Nehemiah 9†

**O our God,
the great, mighty and awesome God,
gracious and merciful;
you keep your covenant of love–
you have acted faithfully
   while we have done wrong.**

**We did not follow your commandment
or pay attention to the warnings you gave us;
even while we were enjoying your great goodness
we did not serve you,
or turn from our evil ways;
because of our sin
our happiness is taken away –
our enemy rules even our souls and bodies
and we are in great distress.**

**Forgive us and restore us
for your name's sake. Amen.**

24.30 ABSOLUTION
From Psalm 51†

God, the righteous judge, remove your sins from you and wash you whiter than snow; may he give you a pure heart, may he strengthen you and renew your spirit, may he restore to you his presence and bring you the joy of his salvation; through Jesus Christ our Lord. **Amen.**

▶ **24.31** COLLECT
Advent, ASB 1980

Almighty God,
give us grace
to cast away the works of darkness
and to put on the armour of light,
now in the time of this mortal life,
in which your Son Jesus Christ
    came to us in great humility:
so that on the last day,
when he shall come again
    in his glorious majesty
to judge the living and the dead,
we may rise to the life immortal;
through him who is alive and reigns
    with you and the Holy Spirit,
one God, now and for ever. **Amen.**

▶ **24.32** PSALM
Psalm 98.1–9†

The congregation may divide at A and B

O sing to the Lord a new song:
for he has done marvellous things.

His right hand and his holy arm:
have brought a great triumph to us.

He lets his salvation be known:
A **his righteousness seen by the world.**

His glory is witnessed by all:
B **to us he continues his love.**

Rejoice in the Lord, all the earth:
ALL **and burst into jubilant song.**

Make music to God with the harp:
A **with songs and the sound of your praise.**

With trumpets and blast of the horn:
B **sing praises to God as your king.**

Let rivers and streams clap their hands:
A **the mountains together sing praise.**

The Lord comes to judge the whole earth:
B **in righteousness God rules the world.**

ALL **Amen.**

24.33 READING: THE COMING OF THE KINGDOM
From Luke 17.20–24, 31–37

Cast: Narrator, Jesus, Person 1, Person 2 (Persons 1 and 2 can be the same as Jesus), Disciple

Narrator
Some Pharisees asked Jesus when the Kingdom of God would come. His answer was:

Jesus
The Kingdom of God does not come in such a way as to be seen. No one will say, 'Look, here it is! or, 'There it is!'; because the Kingdom of God is within you.

Narrator
Then he said to the disciples:

Jesus
The time will come when you will wish you could see one of the days of the Son of Man, but you will not see it. There will be those who will say to you:

Person 1
Look, over there!

Person 2
Look, over here!

Jesus
But don't go out looking for it. As the lightning flashes across the sky and lights it up from one side to the other, so will the Son of Man be in his day. On that day the man who is on the roof of his

451

house must not go down into the house to get his belongings; in the same way the man who is out in the field must not go back to the house. Remember Lot's wife! Whoever tries to save his own life will lose it; whoever loses his life will save it. On that night, I tell you, there will be two people sleeping in the same bed: one will be taken away, the other will be left behind. Two women will be grinding corn together: one will be taken away, the other will be left behind.

Narrator
The disciples asked him:

Disciple(s)
Where, Lord?

Jesus
Wherever there is a dead body, the vultures will gather.

Cast
[This is] the word of the Lord.   OR   This is the Gospel of Christ/
This is the Gospel of the Lord.

All
Thanks be to God.   **Praise to Christ our Lord/**
Praise to you, Lord Jesus Christ.

FURTHER BIBLE READINGS
Readings appropriate to this theme will be found listed in our companion volume, 'The Dramatised Bible' (published by HarperCollins) on index pages 434–436.

▶ **24.34** CREED
From Colossians 1†

God has rescued us from the power of darkness,
and brought us safe
into the kingdom of his dear Son:
in Christ our sins are forgiven,
we are set free. Amen.

▶ **24.35** CREED
Holy Communion, ASB 1980

Let us proclaim the mystery of our faith:
Christ has died,
Christ is risen,
Christ will come again.

24.36   CREED
From Revelation 4 and 5†

We say together in faith:

Holy, holy, holy
is the Lord God Almighty,
who was, and is, and is to come.

We believe in God the Father, who created all things:
for by his will they were created
and have their being.

We believe in God the Son, who was slain:
for with his blood,
he purchased us for God,
from every tribe and language
and people and nation.

We believe in God the Holy Spirit –
the Spirit and the Bride say, 'Come!'
Even so, come, Lord Jesus! Amen.

24.37   ABOUT CHRIST'S COMING
Christopher Idle

O God, who has given us the sure promise that Christ will come to judge the earth: make us ready, we pray, for his royal coming, that we may consider daily what kind of people we ought to be, and as faithful servants wait and work for our Master's return; for his name's sake. **Amen.**

24.38   ABOUT BEING READY
Editor

Lord Jesus Christ, whose advent all shall see: let your coming be with triumph, but not to our shame; let your coming be with glory, but not to our surprise; let your coming be with justice, but not to our judgement. Make our love burn bright for you, our loyalty endure, and our faith increase; that with you we may rejoice on that day, and so enter into your eternal kingdom. **Amen.**

24.39   FOR HELP IN BEING READY
St Simon and St Jude, Southsea

Almighty God, our heavenly Father, as we wait for the return of the Lord Jesus Christ, help us to make the best use of the gifts you have given us – our skills, our time and our possessions; help us to share our good things with those in need as Jesus has taught us to do, and help us to share our faith humbly with those who are not following him, so that they and we may be ready when he appears. We ask these things in his name. **Amen.**

24.40   FOR THE COMING OF THE KINGDOM
Editors

We praise you, Lord God, that all kingdoms of this world are to become the kingdom of your Son. Purge out error in the nations – sweep out corruption, root out the powers of evil, and establish us in grace and goodness. Lord, open the barred doors of human hearts and lives; help us to let the King of glory into our communities.

So let justice overwhelm injustice and peace conquer hostility; so speed the gospel of your grace to every land that all may proclaim Jesus Christ as Lord. **Amen.**

24.41   FOR HOPE
From 1 Thessalonians 4†

Lord Jesus, you will come from heaven with a loud command, with the voice of the archangel, and with the trumpet-call of God: confirm our faith in your death and resurrection so that we shall not grieve as others do who have no hope for those who have fallen asleep in Christ, but believe that you will bring them with you to meet us in the skies and be with you for ever. **Amen.**

▶ **24.42**   ABOUT THE END OF TIME
From Mark 13†

When the skies grow dark and buildings fall, then hear us, Lord:
have mercy on us.

When the deceivers come and the nations rise in anger, then hear us, Lord:
have mercy on us.

When the famines begin, and when the earth shakes to bring the future to birth, then hear us, Lord:
have mercy on us.

When we stand for a witness, when we are arrested and betrayed, then hear us, Lord:
have mercy on us.

When the sun is darkened and the moon fails to give us light, and the stars fall from the sky, then hear us, Lord:
have mercy on us.

When you come in your great power and glory with your angels from heaven; have mercy, Lord:
gather us from the four winds
from the ends of the earth
to be with you for ever. Amen.

▶ **24.43**   ACT OF PRAISE (AT HOLY COMMUNION)
St Catherine's, Houghton-on-the-Hill, Leicester

Jesus, you came to live among us, born of the virgin Mary. We give you thanks:
and praise your holy name.

Jesus, you come to us as we read your story in the Bible. We give you thanks:
and praise your holy name.

Jesus, you come to us as we take in faith the bread and wine. We give you thanks:
and praise your holy name.

Jesus, you will come to reign in glory. We give you thanks:
and praise your holy name.

Amen. Come, Lord Jesus!

▶ **24.44**   THANKSGIVING
Editors

Our gracious God, out of chaos and darkness in the beginning you brought into being the splendour of the universe and the world in all its beauty. God, we praise you:
God, we thank you.

At the right time you sent your Son to be the light of the world, to lead us out of spiritual darkness into the marvellous brightness of your truth. In him has dawned the day of resurrection life. God, we praise you:
God, we thank you.

Above all the noise and movement of this world today, we look for the coming of the new heaven and earth, 'the holy city of God'. Lord Jesus, you are coming again in great power and glory. God, we praise you:
God, we thank you.

We thank you that you are in this world, by your Spirit preparing a people for this next great cosmic event. God, we praise you:
God, we thank you.

We thank you that you are healing lives that have been torn and broken by sin, and that you are filling us with joy and hope. God, we praise you:
God, we thank you.

Lord God, we await the dawning of the new day when the earth shall be filled with the glory of God as the waters cover the sea.
To God be praise and thanks for evermore. Amen.

▶ **24.45   DEDICATION: A PERSONAL PRAYER**
Editors

Call me, infant Lord Jesus;
draw me to the stable
  where your cradle was a manger,
let me kneel before you, God's own Lamb,
and worship you.

Call me, crucified Christ;
draw me to the Cross
  where you suffered and yet still prayed,
let me kneel before your act of pure love
and worship you.

Call me, Prince of Life;
draw me to your side
  for you are risen and here among us,
let me kneel before the light of your holiness
and worship you, and pledge myself anew. **Amen.**

▶ **24.46** INVOCATION (ADVENT)
Liturgical Commission

Come, Lord Jesus, do not delay;
give new courage to your people
who trust in your love.
By your coming, raise us
to the joy of your kingdom,
where you live and reign,
with the Father and the Spirit,
one God for ever and ever. **Amen.**

▶ **24.47** INVOCATION (BEFORE CHRISTMAS)
Editors

Jesus, who came to earth as a helpless baby;
Jesus, the Lamb of God born in a stable;
Jesus, the Prince of Peace who slept on hay;
Jesus, whose birth caused the angels to sing;
Jesus, whose glory lit up the sky;
Jesus, whose coming was foretold;
Jesus, who gave us his life;
Jesus, who draws us with love;
Jesus, our saviour, our king:
come, Lord Jesus, come. Amen.

24.48 BLESSING (ADVENT)
From Isaiah 35†

Strengthen the feeble hands, steady the knees that give way: behold
the glory of the Lord, the splendour of our God. Be strong, do not
fear; your God will come. And his blessing be upon you now and
always. **Amen.**

24.49 BLESSING
From 'Still Waters, Deep Waters'

The dying Saviour's love, the risen Saviour's power, the ascended
Saviour's blessing, and the returning Saviour's glory be the joy and
comfort of *your* hearts now and for ever. **Amen.**

24.50 BLESSING
From 1 Thessalonians 5†

God who gives us peace make you holy in every way: keep your whole being, spirit, soul and body, free from every fault at the coming of our Lord Jesus Christ; and the blessing of God who is faithful, Father, Son and Holy Spirit be with you always. **Amen.**

24.51 BLESSING
From 2 Timothy 4

In the presence of God and of Christ Jesus who will judge the living and the dead, and because he comes as king: preach the word, be prepared at all times whether people will listen or not; always keep control of yourself, endure suffering, share the good news of Christ, do the task that God has given you; and the blessing of God almighty, the Father, the Son and the Holy Spirit be with you always. **Amen.**

God's Word to Us, Proclamation

▶ **25.1** GREETING
From 2 Peter 1†

Grace and peace be yours in full measure through the knowledge of God and of Jesus our Lord. **Amen.**

25.2 SENTENCE
Isaiah 55. 10,11

[The Lord declares:] As the rain and the snow come down from heaven and do not return to it without watering the earth making it bud and flourish, so that it yields seed for the sower and bread for the eater, so is my word that goes out from my mouth: it will not return to me empty, but will accomplish what I desire and achieve the purpose for which I sent it.

OR

25.3 SENTENCE
Isaiah 55.11

[The Lord declares:] My word will not return to me empty, but accomplish what I desire and achieve the purpose for which I sent it.

25.4 SENTENCE
Ephesians 6. 14,17

Stand firm . . . take the sword of the Spirit, which is the word of God.

25.5 SENTENCE
Hebrews 4.12

The word of God is living and active. Sharper than any double-edged sword, it penetrates even to dividing soul and spirit, joints and marrow; it judges the thoughts of the heart.

25.6 SENTENCE
Psalm 95.8

Today, if you hear God's voice, do not harden your heart.

25.7 SENTENCE
Revelation 2.7 etc.

If you have ears to hear, listen to what the Spirit is saying to the churches.

25.8 SENTENCE
Romans 15.4

Everything that was written in the past was written to teach us, so that through endurance and the encouragement of the Scriptures we might have hope.

▶ **25.9** RESPONSE
From 2 Samuel 22†

You are our lamp, O Lord:
turn our darkness into light. Amen.

▶ **25.10** RESPONSE
From 2 Timothy 3 and Psalm 119†

All Scripture is inspired by God, and is useful for teaching the truth, rebuking error, correcting faults, and giving instruction for right living:
your word is a lamp to my feet
and a light for my path. Amen.

▶ **25.11** RESPONSE
From Hebrews 5†

Anyone who has to drink milk is still a baby; solid food is for grown people: let us go forward, then, to mature teaching. Let us go forward:
this we will do, God helping us. Amen.

▶ **25.12** RESPONSE
From Jeremiah 15†

Your words are our joy and our heart's delight:
for we bear your name,
O Lord God almighty. Amen.

25.13 APPROACH
From Hebrews 12†

Come to worship the Lord; to Mount Zion, to the heavenly Jerusalem, to the city of the living God, to thousands upon thousands of angels in joyful assembly, to the church of the firstborn, whose names are written in heaven; to God, the judge of all, to the spirits of the righteous, to Jesus the mediator of a new covenant, and do not refuse him who speaks.

25.14 APPROACH
Editors

Grant, O Lord, that through our worship this day we may be awakened to the wonder of your love for us; that familiar words may shine with new meaning, the habit of worship cleansed of all formality and mere ceremonial observance. Open our eyes to see your loveliness, and make our hearts burn within us as you speak your word to us. May we know ourselves forgiven, and feel our spirits energised with new life, throbbing with new vitality and power through your Holy Spirit; in the name of Jesus Christ our Lord. **Amen.**

▶ **25.15** PRAISE
From Psalm 67†

Let the people praise you, O God;
let all the people praise you!

Let your ways be known on earth;
your saving power in all the world!
Amen.

▶ **25.16** CONFESSION
From 2 Kings 22†

Lord, we have not obeyed your word,
nor heeded
    what is written in the Scriptures:
we repent with all our heart,
and humble ourselves before you.
In your mercy forgive us:
grant us your peace
and the strength to keep your laws;
through Jesus Christ our Lord. Amen.

▶ **25.17** CONFESSION
From Psalm 119†

Lord, we are to blame,
for we have not followed your law,
we have not kept your commandments,
we have not sought for you with all our heart,
we have not walked in your ways,
nor have we fully obeyed you;
Lord, we long to be faithful and obedient:
do not put us to shame.
Give us upright hearts,
teach us obedience
and do not forsake us for ever. Amen.

25.18 ABSOLUTION
From Isaiah 43†

This is what the Lord says – your redeemer, the holy One: 'I, even I,
will blot out your transgressions, and remember your sins no more;
for my name's sake'. **Amen.**

▶ **25.19** COLLECT
A Prayer of Dedication, ASB 1980

Almighty God,
we thank you for the gift of your holy word.
Let it be a lantern to our feet,
a light to our paths, and a strength to our lives.
Take us and use us
to love and serve
in the power of the Holy Spirit
and in the name of your Son,
Jesus Christ our Lord. **Amen.**

▶ **25.20** PSALM
Psalm 111.1–10†

The congregation may divide at A *and* B

Praise the Lord:
praise the Lord!

With my whole heart I will thank the Lord: in the company of
his people. Great are the works of the Lord:
A **those who wonder, seek them.**

Glorious and majestic are his deeds:
B **his goodness lasts for ever.**

He reminds us of his works of grace:
A **he is merciful and kind.**

He sustains those who fear him:
B **he keeps his covenant always.**

All he does is right and just:
A **all his words are faithful.**

They will last for ever and ever:
B **and be kept in faith and truth.**

He provided redemption for his people, and made an eternal
covenant with them:
ALL **holy and awesome is his name!**

The fear of the Lord is the beginning of wisdom; he gives
understanding to those who obey:
ALL **to God belongs eternal praise! Amen**

▶ **25.21** PSALM
Psalm 149.1–9†

The congregation – and ministers – may divide at A *and* B

Praise the Lord:
praise the Lord!

Sing a new song to the Lord:
A **let the people shout his name!**

Praise your maker, Israel:
B **hail your king, Jerusalem.**

Sing and dance to honour him:
A **praise him with the strings and drums.**

God takes pleasure in his saints:
B **crowns the meek with victory.**

Rise, you saints, in triumph now:
A **sing the joyful night away!**

Shout aloud and praise your God!
B **Hold aloft the two-edged sword!**

Let the judgement now begin:
A **kings shall fall and tyrants die.**

Through his people, by his word:
B **God shall have the victory!**

Praise the Lord:
ALL **praise the Lord! Amen.**

25.22 READING: EZRA READS THE LAW
From Nehemiah 8.1–12

Cast: Narrator, Ezra, People (two or more)

Narrator
By the seventh month the people of Israel were all settled in their towns. On the first day of that month they all assembled in Jerusalem, in the square just inside the Water Gate. They asked Ezra, the priest and scholar of the Law which the Lord had given Israel through Moses, to get the book of the Law. So Ezra brought it to the place where the people had gathered – men, women, and the children who were old enough to understand. There in the

square by the gate he read the Law to them from dawn until noon, and they all listened attentively.

Ezra was standing on a wooden platform that had been built for the occasion. Six men stood at his right, and seven stood at his left.

As Ezra stood there on the platform high above the people, they all kept their eyes fixed on him. As soon as he opened the book, they all stood up. Ezra said:

Ezra
Praise the Lord, the great God!

Narrator
All the people raised their arms in the air and answered:

People
Amen! Amen!

Narrator
They knelt in worship, with their faces to the ground. Then they rose and stood in their places, and the Levites explained the Law to them. They gave an oral translation of God's Law and explained it so that the people could understand it. (PAUSE)

When the people heard what the Law required, they were so moved that they began to cry. So Nehemiah, who was the governor, Ezra, the priest and scholar of the Law, and the Levites who were explaining the Law told all the people:

Ezra
This day is holy to the Lord your God, so you are not to mourn or cry. Now go home and have a feast. Share your food and wine with those who haven't enough. Today is holy to our Lord, so don't be sad. The joy that the Lord gives you will make you strong.

Narrator
The Levites went about calming the people and telling them not to be sad on such a holy day. So all the people went home and ate and drank joyfully and shared what they had with others, because they understood what had been read to them.

Cast
[This is] the word of the Lord.

All
Thanks be to God.

25.23   READING: THE SOWER
Matthew 13.1–9, 18–23

Cast: Narrator, Story-teller, Interpreter

Narrator
Jesus left the house and went to the lake-side, where he sat down to teach. The crowd that gathered round him was so large that he got into a boat and sat in it, while the crowd stood on the shore. He used parables to tell them many things.

Story-teller
Once there was a man who went out to sow corn.

Interpreter
Listen, then, and learn what the parable of the sower means.

Story-teller
As he scattered the seed in the field, some of it fell along the path, and the birds came and ate it up.

Interpreter
Those who hear the message about the Kingdom but do not understand it are like the seeds that fell along the path. The Evil One comes and snatches away what was sown in them. (PAUSE)

Story-teller
Some of it fell on rocky ground, where there was little soil. The seeds soon sprouted, because the soil wasn't deep. But when the sun came up, it burnt the young plants; and because the roots had not grown deep enough, the plants soon dried up.

Interpreter
The seeds that fell on rocky ground stand for those who receive the message gladly as soon as they hear it. But it does not sink deep into them, and they don't last long. So when trouble or persecution comes because of the message, they give up at once. (PAUSE)

Story-teller
Some of the seed fell among thorn bushes, which grew up and choked the plants.

Interpreter
The seeds that fell among thorn bushes stand for those who hear the message; but the worries about this life and the love for riches choke the message, and they don't bear fruit. (PAUSE)

Story-teller
> But some seeds fell in good soil, and the plants produced corn; some produced a hundred grains, others sixty, and others thirty.

Interpreter
> And the seeds sown in the good soil stand for those who hear the message and understand it: they bear fruit, some as much as a hundred, others sixty, and others thirty.

Narrator
> And Jesus concluded, 'Listen, then, if you have ears!'

Cast
> [This is] the word of the Lord.   OR   This is the Gospel of Christ/
> This is the Gospel of the Lord.

All
> **Thanks be to God.**   **Praise to Christ our Lord/**
> **Praise to you, Lord Jesus Christ.**

FURTHER BIBLE READINGS

Readings appropriate to this theme will be found listed in our companion volume, 'The Dramatised Bible' (published by HarperCollins) on index pages 436–437.

▶ **25.24** RESPONSE (AFTER A READING)
From Revelation 1–7†

If you have ears to hear, then listen to what the Spirit says to the churches! **Amen.**

▶ **25.25** CREED
From Romans 1†

We believe in the Gospel,
promised by God long ago
through the prophets,
written in the Holy Scriptures.

We believe in God's Son,
**   our Lord Jesus Christ:**
as to his humanity,
born a descendant of David;
as to his divinity,

shown with great power
   to be the Son of God
by his raising from death. Amen.

▶ **25.26** CREED
From 1 Timothy 3†

Let us proclaim the mystery of our faith:

We believe in one Lord Jesus Christ –
he was revealed in the flesh,
attested by the Spirit,
seen by apostles,
proclaimed to the nations,
believed in throughout the world,
and taken up to glory. Amen.

▶ **25.27** THANKSGIVING FOR INSPIRATION
Dick Williams

Thank you, Lord, for the Bible:

For its ability to give us each day new vision and new power: O Lord
of inspiration,
we give you thanks and praise.

For its capacity to enter into our minds and spirits, refreshing them
and fashioning them anew: O Lord of inspiration,
we give you thanks and praise.

For its power to bring faith to birth and to sustain it: O Lord of
inspiration,
we give you thanks and praise.

Thank you, Lord, for the Bible,
through Jesus Christ our Saviour. Amen.

▶ **25.28** THANKSGIVING FOR GOD'S WORD
Emmanuel Church, Northwood.

Let us thank God for all his blessings:

For your creative word, by which the earth and sky were made: we
thank you, Father,
and praise your holy name.

For making us in your own image, able to hear and answer your call: we thank you, Father,
and praise your holy name.

For revealing yourself to people through the ages, and changing their lives: we thank you, Father,
and praise your holy name.

For your word to us in these days, calling us to repentance and assuring us of forgiveness: we thank you, Father,
and praise your holy name.

For promising to hear our prayers, and faithfully meeting our every need: we thank you, Father,
and praise your holy name.

Grant that we may worship you,
not only with our voices,
but in true and willing service,
through Jesus Christ our Lord. Amen.

▶ **25.29**   THANKSGIVING FOR THE BIBLE
J. Meirion Lloyd, adapted

Let us give thanks to God:

For the majesty of the Law, for the power of the Prophets, for the wisdom of the Proverbs and the beauty of the Psalms, and above all for the grace of the Gospel, we lift up our hearts in praise:
thanks be to God!

For the Bible in our own language, for those who long ago gave us translations, for those who down the years improved them, enabling the Scriptures to penetrate deeply into our national life, we lift up our hearts in praise:
thanks be to God!

For the continuing work of revision to match our changing language, for all that the Bible means to Christians throughout the world, we lift up our hearts in praise:
thanks be to God!

For those who interpret, publish and distribute the Scriptures in every tongue, so that all peoples may come to the knowledge of salvation, we lift up our hearts in praise:
thanks be to God!

To you, O gracious Father,
with the living Word,
through the one eternal Spirit,
be glory now and for ever. Amen

25.30 THANKSGIVING FOR GOD'S WORD THROUGH THE BIBLE
British and Foreign Bible Society

We give thanks O God, for the millions of Scriptures which are being distributed, for the new translations which are being produced, and for the dedicated servants who sow the seeds of your word. We pray for those who receive your word; that they may understand all it teaches and through using it discover your living Word, our Lord Jesus, in whose name we pray. **Amen.**

25.31 THANKSGIVING FOR THE MINISTRY OF THE BIBLE
Editors

Father God, we give thanks for our Holy Bible, which contains the good news of Salvation for all and teaches us how to live and respond to you, our Creator. We praise and thank you for the living, active power of the Bible, which constantly ministers love and hope and healing to us. Father, our hearts and minds are filled with joy when we read about your Son, Jesus Christ, who came to set us free to be at one with you. His promises make us secure. Quieten us and bless us that we may often hear you speak to us through your word; and may we always cherish the book which reveals your divine plan of restoration for the whole human family; for Jesus' sake. **Amen.**

25.32 FOR THOSE WHO DO NOT HAVE BIBLES
Editors

O God who has spoken through the Scriptures, we pray for those who are hindered or prevented from receiving your word: strengthen them in times of difficulty, and enable them by the power of your Holy Spirit to grow in knowledge of you. Then give them courage to share their faith with others, for the extension of your kingdom; through Jesus Christ our Lord. **Amen.**

25.33   FOR THE MINISTRY OF CHRISTIAN LITERATURE
Editors

O God, who speaks to us through the printed page, we pray today for the ministry of writers, publishers, book-shops and book agents. We rejoice at the wealth of Christian literature available. Give discernment to those who assess manuscripts, wisdom to editors, tenacity to proof-readers, diligence to typists, type-setters and printers, enthusiasm and graciousness to all who sell books, and diligence to all who read. Hear us as we pray in the name of the great teacher, Jesus our Lord. **Amen.**

25.34   FOR PREACHERS
From Acts 4†

Sovereign Lord, you made the heaven and the earth and the sea, and everything in them; you spoke by the Holy Spirit through the mouth of your servants of old. Enable your servants today to speak your word with great boldness; stretch out your hand to heal and perform miraculous signs and wonders through the name of your holy servant Jesus. **Amen.**

25.35   FOR THE ARTS AND THE MEDIA
St Michael-le-Belfrey, York

Creator God, we pray for all Christians who work in the arts, or in the news media (especially any among us here), for all who design, all who write or compose, and all who direct or perform: help them to grow in their love for you, and let their work always reflect your truth as it is in Christ Jesus; for his sake. **Amen.**

25.36   FOR BROADCASTERS AND JOURNALISTS
From 'New Every Morning'

Almighty God, whose truth has been declared in days past by the voice of prophets and evangelists: direct the minds of those who speak in our time where many listen, and write what many read. We ask for them reverence for the truth, sensitivity to human need, and a true concern for the welfare of all; through Jesus Christ our Lord. **Amen.**

25.37   FOR BROADCASTERS AND JOURNALISTS
From 'New Every Morning'

O God, we thank you that you have spoken to us through the words of Scripture, and chiefly through him who is the living Word of God. We pray for all who, by what they say and write, influence the lives of others; for those whose daily task is the use of words. Grant them your wisdom and the knowledge of your truth that they may be a blessing to us all, and bring glory to your name. **Amen.**

25.38   FOR ALL COMMUNICATORS
Edward Smalley

Our gracious Father, we pray for all who write what many read and speak where many listen. May all engaged in television or radio, all dramatists and actors, all journalists and artists, all preachers and teachers, be enabled in their work by your Spirit; that all who see and hear them, or read their words, may be led in truth and enriched in knowledge and understanding, to the glory of your name; through Jesus Christ our Lord. **Amen.**

25.39   FOR ALL WHO HAVE INFLUENCE
From 'New Every Morning'

We pray, O God, for those who as writers, speakers and entertainers influence the thought of our people through the press, radio and television. Help them to exercise their gifts with responsibility and understanding, that they may enrich the common life of the nation and strengthen the forces of truth and goodness; through Jesus Christ our Lord. **Amen.**

25.40   FOR BLESSING THROUGH THE PRINTED WORD
Editors

Let us in God's presence reflect upon the power of the printed word.

The printed word can give new thoughts and ideas to millions of readers; it can survive to speak across the centuries; it can reach those who are cut off from the influence of the spoken word; it can speak intimately to people in their own homes; it can be left behind to continue its message when the spoken word is silenced. But the printed word can be either poison or food: it can propagate lies, suspicion, and hatred – or truth, trust and friendship.

So we pray for those who are now learning to read, that their new skills may become for them a means of knowing and loving our Lord Jesus Christ.

We pray also for those who teach the illiterate to read; and we remember before God writers and translators, journalists and artists, editors and printers, and publishers and booksellers, that they may make wise and responsible use of their powers.

With thanksgiving to God for what we have been able to do in the past, let us offer ourselves, our gifts, our possessions, to proclaim the good news of the Christian gospel through the printed word.

Lord, your word is truth: let our words spoken and written be ever true. Lord, your word is life: bless all who speak or write in the name of Christ. **Amen.**

▶ **25.41** THAT WE MAY HEAR GOD'S VOICE
Editors

O Lord, voices surround us, always clamouring, directing, imploring, accusing; and our own voices are too strident. May we be quiet and listen, so that you may speak –

In miracle; in the wonders of human courage and hope and endurance and sacrifice that we meet in ordinary people. O Lord, speak to us:
help us to listen.

In Spirit; in the mysteries beyond our comprehension, in the faith that defies all mortal order, in the resurrection truth. O Lord, speak to us:
help us to listen.

In joy; in laughter, in human warmth, in triumph over pain, in the experience of beauty. O Lord, speak to us:
help us to listen.

Speak, O Lord, that we may listen
and tell what great things you have done for us,
in Jesus' name. Amen.

25.42 FOR UNDERSTANDING
Unknown

God our Father, we praise and thank you for the gift of words – the words we hear and read, the words we speak and write. As we handle and use the holy Scriptures, make us more sensitive to what they say, more appreciative of the life and truth in these pages, and of the love and courage of those who wrote them; and open our ears to your voice, and our lives to yourself; through Jesus Christ our Lord. **Amen.**

▶ **25.43** FOR UNDERSTANDING
Michael Botting

Heavenly Father,
you have shown
the wonder of your love for us in Jesus Christ
through the Bible:
help us to understand it with our minds,
and apply it in our lives: for his name's sake. **Amen.**

▶ **25.44** FOR STRENGTH
Editors

We pray for God's help as we read his commands in the Bible, or as we listen to his word:

When we are tempted to do or say wrong things, Lord,
speak to us in our selfishness;
help us to be strong.

When we are anxious or afraid, Lord,
speak to us in our fearfulness;
help us to be strong.

When we are ill or in pain, Lord,
speak to us in our helplessness;
help us to be strong.

When things we have to do seem too hard for us, Lord,
speak to us in our weakness;
help us to be strong.

O God,
we will listen to your word;

and by your strength
we will do what you command,
and bring glory to your name. **Amen.**

25.45   ABOUT OUR RESPONSE
From Matthew 13, Mark 4 and Luke 8†

O God, make us receptive to your words: open deaf ears, soften hard hearts, concentrate distracted minds, deepen shallow emotions; send your Spirit, Lord, that your word may take root and grow in us: so may we flourish in your service to the glory of your name; through our Lord Jesus Christ. **Amen.**

▶ 25.46   ABOUT OUR WITNESS
From 'A New Zealand Prayer Book'

Jesus,
new beginning, heavenly bread, living water,
we hear the word of life,
we see and grasp the truth:
help us to proclaim it. **Amen.**

25.47   THAT WE MAY BE CHRISTIAN COMMUNICATORS
Editors

Lord God, our Father, you speak to us through your written word and through our consciences – above all in Jesus Christ your Son. He is your living Word; he not only brought us in himself the good news, but through the Holy Spirit he speaks to us today. Be with us when we proclaim your love to a loveless world; give us clarity and pertinence with spoken words, give us courage to handle truth, and the ability to feel deeply the needs of those who hear or read our communications. We ask this in Christ's name. **Amen.**

▶ 25.48   ACT OF PRAISE AND PRAYER
Editors

Lord God, you have spoken to us in the Law of Israel:
we praise and adore you.

You have challenged us in the words of the Prophets:
we praise and adore you.

You have shown us in the Gospel of Jesus what you are really like:
we praise and adore you.

Lord God, because you still come to us now:
we praise and adore you.

You come to us through other people, in their love and concern for us:
thank you, Lord.

You come to us through men and women, young people and children, who need our help:
thank you, Lord.

You come to us as we worship you:
thank you, Lord.

**Lord God, come to us now;
in the power of Jesus Christ. Amen.**

25.49   BLESSING
R. Pynson, adapted

God be in *your* head, and in *your* understanding;
God be in *your* eyes, and in *your* looking;
God be in *your* mouth, and in *your* speaking;
God be in *your* heart, and in *your* thinking;
God be at *your* end, and at *your* departing. **Amen.**

OR

▶ **25.50**   BLESSING
R Pynson, adapted

God be in our head, and in our understanding;
God be in our eyes, and in our looking;
God be in our mouth, and in our speaking;
God be in our heart, and in our thinking;
God be at our end, and at our departing. **Amen.**

25.51   BLESSING
From Philippians 4†

Whatever is true, whatever is honourable, whatever is just, whatever is pure, whatever is lovely, whatever is gracious; if there is anything excellent or anything worthy of praise, think on these things: and the God of peace be with you. **Amen.**

25.52 BLESSING
From 2 Thessalonians 2 and 3†

God our Father, who loved *you* and by his grace gave *you* eternal courage and good hope, confirm *your* hearts, and strengthen *you* in every good deed and word; the Spirit of peace give *you* peace at all times in every way; and the grace of our Lord Jesus Christ be with *you* all. **Amen.**

25.53 BLESSING
From Colossians 3†

The word of Christ dwell in *you* richly as *you* teach and admonish one another with all wisdom, and as *you* sing psalms, hymns and spiritual songs with gratitude in *your* hearts to God; whatever *you* do in word or deed, (let us) do all in the name of the Lord Jesus, giving thanks to God the Father through him: and the blessing of God – Father, Son and Holy Spirit be with *you* always. **Amen.**

25.54 BLESSING
From 2 Timothy 1†

Hold firmly to the true words you have been taught as the example for you to follow, and remain in the faith and love that are ours in unison with Christ Jesus, through the power of the Holy spirit who lives in us; and the blessing of God – Father, Son and Holy Spirit be with you always. **Amen.**

25.55 BLESSING
From 1 Thessalonians 3†

God himself, our Father, and our Lord Jesus Christ direct your way together; the Lord make your love increase and overflow for each other and for everyone else, the Lord strengthen your hearts so that you will be blameless and holy in the presence of our God and Father at the coming of our Lord Jesus Christ. **Amen.**

Christmas (and Christmas Readings)

▶ **26.1** GREETING
From Titus 1†

Grace and peace to you from God our Father and Jesus Christ our Saviour. **Amen.**

26.2 GREETING
Editor

Welcome, everybody! At Christmas time we delight again to hear the story of the journey to Bethlehem, the song of the angels, the surprise of the shepherds, and their joy as they found Jesus in the manger. And because he was born to poverty, we remember at this season all who are hungry or cold. And because he became a refugee, we remember the stranger and the homeless among us. And because he felt the pain of life and death, we remember those who are ill, or anxious, or bereaved. And because we know he came for our salvation, let us in heart and mind go once again to Bethlehem, to hear again the message of the angels and worship afresh the Son of God.

26.3 SENTENCE: CHRISTMAS EVE SERVICE
Exodus 16.7

In the morning you shall see the glory of the Lord.

26.4 SENTENCE: 'MIDNIGHT' SERVICE
1 Chronicles 16. 31,33

Let the heavens rejoice, and let the earth be glad before the Lord: for he comes!

26.5 SENTENCE
Isaiah 9.2

The people who walked in darkness have seen a great light: those who dwell in the land of deep darkness, on them has the light shone.

26.6 SENTENCE
2 Corinthians 4.6

God has shone in our hearts to give the light of the knowledge of his glory in the face of Jesus Christ.

26.7 SENTENCE
Titus 2.11

The grace of God has dawned on the world with healing for all people.

26.8 SENTENCE
Luke 2. 10,11

I bring you good news of great joy that will be for all people: today in the town of David a Saviour has been born to you: he is Christ the Lord.

▶ **26.9** RESPONSE
From Isaiah 9†

For us a Child is born:
to us a Son is given. Alleluia!

▶ **26.10** RESPONSE
From John 1†

The Word became flesh and lived among us:
we have seen his glory,
the glory of the one and only Son,
who came from the Father,
full of grace and truth.

26.11 INVITATION
From Exodus 14

Do not fear . . . see the salvation of our God!

26.12 APPROACH: *BEFORE* CHRISTMAS
Joyce Huggett

Heavenly Father, as we await the birthday of your Son, Jesus Christ, give us a glimpse of the mystery of the Incarnation; cause us to wonder that the Creator of the universe emptied himself of the splendour and glory of heaven and took upon himself the feeble frame of a fragile baby; restore to us the ability to stop, the serenity to ponder, and the creativity to gaze in wonder at the Christ-child – the radiance of the glory of God, the flawless expression of the divine nature – at God made man, God in human form, God manifesting himself with a vulnerability which asks to be touched and handled and seen and known and loved. And teach us to love you without inhibition; that this Christmas the glow in our hearts may bring joy to you, Father, Son and Holy Spirit. **Amen.**

26.13 APPROACH: MIDNIGHT
David Jenkins

Jesus, new-born child of all time, we greet your birth with wide-eyed delight: you are precious beyond words, for our world needs your presence more than ever. Let the angels' promise of your good news, offering joy and peace to all the world, be heard by those who lead and guide. Let kings bow down, and all creation greet this holy moment as we seek to grasp its magnitude. For you are God's gift, silently delivered to every human heart; Christ our Lord. **Amen.**

26.14 APPROACH: CHRISTMAS DAY
Editors

With joy we sing aloud our praise today, our God and heavenly Father: for your Son, the Saviour of the world has come. He is the embodiment of your love and grace; in him we see life and hope for the world: fill us today with your Holy Spirit, that we may bow before you and be made alive by your presence. Help us, with the working shepherds of old, to bring our adoration and worship to you with joy and gladness. Receive our praises in the name of Jesus our Lord. **Amen.**

▶ **26.15** PRAISE
From Psalm 100†

Shout for joy to the Lord, all the earth;
serve the Lord with gladness!

Come before him with joyful songs;
give thanks to him and praise his name! Amen.

▶ **26.16** ACT OF PRAISE
From 'Worship Now'

Let us worship the Saviour:

Heavenly king, yet born of Mary; Jesus, Son of God,
we praise and adore you.

Eternal Word, yet child without speech; Jesus, Son of God,
we praise and adore you.

Robed in glory, yet wrapped in infant clothes; Jesus, Son of God,
we praise and adore you.

Lord of heaven and earth, yet laid in a manger; Jesus, Son of God,
we praise and adore you.

To you, O Jesus,
strong in your weakness,
glorious in your humility,
mighty to save,
be all praise and glory,
with the Father and the Holy Spirit,
now and for ever. Amen.

▶ **26.17** CONFESSION
John Searle, adapted

We confess that amid all the joys and festivities of this season we
have sometimes forgotten what Christmas really means, and have
left the Lord Jesus out of our thinking and living:
Father, forgive us.

Help us to remember that you loved the world so much that you
gave your only Son, who was born to be our Saviour:
Lord, help us.

We confess that we have allowed the most important event in history to become dulled by familiarity:
Father, forgive us.

Help us in this act of worship to recapture a sense of wonder, and to discover again the stupendous fact that the Creator of the universe has come to us as a newborn baby:
Lord, help us.

We confess to a selfish enjoyment of Christmas while we do little to help the homeless families of your world:
Father, forgive us.

Fill our hearts with the love that cares,
that understands and gives;
show us how we can best serve those in need;
for the sake of him who was born in a stable,
Jesus Christ our Lord. Amen.

▶ **26.18** CONFESSION
Editors

For our repeated failures to respond to your boundless generosity, in your mercy:
Lord, forgive us.

For our aggressive attitudes which sour human relationships, in your mercy:
Lord, forgive us.

For our self-centredness and lack of love to the less fortunate who struggle in life, in your mercy:
Lord, forgive us.

For our placid contentment in a world of so much hurting and pain, in your mercy:
Lord, forgive us.

Give us more and more your strengthening Spirit
as we open our lives to you;
Help us to fulfil your law of love,
now and always. Amen.

▶ **26.19** CONFESSION
From 'A New Zealand Prayer Book'

God of mercy,
we are sorry that we have not always done
 what you wanted us to do.
We have not loved you with all our heart,
and we have not cared enough for other people.
Forgive us, for Jesus' sake. Amen.

▶ **26.20** CONFESSION
From Job 40–42†

Lord, you are without equal,
everything under heaven is yours:
we are unworthy
and have to answer to you.
We confess our lack of understanding
and repent of all our sin.
Lord, our ears have heard of you,
and now our eyes have seen you
in Jesus our Redeemer. Amen.

26.21 ABSOLUTION
From Isaiah 40†

Hear God's tender words of comfort for his people: your sorrows are
ended, your sin is paid for. God will show you his glory, and you
will receive grace at his hand; through Jesus Christ our Lord. **Amen.**

▶ **26.22** COLLECT
David Silk

Holy Jesus
to deliver us from the power of darkness
you humbled yourself to be born among us
and laid in a manger.
Let the light of your love always shine in our hearts,
and bring us at last
to the joyful vision of your beauty;
for you are now alive
and reign with the Father and the Holy Spirit,
God for ever and ever. **Amen.**

▶ **26.23** PSALM
Psalm 113. 1–8†

The minister/leaders may divide at A *and* B

  A Praise the Lord:
    praise the Lord!

  B You servants of the Lord, praise his name:
    let the name of the Lord be praised,
    both now and for evermore!

  A From the rising of the sun to the place where it sets:
    the name of the Lord be praised!

  B The Lord is exalted above the earth:
    his glory over the heavens.

  A Who is like the Lord our God?
    He is throned in the heights above –

  B Yet he bends down:
    yet he stoops to look at our world.

  A He raises the poor from the dust:
    and lifts the needy from their sorrow.

BOTH Praise the Lord:
    Amen.

▶ **26.24** CANTICLE
From Hebrews 1†

Let us worship the Son of God:

Your throne, O God, will last for ever and ever:
righteousness will be the sceptre of your kingdom.

You have loved righteousness and hated wickedness:
therefore God, your God,
has set you above your companions
by anointing you with the oil of joy.

In the beginning, O Lord, you laid the foundations of the earth:
and the heavens are the work of your hands.

They will perish, but you remain:
They will all wear out like clothing.

But you remain the same;
your years will never end. Amen.

▶ **26.25** READING: JESUS IS BORN
From Luke 2.8–20

Cast: Narrator, Angel, Chorus (three or more including Angel – or congregation) Shepherd 1, Shepherd 2, Shepherd 3, (can be the same as Shepherd 1 and/or Shepherd 2)

Narrator
There were shepherds living out in the fields near Bethlehem, keeping watch over their flocks at night. An angel of the Lord appeared to them, and the glory of the Lord shone around them, and they were terrified. But the angel said to them:

Angel
Do not be afraid. I bring you good news of great joy that will be for all the people. Today in the town of David a Saviour has been born to you; he is Christ the Lord. This will be a sign to you: You will find a baby wrapped in cloths and lying in a manger.

Narrator
Suddenly a great company of the heavenly host appeared with the angel, praising God.

Chorus *(joyfully)*
Glory to God in the highest
and on earth peace to all on whom his favour rests.

Narrator
When the angels had left them and gone into heaven, the shepherds said to one another:

Shepherd 1
Let's go to Bethlehem –

Shepherd 2
and see this thing that has happened –

Shepherd 3
which the Lord has told us about.

Narrator
So they hurried off and found Mary and Joseph, and the baby, who was lying in the manger. When they had seen him, they

spread the word concerning what had been told them about this child, and all who heard it were amazed at what the shepherds said to them. (PAUSE) But Mary treasured up all these things and pondered them in her heart. The shepherds returned, glorifying and praising God for all the things they had heard and seen, which were just as they had been told.

Cast
[This is] the word of the Lord.   OR   This is the Gospel of Christ/
                                              This is the Gospel of the Lord.

All
Thanks be to God.   **Praise to Christ our Lord/**
                                              Praise to you, Lord Jesus Christ.

FURTHER BIBLE READINGS
Readings appropriate to this theme will be found listed in our companion volume, 'The Dramatised Bible' (published by HarperCollins) on index page 437. A complete set of dramatised Christmas readings is included here on pages 494–506.

▶ **26.26**   CREED
From Hebrews 1†

Let us declare our faith in the Son of God:

In the past God spoke to our ancestors
    through the prophets
at many times and in various ways,
but in these last days
    he has spoken to us by his Son,
whom he appointed heir of all things,
and through whom he made the worlds.

The Son is the radiance of God's glory,
the exact representation of his being
who sustains all things by his powerful word.
After he had provided purification for sins
he sat down at the right hand
    of the Majesty in heaven. Amen.

▶ **26.27** CREED
From John 1

Let us declare our faith in the Son of God:

In the beginning was the Word,
and the Word was with God,
and the Word was God.
Through him all things were made;
without him nothing was made
   that has been made.
In him was life,
and that life was the light of all people.

The Word became flesh
and lived for a while among us;
we have seen his glory,
the glory of the one and only Son
who came from the Father,
full of grace and truth. Amen.

26.28 TO RECEIVE JESUS
Editors

Lord Jesus, we praise you even though we cannot fully comprehend how you could leave the spaciousness of heaven and enter into the confined space of a manger in a stable. We know that you left your glory for our sakes, to rescue us from our sin and selfishness and from the power of the evil one. You have taught us that you are Emmanuel, 'God with us': help us to receive you more fully today, that our lives may be strengthened and our love for you deepened; to the glory of your name. **Amen.**

26.29 FOR OUR WORLD
From 'Worship Now'

O God, we thank you for the message of peace that Christmas brings to our distracted world. Give peace among nations; peace in our land, peace in our homes, and peace in our hearts, as we remember the birth at Bethlehem of the Prince of peace, Jesus Christ our Lord. **Amen.**

26.30   FOR THOSE WITHOUT FAITH
Christopher Idle

O Holy Spirit of Christ – teacher, helper, and friend: open the hearts and minds of many this Christmas-time to the good and saving news of Jesus Christ; that those who are insecure, or empty, or aimless, may find in the One from Bethlehem all that they need today, and much more besides; for his name's sake. **Amen.**

26.31   FOR CHILDREN AT CHRISTMAS
Editors

Lord Jesus, bless all children everywhere this Christmas. As they sing their favourite carols and enjoy the Nativity story, may they learn more about you and grow to love and trust you. We pray that this will be a time when seeds of faith are sown and tender young hearts are warmed by your eternal love. Thank you, Jesus. **Amen.**

26.32   FOR POOR HOMES
Eddie Neale

Lord of glory, who for our sakes became poor, born in a backyard stable, laid gently in a feeding trough full of straw: we bring to the heart of your compassion those who live in much worse squalor today – squalor which insults the dignity you gave to humankind: the old lady whose bed is surrounded by pans half full of water, lying among the raindrops which pierce her roof. The family in the slum whose children sleep in the drawers of an old chest. And the millions throughout the world who live in shanty towns or worse, without water taps or sewers. Lord of glory, give us the spirit of your love, never to rest complacent in our luxury, but to care, and to care, and to care; for your glory. **Amen.**

▶ 26.33   FOR THE HOMELESS
From 'New Every Morning'

Lord Jesus Christ, born in a stable:
hear the cry of the homeless and refugee,
and so move our wills by your Holy Spirit
that we may not rest content
until all have found home and livelihood;
for your name's sake. **Amen.**

▶ **26.34** FOR HEARTS AND HOMES OPEN TO CHRIST
Roger Pickering

Loving Father,
we thank you for the gift of your Son,
whose birth at Bethlehem we now prepare to celebrate:
make our hearts and our homes always open to him –
that he may dwell with us for ever,
and we may serve him gladly all our days,
to the honour and glory of your name. **Amen.**

26.35 A CHRISTMAS PRAYER
Editors

Lord Jesus, when we give each other presents at Christmas, please help us to remember why we are giving: it's because you came to earth and gave yourself to us. Thank you for your gift of love, which lasts for ever. **Amen.**

26.36 FOR THOSE WITH SPECIAL RESPONSIBILITIES
         AT CHRISTMAS
From 'Everyday Prayers', adapted

Father, hear our prayers for those for whom Christmas brings added responsibilities and tensions – those who work throughout the holidays: hospital staff, energy workers, police, firemen, travel workers. And we pray for those who find Christmas increases the unhappiness they already have to carry; for the lonely, for divided families, for the ill, for those separated from the people they love, for the depressed and anxious; for those who face the first Christmas following a bereavement. In Christ you embrace our happiness and our need; give to us a love that shall exclude none. Father, hear us and help us, for Jesus' sake. **Amen.**

26.37 THE GREATEST PRESENT
Editors

O God our Father, we praise you for Christmas – our happiness and presents, our families and the friends we see again; and for this greatest present of all we thank you: for the gift of Jesus at Bethlehem to be our saviour and our king. **Amen.**

26.38   FOR A SPIRIT OF WORSHIP
Joyce Huggett

Lord Jesus, this Christmas as we sing the familiar carols, hear the familiar readings and ponder on familiar mysteries, give to us the gift of pure worship – that ability which Mary had; of attributing to you your true worth, your full value, your inestimable greatness. Teach us to be reverent; yet teach us how to express the love that burns within our hearts as we think of your goodness to us – that you have come to be our light in darkness, our hope in despair, our strength in weakness, our shelter in the storm – yes, and our eternal Saviour. **Amen.**

26.39   CANDLE SERVICE
Editors

Father God, as the candles are lit and the first carols are sung, we take this moment of quietness to draw near to you: we thank you for the joy of Christmas that warms our hearts and brings light to our lives; we thank you for the support of church fellowship and for the love of family and friends; we thank you for all blessings, mercies and miracles. Father, help us to keep the Christmas spirit of peace and goodwill all the year round; and may we always rejoice in your gift to us, our saviour, the Prince of peace, the Lord Jesus Christ, who now lives and reigns. **Amen.**

26.40   ABOUT BRINGING LIGHT TO THE WORLD
Editors

Our Lord and Master, Jesus Christ, you have come as the Light of the World to shine in our lives and illuminate our hearts and minds. Thank you, Lord Jesus, for banishing our darkness with your eternal light. As we celebrate your birth this Christmastime, show us how we can share our joy with those who have no joy and to share our wealth with those who have no comfort. Help us to make your love real to them, Lord, and let us reflect your pure light as we proclaim the good news. **Amen.**

26.41 CHRISTMAS THANKSGIVING
From 'Everyday Prayers'

Thank you, Father for this loved and familiar season, for tuneful carols, for reunions with families and friends, for giving and receiving, for a sense of celebration everywhere; for all the ways of saying 'Christ is born'. We ask that the familiarity of Christmas may not smother the truth that we celebrate together. May Christ be among us – as real, as close, as warm as at that first Christmas. With Mary may we open our hearts to the word of God, that Christ may be born in us; with the shepherds, may we hear in the world of our daily work what heaven is saying to us – may our experience of Christ be as real and enduring as theirs. Save us from a faith so shallow that we put away our Christian commitments with the decorations, or discard your revelation like an unwanted present. Hear as we pray in Christ's name. **Amen.**

▶ **26.42** RESPONSIVE THANKSGIVING
From 'Worship Now'

For the birth of Jesus your Son, our Saviour, cradled in the manger at Bethlehem;
we thank you, heavenly Father.

For the love and gentle care of Mary, his mother, most blessed of all women:
we thank you, heavenly Father.

For shepherds keeping watch over their flocks by night, who came with haste to worship Christ, the new-born King:
we thank you, heavenly Father.

For wise men from the East, who followed the star and presented him with their gifts of gold and frankincense and myrrh:
we thank you, heavenly Father.

For the light and love of this Christmas season, in our hearts and in our homes, bringing joy and gladness to us all:
we thank you, heavenly Father.

And in our joyful gratitude we join our voices with the angels who are always singing to you:
Holy, holy, holy Lord
God of power and might,
heaven and earth are full of your glory;
hosanna in the highest. Amen.

▶ **26.43** THANKSGIVING
National Christian Education Council

God our Father, we listen again to the story of Christmas, and we are glad that Jesus has come to be our saviour and our friend.

We hear how Mary laid her baby in a manger. Jesus has come:
thank you, Father.

We hear how the angels sang over the Bethlehem hills: 'Glory to God; peace for the world.' Jesus has come:
thank you, Father.

We hear how the shepherds hurried to see that what the angel said was true. Jesus has come:
thank you, Father.

We hear how the wise men came to bring their worship and their precious gifts. Jesus has come:
thank you, Father.

O God,
we thank you
that Jesus has come to be our saviour and our friend:
we welcome him with love,
and worship him with gladness,
for your glory's sake. Amen.

▶ **26.44** THANKSGIVING
Liturgical Commission

We thank you, Father, giver of all good things,
for the joy of this season of Christmas,
for the good news of a Saviour,
and for the wonder of the Word made flesh,
your Son, Jesus Christ, our Lord. **Amen.**

▶ **26.45** THANKSGIVING AT COMMUNION
Liturgical Commission

We thank you, Father, God of love,
for the signs of your love on this table,
for your love made known through all the world
and shining on us in the face of Jesus Christ, our Lord. **Amen.**

26.46   THANKSGIVING, ADORATION AND DEDICATION
Editors

Our Father God, we thank you for the miracle of Christmas; we thank you for your love made incarnate. When we think of Jesus, come as a baby in a manger to save his people from their sins, we can only worship you in the deep and wonderful mystery of it all. In adoration we bring you our own love-gift – ourselves. Accept us, Father, in the light of your dear Son. **Amen.**

26.47   DEDICATION
Editors

Lord Jesus Christ, Saviour of the world, we praise you as the angels praised you long ago in Bethlehem, because you were given for us, and we were made for you; in gratitude we offer you our loyalty and devotion and love: let all the earth sing for joy, let every living creature bow down and worship you, let all the universe rejoice: for you are the beloved Messiah who was born for us, you are the blest Redeemer who died for us, you are the ascended King who reigns in power and glory, you are God among us, now. **Amen.**

▶ **26.48**   ACCLAMATION
From Isaiah 25†

O Lord,
we exalt and praise your name,
for you are faithful to us
and have done marvellous things –
things promised long ago.
For certain, you are our God:
we trust in you, and you save us;
through Jesus our redeemer. **Amen.**

26.49   BLESSING
Editors

The joy of the angels, the wonder of the shepherds, and the peace of the Christ child, fill *your* hearts this Christmas time; and the blessing of God the Father, God the Son, and God the Holy Spirit, be with *you* now and always. **Amen.**

CHRISTMAS READINGS

CAST OF READERS
for the dramatised Christmas Readings

Sometimes the dramatised Christmas Readings will be used in public at a crowded service where there is little space for a large cast, or where amplification of the cast is needed but only a single directional microphone is available. In such circumstances it will be as well to keep those participating to a minimum. The cast list below (not in order of appearance) is arranged in groupings to allow each reader to take more than one part in the series, but not in the same reading. This is the minimum configuration which also takes into account a male-female balance of voices. Where such a balance is not possible, please ignore the instructions in brackets.

First Reader (*strong female voice*)
Narrator – except in 'Mary visits Elizabeth'
Narrator 1 – in 'The shepherds find the baby'.
Elizabeth

Second Reader (*older male voice*)

Commentator	Teacher 1	Hebrews
Shepherd 1	Simeon	

Third Reader (*male voice*)

Isaiah	Chorus	Colossians
Prophet	Magi 1	

Fourth Reader (*male voice*)

Jeremiah	John
Chorus	Narrator – in 'Mary visits Elizabeth'
Magi 2	Narrator 2 – in 'The shepherds find the baby'

Fifth Reader (*authoritative male voice*)

Micah	Shepherd 2	Philippians
Angel	Herod	

Sixth Reader (*female voice*)

Numbers	Chorus	2 Corinthians
Mary	Teacher 2	

Suggested carols to match some of the Christmas readings will be found at the back of our *Carols for Today* (music edition, from Hodder & Stoughton/Hope Publishing Company). Carols to match the Christmas themes will be found indexed at the back of our *Carol Praise* (music edition, from HarperCollins/Hope Publishing Company). Further dramatised readings are available in our publication *The Dramatised Bible* (published by HarperCollins)

26.50 READING: THE PROPHETS PROMISE THE SAVIOUR
Numbers 24.16–17; Isaiah 7.14; Jeremiah 23.5–6; Micah 5.2, 4; Isaiah 9.6

Numbers

The oracle of one who hears the words of God, who has knowledge from the Most High: I see him, but not now; I behold him, but not near. A star will come out of Jacob; a sceptre will rise out of Israel.

Isaiah

The Lord himself will give you a sign: The virgin will be with child and will give birth to a son, and will call him Immanuel.

Jeremiah

'The days are coming,' declares the Lord, 'when I will raise up to David a righteous Branch, a King who will reign wisely and do what is just and right in the land. This is the name by which he will be called: The Lord Our Righteousness.'

Micah

Bethlehem Ephrathah, though you are small among the clans of Judah, out of you will come for me one who will be ruler over Israel, whose origins are from of old, from ancient times. He will stand and shepherd his flock in the strength of the Lord, in the majesty of the name of the Lord his God.

Isaiah

To us a child is born, to us a son is given, and the government will be on his shoulders. And he will be called Wonderful Counsellor, Mighty God, Everlasting Father, Prince of Peace.

Cast

[This is] the word of the Lord.

All

Thanks be to God.

26.51   READING: MARY HEARS THE NEWS
From Luke 1. 26–38

Narrator

In the sixth month, God sent the angel Gabriel to Nazareth, a town in Galilee, to a virgin pledged to be married to a man named Joseph, a descendant of David. The virgin's name was Mary. The angel went to her [and said]:

Angel

Greetings, you who are highly favoured! The Lord is with you.

Narrator

Mary was greatly troubled at his words and wondered what kind of greeting this might be. But the angel said to her:

Angel

Do not be afraid, Mary, you have found favour with God. You will be with child and give birth to a son, and you are to give him the name Jesus. He will be great and will be called the Son of the Most High. The Lord God will give him the throne of his father David, and he will reign over the house of Jacob for ever; his kingdom will never end.

[Narrator

Mary asked the angel:]

Mary

How will this be, since I am a virgin?

Angel

The Holy Spirit will come upon you, and the power of the Most High will overshadow you. So the holy one to be born will be called the Son of God.

[Narrator

Mary answered:]

Mary

I am the Lord's servant. May it be to me as you have said.

Narrator

Then the angel left her.

Cast

[This is] the word of the Lord.

All

Thanks be to God.

26.52   READING: MARY VISITS ELIZABETH*
Luke 1.39–55 (56)

This reading can be omitted from the series

Narrator
Mary got ready and hurried off to a town in the hill-country of Judaea. She went into Zechariah's house and greeted Elizabeth. When Elizabeth heard Mary's greeting, the baby moved within her. Elizabeth was filled with the Holy Spirit [and said in a loud voice]:

Elizabeth (*delighted*)
You are the most blessed of all women, and blessed is the child you will bear! Why should this great thing happen to me, that my Lord's mother comes to visit me? For as soon as I heard your greeting, the baby within me jumped with gladness. How happy you are to believe that the Lord's message to you will come true!

Mary
My heart praises the Lord;
my soul is glad because of God my Saviour,
for he has remembered me, his lowly servant!
From now on all people will call me happy,
because of the great things the Mighty God has done for me.
His name is holy;
from one generation to another
he shows mercy to those who honour him.
He has stretched out his mighty arm
and scattered the proud with all their plans.
He has brought down mighty kings from their thrones,
and lifted up the lowly.
He has filled the hungry with good things,
and sent the rich away with empty hands.
He has kept the promise he made to our ancestors,
and has come to the help of his servant Israel.
He has remembered to show mercy to Abraham
and to all his descendants for ever!

[**Narrator**
Mary stayed about three months with Elizabeth and then went back home.]

Cast
[This is] the word of the Lord.

All
Thanks be to God.

26.53   READING: JOSEPH LEARNS THE TRUTH
Matthew 1.18–25

Narrator
This is how the birth of Jesus Christ came about. His mother Mary was pledged to be married to Joseph, but before they came together, she was found to be with child through the Holy Spirit. Because Joseph her husband was a righteous man and did not want to expose her to public disgrace, he had in mind to divorce her quietly. But after he had considered this, an angel of the Lord appeared to him in a dream [and said]:

Angel
Joseph son of David, do not be afraid to take Mary home as your wife, because what is conceived in her is from the Holy Spirit. She will give birth to a son, and you are to give him the name Jesus, because he will save his people from their sins.

Narrator
All this took place to fulfil what the Lord had said through the prophet:

Prophet
The virgin will be with child and will give birth to a son, and they will call him Immanuel –

Narrator
Which means 'God with us'. (PAUSE) When Joseph woke up, he did what the angel of the Lord had commanded him and took Mary home as his wife. But he had no union with her until she gave birth to a son. And he gave him the name Jesus.

Cast
[This is] the word of the Lord.

ALL
Thanks be to God.

26.54   READING: JESUS IS BORN*
Luke 2.1–7

*This reading can be omitted from the series

Narrator
The Emperor Augustus ordered a census to be taken throughout the Roman Empire.

Commentator

When this first census took place, Quirinius was the governor of Syria. Everyone, then, went to register himself, each to his own town.

Narrator

Joseph went from the town of Nazareth in Galilee to the town of Bethlehem in Judaea, the birthplace of King David.

Commentator

Joseph went there because he was a descendant of David.

Narrator

He went to register with Mary, who was promised in marriage to him. She was pregnant, and while they were in Bethlehem, the time came for her to have her baby. She gave birth to her first son wrapped him in strips of cloth and laid him in a manger.

Commentator

There was no room for them to stay in the inn.

Cast

[This is] the word of the Lord.

All

Thanks be to God.

26.55 READING: THE ANGELS ANNOUNCE THE BIRTH
Luke 2. 8–14

Narrator

There were shepherds living out in the fields near Bethlehem, keeping watch over their flocks at night. An angel of the Lord appeared to them, and the glory of the Lord shone around them, and they were terrified. But the angel said to them:

Angel

Do not be afraid. I bring you good news of great joy that will be for all the people. Today in the town of David a Saviour has been born to you; he is Christ the Lord. This will be a sign to you: You will find a baby wrapped in strips of cloth and lying in a manger.

Narrator

Suddenly a great company of the heavenly host appeared with the angel, praising God:

Chorus (*cheerfully*)

Glory to God in the highest and on earth peace to all on whom his favour rests.

Cast

[This is] the word of the Lord.

All

Thanks be to God.

26.56 READING: THE SHEPHERDS FIND THE BABY
Luke 2. 15–20

Narrator 1

When the angels had left them and gone into heaven, the shepherds said to one another:

Shepherds 1 and **2**

Let's go to Bethlehem!

Shepherd 1

And see this thing that has happened –

Shepherd 2

Which the Lord has told us about.

Narrator 1

So they hurried off and found Mary and Joseph, and the baby, who was lying in the manger.

Narrator 2

When they had seen him, they spread the word concerning what had been told them about this child, and all who heard it were amazed at what the shepherds said to them.

Narrator 1

But Mary treasured up all these things and pondered them in her heart.

Narrator 2

The shepherds returned, glorifying and praising God for all the things they had heard and seen, which were just as they had been told.

Cast

[This is] the word of the Lord.

All

Thanks be to God.

26.57 READING: THE WISE MEN FOLLOW THE STAR
From Matthew 2. 1–11

Narrator
After Jesus was born in Bethlehem in Judaea, during the time of King Herod, Magi from the east came to Jerusalem and asked:

Magi
Where is the one who has been born king of the Jews? We saw his star in the east and have come to worship him.

Narrator
When King Herod heard this, he was disturbed, and all Jerusalem with him. When he had called together all the people's chief priests and teachers of the law, he asked them:

Herod
Where will the Christ be born?

[Narrator
They replied:]

Teachers 1 and **2**
In Bethlehem in Judaea.

Teacher 2
For this is what the prophet has written:

Prophet
Bethlehem, in the land of Judah, out of you will come a ruler who will be the shepherd of my people Israel.

Narrator
Then Herod called the Magi secretly and found out from them the exact time the star had appeared. He sent them to Bethlehem [and said]:

Herod
Go and make a careful search for the child. As soon as you find him, report to me, so that I too may go and worship him.

Narrator
After they had heard the king, they went on their way, and the star they had seen in the east went ahead of them until it stopped over the place where the child was. When they saw the star, they were overjoyed. On coming to the house, they saw the child with his mother Mary, and they bowed down and worshipped him. Then they opened their treasures and presented him with gifts of gold and of incense and of myrrh.

Cast
[This is] the word of the Lord.

All
Thanks be to God.

26.58 READING: THE CHILD ESCAPES THE SWORD
From Matthew 2. 13–18

Narrator
When the Magi had gone, an angel of the Lord appeared to Joseph in a dream:

Angel
Get up. Take the child and his mother and escape to Egypt. Stay there until I tell you, for Herod is going to search for the child to kill him.

Narrator
So Joseph got up, took the child and his mother during the night and left for Egypt, where he stayed until the death of Herod. And so was fulfilled what the Lord had said through the prophet:

Prophet
Out of Egypt I called my son.

Narrator
When Herod realised that he had been outwitted by the Magi, he was furious, and he gave orders to kill all the boys in Bethlehem and its vicinity who were two years old and under, in accordance with the time he had learned from the Magi. Then what was said through the prophet Jeremiah was fulfilled:

Jeremiah
A voice is heard in Ramah,
weeping and great mourning,
Rachel weeping for her children
and refusing to be comforted,
because they are no more.

Cast
[This is] the word of the Lord.

All
Thanks be to God.

26.59   READING: THE FAMILY RETURN FROM EGYPT*
Matthew 2. 19–23

*This reading can be omitted from the series

Narrator
After Herod died, an angel of the Lord appeared in a dream to Joseph in Egypt:

Angel
Get up, take the child and his mother, and go back to the land of Israel, because those who tried to kill the child are dead.

Narrator
So Joseph got up, took the child and his mother, and went back to Israel.

But when Joseph heard that Archelaus had succeeded his father Herod as king of Judaea, he was afraid to go there. He was given more instructions in a dream, so he went to the province of Galilee and made his home in a town named Nazareth. And so what the prophets had said came true:

Prophet
He will be called a Nazarene.

Cast
[This is] the word of the Lord.

All
Thanks be to God.

26.60   READING: SIMEON RECOGNISES THE MESSIAH
From Luke 2. 25–32

Narrator
There was a man in Jerusalem called Simeon, who was righteous and devout. He was waiting for the consolation of Israel, and the Holy Spirit was upon him. It had been revealed to him by the Holy Spirit that he would not die before he had seen the Lord's Christ. Moved by the Spirit, he went into the temple courts. When the parents brought in the child Jesus to do for him what the custom of the Law required. Simeon took him in his arms and praised God [saying]:

Simeon

Sovereign Lord, as you have promised,
you now dismiss your servant in peace.
For my eyes have seen your salvation,
which you have prepared in the sight of all people,
a light for revelation to the Gentiles
and for the glory to your people Israel.

Narrator

The child's father and mother marvelled at what was said about him. Then Simeon blessed them and said to Mary, his mother:

Simeon

This child is destined to cause the falling and rising of many in Israel, and to be a sign that will be spoken against, so that the thoughts of many hearts will be revealed. And a sword will pierce your own soul too.

Cast

[This is] the word of the Lord.

All

Thanks be to God.

26.61 READING: THE APOSTLES EXPLAIN THE MEANING

John 1.1,3,14; Colossians 1.15,17; Hebrews 1.1–3; 2 Corinthians 4.6; 8.9; Philippians 2.6–7; John 1.11–12

John

In the beginning was the Word, and the Word was with God, and the Word was God. Through him all things were made. The Word became flesh and lived for a while among us. We have seen his glory, the glory of the one and only Son, who came from the Father, full of grace and truth.

Colossians

Christ is the image of the invisible God, the first-born over all creation. He is before all things, and in him all things hold together.

Hebrews

In the past God spoke to our forefathers through the prophets, but in these last days he has spoken to us by his Son, who is the radiance of his glory and the exact representation of his being.

2 Corinthians

God, who said, 'Let light shine out of darkness,' made his light shine in our hearts to give us the light of the knowledge of the glory of God in the face of Christ. You know the grace of our Lord Jesus Christ, that though he was rich, yet for your sakes he became poor, so that you through his poverty might become rich.

Philippians

Christ Jesus, being in very nature God, did not consider equality with God something to be grasped, but made himself nothing, taking the very nature of a servant, being made in human likeness.

John

He came to that which was his own, but his own did not receive him. Yet to all who received him, to those who believed in his name, he gave the right to become children of God.

Cast
[This is] the word of the Lord.

All
Thanks be to God.

At a Baptism

▶ **27.1** GREETING
From Titus 1†

Grace and peace to you from God our Father and Jesus Christ our Saviour. **Amen.**

27.2 SENTENCE
Matthew 16.24

Jesus said to his disciples, 'If you want to come with me, you must forget self, carry your cross and follow me'.

27.3 SENTENCE
Romans 6. 3,4

When we were baptised into Christ Jesus, we were baptised into his death, so that, as Christ was raised from the dead by the Father's glory, we also might walk in newness of life.

27.4 SENTENCE
Romans 8.4

We were buried with Christ through baptism into death in order that, just as Christ was raised from death through the glory of the Father, we too may have a new life.

27.5 SENTENCE
1 Corinthians 12.13

We were all baptised by one Spirit into one body, and we were all given the one Spirit to drink.

27.6 SENTENCE
Titus 3. 5,6

God saved us through the washing of rebirth and renewal by the

Holy Spirit, whom he poured out on us generously through Jesus Christ our Saviour.

27.7 SENTENCE
Mark 10. 14,16

Jesus said, 'Let the little children come to me, and do not hinder them, for the kingdom of God belongs to such as these'. And he took the children in his arms, put his hands on them and blessed them.

▶ **27.8** RESPONSE
From Ezekiel 47†

I saw water flowing from the right side of the temple; the water flowed, it brought God's life and his salvation. The people sang in joyful praise:
Alleluia, alleluia!

▶ **27.9** RESPONSE
From 1 Corinthians 6†

Now you are washed, you are sanctified, you are justified:
in the name of the Lord Jesus Christ
and by the Spirit of our God. Amen.

▶ **27.10** RESPONSE
From Romans 8†

There is now no condemnation for those who are in Christ Jesus:
the Spirit of life has set us free
from the law of sin and death. Amen.

▶ **27.11** RESPONSE
From 1 Samuel 1 and Psalm 127†

Hannah said 'I prayed for this child, and the Lord has granted me what I asked of him':
Children are a gift from the Lord;
they are his blessing. Amen.

▶ **27.12** RESPONSE
From 1 Corinthians 6†

Now you are washed, you are sanctified, you are justified:
in the name of the Lord Jesus Christ
and by the Spirit of our God. Amen.

27.13 APPROACH
From 1 Peter 1†

Praise be to you our God, the Father of our Lord Jesus Christ! In your great mercy you have given us new birth into a living hope through the resurrection of Jesus Christ from the dead, and into an inheritance that can never perish, spoil or fade, kept in heaven for us. Through faith you shield us by your power until the coming of salvation that is ready to be revealed in the last time: for this we praise you through Jesus Christ whom we love, and in whom we believe, though we cannot see him; and our hearts are filled with inexpressible and glorious joy as we receive from you the goal of our faith, the salvation of our souls. **Amen.**

▶ **27.14** PRAISE
From Psalm 34†

Glorify the Lord with me:
let us praise his name together.

▶ **27.15** PRAISE
From Psalm 107†

Give thanks to God, for he is good;
his love endures for ever.

Let those whom the Lord has redeemed repeat these words of praise:
O thank the Lord for his love
and the wonderful things he has done! Amen.

▶ **27.16**   CONFESSION
From 1 John 1†

If we say that we have no sin, we deceive ourselves,
and the truth is not in us:

If we confess our sins,
God will keep his promise
and do what is right –
he will forgive us our sins
and cleanse us from every kind of wrong.

Father, have mercy on us
through Jesus Christ our Lord. Amen.

27.17   ABSOLUTION
From Psalm 51†

God in his goodness have mercy on *you*, wash *you* clean from *your* guilt and purify *you* from *your* sin; God the righteous judge remove *your* sins from *you* and make *you* whiter than snow; through Jesus Christ our Saviour. **Amen.**

27.18   ABSOLUTION
From Psalm 103†

The Lord forgive *you* all your sin, and heal the disease of *your* soul; the Lord redeem *your* life from the grave, and bless *you* with his love and mercy. **Amen.**

▶ **27.19**   COLLECT
Baptism, ASB 1980

Almighty God,
we thank you for our fellowship
in the household of faith
with all those who have been baptized in your name.
Keep us faithful to our baptism,
and so make us ready for that day
when the whole creation
shall be made perfect in your Son
our Saviour, Jesus Christ. **Amen.**

▶ **27.20** PSALM
Psalm 113. 1–9†

The ministers/leaders may divide at A *and* B

A Praise the Lord:
   praise the Lord!

B You servants of the Lord, praise his name:
   let the name of the Lord be praised,
   both now and for evermore!

A From the rising of the sun to the place where it sets:
   the name of the Lord be praised!

B The Lord is exalted above the earth:
   his glory over the heavens.

A Who is like the Lord our God?
   He is throned in the heights above –

B Yet he bends down:
   yet he stoops to look at our world.

A He raises the poor from the dust:
   and lifts the needy from their sorrow.

B He honours the childless wife in her home:
   he makes her happy, the mother of children.

BOTH Praise the Lord:
   Amen.

27.21 READING: JESUS' BAPTISM
Matthew 3. 13–17

Cast: Narrator, John, Jesus, Voice.

Narrator
Jesus arrived from Galilee and came to John at the Jordan to be baptized by him. But John tried to make him change his mind:

John
I ought to be baptized by you, and yet you have come to me!

[Narrator
But Jesus answered him:]

Jesus
Let it be so for now. For in this way we shall do all that God requires.

510

Narrator
So John agreed. (PAUSE)

As soon as Jesus was baptized, he came up out of the water. Then heaven was opened to him, and he saw the Spirit of God coming down like a dove and alighting on him. Then a voice said from heaven:

Voice
This is my own dear Son, with whom I am pleased.

Cast
[This is] the word of the Lord.   OR   This is the Gospel of Christ/
                                          This is the Gospel of the Lord.

All
Thanks be to God.   **Praise to Christ our Lord/**
                                           Praise to you, Lord Jesus Christ.

FURTHER BIBLE READINGS
Readings appropriate to this theme will be found listed in our companion volume, 'The Dramatised Bible' (published by HarperCollins) on index page 419.

▶ **27.22**   CREED
From 1 Corinthians 12†

We believe in one Lord Jesus Christ,
one faith, one baptism,
one God and Father of us all,
who is in all and over all
and through all. Amen.

▶ **27.23**   CREED
ASB 1980

Do you believe and trust in God the Father, who
made the world?
We believe and trust in him.

Do you believe and trust in his Son Jesus Christ.
who redeemed mankind?
We believe and trust in him.

Do you believe and trust in his Holy Spirit, who
gives life to the people of God?
We believe and trust in him.

This is the faith of the Church.
This is our faith.
We believe and trust in one God:
Father, Son, and Holy Spirit. Amen.

27.24   BLESSING OF THE CANDIDATE(S)
From 1 Corinthians 1†

God who raises the dead deliver you from all deadly perils as you
set your hope on him; the Lord grant you his gracious favour in
answer to the prayers of many; and the blessing of God almighty, the
Father, the Son and the Holy Spirit be upon you and remain with
you always. **Amen.**

▶ **27.25**   BLESSING OF THE CANDIDATE(S)
From Colossians 1†

The Lord God fill you with the knowledge of his will;
his Spirit give you wisdom and understanding;
Christ strengthen you with his glorious power
so that you may be able to endure, to be patient
and to give thanks to the Father with joy in your heart(s). **Amen.**

▶ **27.26**   BLESSING OF THE CANDIDATE(S)
From 2 Timothy 1†

Hold firmly to the true words you have been taught
as the example for you to follow,
and remain in the faith and love that are ours
in union with Christ Jesus,
through the power of the Holy Spirit
who lives in us. **Amen.**

▶ **27.27** BLESSING OF THE CANDIDATE(S)
From 2 Timothy 2†

Be strong through the grace that is ours
in union with Christ Jesus;
take your part in suffering
as his loyal soldier;
and remember him who was raised from the dead,
Jesus Christ, our Lord and Saviour. **Amen.**

27.28 BLESSING
From Numbers 6†

The Lord bless *you* and keep *you*; the Lord make his face to shine
upon *you* and be gracious to *you*; the Lord turn his face towards *you*
and give *you* peace. **Amen.**

▶ **27.29** INTERCESSION
From Isaiah 11†

We pray that *N* may bear fruit as a new branch of the Vine which is
Jesus Christ:

May the spirit of the Lord rest upon *him*:
the spirit of wisdom and understanding,
the spirit of counsel and power,
the spirit of knowledge and the fear of the Lord;
may *he* delight in the Lord. Amen.

▶ **27.30** THANKSGIVING
From 1 Peter 1†

We praise you,
O God and Father of our Lord Jesus Christ,
that in your great mercy
you have given us new birth
into a living hope
through the resurrection of Jesus Christ from the dead,
and into an inheritance
that can never perish, spoil or fade –
kept in heaven for us,
who through faith
are shielded by God's power

until the coming of the salvation
that is ready to be revealed in the last time:
in this we greatly rejoice. **Amen.**

27.31   BLESSING
From 2 Timothy 4†

Run the good race to the end, keep the faith, that you may receive
the crown of righteousness which God the righteousness judge will
give on that day to us who have loved him and long to see him: and
the blessing of God – Father, Son and Holy Spirit – be with you
always. **Amen.**

27.32   BLESSING
From 1 Peter 5†

The God of all grace, who called *you* to his eternal glory in Christ,
make *you* strong, firm and steadfast. To him be the power for ever
and ever. **Amen.**

▶ **27.33**   BLESSING
From 2 Peter 3†

May *you* grow in the grace and knowledge of our Lord and
Saviour Jesus Christ:
**to him be glory
both now and for ever. Amen.**

At Holy Communion/The Lord's Supper

▶ **28.1** GREETING
From Romans 15†

Welcome one another as Christ has welcomed you:
to God be the glory. **Amen.**

▶ **28.2** GREETING
From Ruth 2†

The Lord be with you:
the Lord bless you!

28.3 SENTENCE
Psalm 34.8

O taste and see how gracious the Lord is.

28.4 SENTENCE
Luke 22.28,30

Jesus said, 'You are those who have continued with me in my trials;
you shall eat and drink at my table in my kingdom.'

28.5 SENTENCE
1 Corinthians 11.26

Whenever you eat this bread and drink this cup, you proclaim the
Lord's death until he comes.

28.6 SENTENCE
Revelation 3.20

[The Lord says:] I stand at the door and knock. If you hear my voice
and open the door, I will come in and eat with you, and you with
me.

▶ **28.7** RESPONSE
From Matthew 5†

Blessed are the poor in spirit:
for theirs is the kingdom of heaven.

Blessed are those who hunger and thirst for righteousness:
for they will be filled.

Praise the Lord:
The Lord's name be praised! Amen.

28.8 APPROACH

Editors

Our Father in heaven – we come to you this day in the name of the
Lord Jesus Christ. We come hungry for your word, we come
spiritually thirsty; we have had many experiences in the world,
where there is constant and unsatisfied need. We praise you that we
can come to you not knowing how to cope with all life's demands,
but having a deep assurance that you know the end from the
beginning and that you have the solution to those problems which
confront us.

You remind us that not a sparrow falls to the ground without your
knowledge: assure us today that you know about the difficulties, the
sorrows and the challenges ahead, but will enable us so to meet
them that we may grow in patience and increase in spiritual
strength. So let us see your glory, as we have seen it before, that we
may be built up in faith, encouraged in love and equipped to live;
through Jesus Christ our Lord. **Amen.**

28.9 EVENING EXHORTATION/WELCOME
From Psalm 134†

All of you who serve the Lord, praise the Lord; you who come in the
evening of the day to worship in his house, praise the Lord. Lift up
your hands in his holy place and praise the Lord. May the Lord, the
Maker of heaven and earth, bless you here; through our saviour,
Jesus Christ. **Amen.**

▶ **28.10** PRAISE
From Psalm 107†

Let us give thanks to the Lord for his unfailing love
and the wonders he has done for us.

He satisfies the thirsty
and fills the hungry with good things.

▶ **28.11** COMMANDMENTS
From Mark 12†

Jesus said: Love the Lord your God with all your heart and with all your soul and with all your mind and with all your strength; and love your neighbour as yourself.

Lord, we have broken your commandments:
forgive us, and help us to obey;
for your name's sake. Amen.

▶ **28.12** THE TEN COMMANDMENTS
From Exodus 20/Deuteronomy 5†

Let us hear the decrees and laws of the Lord, learn them, and be sure to follow them:

'You shall have no other gods but me':
Lord, help us to love you
with all our heart, all our soul,
all our mind and all our strength.

'You shall not make for yourself any idol':
Lord, help us to worship you
in spirit and in truth.

'You shall not dishonour the name of the Lord your God':
Lord, help us to honour you
with reverence and awe.

'Remember the Lord's day and keep it holy':
Lord, help us to remember Christ
  risen from the dead,
and to set our minds on things above,
not on things on the earth.

'Honour your father and your mother':
Lord, help us to live as your servants,
giving respect to all,
and love to our brothers and sisters in Christ.

'You shall not murder'.
Lord, help us to be reconciled with each other,
and to overcome evil with good.

'You shall not commit adultery':
Lord, help us to realise
that our body is a temple of the Holy Spirit.

'You shall not steal':
Lord, help us to be honest in all we do,
and to care for those in need.

'You shall not be a false witness':
Lord, help us always to speak the truth.

'You shall not covet anything which belongs to your neighbour':
Lord, help us to remember Jesus said,
'It is more blessed to give than to receive',
and help us to love our neighbours as ourselves;
for his sake. Amen.

▶ **28.13** ACT OF COMMITMENT (THE TEN COMMANDMENTS)
From Exodus 20/Deuteronomy 5†

Let us resolve to follow the decrees and the laws of the Lord:

Lord, we will have no other God but you.

Lord, we will not make idols for ourselves,
nor will we worship them.

Lord, we will not dishonour your name.

Lord, we will remember your day and keep it holy.

Lord, we will honour our father and our mother.

Lord, we will do no murder.

Lord, we will not commit adultery.

Lord, we will not steal.

Lord, we will not be a false witness.

Lord, we will not covet anything that belongs to another.

May the awe of your presence and the vision of your glory keep us
from sinning, for the sake of Jesus our redeemer. **Amen.**

28.14 DECLARATION (FOLLOWING RECITAL OF COMMANDMENTS)
From Deuteronomy 26†

You have declared this day that the Lord is your God and that you will walk in his ways, that you will keep his decrees, commands and laws, and that you will obey him. And the Lord declares this day that you are his people, his treasured possession, a people holy to the Lord your God, as he promised in Jesus Christ our Saviour.

Thanks be to God. **Amen.**

28.15 PREFACE
From 'A New Zealand Prayer Book'

We come seeking forgiveness for all we have failed to be and do as members of Christ's body:

▶ **28.16** CONFESSION
BCP, adapted Editors

Almighty God,
Father of our Lord Jesus Christ,
maker and judge of all:
we confess the sins
which again and again
 we have so hurtfully committed
against you, our God and king.
By right you are angry and displeased at us.
We sincerely repent
and are truly sorry
for the wrong things we have done –
their memory is painful
and more than we can bear.
Have mercy on us, most merciful Father;
for Jesus' sake forgive us all that is past,
and renew our lives from this day
that we may serve you and please you,
and bring honour and glory to your name;
through Jesus Christ our Lord. Amen.

▶ **28.17** CONFESSION
From Psalm 51†

Lord God, have mercy on us,
according to your steadfast love;
and in your abundant mercy,
blot out our transgressions:
cleanse us from our sin,
create in us a clean heart and life,
and continually renew
a right spirit within us. Amen.

▶ **28.18** CONFESSION
From 1 John 1†

O God,
you have taught us
    that if we say we have no sin
we deceive ourselves
and the truth is not in us:
we humbly confess our sins to you;
and we ask you to keep your promise
to forgive us our sins
and cleanse us from all unrighteousness;
through Jesus Christ our Lord. Amen.

28.19 ABSOLUTION
From Isaiah 43†

The Lord, *your* Redeemer, the Holy One, blot out *your* transgressions
and remember *your* sins no more; for his name's sake. **Amen.**

▶ **28.20** WORDS OF COMFORT
From Matthew 11, John 3, 1 Timothy 1, and 1 John 2†

Jesus said, 'Come to me, all who are heavy laden, and I will give you
rest':
God so loved the world
that he gave his only Son,
that whoever believes in him
should not perish
but have eternal life.

This saying is true and worthy of full acceptance, that Christ Jesus came into the world to save sinners:
If anyone sins
we have an advocate with the Father,
Jesus Christ the righteous;
and he is the propitiation for our sins.

28.21   WORDS OF COMFORT
After BCP

Hear the words of comfort our Saviour Christ says to all who truly turn to him:

Come to me, all who labour and are heavy laden, and I will give you rest.   *Matthew 11.28*

God so loved the world that he gave his only Son, that whoever believes in him should not perish but have eternal life. *John 3.16*

Hear what Saint Paul says: This saying is true and worthy of full acceptance, that Christ Jesus came into the world to save sinners.
                                                                1 Timothy 1.15

Hear what Saint John says: If anyone sins, we have an advocate with the Father, Jesus Christ the righteous; and he is the propitiation for our sins.   *1 John 2.1*

▶ ### 28.22   COLLECT
Collect for Purity, adapted Editors

Almighty God,
you see into our hearts
and you know our minds;
we cannot hide our secrets from you:
cleanse our hearts and minds
   by the power of your Holy Spirit,
that we may perfectly love you
and worship you as you desire;
through Jesus Christ our Lord. **Amen.**

▶ **28.23** PSALM
Psalm 116.1–19†

The congregation may divide at A, B *and* C

I love the Lord because he heard my voice:
A **the Lord in mercy listened to my prayers.**

Because the Lord has turned his ear to me:
B **I'll call on him as long as I shall live.**

The cords of death entangled me around:
C **the horrors of the grave came over me.**

But then I called upon the Lord my God:
A **I said to him: 'O Lord, I beg you, save!'**

The Lord our God is merciful and good:
B **the Lord protects the simple-hearted ones.**

The Lord saved me from death and stopped my tears:
C **he saved me from defeat and picked me up.**

And so I walk before him all my days:
A **and live to love and praise his holy name.**

What shall I give the Lord for all his grace?
B **I'll take his saving cup, and pay my vows.**

Within the congregation of his saints:
C **I'll offer him my sacrifice of praise.**

Praise the Lord:
ALL **Amen, amen!**

28.24 READING: THE LORD'S SUPPER (GNB)
From Luke 22.14–20 [21–23]

Cast: Narrator, Jesus

Narrator
When the hour came, Jesus took his place at the table with the apostles. [He said to them:]

Jesus
I have wanted so much to eat this Passover meal with you before I suffer! For I tell you, I will never eat it until it is given its full meaning in the Kingdom of God.

Narrator

Then Jesus took a cup, gave thanks to God, and said:

Jesus

Take this and share it among yourselves. I tell you that from now on I will not drink this wine until the Kingdom of God comes.

Narrator

Then he took a piece of bread, gave thanks to God, broke it, and gave it to them, saying:

Jesus

This is my body, which is given for you. Do this in memory of me.

Narrator

In the same way, he gave them the cup after the supper, saying:

Jesus

This cup is God's new covenant, sealed with my blood, which is poured out for you.

Cast

[This is] the word of the Lord.   OR   This is the Gospel of Christ/
                                            This is the Gospel of the Lord.

All

Thanks be to God.   **Praise to Christ our Lord/**
                                            Praise to you, Lord Jesus Christ.

28.25   READING: THE LORD'S SUPPER (NIV)
From Luke 22.14–20 [21–23]

Cast: Narrator, Jesus

Narrator

When the hour came, Jesus and his apostles reclined at the table. [And he said to them:]

Jesus

I have eagerly desired to eat this Passover with you before I suffer. For I tell you, I will not eat it again until it finds fulfilment in the kingdom of God.

Narrator

After taking the cup, he gave thanks [and said:]

Jesus

Take this and divide it among you. For I tell you I will not drink again of the fruit of the vine until the kingdom of God comes.

Narrator
And he took the bread, gave thanks and broke it, and gave it to them.

Jesus
This is my body given for you; do this in remembrance of me.

Narrator
In the same way, after the supper he took the cup.

Jesus
This cup is the new covenant in my blood, which is poured out for you.

Cast
[This is] the word of the Lord.   OR   This is the Gospel of Christ/
This is the Gospel of the Lord.

All
Thanks be to God.   **Praise to Christ our Lord/
Praise to you, Lord Jesus Christ.**

FURTHER BIBLE READINGS
Readings appropriate to this theme will be found listed in our companion volume, 'The Dramatised Bible' (published by HarperCollins) on index page 419.

▶ **28.26**   CREED
ASB 1980, adapted

Let us affirm our faith in God:

**We believe and trust in God the Father
who made the world.**

**We believe and trust in his Son Jesus Christ,
who redeemed mankind.**

**We believe and trust in his Holy Spirit,
who gives life to the people of God.**

**We believe and trust in one God:
Father, Son, and Holy Spirit. Amen.**

▶ **28.27** INTERCESSION
ASB 1980

Let us pray for the whole Church of God in Christ Jesus, and for all people according to their needs:

O God, our creator and preserver, we pray for people of every race, and in every kind of need: make your ways known on earth, your saving power among all nations. (Especially we pray for . . .) Lord, in your mercy
hear our prayer.

We pray for your Church throughout the world: guide and govern us by your Holy Spirit, that all who profess and call themselves Christians may be led into the way of truth, and hold the faith in unity of spirit, in the bond of peace, and in righteousness of life. (Especially we pray for . . .) Lord, in your mercy
hear our prayer.

We commend to your fatherly goodness all who are anxious or distressed in mind or body; comfort and relieve them in their need; give them patience in their sufferings, and bring good out of their troubles. (Especially we pray for . . .) Merciful Father,
accept these prayers
for the sake of your Son,
our Saviour Jesus Christ. Amen.

▶ **28.28** FOR VARIOUS PEOPLE
Editors

God our Father, grant us the help of your Spirit in our prayers for the salvation of humankind. We pray for the whole church, that in faith and unity it may constantly be renewed by your Holy Spirit for mission and service. Lord, in your mercy,
hear our prayer.

We pray for the peoples of the world and the leaders of the nations, that they may seek justice, freedom and peace for all. Lord, in your mercy,
hear our prayer.

We pray for our own country and for all who have authority and influence, that they may serve in wisdom, honesty and compassion. Lord, in your mercy,
hear our prayer.

We pray for the communities in which we live and work, that there we may use your gifts to set people free from drudgery and poverty, and together find joy in your creation. Lord, in your mercy,
hear our prayer.

We pray for those who are ill . . . , for those in sorrow . . . , for the anxious, the lonely, the despairing, the persecuted, and for all who suffer from cruelty, injustice or neglect, that they may find strength and hope. Lord, in your mercy,
hear our prayer.

We pray for the life and witness of this church and all its members, that we may serve you in holiness throughout our lives.
Lord hear our prayers, in the strong name of Jesus Christ. Amen.

28.29   ABOUT COMMUNION
Llewellyn Cumings

Lord Christ, who said 'Do this in remembrance of me': help us at every communion service to look back, and remember your death for us on the cross; to look up, and know that you are the risen saviour among us; to look around, and rejoice in our fellowship with one another; and to look forward in hope to the coming of your kingdom and the heavenly banquet. For your name's sake. **Amen.**

▶ **28.30**   PEACE
From Romans 1†

Grace and peace to you from God our Father and from the Lord Jesus Christ:
peace be with you. Amen.

▶ **28.31**   PEACE
From Romans 15†

The God of peace be with you all. **Amen.**

▶ **28.32** PEACE
From 1 Corinthians 1†

*Here the local community may be named

To the church of God *in . . .** , to those sanctified in Christ Jesus and called to be holy, to all those everywhere who call on the name of our Lord Jesus Christ – their Lord and ours: grace and peace to you from God our Father and the Lord Jesus Christ. Amen.

▶ **28.33** PEACE
From 2 Corinthians 13†

Be of one mind, live in peace; the God of love and peace be with you. **Amen.**

▶ **28.34** PEACE
From Galatians 1†

Grace and peace be with you from God our Father and the Lord Jesus Christ, who gave himself for our sins according to the will of our God and Father; to whom be glory for ever and ever. **Amen.**

▶ **28.35** PEACE
From Galatians 6†

Peace and mercy to the people of God. **Amen.**

▶ **28.36** PEACE
From Ephesians 6†

Peace to our sisters and brothers, and love with faith from God the Father and the Lord Jesus Christ. **Amen.**

▶ **28.37** PEACE
From Ephesians 6†

Grace to all who love our Lord Jesus Christ with an undying love. **Amen.**

▶ **28.38** PEACE
From Philippians 4 and Philemon†

The grace of the Lord Jesus Christ be with your spirit. **Amen.**

▶ **28.39** PEACE
From 2 Timothy 1†

Grace, mercy and peace from God the Father and Christ Jesus our Lord. **Amen.**

▶ **28.40** PEACE
From 2 Timothy 4†

The Lord be with your spirit:
grace be with you. Amen.

▶ **28.41** PEACE
From 2 Thessalonians 1†

Grace and peace to you from God our Father and the Lord Jesus Christ. **Amen.**

▶ **28.42** PEACE
From Titus 1†

Grace and peace from God our Father and Christ Jesus our Saviour. **Amen.**

▶ **28.43** PEACE
From Philemon 1†

Grace to you and peace from God our Father and the Lord Jesus Christ. **Amen.**

▶ **28.44** PEACE
From 1 Peter 1†

Grace and peace be yours in abundance:
praise be to God!

▶ **28.45** PEACE
From 2 Peter 1†

Grace and peace be yours in abundance through the knowledge of
God and of Jesus our Lord. **Amen.**

▶ **28.46** PEACE
From 2 John†

Grace, mercy and peace from God the Father and from Jesus Christ,
the Father's Son, be with you in truth and love. **Amen.**

▶ **28.47** PEACE
From Jude†

You are loved by God the Father and kept by Jesus Christ: mercy,
peace and love be yours for ever. **Amen.**

▶ **28.48** PEACE (EASTER)
From Revelation 1†

Grace and peace to you from him who is, and who was, and who is
to come, [and from the seven spirits before his throne,] and from
Jesus Christ, who is the faithful witness, the firstborn from the dead:
Alleluia! Amen.

▶ **28.49** PEACE (EASTER)
From Revelation 1†

Grace and peace to you from Jesus Christ, who is the faithful
witness, the firstborn from the dead. **Amen.**

▶ **28.50** PEACE
From Revelation 1†

Grace and peace to you from him who is, and who was, and who is
to come. **Amen.**

▶ **28.51** PEACE
From Revelation 22†

The grace of the Lord Jesus be with God's people. **Amen.**

▶ **28.52** PEACE/GREETING
From 1 Peter 5†

Peace to all of you in Christ: greet one another with [a kiss of] love.
Amen.

▶ **28.53** PEACE/GREETING
From 3 John†

Peace to you all ... greet your friends by name.

▶ **28.54** GREETING
From Romans 15†

Welcome one another as Christ has welcomed you:
to God be the glory. Amen.

▶ **28.55** ASCRIPTION
From 1 Chronicles 29†

Yours, Lord, is the greatness, the power,
the glory, the splendour and the majesty:
everything in heaven and on earth is yours.

Everything comes from you,
and of your own do we give you.

28.56 INTRODUCTION
Editors

We have gathered in the name of Jesus our saviour and living Lord.
We recall how Jesus made himself known to his friends in the
breaking of bread, and how their hearts were set ablaze as they
talked and communed with him. May our hearts rejoice and our
tongues be filled with praise as we come to meet him here.

▶ **28.57** INVITATION
Editors

Come to this table, not because you are strong, but because you are
weak; come, not because any goodness of your own gives you a
right to come, but because you need mercy and help; come, because

530

you love the Lord a little and would like to love him more; come, not because you are worthy to approach him, but because he died for sinners; come, because he loved you and gave himself for you:

Your death, O Lord, we commemorate,
your resurrection we proclaim,
your coming again in glory we anticipate:
glory to you, living Saviour and Lord! Amen.

▶ **28.58** PRAYER OF APPROACH
Editors

Jesus,
we come to this your table
not because we are strong,
but because we are weak;
not because any goodness of our own
gives us the right to come,
but because we need your mercy and your help;
not because of anything we have achieved,
but because you died for sinners.
Glory be to you, our living Saviour and Lord. Amen.

28.59 EXHORTATION
Scoltish Baptist Ministers' Handbook

We come to this sacred Table, not because we must but because we may; not to testify that we are righteous, but that we sincerely love our Lord Jesus Christ, and desire to be his true disciples; not because we are strong but because we are weak; not because we have any claim on heaven's rewards, but because in our frailty and sin we stand in constant need of heaven's mercy and help.

Now that the supper of the Lord is spread before us, let us lift up our minds and hearts above all faithless fears and cares; let this bread and wine be for us the witnesses and signs of the grace of our Lord Jesus Christ, the love of God, and the communion of the Holy Spirit. Before the throne of the Heavenly Father and the cross of our Redeemer, let us consecrate our lives afresh to Christian obedience and service, and pray for strength to do and bear the holy will of God. **Amen.**

28.60   INTRODUCTION
Editors

In memory now we travel back two thousand years; in faith Christ comes to us across the ages. We break bread, as he did, and remember his body broken for us; we pour out wine, as he did, and remember his blood poured for us to the ground. We hold out our hands to receive his grace; we eat to feed on his love, and drink to pledge our loyalty; we rise to take up our cross; we go out to serve him in his world.

▶ **28.61**   DIALOGUE
From Ruth 2 and Psalm 107†

The Lord be with you:
the Lord bless you.

Let us give thanks to the Lord for his unfailing love
and the wonders he has done for us.

He satisfies the thirsty
and fills the hungry with good things. Amen.

▶ **28.62**   DIALOGUE
ICET

The Lord is here:
his Spirit is with us.

Lift up your hearts:
we lift them to the Lord.

Let us give thanks to the Lord our God:
it is right to give him thanks and praise.

▶ **28.63**   DOXOLOGY
From Revelation 4 and 5†

Let us give glory to God:

Our Lord and God, you are worthy to receive glory, honour, and power; for you created all things, and by your will they were given existence and life:
Glory to God in the highest!

O Lamb of God, you are worthy to receive wisdom, strength, and

praise, for by your death you bought for God people from every tribe, language, nation and race:
Glory to God in the highest!

You have made them a kingdom of priests to serve our God, and they shall rule on earth:
Glory to God in the highest!

**To him who sits upon the throne
and to the Lamb,
be praise and honour, glory and power,
for ever and ever! Amen.**

28.64   THANKSGIVING
From Ephesians 5†

In the name of our Lord Jesus Christ we give thanks for everything to you, God our Father.

And now we thank you that . . . (*number 28.96*)

▶ **28.65**   THANKSGIVING (END OF YEAR)
Editors

For the year that is past:
Lord, we thank you.

For your mercies every day:
Lord, we thank you.

For new discoveries of your grace, and fresh opportunities to do your work:
Lord, we thank you.

For your strength to survive hurt and sorrow, and that you pick us up when we fall:
Lord, we thank you.

For our life in Christ which gives us hope for the future:
Lord, we thank you.

**Lord, we thank you that you walk beside us –
your mighty hand to uphold us,
your heart of love to guide us,
your outstretched arms to bring us to our journey's end.**

And now we thank you that . . . (*number 28.96*)

▶ **28.66** THANKSGIVING (END/BEGINNING OF YEAR)
Lancelot Andrewes (1555–1626) adapted

Blessing and honour,
thanksgiving and praise,
more than we can utter,
more than we can conceive,
be to your glorious name,
O God, our Father,
by all angels, all people, all creation,
for ever.

And now we thank you that . . . (*number 28.96*)

▶ **28.67** THANKSGIVING (EPIPHANY ETC.)
From Psalm 117†

O Lord of all the nations,
we your people praise you and extol you;
for your love towards us is great
and your faithfulness endures for ever.

And now we thank you (Father) that . . . (*number 28.96*)

28.68 THANKSGIVING (FOLLOWING JESUS)
From Hebrews 4†

'We have a great High Priest who has gone through the heavens:
Jesus, the Son of God.'

Father, we thank you that our High Priest is able to sympathise with
our weaknesses, and has been tempted in every way, just as we are –
yet without sinning; that we can approach your throne of grace with
confidence, so that we may receive mercy and find grace to help in
our time of need.

And now we thank you (Father) that . . . (*number 28.96*)

28.69 THANKSGIVING (PEOPLE OF GOD)
From Psalm 111†

O God our Father, we, the assembly of your people praise you with
all our heart: for great are your works and wonderful the things you

do; all who seek them are delighted. Glorious and majestic are your deeds, and your righteousness is everlasting. Here we remember what you have done for us – your grace and your compassion; you have given this food to us who fear you, and your covenant is for ever. You have provided redemption for your people – an eternal covenant – holy and awesome is your name.

And now we thank you (Father) that . . . (*number 28.96*)

▶ **28.70** THANKSGIVING (LIFE OF PRAYER/FORGIVENESS)
From Psalm 118†

God our Father, we thank you,
for you are good, and your love endures for ever;
we thank you that you have heard our cry to you and set us free;
we thank you that you are with us,
and we need not be afraid;
we thank you that you have answered us and become our salvation.

And now we thank you (Father) that . . . (*number 28.96*)

▶ **28.71** THANKSGIVING (THE FAMILY ETC.)
From Psalm 145†

God our Father,
gracious and compassionate,
slow to anger and rich in mercy:
we thank you that you keep your promises,
and love all that you have made;
you uphold those who fall,
and lift up those who are bowed low;
you open your hand
and satisfy the desires of your people who fear you,
you hear our cry and save us.
Therefore we proclaim your goodness:
let every creature praise your holy name for ever and ever.

And now we thank you (Father) that . . . (*number 28.96*)

28.72   THANKSGIVING (PALM SUNDAY/PASSIONTIDE)
From Ephesians 1†

We praise you, God and Father of our Lord Jesus Christ, for you have blessed us from heaven with every spiritual blessing in Christ; you chose us in him before the creation of the world to be holy and blameless in your sight. We thank you for your glorious grace freely given in your beloved Son – by whose blood we are redeemed, our sins forgiven according to the riches of your grace.

And now we thank you (Father) that . . . (*number 28.96*)

▶ **28.73**   THANKSGIVING (EASTER)
From 1 Peter 1†

Praise be to you, O God our Father:
for in your great mercy
you have given us new birth into a living hope
through the resurrection from the dead
of Jesus Christ our Lord.

And now we thank you (Father) that . . . (*number 28.96*)

28.74   THANKSGIVING (EASTER)
From Luke 24†

Lord Jesus Christ, we are your disciples with whom you desire to eat; and we come to your table. Our hearts were burning within us as you talked with us on the way and opened the Scriptures to us. Now in your name we break bread, and give thanks and receive it: open our eyes, confirm our faith and fill us with your grace, that we may believe and declare to all: 'It is true! The Lord has risen'.

▶ **28.75**   THANKSGIVING (GOD'S CREATION)
Editors

Gracious Father and creator, the variety of beauty and colour in the world often leaves us speechless; the rolling hills, the mighty seas, the desert plains and the succulent green pastures, all proclaim your power and creative provision. O Lord our God:
we praise and adore you.

We praise you for the warming sun, the growth-making rain, the freshness of a new morning and the calm of a still evening: all proclaim your purpose and your pleasure. O Lord our God:
we praise and adore you.

We praise you for your Son, our Saviour, Jesus Christ: through him we have received pardon for our sin and the joy of salvation; for he lived and died and rose again to redeem us. O Lord our God:
we praise and adore you.

For all the work of your hands,
and for every gift from your heart of love,
we exalt your holy name.

And now we thank you (Father) that . . . (*number 28.96*)

▶ **28.76** THANKSGIVING (JESUS IS LORD)
From Revelation 4†

You are worthy, O Lord our God:
to receive glory and honour and power.

For you created all things:
and by your will they existed and were created.

You are worthy, O Christ, for you were slain:
and by your blood you ransomed us for God.

From every tribe and tongue and people and nation:
you made us a kingdom of priests to serve our God.

To him who sits upon the throne, and to the Lamb:
be blessing and honour and glory and might.

And now we thank you (Father) that . . . (*number 28.96*)

28.77 THANKSGIVING (HOLY SPIRIT)
From Isaiah 59†

We thank you, O God our Father, that your arm is not too short to save, nor your ear too dull to hear; that your Son Jesus has come, as you promised, to redeem your people who repent of their sins. We thank you that your Spirit, who is upon us, will not leave us; and your word will not depart from us, nor from our children, nor from their descendants from this time on for ever.

And now we thank you (Father) that . . . (*number 28.96*)

28.78 THANKSGIVING (HOLINESS AND MAJESTY OF GOD)
From 1 Timothy 6†

To you our God and Father, the blessed and only Ruler, the King of kings and Lord of lords, who alone is immortal and who lives in unapproachable light: to you be honour and might for ever.

And now we thank you (Father) that . . . *(number 28.96)*

▶ **28.79** THANKSGIVING (SEA THEME/HOLIDAYS)
From Psalm 136†

O God our Father, we thank you, for you are good:
Lord, your love endures for ever.

We thank you that you are the God of gods; we thank you that you are the Lord of lords:
Lord, your love endures for ever.

We thank you that you do great wonders; that by your understanding you made the skies and spread out the earth and sea:
Lord, your love endures for ever.

We thank you that you made the lights of heaven – the sun to rule the day, and the moon and stars to govern the night:
Lord, your love endures for ever.

We thank you that you have remembered us in our humiliation; that through your Son Jesus Christ you have freed us from our enemies, the powers of evil and of death:
Lord, your love endures for ever.

And now we thank you (Father) that . . . *(number 28.96)*

▶ **28.80** THANKSGIVING
(GOD'S LOVE TO US/HOLY COMMUNION)
From Psalm 36†

We thank you, our Father,
that your love reaches to the heavens,
and your faithfulness to the skies;
that your justice is like the great deep.
Without price are your unfailing mercies;
we feast on your goodness and drink from the river of your blessing.

And now we thank you (Father) that . . . *(number 28.96)*

► **28.81**   THANKSGIVING (INVITATION TO FAITH)
From Psalm 118†

O God our Father, we thank you,
for you are good, and your love endures for ever:
we thank you that you have heard our cry to you and set us free;
we thank you that you are with us,
and we need not be afraid;
we thank you that you have answered us
and become our salvation in Jesus.

And now we thank you (Father) that . . . (*number 28.96*)

► **28.82**   THANKSGIVING (THE CARING CHURCH)
From Psalm 138†

We thank you, God our Father, with all our hearts
and sing to you our songs and hymns;
we bow before you in worship
and praise you because you have loved us
and shown yourself faithful;
your word is as mighty as your name –
and when we call to you,
you answer our prayer
and give us the strength we need.
Though you are very high,
yet you care for the lowly,
and the proud cannot hide from you;
when we are surrounded by troubles
you keep us safe.

And now we thank you (Father) that . . . (*number 28.96*)

► **28.83**   THANKSGIVING
             (MISSIONARY/WORLDWIDE CHURCH)
From Revelation 5†

We thank you, our Father,
that you sent your Son, Jesus Christ
to die for us
and by his blood to ransom us
from every tribe and tongue
and people and nation;

and to make us
a kingdom of priests
to serve our God

And now we thank you (Father) that . . . (*number 28.96*)

▶ **28.84**   THANKSGIVING (RENEWAL)
From 1 Corinthians 12†

We thank you, O God our Father, for our unity in diversity:

For different kinds of gifts:
but the same Spirit.

For different kinds of service:
but the same Lord.

For different kinds of working:
but the same God.

**Thank you, God our Father,
that you work in us in all these ways.**

And now we thank you that . . . (*number 28.96*)

28.85   THANKSGIVING (AT A MUSICAL SERVICE)
From Psalm 150†

* Here may be listed all musical instruments used in the service

O God our Father, we praise you; we praise you in your sanctuary,
we praise you in your mighty heavens. We praise you for your acts
of power; we praise you for your surpassing greatness; with . . . * we
praise you. With every breath your people praise you.

And now we thank you (Father) that . . . (*number 28.96*)

▶ **28.86**   THANKSGIVING (CHURCH ANNIVERSARY)
From Revelation 15†

Glory be to you, O God our Father,
you have power, wisdom and majesty:
receive from us
honour, glory, worship and blessing.
Great and marvellous are your works,
just and true are your ways:

blessing and honour and glory and power
be to him who reigns upon the throne,
and to the Lamb,
through the one eternal Spirit,
now and for ever.

And now we thank you (Father) that . . . (*number 28.96*)

▶ **28.87** THANKSGIVING ('LAMMAS'/HARVEST)
D. L. Couper, adapted

Let us give thanks to the Lord our God:
it is right to give him thanks and praise.

It is indeed right,
it is our duty and our joy,
at all times and in all places
to give you thanks and praise,
holy Father, heavenly King,
almighty and eternal God,
creator of heaven and earth,
through Jesus Christ our Lord:
for you have provided for us and prospered us
and called us to be your fellow-workers.
You have ripened our first-fruits with the spring rain
and the warmth of the summer sun;
you have given us all things richly to enjoy
and have blessed the work of our hands.

And now we thank you (Father) that . . . (*number 28.96*)

28.88 THANKSGIVING (HARVEST)
From Psalm 145†

O God our Father, gracious and compassionate, slow to anger and
rich in mercy; we thank you that you keep your promises, and love
all that you have made; you uphold those who fall, and lift up those
who are bowed low: you open your hand and satisfy the desires of
your people who fear you, you hear our cry and save us.

And now we thank you (Father) that . . . (*number 28.96*)

▶ **28.89** THANKSGIVING
(CHRISTIAN CONFLICT AND CHARACTER)
From Revelation 15†

God our Father,
we thank you with all our heart
and bow before you in worship,
because you have loved us
and shown yourself faithful;
your word is as mighty as your name,
and when we call to you
you answer our prayer
and give us the strength we need;
though you are very high,
yet you care for the lowly,
and the proud cannot hide from you;
when we are surrounded by troubles
you keep us safe:
Father, we thank you
that your love is eternal,
and you will complete in us
the work you have begun.

And now we thank you (Father) that . . . (*number 28.96*)

▶ **28.90** THANKSGIVING (HEAVEN/GOD'S PEOPLE)
From 1 Peter 1†

We thank you, O God our Father:
that in your great mercy
you have given us new birth
into a living hope
through the resurrection from the dead
of Jesus Christ our Lord.

And now we thank you (Father) that . . . (*number 28.96*)

28.91 THANKSGIVING (CHRIST'S COMING/JUDGEMENT)
From Revelation 11†

We give thanks to you, Lord God almighty, the One who is and who
was, because you will take your great power and begin to reign; the

time will come for judging the dead, for rewarding your servants and your saints and those who reverence your name.

And now we thank you (Father) that . . . (*number 28.96*)

▶ **28.92** THANKSGIVING (WORD OF GOD)
From Romans 11†

O Lord God our Father,
we thank you for the riches of your wisdom and your knowledge.
How unsearchable are your judgements;
your paths beyond tracing out!
Who has known your mind or been your counsellor?
Who has ever given anything to you that you should repay?
For from you and through you and to you are all things.
To you be the glory for ever!

And now we thank you (Father) that . . . (*number 28.96*)

▶ **28.93** THANKSGIVING (CHRISTMAS)
Liturgical Commission

For the birth of Jesus your Son, our Saviour, cradled in the manger at Bethlehem;
we thank you, heavenly Father.

For the love and gentle care of Mary, his mother, most blessed of all women:
we thank you, heavenly Father.

For shepherds keeping watch over their flocks by night, who came with haste to worship Christ, the new-born King:
we thank you, heavenly Father.

For wise men from the East, who followed the star and presented him with their gifts of gold and frankincense and myrrh:
we thank you, heavenly Father.

For the light and love of this Christmas season, in our hearts and in our homes, bringing joy and gladness to us all:
we thank you, heavenly Father.

And in our joyful gratitude we join our voices with the angels who are always singing to you:
Holy, holy, holy Lord

God of power and might,
heaven and earth are full of your glory;
hosanna in the highest. Amen.

And now we thank you,
    Father, God of love,
for the signs of your love on this table,
for your love made known
    through all the world
and shining on us
in the face of Jesus Christ.

28.94   THANKSGIVING (BAPTISM)
From 1 Peter 1†

We thank you, O God and Father of our Lord Jesus Christ, that in your great mercy you have given us new birth into a living hope through the resurrection of Jesus Christ from the dead, and into an inheritance that can never perish, spoil or fade – kept in heaven for us, who through faith are shielded by God's power until the coming of the salvation that is ready to be revealed in the last time: in this we greatly rejoice.

And now we thank you (Father) that . . . (*number 28.96*)

▶ **28.95   THANKSGIVING (LOCAL FESTIVALS)**
From 1 Chronicles 29†

Lord God of our fathers,
may you be praised for ever and ever!

You are great and powerful, glorious, splendid and
majestic: Lord God of our fathers,
may you be praised for ever and ever!

Everything in heaven and earth is yours, and you
are king, supreme ruler over all: Lord God of our fathers,
may you be praised for ever and ever!

All riches and wealth come from you; you rule
everything by your strength and power: Lord God
of our fathers,
may you be praised for ever and ever!

Now, our God,
we give you thanks,
and praise your glorious name.

And now we thank you (Father) that . . . (*number 28.96*)

▶ **28.96** WORDS OF INSTITUTION
From 1 Corinthians 11†

[*And now we thank you (Father) that*]

Our Lord Jesus Christ,
in the same night that he was betrayed,
took bread,
and when he had given thanks
he broke it and said,
'This is my body, which is for you;
do this to remember me'.

In the same way, after supper
he took the cup, saying,
'This cup is the new covenant in my blood;
do this, whenever you drink it, to remember me'. **Amen.**

And there may be added:

Whenever you eat this bread and drink this cup, you proclaim the
Lord's death until he comes. **Amen.**

▶ **28.97** WORDS OF INSTITUTION
Song: Janet Lunt, © Mustard Seed Music

And now we thank you for [the symbols of] Christ's body broken
and blood shed:

>Broken for me, broken for you,
>the body of Jesus broken for you.
>He offered his body, he poured out his soul,
>Jesus was broken that we might be whole:
>Broken for me . . .
>Come to my table and with me dine,
>eat of my bread and drink of my wine:
>Broken for me . . .

This is my body given for you,
eat it remembering I died for you:
    Broken for me . . .
This is my blood I shed for you,
for your forgiveness, making you new:
    Broken for me . . .

▶ **28.98** COMMUNION PRAYER
Editor, and others

God our Father, we give you our thanks (at this time especially
for . . .) and we rejoice to praise you through Jesus Christ our Lord.

Through him you made us;
through him you set us free from sin and death.
Through him you gave us your Holy Spirit,
and called us into one family.

So, Father, by the same Spirit, let us who take this bread and wine,
receive the body and blood of Christ.

For when the time came for him to be lifted up to die and so to enter
his glory, he gathered his disciples and took bread and gave thanks
to you; then he broke it and gave it to them saying, 'Take, eat: this is
my body which is given for you; do this to remember me'. After
supper he took the cup and gave thanks. He gave it to them saying,
'Drink this, all of you: this is my blood of the new covenant, shed for
you and for many that sins may be forgiven; do this every time you
drink it, to remember me'.

Now as we look for his coming, we celebrate with this bread and
wine his one perfect sacrifice; proclaiming his death for our salvation
and rejoicing in the power of his resurrection, until we share the
fellowship of his Kingdom.

Father,
accept the thanks and praise of your children
in this sacred feast;
renew us by your Holy Spirit,
and make us one in Christ Jesus our Lord. Amen.

▶ **28.99** RESPONSE (SANCTUS)
From Revelation 5

With the whole family in heaven and on earth we praise and adore
you, saying:

Holy, holy, holy Lord,
God of power and might,
heaven and earth are full of your glory.
Hosanna in the highest. Amen.

▶ **28.100** RESPONSE (SANCTUS)
From Revelation 5

Holy, holy, holy is the Lord
holy is the Lord God almighty,
who was and is and is to come;
holy, holy, holy is the Lord.

▶ **28.101** RESPONSE (SANCTUS)
From Revelation 5

Holy, holy, holy
is the Lord God almighty,
who was, and is
and is to come. **Amen.**

▶ **28.102** RESPONSE (SANCTUS)
From Isaiah 6

Holy, holy, holy is the Lord God almighty:
the whole earth is full of his glory. Amen.

▶ **28.103** RESPONSE
From Revelation 5†

Worthy is the Lamb, who was slain, to receive power and wealth and
wisdom and strength and honour and glory and praise:
To him who sits upon the throne
and to the Lamb
be praise and honour
**   and glory and power**
for ever and ever. Amen.

▶ **28.104**   RESPONSE (ESPECIALLY EASTER)
From 2 Corinthians 13†

In weakness Christ was put to death on the Cross:
by God's power he lives!

▶ **28.105**   FOR CHRIST'S PRESENCE
Robert Runcie

Come, Lord,
in the fullness of your risen presence,
and make yourself known
to your people again
through the breaking of the bread,
and the sharing of the cup. **Amen.**

▶ **28.106**   FOR CHRIST'S PRESENCE
F. W. Street

Come to us, Lord Jesus, in your risen power,
when we receive the bread of life
    and the cup of salvation;
cleanse our hearts from sin,
that they may be worthy of so great a guest;
and keep us firm in your love,
for your great name's sake. **Amen.**

▶ **28.107**   FOR THE HOLY SPIRIT
Editors

Come, Holy Spirit:
speak to us of Jesus,
heal us and renew us,
strengthen our wills to obey,
warm our hearts with love for one another;
bring glory to the name of our mighty God. **Amen.**

▶ **28.108**   THE LORD'S PRAYER
ICET, adapted ASB 1980

Our Father in heaven,
hallowed be your name,
your kingdom come,
your will be done,
on earth as in heaven.
Give us today our daily bread.
Forgive us our sins
as we forgive those who sin against us.
Lead us not into temptation
but deliver us from evil.

For the kingdom, the power,
   and the glory are yours
now and for ever. Amen.

▶ **28.109**   SENTENCE (Especially Lent and Passiontide)
1 Corinthians 11.26†

At the breaking of the bread and the taking of the wine:

Whenever you eat this bread and drink this cup, you proclaim the
Lord's death until he comes. **Amen.**

28.110 RESPONSES
From John 6 and 15†

At the breaking of the bread

Jesus said, 'I am the bread of life: those who come to me will never
grow hungry, and those who believe in me will never be thirsty.'
'Lord, give us this bread for ever.' Amen.

At the sharing of the wine

Jesus said, 'I am the true vine . . . remain in me, and I will remain in
you.' **Amen.**

▶ **28.111** RESPONSES
From Luke 22 and Mark 14†

At the breaking of the bread

Jesus said, 'I have eagerly desired to eat this passover with you before I suffer; for I tell you, I will not eat it again until it finds fulfilment in the kingdom of God.'

'Do this in memory of me.' **Amen.**

At the sharing of the wine

Jesus said, 'I tell you the truth, I will not drink again of the fruit of the vine until that day when I drink it anew in the kingdom of God.'

'Take this and share it among you.' **Amen.**

▶ **28.112** RESPONSES
From 1 Corinthians 10†

At the breaking of the bread

The bread that we break:
is a sharing in the body of Christ. Amen.

At the sharing of the wine

The cup of thanksgiving for which we give thanks:
is a sharing in the blood of Christ. Amen.

▶ **28.113** RESPONSES
From John 6†

At the breaking of the bread

Jesus said, 'The bread of God is he who comes down from heaven and gives life to the world':
Lord, from now on give us this bread. Amen.

At the sharing of the wine

Jesus said, 'Whoever believes in me will never be thirsty'.
Lord, we have seen and we believe. Amen.

▶ **28.114** RESPONSES
From John 6†

At the breaking of the bread

Jesus said, 'Just as the living Father sent me and I live because of the Father, so the one who feeds on me will live because of me'.
This is the bread that came down from heaven. Amen.

At the sharing of the wine

Jesus said, 'Unless you can eat the flesh of the Son of Man and drink his blood, you have no life in you'.
This is the blood of eternal life. Amen.

▶ **28.115** RESPONSES
From 1 Corinthians 10†

At the breaking of the bread

We break the bread and eat:
to share in the body of Christ.

So we who eat are one:
for we share one bread.

At the sharing of the wine

We give thanks for the cup and drink:
to share in the blood of Christ. Amen.

▶ **28.116** SENTENCES
From 1 Corinthians 11

At the breaking of the bread

When he had given thanks, Jesus said 'This is my body which is for you: do this in remembrance of me.' **Amen.**

At the taking of the cup

In the same way he took the cup and said, 'This cup is the new covenant in my blood: drink this always in remembrance of me.'
Amen.

▶ **28.117** INVITATION
From Hebrews 10†

Draw near with a sincere heart and a sure faith, purged from your guilt and washed clean through the blood of Christ; hold on to your hope and trust the promises of God. **Amen.**

▶ **28.118** WORDS OF ADMINISTRATION
Editors

At the giving of the bread

Receive this bread as the token that Jesus loved you and died for you. **Amen.**

At the giving of the wine

Take this wine, and let Christ cleanse you and fill you with his love. **Amen.**

28.119 THANKSGIVING AFTER COMMUNION
From 'Worship Now'

O God, our Father, we thank you for this sacrament. For all who down the centuries at your table have found the light that never fades, the joy that no one takes from them, the forgiveness of their sins, the love which is your love, the presence of their Lord; we thank you in his name. **Amen.**

▶ **28.120** THANKSGIVING AFTER COMMUNION
Liturgical Commission

Eternal Father,
we thank you for refreshing us
with these heavenly gifts:
may our communion
strengthen us in faith,
build us up in hope,
and make us grow in love;
for the sake of Jesus Christ our Lord. **Amen.**

▶ *28.80 may also be used here*

28.121 DOXOLOGY
FromPhilippians 4†

To our God and Father, who meets all our needs according to his glorious riches in Christ Jesus, be glory for ever and ever. **Amen.**

▶ **28.122** DOXOLOGY
From Romans 16†

Glory to God
who alone is all–wise;
through Jesus Christ, for ever! **Amen.**

28.123 BLESSING
2 Corinthians 11†

Be of one mind, live in peace; and the God of love and peace be with you always. **Amen.**

OR

28.124 BLESSING
From 2 Corinthians 13†

Strive for perfection, listen to wisdom, agree with one another, live in peace; and the God of love and peace be with you always. **Amen.**

28.125 BLESSING
ASB 1980

The love of the Lord Jesus draw *you* to himself, the power of the Lord Jesus strengthen *you* in his service, the joy of the Lord Jesus fill *your* hearts; and the blessing of God almighty, the Father, the Son, and the Holy Spirit, be among *you* and remain with *you* always. **Amen.**

▶ **28.126** DISMISSAL
From 'A New Zealand Prayer Book'

Let us bless the Lord:
thanks be to God.

The almighty and merciful God bless us and keep us now and for ever.
Amen.

▶ **28.127** DISMISSAL
From 1 Corinthians 16†

Let all who love the Lord be blessed:
come, O Lord.

Love to you all in Christ Jesus:
the grace of the Lord Jesus be with you. Amen.

At Local Festivals, For the Peace of the World

▶ **29.1** GREETING
From Romans 1

Grace and peace to you from God our Father and from the Lord
Jesus Christ. **Amen.**

29.2 SENTENCE
Psalm 24.1

The earth belongs to the Lord, and all that it contains: the whole
earth, and all who live in it.

29.3 SENTENCE
2 Corinthians 13.11

Be of one mind, live in peace. And the God of love and peace will be
with you.

29.4 SENTENCE
1 Timothy 2.1

I urge that requests, prayers, intercession and thanksgiving be made
for everyone – for kings and all those in authority, that we may live
peaceful and quiet lives in all godliness and holiness.

29.5 SENTENCE
1 Peter 2. 13,16

Submit yourselves for the Lord's sake to every human authority; live
as free people, but do not use your freedom as a cover for evil; live as
servants of God.

29.6 SENTENCE (REMEMBRANCE)
Revelation 12. 11,12

They did not love their lives so much as to shrink from death.
Therefore rejoice, you heavens and all that dwell in them.

▶ **29.7** RESPONSE
From Galatians 1†

Grace and peace to you from God our Father and the Lord Jesus
Christ:
to whom be glory for ever and ever. Amen.

▶ **29.8** RESPONSE
From Amos 5†

Let justice roll on like a river:
**and righteousness
like a never failing stream. Amen.**

▶ **29.9** RESPONSE
From 2 Chronicles †

Lord, God of our fathers, you are the God of heaven; you rule over
all the kingdoms of the nations:
**power and might are in your hand,
and no-one can withstand you.**

We have no power to face the perils that confront us:
**we do not know what to do,
but our eyes are upon you, O Lord. Amen.**

▶ **29.10** RESPONSE
From Revelation 1†

Grace and peace to you from Jesus Christ, the ruler of the kings of
the earth. **Amen.**

▶ **29.11** APPROACH
From Psalm 138†

Lord, we worship you with all our heart; before the powers of the
universe we sing your praises.

We come into your house and honour your name because of your
love and faithfulness; for you have exalted your name and your
word above all things. We worship you with all our heart:
your love endures for ever.

When we called to you, you answered us; you gave us courage. We worship you with all our heart:
your love endures for ever.

O may the leaders of the nations praise you, Lord, when they hear the words of your mouth – let them too sing of your ways, for your glory is very great. Though you are so high yet you look upon the lowly – while you distance yourself from the proud. We worship you with all our heart:
your love endures for ever. Amen.

29.12   APPROACH
Editors

Our loving Father God, we address you by many names and we experience you in a wealth of ways, we thank you that you are Truth. Jesus came bringing that truth to us. We praise you because in every place and at all times we can know you as the God of truth.

We thank you that in all that we do and in all that we see, in our work or rest, our laughter or our tears, in loneliness or in fellowship you remain faithful and true. You never deny your nature. We thank you for what your Spirit's presence does for us and in us, as you come as Truth in every situation.

Grant O Lord, that this day we may be awakened to the truth of your love for us; that familiar words may shine with new meaning and that our worship may be cleansed of mere formality and ceremonial.

Open our eyes to see your true loveliness, and make our hearts to burn within us as you speak your true word to us; that we may know ourselves forgiven, energised with new life, filled with new vitality and power: through Jesus Christ our Lord. **Amen.**

29.13   APPROACH (REMEMBRANCE)
Editors

We come to worship Almighty God who has created the world and whose power continues to sustain it: his love is unfailing.

Today we are here to give thanks for our deliverance in times of war and danger, to remember with deep gratitude the courage, devotion and example of those who laid down their lives for our country, to

557

commend to God all who suffer as the result of war, and to pray for peace and justice in the world.

On this day also let us renew our dedication to the task of bringing the inner peace of Christ to those around us, and the news of his gracious kingdom to the peoples of the world:

Let us worship God. **Amen.**

▶ **29.14** PRAISE
From Psalm 134†

All you servants of the Lord:
praise the Lord.

You who come into his house to worship him:
praise the Lord.

Lift up your hands in his presence:
praise the Lord.

May the Lord, the maker of heaven and earth, bless you in this holy place. **Amen.**

▶ **29.15** PRAISE
From Psalm 67†

Let the people praise you, O God;
let all the people praise you!

Let your ways be known on earth;
your saving power in all the world!

▶ **29.16** CONFESSION
From Jeremiah 14†

O Lord,
we acknowledge our own wickedness
and the guilt of our society;
we have sinned against you.
For the sake of your name do not despise us;
remember your new covenant in Jesus our redeemer
and forgive us our sin;
for his name's sake. Amen.

▶ **29.17** CONFESSION
Editors

We confess our sins and selfishness, our pride, our greed, the evil divisions we create and sustain. O Lord of mercy, we put our hope in you:
**forgive us and help us
for your name's sake.**

We confess our share in the world's wrong and our failure to strive for that universal peace and justice which is your will. O Lord of mercy, we put our hope in you:
**forgive us and help us
for your name's sake.**

We confess we have not loved you with our whole heart nor our neighbours as ourselves. O Lord of mercy, we put our hope in you:
**forgive us and help us
for your name's sake.**

**Release us from our sins by the cross of Christ
and strengthen us for his service
by the power of your Spirit. Amen.**

▶ **29.18** CONFESSION
Editor

Lord God, our maker and our redeemer, this is your world and we are your people: come among us and save us.

Where we have wilfully misused your gifts of creation, be merciful, Lord:
forgive us and help us.

Where we have seen the ill-treatment of others and have not gone to their aid, be merciful, Lord:
forgive us and help us.

Where we have condoned the lie in our society, and failed to achieve justice or compassion, be merciful, Lord:
forgive us and help us.

Where we have heard for ourselves the good news of Christ, but have not shared it with our generation nor taught it to our children, be merciful, Lord:
forgive us and help us.

Where we have not loved you with all our heart, nor our neighbours as ourselves, be merciful, Lord:
forgive us and help us.

O God,
forgive us for our lack of love,
and in your mercy make us
what you would have us be,
through Jesus Christ our Lord. Amen.

29.19   ABSOLUTION
From Isaiah 12

The Lord's anger is turned away and he will comfort *you*. God is *your* salvation – trust and do not be afraid. **Amen.**

29.20   COLLECT
Pentecost 16, ASB 1980

Almighty God, you have taught us through your Son that love is the fulfilling of the law. Grant that we may love you with our whole heart and our neighbours as ourselves; through Jesus Christ our Lord. **Amen.**

▶ 29.21   PSALM
Psalm 122. 1–8†

The congregation may divide at A *– male voices, and* B *– female voices*

I was glad when they said to me:
let us go to the house of the Lord!

Pray for the peace of Jerusalem:
A **may those who love our land be blessed.**

May there be peace in your homes:
B **and safety for our families.**

For the sake of those we love we say:
ALL **Let there be peace! Amen.**

▶ **29.22**   PSALM
Psalm 124. 1–8

The congregation may divide at A, B *and* C

If the Lord had not been on our side – now let Israel say:

If the Lord had not been on our side –
A **when enemies attacked us,**
B **when their anger flared against us,**
C **they would have swallowed us alive.**
A **The flood would have engulfed us,**
B **the torrent would have swept over us,**
C **the waters would have drowned us.**

Praise the Lord:
A **who has not given us up to their teeth.**
B **We have escaped like a bird from the snare:**
C **the snare is broken and we are free.**

Our help is in the name of the Lord:
ALL **who made heaven and earth. Amen.**

29.23   READING: INSINCERE REPENTENCE
Hosea 6. 1–6

Cast: Prophet, Person 1, Person 2 (can be the same as Person 1), The Lord

Prophet
The people say:

Persons 1 and 2
Let's return to the Lord!

Person 1
He has hurt us, but he will be sure to heal us.

Person 2
He has wounded us, but he will bandage our wounds, won't he?

Person 1
In two or three days he will revive us, and we will live in his presence.

Person 2
Let us try to know the Lord. He will come to us as surely as the day dawns, as surely as the spring rains that water the earth.

Prophet

But the Lord says:

The Lord
Israel and Judah, what am I going to do with you? Your love for me disappears as quickly as morning mist; it is like dew, that vanishes early in the day. That is why I have sent my prophets to you with my message of judgement and destruction. What I want from you is plain and clear: I want your constant love.

Cast
[This is] the word of the Lord

All
Thanks be to God.

29.24   READING: ABOUT PAYING TAXES
Matthew 22. 15–22

Cast: Narrator, Spy 1, Spy 2, Jesus

Narrator
The Pharisees went off and made a plan to trap Jesus with questions. Then they sent to him some of their disciples and some members of Herod's party. [They said:]

Spy 1
Teacher, we know that you tell the truth.

Spy 2
You teach the truth about God's will for man, without worrying about what people think, because you pay no attention to a man's status.

Spy 1
Tell us, then, what do you think? Is it against our Law to pay taxes to the Roman Emperor, or not?

Narrator
Jesus, however, was aware of their evil plan:

Jesus
You hypocrites! Why are you trying to trap me? Show me the coin for paying the tax!

Narrator
They brought him the coin. (PAUSE)

Jesus
Whose face and name are these?

Spies 1 and **2**
The Emperor's.

Jesus
Well, then, pay the Emperor what belongs to the Emperor, and pay God what belongs to God.

Narrator
When they heard this, they were amazed; and they left him and went away.

Cast
[This is] the word of the Lord.   OR   This is the Gospel of Christ/
                                                            This is the Gospel of the Lord.

All
Thanks be to God.   **Praise to Christ our Lord/**
                                                        Praise to you, Lord Jesus Christ.

FURTHER BIBLE READINGS
Readings appropriate to this theme will be found listed in our companion volume, 'The Dramatised Bible' (published by HarperCollins) on index pages 419–410.

▶ **29.25**   CREED
ASB 1980

Do you believe in God the Father?
We believe and trust in God the Father,
who made the world.

Do you believe in God the Son?
We believe and trust in his Son Jesus Christ
who redeemed mankind.

Do you believe in the Holy Spirit?
We believe and trust in the Holy Spirit,
who gives life to the people of God.

We believe and trust in one God:
Father, Son, and Holy Spirit. Amen.

▶ **29.26** ACT OF REMEMBRANCE
The congregation stands:

Let us remember in the presence of God those who have died amid the tragedy of war – those whom we knew and whose memory we treasure, those mourned by other loved ones. Let us celebrate all who have lived and died in the service of their fellow men and women.

They shall grow not old,
as we who are left grow old.

Age shall not weary them,
nor the years condemn.

At the going down of the sun, and in the morning, we will remember them:
we will remember them.

Silence is kept

▶ **29.27** FOR THOSE WHO SUFFER (REMEMBRANCE)
Editors

We pray for all who suffer as a result of war:

For the injured and the disabled, for the mentally distressed and for those whose faith in God and in other people has been weakened or destroyed, we lift our hearts to you:
O Lord of mercy, hear our prayer.

For the homeless and refugees, for those who are hungry, and for all who have lost their livelihood and security, we lift our hearts to you:
O Lord of mercy, hear our prayer.

For those who mourn their dead; for those who have lost husband, wife, children or parents, and especially for those who have no hope in Christ to sustain them in their grief, we lift our hearts to you:
O Lord of mercy, hear our prayer.

Here follows a short silence, then:

O Lord, hear our prayer:
for the sake of our Saviour, Jesus Christ. Amen.

29.28 REMEMBRANCE
Unknown

Almighty Father, we remember before you those who sacrificed their lives in the struggle for freedom, and we pray that the justice and peace for which they fought may become established today among the families of the nations: we ask this through him who taught us to pray for the coming of your kingdom on earth as it is in heaven, Jesus Christ our Lord. **Amen.**

▶ **29.29** REMEMBRANCE
Alan Gaunt

As we remember those who died in war for the cause of peace:
Lord, make us peace-makers.

As we look to the future of our children and grandchildren:
Lord, make us peace-makers.

As we think of the war torn, blood-stained, sorrowful world:
Lord, make us peace-makers.

**Lord, hear our prayer
and come to us in perfect love,
to drive away our fear;
in the name of the Prince of peace,
Jesus Christ our Lord. Amen.**

▶ **29.30** INTERCESSION
Alan Gaunt, adapted Gill Tovar

Eternal God, we all need to know the power and the freedom of your healing. We pray for others in the knowledge of your love and forgiveness:

For all who are weighed down by a guilty conscience, for those who lack imagination, and for those who immerse themselves in activities so that they need never stand still to see themselves as they really are, Lord, in your mercy:
hear our prayer.

For those who have been stunned and shocked by death; for widows and orphaned children, especially for those who do not see how they

can put their lives together again; and for those who suffer remorse because of what they did or failed to do, Lord, in your mercy:
hear our prayer.

For those whose bodies are being eaten away by disease – or fighting the invasion of infection; for those who suffer constant pain and continual discomfort, Lord, in your mercy:
hear our prayer.

For those who suffer the effects of war, political oppression or persecution; and for those who are unemployed, hungry, or dying through the failure of economic systems, Lord, in your mercy:
hear our prayer.

As we pray, we ask that we may take the joy and hope of being loved and forgiven and made whole into the world in the name of Christ – who loved life, and loved you, and loved all humankind and proved your love by his own self-sacrifice.

Make us like Christ,
so that through our lives
your love and forgiveness
   may be lived and proclaimed;
and your name honoured. Amen.

▶ **29.31**   FOR FORGIVENESS
Alan Gaunt

For the wounds still inflicted on your children, Lord, forgive us and help us.

For infants who cry for food and get none; for the making of orphans and widows, Lord, forgive us:
forgive us and help us.

For those who mourn and are not comforted, for those who are guilty and are not convicted of sin, Lord, forgive us:
forgive us and help us.

For those who are lost and have no good news proclaimed to them, but are left to think you have rejected them, Lord, forgive us:
forgive us and help us.

Through the cross of Jesus
reconcile us to yourself
and to each other;

so that war may cease,
nation may speak peace to nation,
your will be done on earth
and your name honoured everywhere for ever. Amen.

▶ **29.32** FOR VICTIMS
Editors

Lord God, Father of mercy,
we pray for the innocent victims of war
and those held hostage in any place:
help us to remember them day by day.
May the light of Christ give them hope,
may the love of Christ give them strength,
and may the presence of your Holy Spirit
comfort and sustain them at all times. **Amen.**

29.33 FOR RULERS
Christopher Idle

O God, our Father and Lord, you have taught us that you are the ruler of all, the power above all powers. We commit into your hands all the rulers of the world; and we pray, most merciful Lord, that your will may be done upon earth, that you will raise up those whom you will raise up, and throw down those whom you will throw down. Whenever the peace of our world is threatened, give us the confidence that you alone are the creator and destroyer of kingdoms, even to the end of time: through Jesus Christ our Lord. **Amen.**

29.34 FOR WORLD LEADERS
Beryl Bye

O Lord God, guide the leaders of many different countries at the meetings where they try, by working together, to make the world a better and safer place. Help them to want peace rather than power, and show them how they can share the food in the world so that no one need be hungry. For Jesus' sake. **Amen.**

29.35   FOR THE OPPRESSED
Christopher Idle

We plead with you today, O God for nations and states where oppressive governments give little freedom: for their leaders, we ask that they may learn to govern in justice, mercy and truth; for their people, we ask that they may be able to hear your gospel and heed your word; and for all your servants in these lands, we pray for great faithfulness, great courage, and great love; through Jesus Christ our Lord. **Amen.**

29.36   FOR PEACE IN THE WORLD
Pentecost 15, ASB 1980

Almighty Father, whose will is to restore all things in your beloved Son, the king of all: govern the hearts and minds of those in authority, and bring the families of the nations, divided and torn apart by the ravages of sin, to be subject to his just and gentle rule; who is alive and reigns with you and the Holy Spirit, one God, now and for ever. **Amen.**

29.37   FOR OUR OWN COUNTRY AND ITS GOVERNMENT
Editors

Lord God our ruler, justice and mercy come from you: we bring before you the needs of our country. Give wisdom, insight and a sense of caring responsibility to those elected to authority over us, and grant them true humility in using their power; that our country may be governed and administered for the good of all its inhabitants and for the refuge of those who seek their peace and well-being among us. Grant that all elected to parliament, of whichever party, may put the common good ahead of all ambition and dogma. Lord, watch over our country we pray and may your will be done; in Jesus' name. **Amen.**

29.38   FOR OUR NATION
Unknown

God and ruler of us all, graciously bless this our nation, and send out your light and your truth to lead us in the paths of justice and peace. Give wisdom to those who exercise authority in the government of our land; remove all causes of contention and strife among us; unite us in the service of your kingdom; and make us a God-fearing people, respecting your laws and living together in love and concord; through Jesus Christ our Lord. **Amen.**

29.39 FOR OUR NATION AND RULERS
Editors

We pray you, Lord of all peoples, for our nation, not because we deserve your favour, but because we repent of our sins. Where we need to be disciplined for our misuse of privilege, deal with us in mercy. Where we have strayed from your ways, cause us to return quickly and obey your law.

We pray for the Queen, and for all in authority; we ask for them wisdom, understanding and reliance upon you; cause them to give us a godly example and help us to follow; for the sake of Jesus Christ and his kingdom. **Amen.**

29.40 FOR THOSE WHO GOVERN
From 'A New Zealand Prayer Book'

Eternal God, Fount of wisdom; we ask you to bless the representatives we have elected; grant that through their discussions and decisions we may solve our problems effectively, enhance the well-being of our nation, and achieve together a fairer and more united society. **Amen.**

▶ **29.41** FOR GOOD GOVERNMENT
From 'A New Zealand Prayer Book'

Spirit of justice, creator Spirit:
help us to make and keep this country
a home for all its different peoples,
and grant to our government and all its representatives
imagination, skill and energy
that peace may grow among us,
through Jesus our Lord. **Amen.**

▶ **29.42**   FOR QUEEN AND COMMONWEALTH
Editors

For the blessing of community in our Nation and Commonwealth, and for those who have used your gifts to strengthen and enrich its life, with grateful hearts:
we thank you, Lord.

For our sovereign lady, Queen Elizabeth, for her long and tireless service to our world-wide family of nations, for her profession of faith in you by word and deed, for her example of unselfish devotion to duty, for her care for our people, and for her concern for them at all times and in all places, with grateful hearts:
we thank you, Lord.

Continue in her and her family, we pray, your royal gifts of service, the vision of your will for her people, and wisdom to fulfil her vocation of leadership in a Commonwealth of many races. Give her strength and courage to carry out the duties of her calling.

**Grant her always the assurance of your presence,
your power, and your love,
through Jesus Christ our Lord. Amen.**

▶ **29.43**   FOR OUR NATIONAL LEADERS
Editors

Almighty God,
we pray for our Queen
and all leaders of our country,
that they may govern us wisely and well;
we pray for one another,
that we may live and work together
in love, mutual understanding and peace,
through Jesus Christ our Lord. **Amen.**

29.44   FOR OUR NATIONAL LEADERS
Guy King

Almighty God, we pray for your blessing upon our Queen, upon the Royal Family and upon all the leaders of our land. You have blessed our nation in past days and made it great: bless it now, we pray and keep it ever true to your word and will; that it may still bring blessing to other peoples and honour to your name, through Jesus Christ our Lord. **Amen.**

...NS

...ose who follow a political calling: strengthen ...sponsibility that we place upon them. Guide ...al programmes, that they may plan for the ...t to set neighbour against neighbour, class ...ainst region. Encourage advocates for the ...work for justice. Renew the vision of those ...ve been tarnished by cynicism, and of those ...en sapped by frustration. Give wisdom to ...difficult problems, who must balance the ...e against the ideas in which they believe. And to all your people give a spirit of compassion and mutual affection, so that we may bring glory to your name; through Jesus our Lord. **Amen.**

▶ **29.46** FOR OUR VILLAGE/TOWN/CITY
St Michael-le-Belfrey, York

*Here the local community is named

Heavenly Father,
we thank you for . . . *
and for every person who lives here.
Help us to care more for our community,
to share your love,
and to stand for your truth:
through Jesus Christ our Lord. **Amen.**

29.47 FOR CIVIC LEADERS
Leslie Weatherhead

We lift up our hearts, O Lord, in intercession for all who carry civic and political responsibilities; for all whose words and actions mould public life. Cause them to put aside all merely selfish ambition, to seek to be instruments of your will, and to carry out your purpose for the welfare of your people. Let your grace sustain them, your love work through them, your power uphold them, and let them seek and see your glory in happier human lives; through Jesus Christ our Lord. **Amen.**

29.48   FOR COMMUNITY LEADERS
Collect for Civic Occasions, ASB 1980

Almighty and eternal God, to whom we must all give account: guide with your Spirit the . . . of this *city*, that *they* may be faithful to the mind of Christ, and seek in all *their* purposes to enrich our common life; through Jesus Christ our Lord. **Amen.**

29.49   FOR WORKERS IN THE COMMUNITY
Editors

We pray for your blessing on those who maintain our common life; for teachers, doctors and nurses, for social workers. For those who clean the streets, drive the buses and the trains, and all who in daily duty serve us. Sustain and strengthen them in all their tasks. This we ask in the strong name of Jesus our Lord. **Amen.**

▶ 29.50   FOR THOSE WHO SERVE OUR COMMUNITY
Editors

Almighty God, you have taught us to intercede for others:

For those who guard the health of our people and tend the sick at home and in hospital, for scientists who seek ways of combating disease, and for all engaged in administration, Lord, hear our prayer:
Lord, bless them and help them.

For those who bear witness to Jesus in their work of healing, Lord, hear our prayer:
Lord, bless them and help them.

For police and customs, for ambulance and fire officers, for the military and those in our land who keep us in safety, Lord, hear our prayer:
Lord, bless them and help them.

For those responsible for the maintenance of law and order – legislators, lawyers, judges, probation officers, prison staff and the police, Lord, hear our prayer:
Lord, bless them and help them.

Give to them courage in danger,
alertness of mind
and warmth of heart
that they may be guided to right decisions
for the good of all.

For clergy, ministers and pastors, and all who attend to our spiritual needs and bring to us the saving news, the encouragement, the guidance and the consolation of Christ – Lord, hear our prayer:
Lord, bless them and help them. Amen.

29.51   FOR PEACE IN OUR COMMUNITIES
Editors

Have pity, heavenly Father, on the human race for our failure to follow the Prince of peace, and our inability to seek peace without violence. Be merciful to us in our futile efforts to help the wounded victims of greed and intolerance. Make us effective peacemakers in our own small world, and help us to live at peace with our neighbours. Help us to be calm and unruffled when we are busier than we ought to be, so that we may always radiate your peace and joy, through Jesus our Lord. **Amen.**

29.52   ABOUT RACE RELATIONS
Michael Hollings and Etta Gullick

I see white and black, Lord; I see white teeth in a black face, I see black eyes in a white face: help me to see persons, Jesus – not a black person, but human persons. Thank you, Jesus. **Amen.**

▶ 29.53   ABOUT TERRORISM
Editors

God of peace, we have been shocked by the sheer brutality and callousness of terrorist attacks. We have been numbed by the loss of life, saddened by the hatred of the fanatical, distressed by the power of destruction let loose upon innocent people.

Lord forgive us for any complacency:
Lord, forgive us.

Lord teach us how to love one another:
Lord teach us.

Lord pity us in our weakness:
Lord, pity us.

Lord enlighten us, and show all who are disaffected and embittered that the only remedy for grievance is the justice of the God of love and peace:
Lord enlighten us.

Help us to put our faith in you,
and to work as peacemakers in a distressed world.
We ask this for your glory. Amen.

29.54   FOR OUR NATION IN DIFFICULT DAYS
Editors

In days of trouble we turn to you, O Lord; we do not ask for ease and comfort, but for courage and honesty. Help us to seek the highest good for all, save us from the temporary triumphs of short-lived party success, or the transient pleasure of winning an argument by deception. Banish the language of expediency. Help us to dwell in peace for your glory's sake.

Raise up spiritual leaders who, believing in your word and energised by your Spirit, will seek to win the people to hear your word and obey you. Bless our Queen, the prime minister, the government and all who have political influence and power. We ask this through him who brought truth to light, who contended for justice, admired faith and uprightness, commended peace, and redeemed sinful humanity, Jesus Christ our Lord. **Amen.**

▶ **29.55**   IN TIMES OF TROUBLE
From Psalm 143†

O Lord,
hear our prayer as we cry for your mercy;
in your faithfulness and righteousness come to help us.

Do not bring us to judgement,
for no-one is innocent before you.
We remember days gone by,
and think about all you have done for us:
answer us now, O Lord,
and do not hide yourself from us;
for we put our trust in you.

We pray to you:
show us the way we should go,
rescue us from our enemies,
teach us to do your will,
and by your good Spirit
lead us in a safe path,
for your name's sake. **Amen.**

▶ **29.56** IN TIMES OF TROUBLE
From 2 Chronicles 20†

O Lord God of heaven,
you rule over states and nations;
power and might are in your hand,
and no-one can withstand you.
We stand in your presence and cry out to you
in the name of Jesus;
of ourselves we have no power to face an aggressor,
we do not know what to do –
but our eyes are on you. **Amen.**

29.57 FOR FREEDOM IN OUR SOCIETY
Editors

O God our deliverer, we come to renew our thanksgiving for our inheritance of personal freedom; and we acknowledge our debt to those in every age who have helped to establish it. We ask you to renew our sense of responsibility for extending liberty to other communities through agencies of justice and compassion. Lord Jesus, you are the King of righteousness: lead us in ways of freedom and mercy; inspire us to break down all injustice and oppression, to gain for everyone their due reward, and from everyone their due service; through Jesus Christ our Lord. **Amen.**

29.58 FOR THE DISTURBED AND DELINQUENTS
Editors

Lord Jesus, you never seemed to be crushed by the pressures of life. For the whole of your life on earth you saw hardness and repression; you suffered from the arrogance of others, and you experienced poverty – yet you never allowed these pressures to force you into their mould. We pray for the people of our land who live in difficult circumstances: the young who react with senseless destruction. Vandals who uproot flowers and shrubs, who wreck property and create tension, anger and suffering. We pray for those in bondage to drugs or drink, and those who commit crime to pay for their addiction. We pray for the elderly who are impoverished, isolated, afraid. Strengthen people who are called by the name of Christ to pray and work for the betterment of our society, as well as for the transformation of human life which you alone can give, through Jesus Christ our Lord. **Amen.**

29.59 FOR VICTIMS OF WAR
From 'New Every Morning'

Father of mercies, whose Son here on earth ministered to those in need: remember for good all who suffer through war by loss of home or health, by loss of friends and loved ones, by loss of security and freedom, by loss of faith and hope. Look upon our world, still torn apart by violence, and prosper the work of all who are striving for peace; through Jesus Christ our Lord. **Amen.**

29.60 FOR PITY
From 'New Every Morning'

Have mercy, O God, on those who are victims of our inhumanity – defenceless people in hideous war zones, families robbed of those they love, prisoners of war ill-treated and tortured, old people and children dying of starvation, and those who still bear the scars of former wars. Deepen our pity, O Lord, into creative prayer which will inspire us to positive action, for the sake of our Saviour Jesus Christ. **Amen.**

▶ **29.61** FOR THE JUDICIARY AND POLICE
From 'A New Zealand Prayer Book'

God of truth and justice;
we ask you to help the men and women
who administer and police our laws;
grant them insight, courage and compassion,
protect them from corruption and arrogance
and grant that we, whom they seek to serve,
may give them the support and affection they need;
so may our people be strengthened more and more
in respect and concern for one another. **Amen.**

▶ **29.62** FOR PEACE
Eric Milner-White, adapted David Silk

O God, you desire to enfold
both heaven and earth in a single peace;
Let the design of your great love
lighten upon the waste of our angers and sorrows;
and give peace to your church,
peace among nations, peace in our homes,
and peace in our hearts;
through Jesus Christ our Lord. **Amen.**

▶ **29.63** THANKSGIVING (REMEMBRANCE)
Editors

Our gracious and eternal God, we give you thanks for the world you
have created:

We praise you for your great goodness to your people in sending
Jesus Christ to be the Saviour of those who trust in him. O Lord, we
worship you:
from our hearts we praise and thank you.

Today especially, we thank you for all who courageously served our
country in time of war. O Lord, we worship you:
from our hearts we praise and thank you.

We praise you for the graces of strength and endurance given to our
people in those dark days of danger and sorrow. O Lord, we worship
you:
from our hearts we praise and thank you.

We give thanks for all who laid down their lives for our sake:
make us worthy of their sacrifice,
help us to strive for peace,
make us loyal to each other
and above all to you, our God;
through Jesus Christ our Lord. Amen.

▶ **29.64**   THANKSGIVING
From 1 Chronicles 29†

Lord God of our fathers,
may you be praised for ever and ever!

You are great and powerful, glorious, splendid and majestic: Lord
God of our fathers,
may you be praised for ever and ever!

Everything in heaven and earth is yours, and you are king, supreme
ruler over all: Lord God of our fathers,
may you be praised for ever and ever!

All riches and wealth come from you; you rule everything by your
strength and power: Lord God of our fathers,
may you be praised for ever and ever!

**Now, our God,
we give you thanks,
and praise your glorious name;
through Jesus Christ our Lord. Amen.**

▶ **29.65**   DEDICATION (REMEMBRANCE)
Editors

Lord God our Father, we pledge ourselves to serve you and all
humankind; for the cause of peace, for the relief of need and
suffering, and to the praise of your name:

By your Spirit,
Lord, guide us.

From your wisdom,
Lord, teach us.

With true courage,
Lord, bless us.

In eternal hope,
Lord, keep us. Amen.

▶ **29.66**   ACCLAMATION
From Isaiah 23 and 24†

Lord almighty,
you bring low the pride of all glory
and humble those who are renowned in the earth,
you stretch out your hand over the sea
and make the nations tremble.

To you we raise our voices
and shout for joy,
we acclaim your majesty, we give you praise,
we exalt your name;
from the ends of earth we sing,
'Glory to the righteous One!'
for you will reign among us for ever and ever. **Amen.**

▶ **29.67**   DOXOLOGY
From Revelation 15†

Glory be to you, O God,
Father, Son, and Holy Spirit –
you have power, wisdom and majesty:
receive from us
honour, glory, worship and blessing.

Great and marvellous are your works,
just and true are your ways:
blessing and honour and glory and power
be to him who reigns upon the throne,
and to the Lamb,
through the one eternal Spirit,
now and for ever. **Amen.**

▶ **29.68**   DOXOLOGY
From Romans 11

O Lord our God,
how profound are the riches
of your wisdom and knowledge;
how unsearchable your judgements,
and your paths beyond tracing out!

**Who has known your mind, O Lord;
who has been your counsellor?
Who has ever given to you,
that you should repay?**

For from you and through you and to you are all things:
yours be the glory for ever! Amen.

29.69 BLESSING
From Deuteronomy 28†

The Lord our God open his storehouse of heaven and send his
blessing on our land: bless us in the city, bless us in the country; bless
our homes with children; bless our farms with crops, our orchards
with fruit; bless our industry with produce, our commerce with
trade; bless us in our coming in and going out; bless us in obedience
to his will, grant us his prosperity, and lead us to follow him alone
for ever. **Amen.**

29.70 BLESSING
St George's Windsor

Upon all people of this *nation* whose lives are dedicated to the
service of others, may God bestow his blessings of faithfulness and
peace. **Amen.**

29.71 BLESSING
From Psalm 37†

Trust the Lord and do right. find in him your happiness and
your heart's desire, give yourself to him, wait patiently for him;
and the Lord God almighty bring you prosperity and peace.
Amen.

Acknowledgements

The Editors are grateful to all authors, publishers and other copyright–holders who have given permission for their works to be reproduced in this book. In many cases the attribution has been short enough to be included with the prayer. Where a longer credit was required full details are printed here.

Prayers by Frank Colquhoun are from the *Contemporary Parish Prayers* and are reproduced by permission of the author.
Prayers by William Barclay are reproduced by permission of SCM Press.

Prayers by Michael Hollings and Etta Gullick are from *The One who Listens* and are reproduced by permission of McCrimmon, Great Wakering, Essex.
The prayer by George Appleton from *One Man's Prayers* is reproduced by permission of SPCK.

Prayers from *Everyday Prayers, Further Everyday Prayers* and *When you pray with 7's to 10's* edited by Hazel Snashall are reproduced by permission of the National Christian Education Council

The Prayer by Zinnia Bryan is from the *Prayers for Children* and is reproduced by permission of Scripture Union.

Prayers from *The Promise of his Glory: services and prayers for the season from All Saints to Candlemas* are copyright © The Central Board of Finance 1990, 1991 and are reproduced by permission.

Prayers drawn from the *Alternative Service Book* 1980 (ASB) are © The Central Board of Finance of the Church of England 1980, and may not be reproduced without permission. Inclusive language variations are those proposed by the Liturgical Commission of the General Synod of the Church of England in the paper GS 859 *Making Women Visible* which has only the authority of the Commission by which it was prepared. The variations have no legal standing at the present time but, in an answer to a Question in General Synod, the then president (Archbishop Robert Runcie) expressed the view that such amendments might be made in local circumstances.

Prayers from the *Contemporary Prayers for Public Worship*, and *More Contemporary Prayers* edited by Caryl Micklem are reproduced by permission of SCM Press.

Acknowledgements

Prayers by Elizabeth Goudge are from *A Diary of Prayer* and are reproduced by permission of David Higham Associates Ltd.

Prayers from *Worship Now* are reproduced by permission of St Andrews Press.

Prayers by David Silk are from *Prayers for use in the Alternative Services* and are reproduced by permission of Mowbray, a division of Cassell plc.

Prayers by Joyce Huggett are from *Approaching Christmas* and are reproduced by permission of Lion Publishing plc.

The prayer attributed to Edinburgh House Press is from *Daily Prayer and Praise* and are reproduced by permission of Lutterworth Press.

The song by Janet Lunt is reproduced by permission of Mustard Seed Music, PO Box 356, Leighton Buzzard LU7 8WP.

Scripture quotations taken from the *Holy Bible, New International Version* are copyright © 1973, 1978, 1984 by the International Bible Society, and are used by permission.

Scripture quotations taken from the *Good News Bible (Today's English Version), British usage edition* published by the Bible Societies and Collins, are copyright © American Bible Society 1966, 1971, 1976 and are used with permission.

The Jubilate Liturgical Psalms, also available in *The Dramatised Bible* published by HarperCollins, *Psalms for Today* and *Songs from the Psalms* published by Hodder & Stoughton, are copyright © 1986, 1989, 1992, Michael Perry/Jubilate Hymns; © 1986, 1989, 1992 Hope Publishing Company.

Readings from *The Dramatised Bible* published by HarperCollins and the Bible Society are copyright © 1986, 1989 Michael Perry/Jubilate Hymns; © 1986, 1989 Hope Publishing Company.

Prayers prayers and responses marked '†' are from *Bible Praying* published by HarperCollins and are copyright © 1992 Michael Perry/Jubilate Hymns.

For assistance in preparing the manuscripts of *Prayers for the People*, People's Edition and Leaders' Edition: Rev Jane Austin, Bunty Grundy, Emma Hewlett, Isabel Izatt and Valerie Parker. For the sympathic and careful design: Claire Brodmann.

Bible Index to Prayers, Readings and Responses

* indicates item appears both in People's and Leader's Editions

2 Peter
1 Greeting - *25.1
   Peace - *28.45
3 Blessing - *27.33

1 John
1 That We May Walk in God's
     Light - *16.39
   Confession - *27.16, *28.18
2 Words of Comfort - *28.20, 28.21
4 Response - *15.9, *15.10, *18.10

2 John
   Greeting - *2.1
   Peace - *28.46

3 John
   Greeting - *6.1
   Peace/Greeting - *28.53

Jude
   Ascription - *1.37, *5.46
   Blessing - 5.47, 20.64
   Greeting - *15.1
   Peace - *28.47

Revelation
1 Response - *1.6, *17.16, *20.15,
     *24.21, *24.22, *29.10
   Response (After a Reading) -
     *25.24
   Ascription - *8.48
   Greeting - *9.1, *9.2, *22.1, *24.1
   Thanksgiving - *11.29
   Creed - *12.19, *20.38, *22.22
   Peace - *28.50

   Peace (Easter) - *28.48, *28.49
2 Response (After a Reading) -
     *19.40
   Promises/Thanksgiving - *20.47
   Creed - *23.27
3 Response (After a Reading) -
     *19.40
4 Ascription - *11.32, *17.72
   Creed - *24.36
   Doxology - *28.63
   Thanksgiving (Jesus is Lord) -
     *28.76
5 Ascription - *3.48, *11.32
   Creed - *24.36
   Doxology - *28.63
   Thanksgiving (Missionary/
     Worldwide Church) - *28.83
   Response - *28.103
   Response (Sanctus) - *28.100,
     *28.101
7 Response - *22.7
11 Response - *11.8, *11.9, *17.15,
     *24.23
   Thanksgiving (Christ's
     Coming/Judgement) - 28.91
12 Response - *11.10
15 Ascription - *13.32, *13.34
   Thanksgiving (Church
     anniversary) - *28.86
   Doxology - *29.67
19 Praise - *3.18, *13.35
21 Reading: The New Heaven and
     the New Earth - 23.25
22 Greeting - *7.1
   Peace - *28.51

Subject Index to Prayers, Responses and Readings

indicates item appears both in People's and Leader's Editions

Liturgical Bible Index

indicates item appears both in People's and Leader's Editions

Greeting/Invitation
Genesis 33 - *21.26
Exodus 14 - *26.11
Ruth 2 - *28.2, *28.61
Nehemiah 9 - *10.11
Psalm 107 - *28.61
Psalm 134 - *20.2
Song of Songs 2 - *10.12
Isaiah 55 - 16.18
Romans 1 - *29.1
Romans 15 - *1.1, *28.1, *28.54
1 Corinthians 1 - *20.1
2 Corinthians 13 - *23.1
Galatians 1 - *8.1
Galatians 6 - *3.1
Ephesians 2 - *17.2
Ephesians 6 - *4.1, *17.1
Philippians 4 - *19.1
2 Thessalonians 1 - *13.1
2 Timothy 1 - *11.1
2 Timothy 4 - *5.1, *12.1
Titus 1 - *14.1, *16.1, *26.1, *27.1
Philemon - *19.1, *21.1
Hebrews 10 - *28.117
1 Peter 1 - *10.1
1 Peter 5 - *18.1
2 Peter 1 - *25.1
2 John - *2.1
3 John - *6.1
Jude - *15.1
Revelation 1 - *9.1, *9.2, *22.1, *24.1
Revelation 22 - *7.1

Approach to God/Approach to worship
Deuteronomy 12 - *6.11, 20.21
1 Kings 8 - 20.22
Job 38 - 14.11
Psalm 100 - 3.13
Psalm 105 - 1.11
Psalm 108 - 15.11
Psalm 113 - 13.11
Psalm 118 - 2.10
Psalm 134 - 28.9, *20.20

Psalm 138 - *29.11
Psalm 139 - 5.13
Psalm 148 - 10.13
Ecclesiastes 52 - 13.12
Matthew 10 - 28.8
Matthew 24 - 24.24
John 1 - *2.11
Colossians 1 - *2.11
Hebrews 1 - *2.11
Hebrews 12 - 25.13
1 Peter 1 - 27.13

Commandments:
The Ten Commandments
Exodus 20 - *3.44, *28.12
Deuteronomy 5 - *3.44, *28.12

Commandments to Love
Mark 12 - *28.11

Act of Commitment
Exodus 20 - *3.46, *28.13
Deuteronomy 5 - *3.46, 28.13

Confession
2 Kings 22 - *25.16
Ezra 9 - *16.24
Nehemiah 9 - *24.29
Job 40 - *26.20
Job 41 - *26.20
Job 42 - *26.20
Psalm 10 - *4.14
Psalm 51 - *5.17, *24.28, *28.17
Psalm 106 - *10.17
Psalm 109 - *23.19
Psalm 119 - *25.17
Psalm 130 - *14.17, *15.18
Psalm 142 - *16.25
Psalm 143 - *8.17, *19.28
Isaiah 6 - *13.17
Isaiah 43 - *21.14
Isaiah 57 - *13.18
Isaiah 59 - *3.21

Isaiah 64 - *7.14
Jeremiah 14 - *29.16
Lamentations 5 - *11.15
Daniel 9 - *3.20
Jonah 2 - *19.32
1 Corinthians 13 - *20.26
Ephesians 5 - *6.14
Ephesians 6 - *6.14
1 John 1 - *27.16, *28.18

Absolution

Ezra 9 - 16.26
Psalm 31 - 5.19, 20.28, 8.20, 12.14,
  24.30, 27.17
Psalm 103 - 5.20, 10.18, 17.24, 18.19,
  23.20, 27.18
Psalm 116 - 4.16
Psalm 118 - 2.16
Psalm 130 - 15.19
Psalm 140 - 1.15, 11.16
Psalm 142 - 19.34
Psalm 145 - 6.16
Isaiah 12 - 3.22, 29.19
Isaiah 25 - 19.35
Isaiah 38 - 18.20
Isaiah 40 - 7.15, *26.21
Isaiah 41 - 22.13
Isaiah 43 - 25.18, 28.19
Isaiah 49 - 21.15
Isaiah 53 - 9.22
Isaiah 59 - 14.18
Lamentations 5 - 13.20
Jonah 1 - 19.33
John 8 - 5.18
Romans 8 - 5.18
Hebrews 10 - 16.27

Response (After a Reading)

Revelation 1 - *25.24
Revelation 2 - *19.40
Revelation 3 - *19.40
1 John 1 - *16.39

Creed

Psalm 65 - *21.24
Psalm 145 - *13.25
Isaiah 43 - *17.29
Isaiah 44 - *10.24, *10.25
John 1 - *15.24, *26.27

Romans 1 - *25.25
Romans 4 - *9.31
Romans 8 - *9.31
1 Corinthians 8 - *3.28, *4.22, *4.22
1 Corinthians 10 - *17.30
1 Corinthians 12 - *3.28, *4.22, *19.41,
  *27.22
1 Corinthians 15 - *9.30
2 Corinthians 1 - *1.21
2 Corinthians 4 - *23.26
Galatians 2 - *8.27, *11.23, *16.32
Ephesians 3 - *6.25
Ephesians 4 - *3.29
Philippians 2 - *7.20
Colossians 1 - *10.26, *11.24, *20.37,
  *24.34
2 Thessalonians 2 - *23.28
1 Timothy 3 - *16.34, *22.21, *25.26
2 Timothy 2 - *22.21
Titus 2 - *2.24
Titus 3 - *2.24, *16.33
Hebrews 1 - *26.26
Hebrews 4 - *5.25, *22.20
1 Peter 1 - *9.31
1 Peter 3 - *8.28
Revelation 1 - *12.19, *20.38, *22.22
Revelation 2 - *23.27
Revelation 4 - *24.36
Revelation 5 - *24.36

Before Prayer

Hebrews 4 - 5.26

Peace

Romans 1 - *28.30
Romans 15 - *28.31
1 Corinthians 1 - *28.32
2 Corinthians 13 - *28.33
Galatians 1 - *28.34
Galatians 6 - *28.35
Ephesians 6 - *28.36. *28.37
Philippians 4 - *28.38
2 Thessalonians 1 - *28.41
2 Timothy 1 - *28.39
2 Timothy 4 - *28.40
Titus 1 - *28.42
Philemon - *28.38, *28.43
1 Peter 1 - *28.44
1 Peter 5 - *28.52

2 Peter 1 - *28.45
2 John - *28.46
3 John - *28.53
Jude - *28.47
Revelation 1 - *28.48, *28.49, *28.50
Revelation 22 - *28.51

Doxology

Psalm 63 - *10.46
Romans 11 - *13.36, *14.35, *16.53, 18.76, *29.68
Romans 16 - 28.121
Revelation 4 and 5 - *28.63
Revelation 15 - *29.67

Offering Prayer

Genesis 33 - *21.26, 21.27

Ascription

Exodus 5 - *3.49
1 Chronicles 29 - *14.36, 28.55
Nehemiah 9 - *10.44
Ephesians 3 - *20.61
Philippians 4 - *23.62
1 Timothy 1 - *18.77
1 Timothy 6 - 13.33
Jude - *1.37, *5.46
Revelation 1 - *8.48
Revelation 4 - *11.32, *17.72
Revelation 5 - *3.48, *11.32
Revelation 15 - *13.32, *13.34

Blessing

Numbers 6 - 1.39, 1.40, 3.55, 21.41, 27.31
Deuteronomy 10 - 3.56
Deuteronomy 28 - 10.47, 29.69
Joshua 1 - 22.60
1 Kings 8 - *3.51
Psalm 8 - 13.39
Psalm 19 - 10.48
Psalm 37 - 21.42, 29.71
Psalm 102 - 5.48
Psalm 115 - 6.67
Psalm 121 - 10.49
Psalm 128 - *3.57, *3.60, 6.66, *20.62
Psalm 134 - 20.65
Isaiah 26 - 23.68

Isaiah 35 - 24.48
Isaiah 40 - 15.44
Isaiah 57 - 18.79, 18.80, 23.72
Isaiah 57 - 23.72
Isaiah 61 - 17.74
Matthew 28 - 17.75
John 14 - 23.71
John 21 - 9.44
Romans 1 - 10.50
Romans 15 - 3.58, 3.59
Romans 15 - 3.52, 16.54, 16.55, 23.70
1 Corinthians 1 - 27.24
1 Corinthians 13 - 6.68
1 Corinthians 16 - 3.53, 22.61
2 Corinthians 1 - 23.74
2 Corinthians 3 - 19.86
2 Corinthians 4 - 22.69, 23.76
2 Corinthians 6 - 19.81, 19.82
2 Corinthians 11 - 3.54, 4.46, 28.123
2 Corinthians 13 - 28.124
Ephesians 1 - 16.56
Ephesians 3 - 19.83
Ephesians 5 - 12.34, 19.84
Ephesians 6 - 20.63
Philippians 4 - 1.40, 5.49, 11.34, 23.69, 25.51
Colossians 1 - 22.68, *27.25
Colossians 3 - 5.50, 11.35, 18.81, 25.53
1 Thessalonians 3 - 11.36, 18.78. 25.55
1 Thessalonians 5 - 12.33, 19.85, 24.50
2 Thessalonians 2 - 18.82, 22.58, 25.52
2 Thessalonians 3 - 15.43, 22.59, 23.75, 25.52, 28.125
1 Timothy 6 - 4.47. 16.57
2 Timothy 1 - 25.54
2 Timothy 2 - 22.70, *27.26
2 Timothy 4 - 22.71, 22.72, 24.51, 27.27, 27.28
Hebrews 12 - 4.44, 7.26, 11.37, 22.65, 22.66
Hebrews 13 - 9.43
1 Peter 5 - *22.67, 23.73, 27.32, *27.33
Jude - 5.47, 20.64

Dismissal

John 20 - 17.77
1 Corinthians 16 - *28.127

Index to Dramatised Bible Readings

Index to Responsive Psalms *with subjects*

A Short Service

INVITATION
From Psalm 98†

Sing to the Lord, all the world,
for the Lord is a mighty God.

Sing a new song to the Lord,
for he has done marvellous things.

Proclaim his glory among the nations,
and shout for joy to the Lord our king.

GREETING
From Romans 1 etc.†

Grace and peace to you from God our Father and from the Lord
Jesus Christ. **Amen**

APPROACH
From Psalm 118†

Lord,
this is the day you made;
we rejoice and are glad in it:
help us and bless us
as we come into your presence -
we praise you and exalt you,
we celebrate and thank you;
for you are our God
and your love endures for ever. **Amen.**

CONFESSION
From Psalm 51†

Lord God, be gracious to us
because of your great love for us;
in your great mercy
wash away our sins -
for we are weighed down by them,
and we know we have failed;
we have offended against you

618

and done evil in your sight:
create in us a pure heart,
put a loyal spirit in us,
and give us again the joy
    that comes from your salvation. Amen.

ABSOLUTION
From Psalm 103†

The love of God for those who seek him is as great as the heavens are high above the earth: as far as the east is from the west he removes *your* sins from *you*, and he will remember them no more. **Amen.**

EXHORTATION
From Revelation 19†

Let us rejoice and be glad,
and give God the glory. Amen.

BEFORE READING
From 2 Samuel 22†

You are our lamp, O Lord;
you turn our darkness into light.

AFTER READING
From Mark 4†

Those who have a mind to hear,
let them hear!

CREED
From 1 Corinthians 8 and 12†

We believe in one God and Father;
from him all things come.

We believe in one Lord Jesus Christ;
through him we come to God.

We believe in one Holy Spirit;
in him we are baptised into one body.

We believe and trust in one God,
Father, Son and Holy Spirit. Amen.

THE LORD'S PRAYER
From Matthew 6 and Luke 11

**Our Father in heaven,
hallowed be your name,
your kingdom come,
your will be done,
on earth as in heaven.
Give us today our daily bread.
Forgive us our sins
as we forgive those who sin against us.
Lead us not into temptation
but deliver us from evil.**

**For the kingdom, the power,
and the glory are yours,
now and for ever. Amen.**

BEFORE PRAYER
From Hebrews 4†

Let us approach God's throne with confidence:
**we shall receive mercy,
and find grace to help us. Amen.**

FOR OTHERS: IN TROUBLE
From Psalm 31†

Be merciful, Lord,
to all those in trouble:
those who are ill or weary,
those who are deep in sorrow,
those whose life is ebbing away,
those who are without friends,
those who are forgotten by the world:
Lord, we entrust them to your care;
in Jesus' name. **Amen.**

FOR OURSELVES
From Isaiah 33†

Lord, be gracious to us,
for we long for you:
be our strength every day,

our salvation in time of trouble,
our greatest treasure in life,
and our reward in heaven;
through Jesus our redeemer. **Amen.**

THANKSGIVING
From Isaiah 63†

Our God,
we thank you for all your kindness,
and we praise you
for all the good things
    you have done for us:
you are our saviour -
in our distress
you too were distressed,
in your love and mercy you redeemed us;
through Jesus Christ our Lord. **Amen.**

THE GRACE
From 2 Corinthians 13

The grace of our Lord Jesus Christ,
and the love of God,
and the fellowship of the Holy Spirit,
be with us all evermore. **Amen.**

DOXOLOGY
From Romans 16†

Glory to God
who alone is all-wise;
through Jesus Christ, for ever! **Amen.**

BLESSING
From Numbers 6†

The Lord bless *you* and keep *you*, the Lord make his face to shine
upon *you*, the Lord be kind and gracious to *you*, the Lord look upon
you with favour, and give *you* peace. **Amen.**

A Communion Service

INVITATION
INVITATION
From Psalm 96†

Sing to the Lord a new song:
proclaim his salvation each day.

Declare his glory to all:
he is great and worthy of praise. Amen.

GREETING
From Ruth 2†

The Lord be with you:
the Lord bless you.

APPROACH
From Psalm 26†

Lord God,
we are here to worship you -
let your love guide us,
and your faithfulness lead us;
we come to ask for your forgiveness,
to gather round your table,
to bring you our thanksgiving,
and to proclaim your redemption:
receive the praise of your people. **Amen.**

COMMANDMENTS
From Mark 12†

Jesus said: Love the Lord your God with all your heart and with all
your soul and with all your mind and with all your strength; and
love your neighbour as yourself.
Lord,
we have broken your commandments:
forgive us, and help us to obey. Amen.

CONFESSION
From 1 John 1†

**God our Father,
you have taught us
that if we say we have no sin
we deceive ourselves
and the truth is not in us:
we humbly confess our sins to you,
and we ask you to keep your promise
to forgive us our sins
and to cleanse us
  from all unrighteousness;
through Jesus Christ our Lord. Amen.**

ABSOLUTION
From Psalm 6†

The Lord God be merciful to *you* and heal *you*; the Lord turn his face towards *you* and deliver *you*; the Lord save *you* in his unfailing love; through Jesus Christ. **Amen.**

EXHORTATION
From Psalm 107†

Let us give thanks to the Lord:
his mercy lasts for ever.

He satisfies the thirsty:
and fills the hungry with good things. Amen.

BEFORE READING
From Jeremiah 9†

Let us listen to the Lord,
let us pay attention to his word.

AFTER READING
From Revelation 1-7†

Hear what the Spirit is saying to the churches:
thanks be to God. Amen.

CREED
From Titus 2 and 3†

Let us confess our faith in one God, whose grace has dawned upon the world.

**We believe in God the Father,
who has revealed his loving kindness
    to us,
and in his mercy saved us -
not for any good deed of our own,
but because he is merciful.**

**We believe in God the Son,
who sacrificed himself for us
to free us from our sin,
and make us his own people,
holy, and eager to do good.**

**We believe in one Holy Spirit,
whom God poured out on us
    generously
through Christ our saviour;
so that justified by his grace
we might become heirs of eternal life.
Amen.**

INTERCESSION
From Hebrews 4 etc.†

Let us approach God's throne with confidence:
**we shall receive mercy,
and find grace to help
in time of need. Amen.**

Upon . . . have mercy, Lord;
we entrust them to your care.

In . . . Lord, may peace and justice rule:
let your love prevail.

To God be glory in the Church and in Christ Jesus:
for ever and ever. Amen.

PEACE
From 1 Peter 5†

Peace to you all in Christ: greet one another in love. **Amen.**

ACCLAMATION
From 1 Chronicles 29†

Yours, Lord is the greatness,
the power and the glory,
the splendour and the majesty;
everything comes from you,
and of your own do we give you. **Amen.**

GREETING
From 2 Timothy 4†

The Lord be with your spirit:
grace and peace be with you.

THANKSGIVING
From Ephesians 5, Isaiah 6, Romans 5,
John 6, 1 Corinthians 11, and Psalm 19†

In the name of our Lord Jesus Christ we give thanks for everything
to God the Father. Father, we thank you for all your
goodness, especially for . . .

Lord, high and exalted, yet present among us, with angels and saints
in heaven we call to each other:
Holy, holy, holy,
the Lord almighty is holy,
his glory fills the world. Amen.

Pour out your love into our hearts by the Holy Spirit whom you
have given to your people. Let this bread and wine be to us the body
and blood of Christ, food of our eternal life.

For our Lord Jesus Christ
in the night he was betrayed,
took bread,
and when he had given thanks,
he broke it and said,
'This is my body, which is for you;
do this to remember me'.

In the same way, after supper,
he took the cup, saying,
'This cup is the new covenant
    in my blood;
do this, whenever you drink it,
to remember me.

So may our remembrance
be acceptable in your sight,
O Lord our strength and our redeemer. **Amen.**

THE LORD'S PRAYER
From Matthew 6 and Luke 11

**Our Father in heaven,
hallowed be your name,
your kingdom come,
your will be done,
on earth as in heaven.
Give us today our daily bread.
Forgive us our sins
as we forgive
    those who sin against us.
Lead us not into temptation
but deliver us from evil.**

**For the kingdom, the power,
    and the glory are yours,
now and for ever. Amen.**

BREAD AND WINE
From John 6†

Jesus said, 'If you come to me you will never go hungry.' **Amen.**

Jesus said, 'If you believe in me you will never be thirsty.' **Amen.**

DOXOLOGY
From Romans 16†

Glory to God
who alone is all-wise;
through Jesus Christ, for ever! **Amen.**

BLESSING
From 2 Thessalonians 3†

The Lord of peace give *you* peace
at all times and in every way;
and the blessing of God almighty,
the Father, the Son and the Holy Spirit,
be with you always. **Amen.**

DISMISSAL (MORNING)
From John 20†

Jesus said, 'As the Father has sent me, so I am sending you.' Go in the name of Christ. **Amen.**

DISMISSAL (EVENING)
From Exodus 33†

The presence of the Lord go with you:
the Lord give us rest. Amen.

The resources for Holy Communion within this volume have been devised to meet a need in some free churches. In the Church of England, elements may commend themselves for use where the rubrics or canons allow.